D0871132

Dying for Joe McCarthy's Sins:

The Suicide of Wyoming Senator Lester Hunt

RODGER MCDANIEL

Recipient of Wyoming State Historical Society
Lola Homsher Endowment Grant

ISBN: 9780983027591

Published by WordsWorth,
1285 Sheridan Avenue, No. 275,
Cody, Wyoming 82414

Cover Photo: U.S. Senate Historical Office
Author photo: Ken Burns Studio-Cheyenne
Book design by R.C. Tafoya

Dedicated to my wife Patricia,
a patient, loving and encouraging soul;
to my brother Bob for the inspiration of his life, God rest his soul;
and to Lester C. Hunt, Jr., a kind and decent soul.

Table of Contents

Foreword by
Former US Senator Alan K. Simpson

Brother Pete and I knew Lester Hunt and always enjoyed our time with him. He and our dear Dad were contemporaries. Both played baseball – loved it – and played it well. Both had wonderful intellects, minds that housed great curiosity as well as humor. They were of different political parties and had different ideas about what was best for America. Yet, if you judge by the letters exchanged between the two, they enjoyed a warm, respectful relationship. When our dad was reelected chairman of the Board of Trustees of the University of Wyoming, Senator Hunt sent him a letter of congratulations. Dad reciprocated. "If the University has gone to town while I was president of the board, it is because I had good support from the board members and especially from one Governor Hunt, who did a magnificent job in that capacity." On another occasion, Dad responded to a kind letter from Lester who sent his condolences on the occasion of our Aunt Virginia's death. "Frankly, Les, you do a hell of a lot of things that I think are pretty fine. You are still the same cool, level-headed, far-seeing guy we all know and respect."

Both were in politics for only one reason, to do what was right for Wyoming and the nation. They understood the political arena was a plenty tough place. Each felt strongly that issues were too important to pull their punches or walk away from an honest argument. They both felt a calling to put their own reputations at risk by placing their names on the ballot. Each of them served Wyoming as a governor and a United States senator and, I believe history shows, the state was the better for it.

I always say: "In politics there are no right answers, only a continuing flow of compromises among groups, resulting in a changing, cloudy and ambiguous series of public decisions – where appetite and ambition compete openly with knowledge and wisdom." That's politics; there is no other good definition for it. And it's sloppy, and it's crude, and it's silly, and it's bizarre, and banal and squirrelly and stupid – but it works!

There is much handwringing going on today regarding incivility in public dialogue. We pine nostalgically for a time when politics was more civil, less nasty, and more decent. Joseph Cummins wrote a history of American politics called *Anything for a Vote: Dirty Tricks, Cheap Shots, and October Surprises.*[1] He demonstrates that the dirty tricks and the outrageous smears didn't just begin in this generation. They were spawned at the dawn of the Republic. According to Cummings the election of 1800 was one of the "dirtiest" in American history. A scribe working for Thomas Jefferson called Jefferson's opponent, President John Adams, a "repulsive pedant" and "a hideous hermaphroditical character." You have to wonder who might have even known what that meant!

Martin Van Buren, it was alleged, enjoyed wearing women's corsets and James Buchanan (whose head tilted to one side as a result of a congenital defect), was purported to be mentally imbalanced. The Presidential race of 1864 was one of the most hideous. The supporters of James G. Blaine, the candidate, accused the other of being the candidate of "Rum, Romanism, and Rebellion"—another memorable slogan. Meanwhile, Grover Cleveland was accused of fathering a child out of wedlock. "Ma! Ma! Where's my pa?" his detractors would holler out at Cleveland's rallies!

The premise of Cummins' book is that campaigns were just as "dirty" and unpleasant before as they are today. I have always said that "politics is a contact sport," no less than football. My friend Rodger McDaniel's mentor, former Wyoming congressman Teno Roncalio, and my father sure played the game that way. Teno was the chairman

1   Quirk Books; 1st edition, (August 1, 2007)

of the Wyoming Democratic Party in 1958. He helped engineer my father's defeat in a bid for a second term as governor. In 1966, Dad had the opportunity to return the favor. By then he was a United States senator and Teno was running for the Senate against Governor Cliff Hansen. Dad said Roncalio "took credit for everything from the rising of the sun to the shifting of the sands." He thrashed Teno for his voting record, both votes made and votes missed.

For a while Teno ignored Dad, taking aim only at Hansen. But eventually, he exploded. Roncalio called the attacks "vicious." He said he "welcomed Simpson's return to his traditional role as the hatchet man of the Republican Party." The next day a reporter asked Dad if it was true. "Are you really nothing more than a hatchet man for Cliff Hansen?" he inquired. "You bet I am," grinned Dad. "And I am never any happier than when my little old hatchet is banging on Teno's bald head." Teno lost and he knew what hit him. He and Dad both left this life as good friends and Teno smoothed my path and helped me greatly in my first years in the Senate.

The issues are important yet there are consequences to elections. Who wins and who loses matters enough that if you choose to get into the arena, you'd better "buckle up your guts" as my old U.W. football Coach Bowden Wyatt would urge. As a politician you get your skin ripped off, but it grows back double strength. You're on the cover of TIME one month and six months later you're doing it. Still, as with war, there are rules of engagement. There are boundaries – though at times they can be almost anything but black and white.

The 1954 campaign for the United States Senate in Wyoming went beyond anything even the toughest, meanest, most negative politicians would have recognized as being acceptable. What was done to Lester Hunt passed all boundaries of decency and exposed an evil side of politics most would always seek to avoid. Lester Hunt was a decent man who spent 22 years of his life in public service. He understood the arena could be a rough-and-tumble place. He was not prepared politically or emotionally for the savagery and cruelty that was hurled at him. Not one of us would have been. He chose to voluntarily and sadly end his own life rather than to take any further part of such foul ugliness.

Parts of the story of Lester Hunt's suicide have been told before. Rodger's book adds vital and important facts to the historical record of that tragedy. More importantly, this book tells the story not only of Hunt's death but also of his life. One cannot fully gauge the venom in those who drove him to voluntarily end his life unless you also know how Hunt lived, his commitment to family, to Wyoming and to the nation.

Lester Hunt's story is also about the real dangers of demagoguery. It's always a threat in any democracy that some political or religious leader or media personality will play on the fears of the people in order to create targeted hate. When Lester Hunt arrived in Washington in 1949, he witnessed the rising tide of McCarthyism. His was one of the few early voices to call it for what it was. The so-called "Red Scare" has been a main focus of most historians of that period of time. A lesser-known element of that history and one that harmed far more people was the witch-hunt McCarthy and others conducted against homosexuals.

Homophobia was then, and cruelly and unfortunately continues to be, a convenient launching pad for some of the worst kinds of stereotyping and political opportunism. That aspect of McCarthyism is a critical element of the suicide of Lester Hunt. Rodger McDaniel has researched it so well and clearly documents this irony. Senators Joe McCarthy, Styles Bridges and Herman Welker poisoned people to believe that homosexuals were not only "sexual perverts" but that they were dangerous security risks. They argued that those with a same-sex attraction were vulnerable to blackmail by all of those who would do harm to the United States. These same men then used a deeply personal family tragedy to blackmail Hunt in the effort to force the popular Wyoming senator to resign.

The full story of Lester Hunt's death should be told. It is, here in these pages, and told by a writer well qualified to tell it. Rodger McDaniel has served in elective office, spent nearly 20 years as a trial lawyer, directed the state's mental health administration and is also an ordained minister. Rodger brings to this book the fine skills he learned in all of the paths of his own journey. Beyond the rare ability to research, investigate and write a gripping story, Rodger also brings a level of empathy to Lester Hunt's life story that he richly deserves. The result is this book that finally offers Lester Hunt's remaining family some form of justice – though belated. Wyoming was well served by Hunt's youthful choice to make our state his home. He was one of those courageous people who "stepped up" in the earlier history of the state to make it what it is, to help create the sense that Wyoming is a special place.

This story must be read and its lessons heeded. It is a parable exposing the risks inherent in a democracy when personal power becomes more important than the good of our country. It teaches that even in politics, the boundary lines matter and the crossing of them "reaps the whirlwind."

Alan K. Simpson
United States Senator
Wyoming (1979-1997)

Prologue

Joe McCarthy's Cold War witch-hunts targeted people with same-sex attractions as much, maybe more than those with Communist sympathies. The rationale for the witch-hunts and the laws criminalizing sexual acts between consenting gay and lesbian adults was a claim that homosexuals were security risks. It was said they could be easily blackmailed into giving up America's secrets. But the laws enacted in the late 1940s and early '50s to prevent that from happening had an unintended consequence.

Dr. Morris Plascowe's 1951 landmark study "Homosexuality, Sodomy, and Crimes Against Nature," provided decisive evidence that these laws "benefit no one except the blackmailer."[1] Lester C. Hunt's story gives witness to the truth of Dr. Plascowe's work while demonstrating an even greater irony. The same demagogues who alleged homosexuals were subject to being blackmailed were, themselves, the perpetrators of one of the vilest blackmails in American political history.

The Lester Hunt story is as old as the story of Job of the Bible, a story constructed around a mythological wager. God lays a bet that good people will hold onto their beliefs in spite of being plagued with undeserved suffering. Satan calls God's bluff. They both double down on the life of Job. Job was unlike the rest of us. God said Job was "blameless and upright." Lester Hunt may not have reached that standard, although one of his colleagues eulogized Hunt, "He was wholly without guilt."[2] There was never a hint of personal scandal in his per-

---

1 Dr. Morris Plascowe, *Homosexuality, Sodomy, and Crimes Against Nature*, Pastoral Psychology 1951, 2 (18), 40-48, File 33 "Bibliography on Homosexuality" Box 6, Papers of Donald S. Lucas, GLBT Historical Society, San Francisco
2 *Memorial Services Held in the Senate and House of Representatives of the United States, Together With Remarks Made in Eulogy of Lester C. Hunt, Late a Senator From Wyoming*, United States Government Printing Office, (1955), 25

sonal or political life for the first sixty-one of his years. He was quite simply an honest, decent human being, whose suffering, like Job's, was undeserved.

Lester C. Hunt (1892-1954)

Our lives are bookended between two dates – that of our birth and that of our death, dates separated by a small dash. For Hunt, the dash was nearly 62 years long. Yet the darkness of the last few hours had no beginning and no end. People who choose when to die are seldom able to place those last hours in the broader context of their lives no matter how well lived. The time from birth to death is compressed, made infinitely smaller than one's life, crystallized into that one moment.

It is not surprising that most of what is remembered of Lester Hunt is about that moment. Hunt's death was, in important ways, a metaphor for the times. Hunt's last hours were a part of the horror of the McCarthy years, the end of which may well have been hastened by Hunt's suicide.

Knowing how his life ends casts a shadow over the entire story, a shadow so dark as to sometimes eclipse the fascinating and engaged life Hunt led prior to those last few moments. Lester Hunt's life is a far more sustaining metaphor than was his death. The nefarious conduct of some of his senate colleagues leading Hunt to choose death deserves to be condemned by exposure. The truth about his death should be told. But, it is not possible to understand his death without knowing more about his life. Perhaps in those last few hours, Hunt was overcome with a sense that the meaning of a lifetime of public service, loyalty to his family and his country, had been lost to the plans of a few villains. Those last hours may have seemed so dark that Lester Hunt was unable to see how bright a light his life had cast.

Perhaps in those last few hours, Lester Hunt made peace with the idea that there is something bigger to life than our few days on this earth. Lester Hunt had a deeper sense of purpose, what Joseph Campbell called "the mythologically inspired life."[3] The real heroes among us, Campbell said, know when and to what to surrender.[4] More than 2300 years earlier, Socrates took his own life. The great philosopher was accused of refusing to recognize the gods recognized by the state.[5] It was the same charge leveled against Lester Hunt. For Socrates, it was the age of Apollo. For Hunt, it was the age of Joe McCarthy.

Fate had it that Lester Hunt's days in the United States Senate overlapped McCarthy's reign of terror. As Hunt arrived in Washington, McCarthy was beginning his melodramatic career as an unprincipled demagogue. Within days after Hunt's death, McCarthy was discredited. He was abandoned, even by most of those whose political careers had benefited from the drafting effect created by allowing him to run at the head of their pack.

Hunt refused to worship the gods of fear unleashed by McCarthy and his fellow travelers, gods who ruled over American politics, seeking to destroy the lives of good and decent people like the Wyoming senator. A century before Hunt came to Washington, a southern colleague who was unhappy with Missouri senator Thomas Hart Benton's refusal to support slavery confronted him on the floor. Senator Henry Foote of Mississippi "whipped out a pistol and pointed it at Benton, who dramatically threw open his coat and cried, 'I have no pistol. Let him fire, let the assassin fire!'"[6] Not since had a senator shown such courage in the face of a wanton attack as did Lester Hunt in the face of his character assassins.

When Socrates was convicted, he quietly acquiesced. He agreed to end his life by drinking poison. "I understand," he said. "I under-

3   Campbell, Joseph, *The Hero's Journey: Joseph Campbell on His Life and Work,* Edited by Phil Cousineau, New World Library (1990), 64
4   Id. 12
5   Plato, *Apology,* 24-27
6   John F. Kennedy, *Profiles in Courage* Harper and Row (1955), 117

stand." History has been more kind to Socrates than to his accusers just as history will be more kind to Hunt than to his. As night fell on that sunny June morning, Lester Hunt may well have said something similar to the last words of the Greek philosopher. "I understand."

Mythological heroes often leave everything familiar, go to a new land and achieve extraordinary success. Lester Hunt was such a figure. As a young man with immeasurable optimism, he hopped a train and left behind everything familiar to begin life anew in Lander, a small Wyoming frontier town in the middle of nowhere.[7] At first his new fellow-townsfolk simply wanted him to come and play baseball for their small town team. In a few short years, they chose him to serve in high public office. Lester Hunt's story should have been a story of how hard work, decency, and honesty are rewarded. It would have been if not for the last year of his life. Lester Hunt's story will end violently. It is not the ending you might anticipate when walking through Hunt's early years in Illinois, watching him play baseball, excelling in school, and preparing for the extraordinary life ahead.

All of which bring us back to Socrates and the last words he spoke as he drank the poison. "We can and must pray to the gods that our sojourn on earth will continue happy beyond the grave. This is my prayer, and may it come to pass." The stories of real life heroes do not often have happy endings. "For the Greeks, such a resolution (a happy ending) made for a comedy, whether it was funny or not, in contrast to a tragedy, which ended with a negative resolution," author Jack Hart has written.[8] Lester Hunt's life story is not a Greek comedy. It's an American tragedy. Though it is without the happy ending he deserved and we might prefer, it should be told so that, as Socrates prayed, his "sojourn on earth will continue happy beyond the grave."

7   Emily Nathelle Higby Hunt, Autobiographical Essay (unpublished manuscript undated) provided to the author by Lester C. Hunt, Jr., MS Word File

8   Jack Hart, *Storycraft: The Complete Guide to Writing Narrative Nonfiction*, University of Chicago Press (2011), 26

I have been asked frequently why I chose to write about Lester Hunt. It's a reasonable question given that no one has written about so many of the great political personalities of the state's history. Indeed, how unfortunate it is that the shelves of the public libraries across the state have so few books about the rich political history of Wyoming. So, I am asked, "Why Lester Hunt?"

I grew up in Wyoming. In high school and college, I took yearlong courses on Wyoming history. I devoted many of my years to politics, serving ten years in the state legislature and running as the Democratic Party nominee for the U.S. Senate. Yet, I never heard the story of the suicide of one of Wyoming's United States senators. Dr. T.A. Larson wrote the textbook most widely used in Wyoming history courses. Dr. Larson's book simply says, "On June 19, 1954, Senator Lester C. Hunt, overwhelmed by political and personal problems, committed suicide."[9] Dr. Larson wrote nothing more about the "political and personal problems" that overwhelmed Hunt. There is a fascinating story about why Larson left it at that. When I learned the nature of those problems, I wanted to tell the story.

There is another reason. Americans need to know this story, not only for the sake of Lester Hunt and his family, but for the realization it carries that the current lack of civility in the public arena is dangerous and that it has longer roots than we might think. Joe McCarthy is a long time dead and gone but his heirs are alive and well. The ruthless tactics honed by McCarthy and others named in this book continue to be a part of American politics. Today those who use such tactics benefit from having a 24-hour a day, seven-days-a-week news cycle complete with entire radio and television networks dedicated to stretching and denying the truth in order to accomplish questionable ends.

McCarthy and the others would not have chosen the path they chose unless it worked for them and achieved their selfish ends. It con-

---

9   T.A. Larson, *History of Wyoming*, University of Nebraska Press (1965), 520

tinues to work today because a lazy, ill-informed electorate is willing to abdicate its responsibility to the agenda of others. If Lester Hunt's story had been told honestly in 1954, perhaps Americans would have been shocked into taking responsibility for the way in which their vote produced that outcome. It is difficult to imagine what it might take today to change the current ugly course of American discourse. It is, unfortunately, equally difficult to imagine that any democracy can survive this course.

These pages tell of Lester Hunt's ordeal because Americans must wrestle with the fact that the incivility we bemoan today started long ago and has become so much an accepted part of politics as to endanger the very survival of the republic. During the memorial service the Senate conducted for Hunt, "Big Ed" Johnson of Colorado said of his dead colleague, "Lester Hunt was a warm-hearted friendly soul. In his beloved Wyoming he respected and loved everyone, and everyone respected and loved him. Politics to him, as was his religion, was based on warm friendship, courtesy, kindness, gentleness, and good will toward all men."

We should all long for another day when public servants earn such a eulogy.

Nearly six decades have come and gone since Lester Hunt died. Many, if not all, of those who knew Hunt have followed him into the next world. Some, but not all, have left behind records that have been made available. Some of the records left behind are sealed from public review or were destroyed.

For example, the severe limitations imposed on access to the "private files" of Senator McCarthy pose a problem of potential, but uncertain, significance as does the fact that the Federal Bureau of Investigation and Bethesda Naval Hospital destroyed records that would have shed light on the blackmail of Lester Hunt.

The historical record leaves tantalizing evidence of Joe McCarthy's role in Lester Hunt's death. McCarthy's diaries, letters, journals and notes are deposited at Marquette University in Milwaukee. But by agreement with the family of the late Senator, these records, with the exception of newspaper clippings, are sealed until the death of his daughter whom Joe and Jean McCarthy adopted in 1957, when she was five weeks old. We are left to imagine what stories those papers tell that would give McCarthy's family a reason to seal them from public review so long as his daughter is alive. Without access to these papers, an important gap is left in the historical record. In the meantime, only the newspaper stories covering his capers have been studied in an attempt to make this account as complete as currently possible.

A Freedom of Information request seeking FBI records regarding Senator Hunt and his son resulted in disappointment. It would hardly be a surprise that J. Edgar Hoover would have had such files, given the director's penchant for collecting that kind of information. However, the agency lawyers said the records might have once existed but do not now. "Records which may be responsive to your FOIPA request were destroyed between August 1, 1993, and May 16, 2008."[10]

Lester Hunt told constituents he had decided to withdraw from the 1954 Senate race because of health problems. His wife and others attributed his suicide to health problems. There is stronger evidence he didn't actually have serious health problems at all. In order to clarify this issue, copies of his medical records were sought. Despite the extraordinary help of the staff of Wyoming Senator John Barrasso, the records were not located and were likely shredded years after Hunt died.

Regardless of these regrettable holes in the historical record, this book has benefited from my trips to New Hampshire and San Francisco. In Concord I was able to study the massive collection of papers left by the late senator Styles Bridges with the state's Division

10   Letter to author from David M. Hard, Section Chief, Record/Information
Dissemination Section, Federal Bureau of Investigation. March 9, 2012

of Archives and Records Management. The collection of the GLBT (Gay, Lesbian, Bi-sexual and Transgendered) Historical Society in San Francisco provided significant background on Cold War attitudes toward the gay community. Important documents were also obtained from the Presidential libraries of Harry Truman, Dwight Eisenhower and Lyndon Johnson.

In the days before his death, Hunt entrusted 51 boxes of letters, speeches, scrapbooks and other personal papers to the American Heritage Center at the University of Wyoming. I have carefully sorted through every single one of them, reading each and learning a great deal about this man and his times.

Hunt's two children were of immeasurable assistance. Elise Chadwick spoke willingly and lovingly about her parents and their lives. She provided a wonderful glimpse into the family's life in Lander before politics.

I have added Senator Hunt's son to the short list of those to whom this book is dedicated. I could not have undertaken this project without the support and help of Lester C. Hunt, Jr. He has been a most open source of information on his father and the events surrounding his death. A delightful and honest man of 85 years, Lester has encouraged me to "follow the facts" and he has helped me along the way, even when the search may have become personally painful. The ability to tell this story fully and honestly depended entirely on him. Lester Hunt, Sr. was an open and honest man who would be proud of the fact those traits were inherited by his son.

I have a deep sense of regret that I did not personally know Lester Hunt. Yet it is not possible to spend this many hours reading, talking, thinking, and writing about a person without getting to know him. Having been integrally involved in Wyoming politics for much of my life, I am familiar with many of the issues occupying his time and the communities he served, as well as many of those with whom he worked. Before their deaths, I knew many of the people with whom Lester Hunt was engaged. Knowing them, their passions and pursuits provided me with a deeper understanding of the motivation each brought to the work they accomplished together with Hunt.

And so, the story of Lester C. Hunt should be heard not only as history but also as parable. The Hebrew scripture includes the Book of Job, a parable of human response to suffering. Let us begin, for our purposes, by paraphrasing God as he agreed with Satan to visit undeserved suffering on Job.

"The Lord said to Satan, 'Where have you come from?'
Satan answered the Lord, 'From going to and fro on the earth,
and from walking up and down on it.' The Lord said to Satan,
'Have you considered my servant Lester?'"[11]

---

11   Author's paraphrase of Job 1: 7-8

CHAPTER ONE

"Night Falls Fast"[1]

Lester Hunt quietly got out of bed early on the morning of the last day of his life. The Senator hadn't been able to sleep much anyway and he needed to leave without awakening Nathelle. He dressed quickly, stopping to look at her face and assuring himself one last time this was best for her. Walking by the kitchen window, he permitted himself a quick glance across the backyard to where Joe McCarthy lived in a small apartment below. Hunt's lip curled slightly as he remembered the times he had watched Joe and his girlfriends drinking and cavorting on the patio.

McCarthy offended Lester's personal sensibilities of what a senator should be, of what a man should be. The previous day, McCarthy had made public a threat to investigate a senator he didn't name, one he said was involved in a bribe. When Lester Hunt first heard that, he briefly wondered whether he was the target. Now he allowed himself a sneer, an expression that softened as he remembered McCarthy had his own problems. The "Army-McCarthy" hearings had ended two days earlier. He remembered Joe Welch demanding that McCarthy listen. "Senator," he said, "I think I never really gauged your cruelty, or your recklessness."

Then Lester Hunt went on with what remained of his life.

1   The title of a book by Kay Redfield Jamison, *Night Falls Fast: Understanding Suicide,* Alfred A. Knopf (1999)

He quietly opened the closet door and retrieved an old rifle he and Nathelle kept handy in the event that intruders broke into their home again as they had the previous December. As he walked to his car, he loaded the rifle and placed it in the back seat. As Lester Hunt drove one last time down Connecticut Avenue, he looked to his right at the beautiful towers of Washington's National Cathedral just before passing by the Naval Observatory. Minutes later he turned left onto Constitution Avenue and passed by the monuments and memorials that had inspired him, just as they had inspired millions of Americans, over many decades; the Lincoln Memorial, the Washington Monument, the White House in the background. This morning he took little notice and received no inspiration.

Saturday morning traffic was light, the last couple of miles passing so quickly he didn't have to look at the Capitol Building. Hunt's car took him to the rear of the Senate Office Building, and seemed to park itself in the area reserved for "Senators Only." His arms were full of boxes and papers as he walked the long sidewalk to the main door of the building. A young Capitol police officer asked if he could help. Hunt handed him the rifle.[2] The officer carried the gun as he walked beside Hunt until they got to the elevator. Neither man spoke after each acknowledged it was a nice day.

Ronald Maurice, the usual elevator operator, was on duty. He smiled broadly when he saw his passenger was the genial Wyoming Senator.

"How about those Senators," beamed Maurice, referring to the Washington Senators baseball team. "Did you see the game yesterday? They finally won one. 7-5. Beat the Orioles. If I'd had the day off, I'd have taken the train down to Baltimore."

Senators engaged in countless hours of small talk aboard this very

---

2 "Leonard H. Ballard, Inspector, United States Capitol Police, 1947-1984," Oral History Interviews, Pages 216-217, Senate Historical Office, Washington, D.C.

elevator and Hunt, known fondly as the "Pitcher from Atlanta," was always good for some baseball talk. This morning, however, there was none. Hunt didn't respond. Maurice thought the senator looked "right through me." Though Hunt smiled, he didn't seem to have heard a word. It struck Maurice as odd. Yet, the barrel of a rifle sticking out from the bottom of the Senator's coat didn't seem at all odd. "He's from Wyoming," Maurice told himself. "Of course he has guns." The truth is neither an elevator operator nor a security officer would have ever considered questioning a United States senator about what he was carrying or wearing even though the rifle Hunt carried was mostly covered by the heavy top coat he wore on that warm June morning.[3]

Maurice looked at his watch as he reached for the handle to open the elevator door when they stopped at the third floor. It was 8:30. Hunt thanked the operator warmly as always and turned toward his office. Stopping abruptly, he looked back to Maurice and said, "You know Ron, it's only June and those boys are already 17 ½ games out." He continued walking down a hallway that somehow seemed to grow darker.

Those who study these kinds of tragedies tell us that those who take their own lives often choose a time and a place where their bodies will be found first by someone other than beloved family members, someone they trust to compassionately inform a spouse and children. It's not uncommon for people planning to die to "take steps to lessen the impact" on those they love.[4] It's an illogical moment when one about to kill himself believes he can lessen that impact.

Night falls fast and it had fallen for Lester Hunt before Mike Manatos turned his key in the lock of the door to the Senator's office. Hunt timed the morning so that he would arrive only a few minutes before his aide. He made sure he didn't arrive so early that he might have too much time to think about it, though he wanted to give himself

3   *New York Times*, June 20, 1954, Page 1
4   Joiner, *Myths About Suicide*, supra. 41

enough time to get it done before his old friend came through that door. He wanted to be found first by someone he trusted to take care of what necessarily followed.

We'll never know what thoughts and images entered and departed Lester Hunt's mind in those final minutes. We know that in the moments after he arrived and before he knew Manatos would, he moved two photographs, one of son Buddy and the other of daughter Elise, from the cabinet on the far side of the room. He sat them on his desk in front of the chair in which he was found a few minutes later.[5] He wrote four final notes of assurance. A note to his wife assured her of his love and another to his son assured him this was not his fault. Suicide notes seldom, if ever, reveal a great deal about motive. The mind that has decided to kill itself is likely not rational enough to coherently explain the reasons. But Hunt was rational enough to know what the cause was not.

As close as we may get to Hunt's thoughts at that moment are the words Allen Drury ascribed to the fictionalized account of the tragedy. Drury's 1959 Pulitzer Prize winning novel, *Advise and Consent,* is both art and a credible imitation of life.

> *It was late, the time for philosophizing was over, there was little left to do and he did it with a dreamlike efficiency that was the only way it could be done. He closed the venetian blinds, turned off all the lamps but one, unlocked the outer door, so they would not have to break it when (they) came for him, got a towel from the washroom, returned to his desk, and sat down; saying to the Deity to whom he had been taught to pray as a very little boy, God, please help me. Please let me be brave just a little while longer. Please. He wanted to cry and he tried to, but the agony was too deep, the tears would not come.[6]*

5 "Senator Hunt Ends Life With Rifle" *The Washington Evening Star,* June 19, 1954, page A-3
6 Drury, Allen, *Advise and Consent,* Doubleday (1959) Page 547

No one, likely not even Lester Hunt, heard the shot ring out.

It was about a quarter to nine when Mike Manatos fumbled his key into the lock. He was surprised to find the door unlocked that early on a Saturday morning. He'd just walked in from a bright June day, the sun shining brightly in one of those especially blue Washington skies. Inside the sky darkened. A thick fog descended over all who entered Room 304. It was the fog of the horror of what they found that manifested itself in a multitude of mutually irreconcilable memories.

Four envelopes caught his eye as he walked across the threshold. Four envelopes were neatly arranged in the middle of his desk, one on top of the other. In handwriting he recognized, the top envelope was addressed to "Mike." He picked it up. As he peeled back the flap, he saw the second. It was addressed to Senator Hunt's wife Nathelle.

His mind rushed to judgment. His heart began to pound. His breathing deepened. The clock above his desk that usually moved to the next minute every sixty-seconds slowed perceptibly. Mike feared what had happened before he read the name on the third envelope. "To Buddy." He didn't bother with the fourth.

The high ceiling of the ornate office seemed to collapse on him. The walls narrowed to a long tunnel. The short space to Hunt's office suddenly telescoped, leaving him standing on the edge of an abyss, any bridge gone, and below a bottomless pit. His feet knew what to do though his mind struggled to grasp what had happened as his heart began to break. Mike turned and walked dutifully toward the closed door. Time contradicted itself. The short walk to Hunt's door took too much time, so much time to feel the guilt for having not been there earlier that day, for not having been there when the Senator needed him yesterday, last month, time enough to remind Manatos how long the last year had been, filled as it had been with extraordinary emotional demands on this man whom he had grown to love.

But there was not enough time to avoid how fast his life and that of others was about to change. His hand was trembling as he opened the door, knowing already it was too late to change anything. The only light in the room was the sunshine coming through a large window. It provided a haunting backlight as it spread eerily across the face of the Senator. The body of his boss was draped limply across his old leather chair. His head hung over the back, leaning too far to one side. A rifle lay at Hunt's feet, a trickle of blood emerged slowly from his right temple. Manatos hoped for a pulse. Hearing someone walk through the door, he cried out, "Call the senate doctor. Get him up here now."

His head began to spin. The room began to spin faster as it filled with people who were as confused and stunned as was he. Someone began to cry. Someone lifted Hunt's body from the chair to the floor. Someone grabbed a telephone and started yelling through the receiver. Sergeant Leonard Ballard, the security officer on duty, answered the phone. The sergeant didn't want to waste his time waiting for an elevator. He ran up the stairs to the third floor. Entering the suite, he saw Hunt's body stretched out on the carpet. A Winchester Bolt Action .22 rifle lay next to the Senator. Ballard called his friend Jack Frost, a Springfield, Virginia, detective. Frost arrived within minutes. He suggested a flower truck ruse in order to buy Hunt's staff some time to inform family and prepare a statement for the press.[7] The truck arrived shortly and quickly backed up to the loading dock at the rear of the Senate Office Building. The driver was confused about why he'd been asked to go there in an empty van. The assignment may have seemed unusual to him but what mattered was that it was not unusual for his truck to be at that loading dock. A flower truck in the delivery zone of that building would not have drawn any attention. An ambulance or

7   Leonard H. Ballard, Inspector, United States Capitol Police, 1947-1984, "Oral History Interviews, Pages 217-219, Senate Historical Office, Washington, D.C.
8   *Washington Evening Star,* June 19, 1954.

worse yet, a hearse would have, and Senator Hunt's staff was hoping to avoid any attention until his wife and children could be notified of Lester's suicide.

Ballard remembered ordering the flower truck to remove Hunt's remains saying that when he arrived at suite 304 shortly after the shooting, "They took me back in the Senator's office and the Senator was stretched out on the floor dead as a door nail." Others' memories conflicted. Soon Washington's late day newspaper, *The Evening Star*, hit the streets in front of the Senate Office Building, reporting the "Metropolitan Police got their report deviously." The police, they said, received a call from an unnamed Washington doctor asking for a police escort to Casualty Hospital "because he had heard Senator Hunt had shot himself."[8] Contrary to Ballard's "dead as a door nail" report, the *Star* reported Hunt had been found "wounded." By it's account, he died three and a half hours later, having been taken to Casualty Hospital. The *Star* said Mrs. Hunt was with her husband at the hospital as he was wheeled hurriedly into the operating room at 11 A.M. The paper was up against a deadline. The printing presses were about to run. There was no time to change the body of their story. The editor hastily tacked on a short paragraph ahead of the first. "Senator Hunt, Democrat of Wyoming died at 12:32 p.m. today of a bullet wound which, Capitol police said, apparently was self-inflicted."[9]

That report differed from yet another which was interpreted by one newspaper to have been an effort to deceive reporters to "conceal the fact of the shooting.[10], [11] One of Hunt's staff was said to have told the capitol police her boss had suffered a heart attack. The staffer said that Lieutenant Ed Adams and Private James Goodall of the Senate

9   *Washington Evening Star*, June 19, 1954
10   Pvt. Edward R. Murray, Senate Office Detail, Statement to William J. Broderick, United States Capitol Police, June 19, 1954.
11   *Washington Evening Star*, June 19, 1954

Security Detail had immediately rushed to the office, hoping to help save Hunt's life. By the time they arrived, so had a member of the senate medical staff.[12] Officers from the U.S. Capitol and the District of Columbia Police Departments were also on the scene.

Hunt's office was swarming with dazed, confused people. It was one of those times when it was possible that different perceptions of what happened could all be true. Perhaps none was completely accurate. Within minutes, the office and the hallway in front of it were filling with noise of all sorts; sobs, orders being shouted from and to Hunt's staff and the staff of other members of the Senate, capitol and metropolitan police, a doctor from the senate medical staff and others. In the moments following the horror there was more than an expected amount of confusion.

As the fog slowly began to lift, Captain Broderick of the U.S. Capitol Police Department took charge of the investigation. The elevator operator who had delivered Hunt to the third floor was summoned. Ronald Maurice told investigators he had seen the rifle but had thought nothing of it.[13] Private Paul Flynn of the Capitol police said he'd seen the Senator arrive at the Senate Office Building around 8:15 that morning. The senator was in "exceptional spirits," according to Flynn who added, "He commented pleasantly on the weather and then entered the building."[14]

Manatos took charge of the Senator's staff. Mike gave assignments to the few staffers who were there on a Saturday morning. He called Mrs. Hunt. Ira Whitlock drafted a statement for the press. Stewart McClure, who was an aide to Senator Guy Gillette of Iowa, heard the

12   Pvt. James L. Goodall, Senate Office Detail, Statement to William J. Broderick, Captain, United States Capitol Police, June 19, 1954.
13   Lt. Edward B. Adams, Senate Office Detail, Statement to William J. Broderick, Captain, United States Capitol Police, June 19, 1954
14   Pvt. W. Paul Flynn, Senate Office Detail, Statement to the captain, United States Capitol Police, June 19, 1954.

commotion and arrived, asking what he could do to help.[15]

There was no standard operating procedure for handling the suicide of a U.S Senator. In the history of the Republic, nearly 2000 men and women have served in the Senate. Hunt was only the fifth to take his own life while yet in office.[16] The staff simply reacted, doing what they had always done. They protected the image of their boss as they told the story of his suicide. A statement was released. Ironically, Manatos used the same words Hunt used ten days earlier in his statement announcing a decision to withdraw from the senate race. Both statements blamed medical problems. "Senator Lester Hunt has been undergoing extensive medical examinations at the Bethesda Naval Hospital throughout June and for some time before."[17] Manatos told the *New York Times* his boss "apparently suffered from a kidney affliction which had given him great cause for concern."[18]

Hunt's colleagues followed his lead. Former Wyoming Senator Joe O'Mahoney said he had visited Hunt the previous day, finding him "pale and depressed."[19] Senator Earl Campbell of Kentucky told the press "close associates had recognized some indications of his being depressed over his health."20 At the hospital Mrs. Hunt told reporters her husband was "a very, very sick man."[21] News reports disclosed the

15   Stewart E. McClure: Chief Clerk, Senate Committee on Labor, Education and Public Welfare (1949-1973), "Oral History Interviews", Page 148, Senate Historical Office, Washington, D.C.

16   Thomas Jefferson Rusk was the first. Rusk was a U.S. Senator from Texas who committed suicide while in office in 1857. James H. Lane was a Kansas senator who shot himself to death on July 1, 1866. U.S. Senator Frank Brandegee of Connecticut committed suicide by inhaling from a gaslight in Washington, D.C. on October 14, 1924. Joseph McCormick, a Senator from Illinois, took his own life in 1925. Lester Hunt was the fifth and Senator John Porter East of North Carolina the sixth and the most recent. He died at his own hand in 1986.

17   *New York Times*, June 20, 1954, Page 1

18   *New York Times*, June 20, 1954, Page 1

19   *New York Times*, June 20, 1954

20   United Press Story printed in the *Pantagraph* Newspaper in Atlanta, Illinois, June 20, 1954, Page 5

21   Evening Star June 19, 1954

Senator's brother Clyde had also "died at his own hand – two years ago."[22]

Hunt's body had not yet been delivered to the Gawlers Funeral Home when the speculation began about who might replace the Democrat. Hunt's death left the Senate at 47 Democrats and 47 Republicans. If Hunt were to be replaced with a Republican, the GOP would regain the majority they'd lost when Robert Taft of Ohio died the year before. Wyoming Governor C. J. Rogers quickly erased any doubt. A Republican would be appointed.[23] Other Wyoming Republicans guessed, mistakenly, that a former GOP senator, E.V. Robertson, whom Hunt had defeated in 1948, would be chosen. Governor Rogers instead chose Edward Crippa, a Republican Party stalwart.[24]

While family and friends, some reporters and colleagues, were willing to accept the "health" story as the reason for Hunt's suicide, others were more certain there was something far more sinister in the story. The Washington underground knew what Hunt's staff and colleagues were unprepared that day to discuss. Lester Hunt was one more casualty in Joe McCarthy's war on democracy.

22   The *Pantagraph*, June 20, 1954, Page 5 and the New York Times, June 20, 1954, Page 72

23   *New York Times*, June 20, 1954, Page 1

24   Letter Dated June 20, 1954, signed "Edward D. Crippa, USS" thanking Alice Winter of Casper for her congratulatory letter, File "Correspondence June, 1954" Papers of Edward D. Crippa, Collection No. 5848, American Heritage Center, University of Wyoming

CHAPTER TWO

The Pitcher From Atlanta Comes to Wyoming

In 1902 there wasn't much to distract a ten-year-old boy from his schoolwork in Atlanta, Illinois. No picture shows, certainly no television, not even a radio. A couple of young fellows up the road in Springfield had invented a new mode of travel. They said horses would soon be almost useless. As late as 1908, it was front-page news in the *Atlanta Argus* when a few candidates for political office toured the county in automobiles. Horses still provided most of Logan County's transportation when Lester Hunt, his father William, Mother Viola, brother Clyde and sister Nila Elise arrived.

All communities have landscapes. Landscapes are more than vistas. Landscapes include the people of a community, their values, and the way in which their lives and fortunes are formed by their historic responses to the land around them. Children who grow up in an urban landscape often differ considerably from those who grow up in a rural landscape. The landscape of the early years often puts a youngster on a certain path as it establishes personality and values. Hunt was born in Isabel, Illinois, but it was the "community landscape" of Atlanta, with the values Americans generally attribute to small towns, which largely determined whom he would become in his twenty two years of public service. It was those years that caused him to be so fond of the new

11

life he found on the Wyoming prairie a decade later. The similarities between the landscape of the life Hunt enjoyed in Atlanta, Illinois, and the landscape of the life he later adopted in Lander, Wyoming, are striking. Atlanta is one of seventeen townships in Logan County, Illinois. Early in the twentieth century, county historians described the county's "gently undulating character, covered here and there with beautiful groves of timber."[1] The fertile land and streams created an ideal setting for early settlers looking for a place to make a new life. Lester Hunt fell in love with Wyoming's mountains and prairies, but he first learned to appreciate those open landscapes by looking across the Illinois vistas. One enthusiastic Logan County historian said, "From the summit of many of the slight eminences, found everywhere throughout the county, charming views of prairie scenery can be obtained."[2]

In 1839, State Representative Abraham Lincoln, then a member of the General Assembly, sponsored legislation establishing the county. Lincoln chose the name. Logan County honored his friend Dr. John Logan, a well-known Illinois pioneer and fellow legislator who didn't live in Logan County. He lived in Jackson County.[3] Still, Lincoln thought the county should bear his name and so it does.

Many of Hunt's Illinois neighbors, like his neighbors in Wyoming, eked out a living raising livestock and crops. Three quarters of the land in the county was under cultivation. Maize was the primary crop. Because it was plentiful, farmers were able to raise large numbers of cattle and hogs as well. County fairs were occasions of great community fun, an opportunity to show off a farmer's successes. In addition, a nearby coal mine provided a few jobs there just as a coal mine near Lander did for that community. Such were the parallels between the landscape Hunt grew up around in Atlanta and the landscape he later

1 Anonymous Author, *History of Logan County: Its Past and Present,* reproduction of 1923 book, Nabu Publishing (2010), 173.
2 Id. 173
3 Logan Illinois ILGENWEB Project, accessed at logan.ilgenweb.net on October 27, 2011

adopted in Lander. Small towns, farms, and working people making their life from the earth characterized both.

As a United States Senator, Hunt remembered the "fine, wholesome, intellectual atmosphere" of Atlanta. The community took both politics and religion seriously. In those days, neither religion nor politics had yet been demeaned by television. State and national political figures found their way to Atlanta frequently, appearing in person, debating, speaking, and sometimes preaching.

One Sunday evening in September of 1910, the usual quiet was broken by a political rally. A socialist candidate for President came to town to give a speech. Candidates often passed through the small towns of Illinois but having one show up on a Sunday was unusual. He was likely unaware of a local ordinance prohibiting political speeches on the Sabbath. When a policeman arrived to enforce the law, the quick thinking politician claimed he was actually giving a sermon which, of course, was allowed, even encouraged on a Sunday in Atlanta. "It was now up to the cop to decide whether the oration was a really truly Bible sermon or a political speech," wrote a local newspaper reporter covering the confrontation. "This was a difficult matter as it had been a long time since one of the force had heard a sermon." The issue was decided in the politician's favor when the Socialist passed a collection plate.[4]

The people of Atlanta were, Hunt thought, "the finest people with whom my life's journey has brought me into contact." He felt much the same about the people of Wyoming. He was a fourth grader when his family moved from Isabel to Atlanta in 1902. Atlanta schools were serious about their responsibility to educate youngsters. When the superintendent of the schools was charged with assault for chastising one of Hunt's schoolmates "more than was necessary," the judge ruled, "The boy got no more than was coming to him."[5]

4 *Atlanta Argus* Newspaper, September 2, 1910
5 *Atlanta Argus* Newspaper, December 4, 1908

Soon young Lester was demonstrating the skills that would underlie a lifetime of achievement. In 1911, competing against students from 10 area schools, Hunt won third place in the Corn Belt Oratorical and Athletic Association oratory contest. He was the quarterback of his high school football team. In 1910 his team defeated their rival Lincoln High by a score of 56-0. He lettered in football and track, winning second place in the pole vault at the annual Corn Belt Athletic Association track meet.[6]

Lester's mother, Alvira Viola Hunt, role modeled an engaged civic life. She was the superintendent of the Sunday school at the Methodist church. Mrs. Hunt served as the "vice oracle" of the Royal Neighbors, a women's empowerment organization with nineteenth century Midwest roots. She was one of the leaders in the local chapter of the Women's Christian Temperance Union, undoubtedly having a lasting influence on her son. As governor of Wyoming he proudly called himself "a prohibitionist."

Just before Hunt was reelected governor of Wyoming in 1946, a flattering three-part story of his life was published in the Cheyenne newspaper, verifying how significant Hunt's deep roots had been to his success. "To understand the personality of the man who left home as a young kid to pitch baseball and who later sacrificed his dental practice to enter politics and government," explained the newspaper, "one has to go back to his earlier years to the little town of Isabel, Ill., where Lester Hunt was born of sturdy stock."[7]

Family Roots

Viola Hunt, like her son, was born in Isabel, Illinois, in 1871, the ninth child of William and Margaret Calloway.[8] William's father, Elijah

---

6 *Atlanta Argus* Newspaper, June 3, 1910
7 "The Kid Pitcher from Atlanta" *Wyoming Eagle,* October 18. 1946, 2
8 The genealogical and family history information contained in this chapter is derived

Washington Calloway, was born in Sussex County, Delaware a year before the colonies declared their independence from Britain. Elijah married Elizabeth Pack in 1804. They moved west to Illinois around 1833. Hunt's son, Lester Hunt, Jr. (Buddy), called it his "best guess" that his father's side of the family was of Scots-Irish ancestry, an educated guess based on considerable research placing the earliest family members in Ireland's County Ulster. He described his father's early ancestors as living a "hill billy' life very typical of the Scotch-Irish." Hunt's middle name was derivative of these folks. Peter Callaway emigrated from England in 1649. Peter was the great-great grandfather of Lester Hunt's great-great grandfather Elijah Callaway.

Peter Callaway[9] lived first in Somerset County, Maryland as an indentured servant. It was common for immigrants, who could seldom afford the voyage to America, to commit to work for a farmer or craftsman in the New World. In the seventeenth century, two-thirds of all immigrants arrived owing a term of indentured servitude. [10] Indentured servants, like slaves, received food and board. Unlike slaves, they were freed at the end of the agreed term of servitude. If servants worked their full indenture, they were given their freedom based loosely on Old Testament teaching.[11] In some cases, freed servants were also granted land.

Peter's servitude lasted eighteen years, from his arrival in 1649 until 1667. During those years he was not permitted to marry. As a

from the extensive research and unpublished documentation of Lester C. Hunt, Jr. provided to the author in September of 2010.

9 A careful reader might have already noted that at times, the name is spelled with an "o" as in Calloway, and at others with an "a" as in Callaway. Lester Hunt, Jr.'s family history explains that his father changed the spelling from "o" to "a" after a "trip to Kentucky where he saw some murals of famous "Callaways" and decided that was how it should be spelled."

10 Deanna Barker, *Indentured Servitude in Colonial America*, Frontier Resources, accessed at webcitation.org on October 28, 2011

11 Deuteronomy 15:12 "If a member of your community, whether a Hebrew man or a Hebrew woman, is sold to you and works for you six years, in the seventh year you shall set that person free."

consequence of this long wait, Peter and Elizabeth, with whom he had fallen in love, found themselves in front of a judge. Each was convicted and fined. Elizabeth was found guilty of "bearing a bastard child," and Peter of "getting a bastard child." The court records include a report of Elizabeth's "peculiar conduct." She had been observed wandering "amongst ye Indians and layeth in ye marshes." As a result, she was required to undergo what was apparently counseling or a form of probation to correct her "idleness alsoe to provide her a service that she may worke for her living."

Peter and Elizabeth were at long last married in 1667, and had four children. The last was William Callaway whose grandson was Isaiah. Isaiah's 1775 baptism in the Lewes Presbyterian Church was dramatic. The Callaways were in the sanctuary of the Maryland church. The ritual had just begun when it was "interrupted by certain intelligence that the Tories would kidnap and send me (the minister) to ye enemy at New York for Exemplary Punishment." The record doesn't disclose whether young Elijah was ever properly baptized. He moved the Callaway family to Illinois early in the nineteenth century, settling in the fertile lands of Edgar County where they lived in a log cabin within walking distance of one owned by Abraham Lincoln's father, Thomas.

Lester Jamison Is Surnamed Hunt

Lester Hunt's father William was born in DeWitt County, Illinois in 1867. When he was 21, he and Alvira Calloway were married in the small town of Paris in Edgar County, Illinois. Like the Lincolns and so many others, the stories of the Calloway and Hunt families are the stories of America's progressive and relentless movement into the frontier.

Hunt's grandmother Julia Ann Campbell was born in Bourbon County, Kentucky on June 26,1828. She married Samuel Hunt on December 7, 1841. They moved to Illinois, where Samuel Hunt died in 1858. He was just 30 years old. Samuel and Julia Hunt had six children, none of whom was Lester's father, William. Following Samuel's death, Julia Ann married Harvey Jamison in August of 1859. Three children were born to the couple. One was William.[12]

The 1860 Federal Census lists Julia Ann as living with son William and husband Harvey Jamison in DeWitt County, Illinois. A decade later Harvey is no longer listed. Mr. Jamison has, for an unknown reason, disappeared. Julia Ann Jamison is listed as "head of household." The three children are listed with Jamison's surname but when the 1880 Federal Census was published, Julia had become the "Widow Hunt." She was now living with John Hunt in Springfield, Illinois, along with the two youngest children, Franklin and William. The children are also listed as "Hunt." Both kept the surname. The man who might have been known as "Lester C. Jamison" became instead Lester C. Hunt.

Lester Hunt's Birth and Early History

The branches of the Calloway and Hunt family trees converged in the marriage of William Hunt to Alvira Viola Calloway on October 17, 1888. Of that union, Lester Calloway Hunt, the future governor and United States Senator from Wyoming, was born on July 8, 1892 in Isabel, Illinois. William and Alvira moved their young family to Atlanta, Illinois in 1902. Atlanta was a formative experience for the young lad. Patriotism was wildly celebrated in Atlanta. Lester remembered with great detail the first 4th of July he spent there. "Captain Trout leading the parade on a white horse, a small colored man, wearing a Yankee blue uniform with a pointed Yankee blue hat, carrying the American flag. I can still hear the chug of Doctor Burke's Oldsmobile, the first car in Atlanta."

In the "intellectual atmosphere" of Atlanta, young Lester heard some of the great orators of the day. His mother took sister Nila Elise,

12 Adelia was born in 1859, Benjamin Franklin in 1865, and William on April 14, 1867

brother Clyde and Lester to hear the Reverend Billy Sunday speak at the nearby Lincoln County Chautauqua in August of 1908. Reverend Sunday, the "Billy Graham" of his day, was a one-time major league baseball star who became one of the most famous Evangelical Christian preachers in America.

Young Lester also heard William Jennings Bryan give his famous "Cross of Gold" speech. Bryan was a one-time Nebraska congressman who railed against the nation's gold standard, crying, "You shall not crucify mankind upon a cross of gold." The speech carried Bryan to the 1896 Democratic Party's nomination for President but not to the White House. Bryan lost to William McKinley. Still, it must have been inspirational to young Lester Hunt to hear this great orator. A year later, Carrie Nation was the featured speaker in 1910. She proclaimed herself "a bulldog running along at the feet of Jesus, barking at what He doesn't like." Nation was one of the more radical leaders of the pro-temperance and prohibition movement.[13]

Readers of the local newspaper quickly became familiar with young Lester. The paper frequently printed stories of his athletic and scholastic feats. Hunt's name appeared first as a member of the Atlanta baseball team that won both ends of a doubleheader. He hit a home-run in the second game helping Atlanta to a 19-0 victory. Atlanta High School's annual "Old Timers Game" pitted alumni against the school's varsity team. Despite what the *Argus* called "the custom for the high school team to be beaten" the high school boys prevailed in the 1909 game because, the paper reported, of the excellent play of Lester Hunt and his friend "Muggs" Dunham.

Lester not only won awards for athletic accomplishments and oratory while attending school in Atlanta, he also established his lifelong work ethic. "During these very interesting times, I felt quite important

13 Keven McQueen, *"Carrie Nation: Militant Prohibitionist"*. *Offbeat Kentuckians: Legends to Lunatics*. McClanahan Publishing House (2001)

being the official janitor for the little library by Murphy Hall, sweeping out each Saturday morning and building a fire for Miss Spindler, and receiving the exorbitant sum of ten cents per week. And when the new library was built, I was promoted to a like job in the new library and my salary increased to twenty-five cents a week."[14]

Lester's father William worked for the Vandalia Railroad Company, acquired later by the Pennsylvania Railroad. The hard-working and well-liked William was elected mayor of Atlanta only a few years after arriving.[15] Mayor William Hunt was in much the same political environment in which his son would later find himself. Logan County was heavily Republican. He was a Democrat. He was defeated in a bid for re-election in 1909. In the analysis of the local newspaper editor, "There appeared to be no live issues at stake and in most cases party preference seemed to be the deciding factor."[16] Lester was later determined that political preference would never be the deciding factor in any of his political contests.

William Hunt was, his reelection loss notwithstanding, beloved in Atlanta. One time the newspaper got wind that Hunt had been offered a higher salary to move to Oakland, Illinois and later happily announced Atlanta's "accommodating station agent" had turned down the offer.[17] But on March 18, 1910, the *Argus* ran an article on the center of the front-page with William's portrait. "Agent Hunt Will Leave Atlanta." Mr. Hunt had been named station agent in Arthur, Illinois, a small farming community about 60 miles southeast of Atlanta. Hunt left immediately and the rest of the family followed once Lester completed high school. The *Argus* thanked them for being "active in the religious and social life of the city" and grieved that the departure of

14 Speech dedicating memorial to WWI and WWII veterans in Atlanta, IL, November 1, 1947, File: "National Defense Speeches (2)" Box 3, LCH Papers
15 Legal Notice, *Atlanta Argus* Newspaper, June 5, 1905
16 *Atlanta Argus* Newspaper, March 19, 1909.
17 *Atlanta Argus* Newspaper, December 11, 1908.

Hunt and his family would be "keenly felt."

William Hunt worked for the railroad for 50 years before his retirement. Lester Hunt never forgot his roots in that union family. He was always a strong union supporter, a direct result of watching his father struggle. William's right arm was amputated at the shoulder following an accident while he was attempting to decouple two train cars at a crossing in Lovington, Illinois in 1902.[18] Although he was right handed, he quickly adapted, learning to write and use a telegraph with his left hand. He was then sent to the train station at Atlanta.[19] His lifelong friend, a Mr. Fitzpatrick, had likewise lost an arm, his left. Each Christmas the two exchanged gifts, a pair of gloves. William kept the left-hand glove and gave the right- handed glove to his friend.

William was an unapologetic union activist, chairing the Grievance Committee, advocating for fellow union members. He never missed a day's work but was retired in 1936 with little to show for five decades of devotion to the job. "Practically all he had to leave for we (sic) kids was his fifty-year pin."[20]

Tragedy struck in December of 1910. Following gall bladder surgery, Alvira experienced severe complications, possibly infection. She died on Christmas Eve. Lester was 18 years old when he lost his mother "and he learned the meaning of responsibility early in life."[21] The Hunt children were sent to live in the homes of different relatives. Young Lester landed in the home of an aunt with whom he had conflict. He soon left to live with another aunt. In spite of such problems in his life, Lester continued to excel in his studies and on the baseball field. The summer following the loss of his mother, Lester delighted a crowd in Atlanta by pitching a no-hitter. The cheer was loud enough to be

18 *Atlanta Argus* Newspaper, March 18, 1910, page 1
19 Letter from US Senator Lester C. Hunt to W.P. Kennedy, Brotherhood of Railroad Trainmen, October 21, 1953, File: "Hunt-Personal-1953" Box 19, LCH Papers
20 Id.
21 "The Kid Pitcher from Atlanta" *Wyoming Eagle,* October 18, 1945, 2

heard all the way to Wyoming. Somehow in an era long before ESPN, word traveled about this young ballplayer in rural Illinois. He was soon recruited to play baseball 800 miles away in Lander, Wyoming.

The "Pitcher from Atlanta" heads west

Lester likely had some familiarity with Wyoming. In 1908, an Atlanta businessman partnered with a Wyoming company to promote the sale of Wyoming land. Ads covering a quarter of the front-page frequently appeared in the *Atlanta Argus*. "Under the Carey Act a person entering this land receives a title from the United States government through the State of Wyoming," read one such ad on September 25, 1908. "You can take 40, 80, 120 or 160 acres. At the time of filing you pay the State of Wyoming 25 cents per acre, and pay $5.00 per acre on your perpetual water right. You pay an additional payment of $5.00 per acre on or before May 1, 1909, the balance you pay in 10 equal annual installments of $2.50 per acre, which is less than rent in older states. You then own the land and perpetual water right and a proportionate interest in the ditches, reservoirs, canals and irrigation systems."[22]

Regardless of how much or how little Lester knew about Wyoming, the people of Lander knew enough about him. They'd heard of that no-hitter. They wanted him on their roster. Lander was as enthused about baseball as most of America in the early part of the twentieth century.

Today it may be difficult to appreciate what baseball meant to most people in the years in which Emily and Lester were teenagers, years before television. Baseball had a national stage, but was a more popular pastime in local communities. Ken Burns, the baseball documentarian and filmmaker, observed, "Home town baseball in the nineties was rough and rowdy and hugely popular. Everybody seemed to play baseball. "Marrieds" played "singles," the "Fats" took on the "Leans," and

---

22 *Atlanta Argus* Newspaper, September 4, 1908

big crowds turned out to see "Mother Hubbard" teams, men playing in women's clothing. Under guard at Fort Sill, Oklahoma, Geronimo's Chiricahua Apaches played ball."[23]

Baseball news made headlines everywhere. Newspapers featured stories about the major league teams on pages four or five but the local teams made the front page. The publicity inspired folks to play and to cheer. The frenzy of the spectators prompted George Bernard Shaw to exclaim, "What is both surprising and delightful is that spectators are allowed, and even expected, to join in the vocal part of the game. There is no reason why the field should not try to put the batsman off his stroke at the critical moment by neatly timed disparagements of his wife's fidelity and his mother's respectability."

A song written by vaudevillian Jack Norworth was on its way to becoming baseball's national anthem.

"Katie Casey was baseball mad, had the fever and had it bad.

Just to root for the hometown crew, every sou- Katie blew.

On a Saturday her young beau called to see if she'd like to go to see a show

but Miss Kate said, No!" I'll tell you what you can do.

Take me out to the ball game,

take me out with the crowd.

Buy me some peanuts and cracker jacks.

I don't care if I never get back.

Let me root, root, root for the home team.

If they don't win, it's a shame.

For it's one, two, three strikes, you're out...at the old ball game."[24]

23 Ken Burns and Geoffrey C. Ward, *Baseball: An Illustrated History*, Knopf (1994), 45
24 Id. 96

Undoubtedly young Emily Higby and her friends knew the words and sang the song as they cheered the hometown team. "Like many small communities throughout the nation, Lander had gone wild over baseball. Sheep wagons lumbered into town on Sunday to watch the home-town boys perform on a baseball diamond carved out of the virgin prairie."[25]

Lander lost a couple of its most talented players in 1911 when the Chicago White Sox signed Jim "Death Valley" Scott and "Greasy" Farthing.[26] Though folks in Lander were delighted to have their two young stars go to the big leagues, there "was no joy in Mudville." Their departure left a big hole in Lander's hopes. Someone told club manager Charles "Ikey" Thomas, "Ikey, looks like you may have to get a pitcher from Peoria." And that's where Ikey went looking. He found more than what he was looking for in the Central Illinois Baseball League. Ikey scouted a pitcher-catcher combination that was setting the league on fire.[27] Lester Hunt had pitched his no-hitter with his close friend Muggs Dunham doing the catching. Lander asked Hunt to come to Wyoming. He agreed on condition that Muggs also be invited.

The deal was struck and both young men packed their bags, hopped a train and headed out west with Uncle C.E. Huffield as their chaperone. The three eventually arrived at the Chicago and Northwestern train station in Riverton, Wyoming, twenty-five miles northeast of

25 "The Kid Pitcher From Atlanta" *Wyoming Eagle*, October 18, 1945, 2

26 "The Chicago White Sox won its only two championships of the 20th century in 1906 and 1917. In between those two glorious seasons, the team fell back to the middle of the pack in the American League, but were always competitive, due in large part to the unheralded and hard luck hurling of a burly right-handed pitcher from Wyoming, Jim "Death Valley" Scott. Although more often than not ending up on the wrong end of the score, Scott spent 25 years working in major and minor league baseball as a pitcher and umpire, and remains as one of the leading pitchers in franchise history." *JIM SCOTT* by John Bennett http://bioproj.sabr.org/bioproj. Scott pitched 9 major league seasons, ending his career with nearly 1000 strikeouts. *The Baseball Encyclopedia*, 9th Edition, MacMillan Publishing (1993), 2231

27 Lewis Nordyke, *Rocky Mountain Empire Magazine*, "The Pitcher From Peoria," September 19, 1948.

Lander, the station closest to their future ballpark.[28] As the two young men "got off a freight train on an evening in early June of 1911" they saw "a few shacks in a place called Riverton," a community that was but five years old. Governor Hunt told the story often to his Riverton constituents reminding them of how much they had accomplished since 1911.[29] As a candidate for the U.S. Senate in 1948, Hunt made a nostalgic visit to nearby Lander, his old hometown. He recalled his first walk "down Main Street, lined with tall shade trees, saloons, bars, and cafes and with horses standing at the hitching racks. He remembers that the cool, dry air of an especially pleasant Wyoming evening carried with it a faint tinge of beer and cigar smoke."[30]

Emily Nathelle Higby

It wasn't long before Lester caught the eye of a pretty, young local "gal" by the name of Emily Nathelle Higby. Over the next 40 years, Nathelle, as he called her, would be an important part of all of Lester's achievements, from dentistry to politics and, most important, raising their children. Her family history would have signaled that. Her ancestors participated in many of the hallmarks of early American history. Her family tree branched back to the Mayflower when Edward Fuller arrived on its board in 1620. Edward was the 21 signer of the Mayflower Compact and a friend and contemporary of Captain Miles Standish, best known as the character cast by Henry Wadsworth Longfellow in his book *The Courtship of Miles Standish*. Standish was hired by the Pilgrims to be the military advisor for Plymouth Colony. Edward Fuller and his wife were among a large number of colonists who failed to survive that first winter in the New World.

Nathaniel Seeley was another of Nathelle's ancestors. He was an

28 Autobiographical essay of Emily Nathelle Higby Hunt, supra.
29 Lester Hunt, Jr.'s "Family History" supra
30 "Hunt Visits, Recalls How He Came To Lander As Youth To Play Baseball" *Wyoming State Journal*, August 17, 1948, 1

army captain who took part in "King Phillip's War" against an upris-
ing of the Wampanoag Indians.[31] Captain Seeley fought in the "Great
Swamp Fight" at Narragansett Bay, Rhode Island, in 1675. Seeley was
ordered to lead his regiment in an attack on a fort held by the Indians.
They ran unaware into "fire so deadly that four of the five Connecticut
captains were killed."[32] Captain Seeley was, unfortunately, one of the
four.

His descendants include the grandmother for whom Emily Nathelle
was named and who, in 1858, married Edward Oliver (E.O.) Wright.
In the spring of 1879, E.O. loaded a covered wagon and moved their
family to York, Nebraska and opened the Red Lyon Flouring Mill. The
mill was quite successful, grinding more than 100,000 bushels of grain
each year and turning out 100 barrels of flour each day.

Among the Wright children was Maude who married Guy Higby.
Guy and Maude raised three children. One was Emily Nathelle who, in
1911, set her eyes on the future governor of Wyoming. She was born on
March 5, 1895. The earliest "recollections of my life in York, Nebraska
where I was born," she wrote in her autobiography, "were of close family ties with my maternal grandfather, Edward Oliver Wright, pioneer
and proprietor of Seeley Mills and paternal grandmother, Hannah
Elizabeth Higby, several aunts, uncles and a number of cousins."[33] She
was deeply moved by the kindness her grandfather showed the children of Russian immigrants. He quietly purchased shoes for the young
barefoot Russian children as he came across them on cold winter days
in York.

Nathelle had memories of being one of the first to be vaccinated
for measles while in York. She learned to read earlier in her life while
confined to her bed with the measles. "This time I was vaccinated on

31 Nathaniel Philbrick, *Mayflower*, Penguin Books (2006), 266.
32 Id. 273.
33 Information in this section comes from Mrs. Hunt's autobiographical essay

the arm with resulting large scar, the theory being that if infection took place, it was better to lose an arm than a leg."

When Guy developed a lung disease, doctors advised him to "live an outdoor" life. His job as a civil engineer allowed him to work outdoors for prospectors searching for gold and farmers developing water rights. Guy relocated his family from York to Deadwood, South Dakota for a short time before Guy was hired to survey the planned railroad track from Casper to Lander, necessitating the move that brought them to Lander.

The Higbys moved from Deadwood to Lander, traveling by train as far as existing tracks allowed. The last train stop was at Casper, Wyoming. There they loaded everything into covered wagons for the final 120 miles. A heavily loaded covered wagon in those days moved more slowly than a person could walk. If all went well and they experienced neither breakdowns nor bad weather, a wagon averaged about two miles an hour.[34] Given they had to stop before the sun went down in order to prepare for the evening, this trip likely took a week or more.

The Higby wagon train stopped one evening to make camp. As they struggled to put up a tent, two Indians on horseback appeared from over a nearby rise. The Indians watched them for a short while before riding away. Although the incident momentarily raised her heartbeat, Nathelle later mused the Indians must have laughed aloud watching these white folks struggle with the tent.

The presence of the Indians signaled that the Higby wagon train was near Lander, close to the Wind River Indian Reservation where the Northern Arapaho Tribe was assigned to share land with its ancient enemy, the Eastern Shoshone. As their covered wagon rolled into the Lander Valley, young Emily Nathelle was smitten as much as was Lester

---

34 "On the Oregon Trail" Katherine A. Young and Virgil M. Young Producers, Designers, Writers, and Websters in cooperation with Boise State University, accessed at education. boisestate.edu/compass on October 26, 2011

a few years later. "My father," she wrote, "had told us about the beauties of the Lander valley and the Wind River Range of the Rockies, but coming over the hill into town was a sight which thrilled my mother and greatly pleased my father."

It was that same mountain range that so moved Lester years later when he came west. "They're never the same, he said. "There is surely nothing on heaven or earth to compare with them." [35] His love of that landscape never faltered. To a radio audience at the dedication of Lander's first radio station on November 14, 1948, Wyoming's newly elected Senator heralded "the brightness of our sunshine, the brightness of our air, the music of our refreshing breezes, the majestic grandeur of the Wind River Mountains, the beauty of our lakes and rivers," concluding, "time has not changed the peace and security of our wide open spaces."

This was the Lander Valley into which the Higby family drove their covered wagon and started a new life.

Lester and Emily Nathelle

In 1911, Emily Nathelle was a student at Lander High School when the "pitcher from Atlanta" and his catcher, Muggs Dunham showed up that summer day. She was 16. Lester was 19. "These boys were attractive and good-looking, liked to dance and go on picnics between practices," Mrs. Hunt later recalled. Hunt played ball that summer, returning the following year as well, staying in the home of the mayor, Jacob Delfelder.[36] There is little to indicate a romance between Nathelle and Lester caught fire before each took separate paths to college. After graduating from Lander High School, she attended South Dakota State College, majoring in music.

35 Paper entitled "Hunt and Sacajawea" page 10, File "Hunt, Lester C." Box 3, Papers of Blanche Schroer, Collection No. 10575, American Heritage Center, University of Wyoming
36 Letter from Hunt to Mrs. J.A. Delfelder dated January 11, 1954, File: "Hunt-Personal-1954" Box 19, LCH Papers

Lester returned home and then headed to Valparaiso University in Indiana and enrolled in pre-med classes. He had saved for college, working summers as a migrant worker in the wheat fields of the Dakotas, but his father used that money to make ends meet. Lester was unable to continue his medical studies. [37] He told newscaster John Cameron Swayze in 1953 it was, "The greatest disappointment of my life, which ultimately turned to be the most significant in my adult life." [38] Hunt went to work, as had his father, on the railroad. Mr. Fitzpatrick, William's old friend and fellow amputee, helped young Lester get a job with the Pennsylvania Railroad in East St. Louis in 1912 where he worked until 1913.

"I went to work trucking freight out of cars at the inbound platform of the Vandalia railroad on the east end of Eads Bridge," Hunt remembered. "Sometimes I was so tired at midnight, I used to look at the Mississippi River and the Eads Bridge and wonder if I had the strength left to walk across that bridge." [39] After a couple of years on the railroad, he was determined to complete his schooling and become a dentist.

"One Sunday morning I called the dean of Washington University and inquired if it would be possible to enter the College of Dentistry and carry on my work with the railroad. The dean thought it impossible." Hunt didn't give up. "I proceeded to the office of Dean Harper of our university (St. Louis University) and after presenting my situation to him, he simply remarked, 'Hell yes! You can make it.' And while I occasionally missed a meal, I did graduate in 1917."

Hunt came to understand why the first dean thought it couldn't

37 Oral history, Personal interview of Lester C. Hunt conducted by Richard Ewig on December 29, 1979 in Chicago, Illinois.

38 Memo to John Cameron Swayze, January 14, 1953, File: "Personal Statement of John Cameron Swayze" Box 36, LCH Papers

39 Newspaper Article written by Joseph Driscoll, St. Louis Post-Dispatch (undated), File: "Hunt-Personal-1950" Box 19, LCH Papers

be done. "After a hard day at dental college," Senator Hunt later told a newspaper reporter, "I worked from 3 to 11 p.m. six days a week. Sunday mornings I would hurry over to Vandalia to make some real money. I had been promoted from loader and now was a checker and claims clerk. I was paid 7 cents for every claim I checked. Most of the claims were easy, but some days I would work the whole day for 7 cents."[40]

During the summer of 1916, Lester returned to Lander between his junior and senior years to intern with Dr. Stanley J. Roberts, an established Lander dentist. That summer was memorable for a trip the two made to Pinedale, Wyoming. "As I remember the trip...the trip to South Pass City (about 35 miles) took all of our first day and we made it with a team (of horses) and light wagon...the rest of the trip to Pinedale (103 miles) was made in an open Ford. Some place along the line, near the Big Sandy, we stopped at a ranch house and extracted teeth for a farm hand. We anesthetized the area around the tooth to the best of our ability and then each of us took turns attempting to extract the trouble-causing molar. The rancher was seated in a dining room chair by the dining room table, but so help me, the two of us taking turns, were never able to extract that tooth."[41]

Along the way they saw a woman off in the distance. She was waving her arms frantically, trying to get their attention. Somehow she'd learned the two dentists were traveling through those mountains. Her disabled daughter needed dental care. After extracting some teeth, they continued their journey finding that "all the people along the route knew of our coming."[42]

Dr. Roberts remembered that summer and the young dental student with whom he shared it. Years later, after sitting through a lecture

---

40 *Pantagraph* Newspaper, June 20, 1954, 5.

41 Letter from Senator Hunt to Mr. C. Watt Brandon dated March 8, 1951, File "BL-BRI 1951" Box 9, LCH Papers

42 Letter from Dr. Stanley J. Roberts to Hunt, April 6, 1951, File: "RI-RY" Box 31, LCH Papers

about how we are all surrounded "by acres of diamonds," Roberts told his old intern who had now become Senator Hunt, "I am reminded of the young man whom I met in Lander, Wyoming in 1916, who was a good dentist, and one who has gone far in public life to stand for the good things that have made this country great."[43]

Hunt returned to his dentistry studies at the end of that summer. Emily Nathelle Higby had meanwhile returned from college and taken a job in the Lander post office. "By this time Lester Hunt, the professional baseball player from Illinois, had become Dr. Hunt, having graduated from St. Louis University Dental School."[44] Hunt graduated on June 9, 1917[45] and was soon back in Lander working again with Dr. Roberts.

World War I

It wasn't long before the romance between Lester and Emily blossomed. By then the United States had entered the First World War. Dr. Hunt left his new practice in Lander to enlist in the Army. "Dr. Hunt left Wednesday morning for the Presidio, California, where he will formally enlist. He received this week an appointment in the medical corps with a rank of lieutenant," reported the *Wyoming State Journal* on September 14, 1917.

Hunt was ordered to Camp Harry J. Jones on the Mexican border east of Douglas, Arizona. The camp was opened to address the threat posed by Pancho Villa, the infamous Mexican bandit. At Camp Jones an Army chaplain married Nathelle and Lester on February 3, 1918. Later they were transferred to Globe, Arizona as a part of a unit assigned to "protect the big copper mine there."[46] The Arizona Mining

43 Id.
44 Mrs. Hunt's autobiographical essay
45 Records of the Office of the Registrar of St. Louis University
46 Family history compiled by Lester C. Hunt, Jr.

Association historians say the "protection" was necessary because "a new, militant, communistic union, the Industrial Workers of the World (the I.W.W. or Wobblies), came into existence. The years between 1905 and 1920, especially during World War I, were marked by bitter conflict."[47] Nathelle's family history does not record what her husband, the union man, felt about this assignment, though she fondly recalled volunteering many hours to the work of the Red Cross in those days. Later Hunt was transferred to Fort Apache, Arizona, and his final military assignment.

After the war, Lester completed post-graduate studies at Northwestern University. In 1920, he and Emily returned to Lander where Dr. Hunt hung out a shingle. He returned home with a wife and a special affinity for the men and women who serve in the armed forces, one that could be traced throughout the coming years in public service. Whether as governor or a United States Senator, Hunt forever kept foremost the needs of veterans and their families.

The young couple bought their first home and laid stake to a life in the beautiful Lander Valley.

47 Arizona Mining Association History accessed at www.azcu.org/ publicationsHistory6. php on October 27, 2011.

CHAPTER THREE

Entering Politics

If you're elected to the state legislature in a large, urban community it's because the voters know your name. If you're elected to the state legislature in a small, rural community it's because they know you. That is especially true when you're a Democrat and nearly all your Wyoming neighbors are not. As one of Lester Hunt's life-long friends put it, "The only way a Democrat could get elected from Fremont County was if he was really well liked. Dr. Hunt was."[1] It helped that he married a popular local girl. Emily Higby, or Nathelle as everyone called her, had lived in Lander since her high school days.

Wyoming had been a state for little more than two decades when Hunt came to play baseball in 1911. Its 1890 population was "just a whistle over the minimum that the Northwest Ordinance had required."[2] Territories with considerably higher populations were denied statehood while the Republican-controlled Congress agreed to admit Wyoming to the Union because it was "safely Republican."

Regardless of party affiliation, folks in small communities tend to look with suspicion on transplants. People who've live in Wyoming for more than 20 years are still considered outsiders if they seek pub-

---

1 Charlotte Dehnert, "Came As A Baseball Player-Went to Washington As A Senator" *Wyoming State Journal,* July 2, 1984
2 Walter T. K Nugent, *Into the West,* Knopf (1999), 126

lic office. But in the early 1930s, with the exception of the Northern Arapaho and Eastern Shoshone tribal members on the Wind River Indian Reservation, almost everyone in Fremont County was a fairly recent arrival, so it didn't seem presumptuous of Dr. Hunt to run for a seat in the legislature in 1932, when he'd been a resident for little more than a dozen years. Besides, most folks had gotten to know him long before that and they liked him and were probably surprised to learn he was a Democrat. By then his party affiliation mattered little. They became acquainted with Lester when he played baseball and they still talked of his exploits on the diamond. "Doc" Hunt was their dentist before he enlisted in the Army in 1917. Lander welcomed him and his new bride when they returned following World War I. Life in Lander offered the young couple a promising future.

The war years were good to Wyoming. An editor in Laramie wrote, "Never in the history of Wyoming has the entire people been more prosperous than now."[3] The thin mountain air was filled with optimism. Town fathers predicted Lander's population would "double within the next 12 months."[4] The small town numbered only 525 souls when Wyoming became a state in 1890. When Lester Hunt first played for its baseball team in 1911, Lander's population had grown to over 1800. When he and Nathelle returned, it was 2,133. But, it didn't increase as quickly as the optimists predicted. By 1930, Lander's population actually declined by ten percent and didn't double the 1920 count until 1940.[5]

As the "Roaring '20s" opened, there appeared to be every reason for optimism. The state of Wyoming announced a boom in oil drilling with 202 new leases issued between March and May alone. The Wyoming Farm Bureau was organized and elected a Lander-area farmer, John Gronin, its first president. The Lander town council was

3 *Laramie Republican*, September 1917
4 *Wind River Mountaineer*, January 2, 1920.
5 Staff note, File: "Hunt-Personal-1953" Box 19, LCH Papers

so eager to be a family-friendly community they banned minors from entering the local pool hall. The American Laundry on Main Street advertised a new service offering to help women by picking up, washing and delivering ten pounds of their family's dirty laundry for a dollar. New schools were being built throughout Fremont County and a growing tax base allowed the school board to raise teachers' salaries by as much as 35% to 125 dollars a month. Hunt's old baseball team still made the front page with a string of victories over its rivals.

A full-page ad in the November 29, 1921 *Lander Evening Post* was a sign of both the optimism of the day and of the looming economic disaster of Black Tuesday just eight years away. The Finance Corporation of America solicited Fremont County investors to buy preferred stock in its new bank. "This opportunity may mean to you the difference between wealth and poverty." Stock could be purchased with as little as "$5 down and $5 a month."

The Hunts Set Up Housekeeping

When Doctor and Mrs. Hunt returned to Lander, he resumed his dental practice. By June, he was running newspaper ads inviting patients to take advantage of the "special attention to plate work" provided in his Lander office. Dr. Hunt installed the most modern, state-of-the-art dental equipment on the market. The local newspaper claimed his dental office was "second to none in the state" and that "it is almost a pleasure to have an aching tooth treated."[6] His prospects for a successful dental practice could not have been more promising. Mrs. Hunt recalled the couple "started housekeeping in the O'Brien Flats but later bought a house where we lived from 1921 to 1934."[7] A daughter, Elise Nila Hunt (Chadwick) was born on December 30, 1921. Lester

---

6 Newspaper clipping from unidentified newspaper, dated May 12, 1912, Lester Hunt files of the Pioneer Museum, Lander, Wyoming
7 Autobiographical Essay written by Emily Nathelle Higby Hunt

Calloway Hunt, Jr. arrived nearly six years later on September 5, 1927.

The Hunt children, even in their 80s and 90s, recalled the idyllic years of a childhood in Lander, surrounded by loving parents, grandparents and friends. Horse pasture bordered their home on two sides and a picturesque creek ran through their property. One day little Elise watched from the porch as her father visited with a man holding the reins of two horses. The man turned and walked away with his horses. The next day her father presented her with the black-and-white horse as a birthday present. She rode that horse everywhere, often stopping outside the office where her father worked. He would toss a nickel out the window of his second floor office so that she could go for an ice cream.

Grandfather Higby, a civil engineer, would holler, "C'mon schnooks!" Together they surveyed what became Third Street in Lander. "Schnooks" held the surveyor's perch while grandpa stood at his tripod. There was a yearly road trip to Yellowstone National Park and the Grand Tetons, regular picnics at Sinks Canyon and day trips to Bull Lake in the family's open-sided Essex. When the lake was frozen over, Elise recalled, "Father would drive out onto the ice, get up to 25-30 miles per hour, and throw on the brakes." Elise and Lester, Jr., "Buddy" as they all called him, howled joyously as the car skidded, making large circles across the ice.[8]

As Nathelle and Lester bought their first home and started a family, there were hints of Lester's interest in politics. He always had an interest but, growing up poor, his first priority was making a living. He saw dentistry as a path to an income sufficient to provide for his family.[9]

Lester tried his hand in other ventures including ranching. Much later he admitted to being a greenhorn when it came to the cattle business. "All I know about the livestock industry," Hunt once said, "is that

8 Personal interview with Elise Hunt Chadwick, December 19, 2011.
9 Oral interview with Lester C. Hunt, Jr., by Rick Ewig, December 29, 1979, 1

between the years of 1922 and 1927, I lost every cent I put into livestock out on the Sweetwater. My unhappy association with the livestock industry consisted of buying cows with calves to stock a ranch with the agreement that the owner of the ranch was to have half the increase and I was to have the other half, and at the end of the five years I was to receive back the original number purchased plus half the unsold cattle. Through the entire five years, whenever a calf died of blackleg... it was my calf. When an old cow bogged down in the Sweetwater, she was my cow. And when we shipped in the fall, my half for various reasons was not ready to market. And at the end of the five years, I lost my total investment."[10] In those years Doc Hunt was involved in a variety of other moneymaking ventures including mining and oil development, a drug store, a lodge and a building and loan institution.[11]

The Unfortunate Start Of A Political Career

It was apparent from the time young Lester had won oratorical contests back in Atlanta, Illinois, that he had an aptitude for politics. In the Lander years, he served on the local school board, was president of the Chamber of Commerce and the Kiwanis Club. Hunt was elected president of the Wyoming Board of Dental Examiners in 1924 and became president of the Wyoming Dental Association two years later.[12] There he acquired a taste for politics and public office. As the chief advocate for his profession, Hunt became a lobbyist, meeting many of the political figures in the state as he learned more about government. Dentistry gradually gave way to politics as the 1920s moved forward.

10 Undated speech while Governor to Farm Bureau at Hillsdale, File: "Hunt Speeches" Box 3, LCH Papers

11 Response to a Dental Society questionnaire in 1949, asked to identify all "business interests in which you have been involved," File: "Hunt-Personal-1950-1953" Box, 19, LCH Papers

12 "Memorandum for a Biography of U.S. Senator Lester C. Hunt" File: "Hunt Personal-1950-1953" Box 19, LCH Papers

Hastening the transition was a family crisis. "Buddy" was four years old in the fall of 1931 when he suffered what his father called "a pathological fracture of the upper third of his right femur."[13] Buddy experienced ongoing, benign bone cysts. Lander physicians recommended the leg be amputated. The Hunts wanted a second opinion. They took Buddy to the Mayo Clinic in Rochester, Minnesota.

Over the next four years, the doctors at Mayo attempted three grafts using bone from his father's shin. Lucile McGuire, a family friend and nurse, said Hunt "put his own health in jeopardy by being donor for a new form of grafting."[14] Three times the grafts were rejected. Finally, a fourth was successful.[15] "Between these various operations it was necessary that I stay off of my leg, therefore," wrote Lester, "I was unable to practice my profession for some two to three months after each operation."[16] The bone grafts left Hunt unable "to stand day after day beside a dentist's chair." Hunt "decided to shift from the toothaches of dentistry to the headaches of politics."[17]

Hunt's assimilation into Wyoming politics came when many of the state's most historic figures were serving in political office. Two of them held seats in the United States Senate and some of the most popular people of the state's colorful history served elsewhere.[18] One was John Kendrick, a Democrat who served as governor from 1915 until he was elected to the United States Senate. Kendrick served 17 years as a

13 Memorandum, File: "Hunt-Personal 1950-1953" Box 19, LCH Papers

14 Undated Manuscript, File "Hunt, Lester C." Box 3, Papers of Blanche Schroer, Collection No. 10575, American Heritage Center, University of Wyoming

15 Transcript of responses by Lester Hunt Jr. to questions posed by author, December 2, 2011.

16 Memorandum, File "Hunt-Personal 1950-1953" Box 19, LCH Papers

17 Lewis Nordyke, article entitled "Pitcher From Peoria" *Rocky Mountain Magazine*, September 19, 1948, file "Hunt Biographies" Box 19, LCH Papers

18 Both were "outsiders." Kendrick "was a cowboy who became one of Wyoming's governors, came to Wyoming as a cowboy hired to drive a herd of cattle from Texas." Warren "farmed and raised stock in Massachusetts before heading west in 1888 to what was then part of Dakota Territory." wyomingarchives.state.wy.us

Senator before his death in 1933.

The second was Francis E. Warren, who entered politics in 1890, on "day one" of Wyoming's political history. President Chester Arthur named Warren governor of the Territory. As a political appointee, he lost the job when Democrat Grover Cleveland was elected President in November 1886. President Benjamin Harrison, a Republican, reappointed him in March 1889. The following year, the Territory became a state. Warren was its first elected governor. He didn't serve long. Warren resigned in November of 1890 to become a Senator, serving until March 4, 1893. He resumed former business pursuits but returned to the Senate two years later where he remained until his death. Senator Warren was chairman of several committees including the powerful Appropriations Committee as well as the Senate Committee on Military Affairs. Francis Warren died on November 24, 1929. His colleagues gave him the high honor of a funeral service in the chambers of the United States Senate. At the time of his death, Warren had served 37 years, longer than any other Senator.

Although Kendrick and Warren were indeed giants, other important figures were involved in Wyoming politics as Hunt came of age politically, including Nellie Tayloe Ross who, in 1925, became the first female governor in the nation. This was the exciting environment in which Lester Hunt developed his own interest in Wyoming politics. The Great Depression and the nation's response to the presidential candidacy of Franklin Roosevelt set the stage.

State Representative Lester C. Hunt

It was 1932. Lines formed at soup kitchens across Wyoming. Oil prices dropped rapidly along with the prices paid for agricultural and ranching commodities. Years later a Wyoming historian wrote of those years. "It was said that a farmer could trade a chicken to a gas station owner for a gallon of gasoline and both people lost money on the transaction."[19] The state's unemployment rate hit 25%. Communities were asked to shoulder heavy burdens, caring for the unemployed, the poor, the elderly and others left behind in the Great Depression. Hunt ran for the legislature in 1932. His timing could not have been better. The Depression began under the presidency of Herbert Hoover, a Republican. In 1932, Hoover's opponent was Franklin Roosevelt who became only the third Democrat to win the state's electoral votes since Wyoming had become a state forty two years earlier.[20] The Roosevelt bandwagon ran over the Republican Party in Wyoming. "Republicans to Lose Their Grip on Legislature" barked the headline in the November 17, 1932, *Riverton Review*. The 1933 session of the legislature was the first time since statehood that the GOP did not hold majorities of both houses. Fremont County was reliably Republican but that year it elected Democrats to every single county office. Among those swept in was Lester C. Hunt.[21]

Despite limiting his campaign to a single newspaper ad placed three days before the election, promising "Reduction Thru Economy," Hunt was the top vote getter.[22] The editor of the *Riverton Review* felt Hunt could accomplish a great deal with his committee assignments. "Dr. L. C. Hunt's position on the Corporations Committee is a significant one," he wrote.[23] Hunt was also appointed to the Committee on Bridges and Highways and the Military Affairs Committee. Those committee assignments educated him well on issues with which he'd become more involved in the coming years.

19 Phil Roberts, Ph. D. University of Wyoming, "The Great depression and the New Deal in Wyoming" http://uwacadweb.uwyo.edu/ROBERTSHISTORY/great_depression_and_the_new_dea.htm
20 http://www.uselectionatlas.org/RESULTS/compare.php?year=1928&fips=56&f=0&off=0&elect=0&type=state
21 *Riverton Review* Newspaper, November 17, 1932
22 *Riverton Review* Newspaper, November 5, 1932
23 *Riverton Review* Newspaper, January 19, 1933

Lester Hunt and the Eugenics Movement

During the legislative session Doc Hunt introduced what proved to be a highly controversial bill providing for the sterilization of inmates at state institutions. Hunt's proposal was a part of the national movement known as eugenics. The goal of eugenicists was to improve the gene pool by sterilizing those who might pollute it.

Eugenics has a history Americans wanted to forget following the post-World War II disclosures of the horrors wrought on Jews and others by the German Reich. "Eugenics quickly faded from the public view after World War II. Few people discussed the quests for racial purity in other countries, especially the history of forced sterilization in the United States. After what would be called the Holocaust, Allied nations could only look away from the recognizable underpinnings that had helped to create it."[24]

Eugenics is a term first used in 1883 by Charles Darwin's cousin Sir Francis Galton. The eugenics movement established itself in the United States in the early decades of the twentieth century. Such reputable institutions as the Carnegie Foundation supported eugenics policies. In 1911, the president of the Immigration Restriction League, Prescott Hall, asked Charles Davenport of the Eugenics Records Office to help develop ideas for influencing state and federal legislation. Davenport seized on the growing concerns about immigrants and suggested a study to connect the characteristics of foreign-born inmates of insane asylums and prisons with origin of birth.

"It appears probable," Davenport concluded, "from extensive pedigrees that have been analyzed, that feeble-mindedness of the middle and higher grades is inherited as a simple recessive or approximately so. It follows that two parents that are feeble-minded shall have only

---

24 Harry Bruinius, *Better for All the World: The Secret History of Forced Sterilization and America's Quest for Racial Purity*, Vintage Books (2007), 310

feeble-minded children, and this is what is empirically found."[25]

Another adherent was Charles Fremont Dight, a leading advocate for the passage of state eugenics laws. He claimed existing institutions such as schools, churches and government programs failed to reduce "degeneracy" and crime. Sterilization, he concluded, was the best alternative. "If the basement of your house was being flooded from an open water tap, would you keep a person there to bail out the water, or would you close the tap and stop the flow?"[26] Dight told lawmakers the feeble and criminal minded "inherited their bad mentalities which make them socially unfit." He believed these traits could not be corrected and that sterilization was required. "A good house," he said rather crudely, " cannot be made out of rotting lumber."[27]

Before the atrocities of the Third Reich, the movement achieved a great deal of support across the United States. By the time State Representative Lester Hunt introduced his bill in the Wyoming legislature, most surrounding states had already enacted laws allowing for the forced sterilization of certain classes of people. Nebraska was first. Its legislature enacted a law in 1915 allowing the state to sterilize people deemed "insane and feeble-minded." In 1929, the law was expanded to include "habitual criminals, moral degenerates, and sexual perverts."

South Dakota was next, passing a similar law in 1917. Montana followed in 1923. Two years later, Utah's legislature passed a eugenics law. Idaho legislators went next. They targeted "all feeble-minded persons, the insane, epileptics, moral degenerates, and sexual perverts who

25 Charles B. Davenport, "Research in Eugenics," in Eugenics, Genetics and the Family: Volume I. Scientific papers of the Second International Congress of Eugenics, American Museum of Natural History in New York. September 22-28, 1921, ed. International Eugenics Congress, 20-28. Baltimore: Williams & Wilkins Co., 1923. http://hdl.handle.net/1805/1143

26 Charles F. Dight, "Protect at the Danger Point" Dight Papers, Minneapolis Historical Society, Box 5.

27 Charles F. Dight, "Human Betterment and Crime Prevention Through Eugenics" File: "Eugenics: corresp. and misc., 1925" Box 5, Charles Fremont Dight Papers, Minnesota Historical Society

are a menace to society.[28] Only Colorado and Wyoming remained and Lester Hunt wanted to add Wyoming to the list.

In 1927, the United States Supreme Court held that forced sterilization was permissible under the U. S. Constitution. Upholding a Virginia eugenics statute, Justice Oliver Wendell Holmes wrote: "We have seen more than once that the public welfare may call upon the best citizens for their lives. It would be strange if it could not call upon those who already sap the strength of the state for these lesser sacrifices, often not felt to be such by those concerned, to prevent our being swamped with incompetence. It is better for all the world, if instead of waiting to execute degenerate offspring for crime or to let them starve for their imbecility, society can prevent those who are manifestly unfit from continuing their kind."[29] Justice Holmes concluded, "Three generations of imbeciles are enough."[30] While many states had already enacted forced sterilization laws, the Supreme Court gave a green light to many more.

Adolf Hitler based Germany's *Law for the Prevention of Hereditary Diseased Offspring* on a "model law" drafted by one of Charles Davenport's Eugenics Office colleagues, Harry L. Laughlin. In 1936, Laughlin was awarded an honorary doctorate from Heidelberg University.[31] "I consider the conferring of this high degree upon me not only as a personal honor, but also as evidence of a common understanding of German and American scientists of the nature of eugenics as research and the practical application of the fundamental biological and social principles which determine the racial endowments and the racial health-

---

28 University of Vermont, "Eugenics: Compulsory Sterilization in 50 American States" http://www.uvm.edu/%7Elkaelber/eugenics/

29 Buck v. Bell, 274 U.S. 200, 207 (1927)

30 Bruinius, *Better for All the World: The Secret History of Forced Sterilization and America's Quest for Racial Purity*, 7

31 Bruinius, Id., 293-294

physical, mental and spiritual-of future generations."[32]

The Nazi crimes against humanity had not yet changed the debate. Hunt had the legal and cultural winds at his back as he introduced his first bill as a member of a lawmaking body. Hunt's bill gave state officials the authority to "sexually sterilize" inmates at the Wyoming State Hospital and the Wyoming State Training School at Lander if "such inmate (was) afflicted with insanity, idiocy, imbecility, feeblemindedness, or epilepsy."[33] Given the national mood on this issue and the fact that Wyoming was one of the last holdout states, Hunt was greatly surprised by the firestorm his bill created. The Speaker of the House referred the bill to one committee and later decided it was appropriate to transfer it to another. Finally, the bill was reported out of the Committee on Medical Affairs with a recommendation it "Do Not Pass." This recommendation required the bill be placed at the end of the list of bills coming from any committee. It would therefore, be debated by the entire House only after all other bills had been considered.

But the idea enjoyed too much popular support to simply die on a parliamentary maneuver. Reverend J.B. Wood of the Cheyenne Methodist-Episcopal Church voiced the approval of the religious community. Reverend Wood told his congregation that if he were a member of the legislature, he would vote for Hunt's bill. "Most of the members of our state legislature probably pray, 'Thy kingdom come, Thy will be done.' If they are sincere when they pray, they should surely work and vote for the measure providing for the sterilization of the unfit. When we learn of a single family of father and mother and their unfortunate offspring in state institutions, at a cost of tens of thousands of dollars to the state it is difficult for us to understand why any thoughtful person should oppose an act which would do no harm to unfortunate indi-

32 Bruinius, Id., 294
33 House Bill 52 as introduced by "Mr. L.C. Hunt" on January 14, 1933, Wyoming State Archives.

viduals but which would make it impossible for them to inflict feeble-minded, insane, or degenerate children upon society."[34]

The bill came to the House floor for a full debate on January 24, 1933. Representative Hunt told his colleagues that 27 states had already passed similar legislation. He estimated the numbers of "feeble-minded persons" in the state to be about 2,500. "The sterilization of 300 of them would benefit the state," he argued, identifying at least 25 people in the State Training School whom he felt should be relieved of their ability to reproduce. Hunt cited the case of one woman who had "borne 13 children, as many as eight of whom had been at one time inmates" of the institution. Five of them remained in state care. Hunt calculated the annual cost, multiplied by the life expectancy of the "offspring" of this one woman, as the basis for his proposed legislation.[35] It was simple math.

As Hunt finished his speech, Representative Charles P. Scott, a particularly influential member of the House, rose to speak. Scott was the lone voice against the bill that morning. He challenged Hunt's claim that the surgical procedure used to sterilize a female was "simple" telling the House it was "a double abdominal operation." Another member of the House, "a minister of the Gospel," spoke for the passage of the bill, as did one who was a physician and another who was a nurse. Mrs. Thomas Fagan, as she referred to herself, implored, "We don't get healthy animals from scrubs." She argued forced sterilization was inevitable in Wyoming and that if this legislature didn't pass the Hunt bill, another would.[36] She was mistaken in her prediction.

The headline in the January 26th *Wyoming State Tribune* told the story of the bill's demise. "Sterilization Bill is itself 'Sterilized' in Course

34 "Sterilization of 'Socially Unfit' Approved by Minister" *Wyoming State Tribune*, January 16, 1933, 1

35 "Lone Voice Argues Against Sterilization Bill in House" *Wyoming State Tribune*, January 25, 1933, 1

36 Id.

of House Fight." Not many were comfortable speaking publicly against such a popular bill, but they found a way to kill it with "friendly" amendments. "There are two ways to kill a bill," Hunt said. "Vote it down or amend it to death." That's what the House did before finally passing the bill over to the Senate. There the bill died a quiet and final death.

The following July, Hitler announced the Third Reich had officially adopted its own legal practices for forced sterilization.[37] Although some American eugenicists thought the German law provided sound medical and legal patient protections,[38] it was not long before news coming from Europe began to turn American opinion and stomachs. The eugenics idea fell out of favor.

Hunt changed his mind, influenced by religious leaders who began to coalesce in opposition. Governor when the issue was raised again, he received a letter from Reverend George P. Prendergast, S.J. of St. Stephen's Mission advising him of religious objections to eugenics. Governor Hunt acknowledged he had introduced such a bill in 1933, "having been employed at the feeble-minded institution in Lander" but said he was unaware "there were religious objections" at the time. Now, he said, he was pleased the bill did not pass.[39] Wyoming remained one of the few states never to enact a eugenics law.

A Rising Political Star

Despite this setback, Lester Hunt's stock was quickly rising in value. He impressed his colleagues with his oratorical abilities and his hard work and willingness to take on tough issues. He felt comfortable enough in his new role to openly challenge his colleagues who took their marching orders from lobbyists during house debates.[40]

37 Bruinius, Supra, 274
38 Bruinius, Supra, 273-275
39 Letter from Hunt to Rev. George P. Prendergast, SJ of St. Stephen's Mission, File: "Legislature" Box 2, LCH Papers
40 "Unprecedented Event is Witnessed In House When Sergeant-at-Arms Speaks" *Wyoming State Tribune*, January 27, 1933

The legislature was called back into a special session at the end of the year. Hunt, though a freshman, was named chairman of the Committee on Oil and Gas. He left a lasting impression on state Democratic Party officials. Party leaders began to notice Lester Hunt as an up-and-comer, someone who could win a statewide campaign.

CHAPTER FOUR

Becoming Governor

Lester Hunt had the good fortune in his early career to ride the FDR wave. But it was as much Hunt's local appeal as FDR's national appeal that landed Hunt a seat in the state legislature in 1932. Hunt's first victory in a statewide race in 1934 likely had more to do with the nation's mood and FDR's popularity. A Cheyenne newspaper called Hunt "the gentleman who holds the secretary-of-stateship by grace of a couple of New Deal landslides."[1] Roosevelt carried Wyoming by a 56-40 per cent margin in 1932 and although he was not on the ballot in 1934, his New Deal was increasingly popular in Wyoming. By 1936 his margin of victory in the Republican-dominated state widened to 61-31%.[2]

As Hunt mulled a decision of whether or not to seek statewide office after only one term in the legislature, he polled his colleagues in the legislature. With a single exception all pledged their support. One colleague asked why he'd even want the job, advising him that if he lost he'd be out the $1500 a campaign was likely to cost. The letter writer added, "God have mercy on the next fifteen hundred patients of Doc Hunt."[3]

1 "Honey and Vinegar" *Wyoming State Tribune*, Editorial May 15, 1942

2 It was not until FDR's fourth campaign in 1944 that he lost Wyoming's electoral votes. By then Hunt had gained his own political standing in the state.

3 Letter to Hunt from Riley Wilson of Greybull, March 18, 1943, File: "Senate Campaign and Other Campaigns 1943-1948" Box 33, LCH Papers

The Democrats swept all state offices in the 1934 Wyoming elections while Democrats Joseph C. O'Mahoney and Paul Greever were elected to the U.S. Senate and U.S. House respectively. Leslie Miller won the governorship, heading the first all-Democratic administration in the state's history.

Hunt survived a primary and general election challenge from the same popular politician. A former Republican state legislator, Clifford A. Miller, switched parties and ran against Hunt in the Democratic primary. He finished second, but the showing apparently inspired him to give it another shot. Miller ran against Hunt in the general election after switching back to the GOP, becoming the only person in Wyoming history to lose two elections for the same office in the same year to the same man.[4] The 1934 General Election ballot for secretary of state also included both a Socialist and a Communist Party candidate. Together they amassed 679 votes. Hunt received nearly 50,000 and became only the second Democrat elected to the position in the state's history.

Lester fully intended to return to Lander soon enough that he kept his dental office open.[5] He thought he'd be away for only the four-year term he'd won. He would never return except for brief visits. In December of 1934, he and Nathelle packed up their belongings, 13 year-old Elise and seven year-old Buddy and the family moved to Cheyenne.

Located at the southeast corner of the state, Cheyenne differed from Lander in some ways but was quite similar in others. For one, its population was more than 17,000 while Lander's was closer to 2,000. It's an old Wyoming political cliché that "Wyoming is just a small town with very long streets." Hunt's old friends in Lander differed little from their new friends in Cheyenne. He had lived in Cheyenne through two

4 Virginia Trenholm, Editor, *Wyoming Blue Book*, Vol. II, 633, 634
5 Article titled "Meet the Senator" page 4, File: "Hunt-Personal 1950-1953" Box 19, LCH Papers

sessions of the legislature and had long been involved in professional and political endeavors over the previous few years, integrating him into the Cheyenne community.

While Lander sat in a valley surrounded by mountains, Cheyenne sits on the high plains at a place where the west winds gather strength as they come off the mountains and cross the high plateau surrounding the city. Nathelle said she never got used to the wind blowing across those flat prairies. She missed the milder weather of the Lander Valley. But Cheyenne was the capital city and that is where the secretary of state was expected to live.

A New Home In Cheyenne

They settled into a nice home on Third Avenue in an old, established tree-lined neighborhood less than half a mile north of the Capitol building. Although the Cheyenne chief of police was concerned about an increase in juvenile crime, complaining loudly about "damage inflicted on porch lights, windows and street light globes by BB guns,"[6] the city was a good place to raise a family. The Hunt children loved their new home and made friends quickly.

Hunt assumed his official duties and Nathelle quickly and graciously assimilated herself into the Cheyenne civic and social community. She joined two bridge clubs, transferred her Lander P.E.O. membership where she'd been a charter member to Cheyenne, and traveled the state supporting her husband's political efforts.[7] The family joined St. Mark's Episcopal Church, worshipping in the first church building ever erected in Wyoming.

The secretary of state's office in Wyoming is one of those jobs in

6 "Parents Blamed for Rising Juvenile Delinquency Here" *Wyoming State Tribune,* February 1, 1935, 3

7 Emily Nathelle Higby Hunt, *Autobiographical Essay, 21* (P.E.O. is the Philanthropic Educational Organization, one of the pioneer societies for women, founded in1869, to promote the advancement of women.)

which the officeholder must work hard in order to make it interesting. The job was called "a dull slot. Not one voter in a hundred knew of the duties of the office."[8] The first and foremost duty of a secretary of state is to inquire after the health of the governor. The first Wyoming secretary of state, Amos Barber, became the second governor when Wyoming became a state and Governor Francis Warren was chosen U.S. Senator. Wyoming has never had a "lieutenant-governor" as do many states. The secretary of state's job fills many of those functions, including ascending to the governorship if the incumbent is unable to fill his or her term. During the early years of statehood, the secretary of state's job proved to be a steppingstone to the governorship. There had been nine men elected secretary of state ahead of Hunt. Five of them became governors. Although there is no record of just when Hunt first contemplated the governorship, the potential occurred to others quite early. By the time Hunt announced in May of 1942 that he planed to run for governor, the *Wyoming State Tribune* said it had been obvious to "every Wyomingite that is at all observant...for eight to ten years that 'Doc' Hunt was a candidate for governor."[9]

The editor of the *Lovell Chronicle,* a conservative weekly newspaper in rural northwest Wyoming saw it coming and was not disappointed. More than two years before Hunt threw his hat in that ring, the editor commended Hunt, calling him "Wyoming's able Secretary of State." He added, "Most people remember that he proposed the present four-year terms for county officials. Others recall his outstanding work on highway safety. Still others who know of his activities in the legislature think of him as a wise statesman. Wyoming has probably never had a high official who has accomplished so much more than was expected of him. Many come and go in public office, living up to the statute governing their activities, but seldom giving a thought to the welfare of

8 Lewis Nordyke, *"Pitcher from Peoria"* Rocky Mountain Empire Magazine, September 19, 1948

9 "Honey and Vinegar" Editorial, *Wyoming State Tribune,* May 15, 1942, 4

the state as a whole. Secretary of State Hunt is a good secretary, and a great Wyoming booster and builder as well."[10]

Having served only two short years as a member of a legislature that met only 40 days every other year, Hunt was short of knowledge of what it meant to be a statewide political figure. He decided to approach his new office as he had his dental practice. "If teeth had to be pulled, the job should be as painless as possible."[11]

Eight years as secretary of state served as a kind of "graduate course" on government and politics giving him time to sit on the sidelines. As he waited his turn, he watched and learned. They were the challenging days of the Great Depression and the years leading up to the Second World War. Hunt studied the way in which Franklin Roosevelt addressed difficult issues on a national level and how Governor Leslie Miller approached them closer to home.

The national economic crisis caused hardship in Wyoming as it did in every state. Retail sales dropped from more than 103 million dollars in 1929 to under 60 million in 1933. Agricultural production declined by as much as one-half. As the need for state programs grew the budget had to be cut because of withering revenues. The state's historical revulsion at accepting federal subsidies gave way to the new reality. By the mid-1930s it was largely New Deal dollars coming from Washington that were credited with road construction, water conservation efforts, charitable programs and more. Governor Miller's first budget proposal totaled 2.9 million dollars while Wyoming received over 12 million from the federal government.[12]

As though all of that was not a heavy enough load, the war clouds had begun to gather over Europe. Increasingly bad economic news was peppered with stories about the German Reich. Hitler was testing

10 "A Wise Suggestion" Editorial, *Lovell Chronicle* February 29, 1940
11 Nordyke, supra.
12 "Ill Fortunes of Last Year Fail to Lessen Confidence of Wyoming in its Destiny" *Wyoming State Tribune*, January 1, 1935, 7

the will of the Allies to enforce the Treaty of Versailles by significantly strengthening Germany's naval and land forces in violation of the pact. Knowledgeable observers predicted it would not be long before another war broke out.

Against this background Lester Hunt was sworn in as Wyoming's 10th secretary of state, embarking on the most important eight years of study in his life even as he set about doing the job to which he had been elected. A campaign supporter said Hunt took "the office of Secretary of State, which has always been a rather dull, unimportant office, and has made it a live, wide awake, going concern of service to the people."[13]

The secretary of state performs a handful of duties spelled out in statute. In 1935, they included taking "care and custody" of the Seal of the state and all of the public records of the legislature, keeping a register of commissions issued by the state and "such other duties as are required by law."[14] Hunt started by taking his statutory responsibilities seriously. As the caretaker of the state's records, he asked to see them beginning with the original copy of the State Constitution. Surprisingly, it was nowhere to be found. Hunt launched a search for this historic document that quickly caught the attention of the public. "Wyoming was soon in a lather over the lost document."[15]

With suspense building, Hunt found the parchment "in the vault in the basement (of the Capitol) ... lying on the floor of the vault under literally tons of old records, entirely unprotected."[16] He framed it and put it on public display as dozens of thankful citizens came to the Capitol to see the formerly lost piece of Wyoming history.[17] Hunt then located another long-lost document of enormous historic interest, the

13 Undated 3 page speech by an unidentified supporter of Hunt's 1940 campaign for re-election as Secretary of State, File: "Campaign 1944-1948" Box 1, LCH Papers

14 Wyoming Revised Statutes 1931, 109-201 through 109-216

15 Nordyke, supra.

16 Constitution Day Speech, September 17, 1937, File: "Government-State and National Speeches" Box 3 LCH Papers

17 Nordyke, supra.

first act of the 1869 Territorial legislature granting women equal suffrage.[18] These discoveries meant a great deal to the people of the state and brought attention to Hunt, elevating the importance of the office he held.

The Bucking Horse Controversy

In 1930 the state legislature added a requirement to oversee the sale of license plates for automobiles to the list of the secretary of state's responsibilities.[19] Although a source of revenue for nearly 20 years, the business of selling and issuing license plates had been a mixed bag. In the early years, the state simply issued a permit and the driver was expected to craft his or her own license plate. Some used leather or metal. Some affixed common house address numerals. In 1913, the legislature mandated uniformity, requiring metal plates be issued although in 1916, the state conducted a failed one-year experiment with porcelain.

As the number of vehicles on the state's roads increased so did the problem of counterfeiting. The legislature instructed the secretary of state to develop a unique design in an effort to limit counterfeiting. Hunt saw the problem itself as an opportunity. He wanted to use the license plate not just to assure registration fees were paid, but also to promote Wyoming at a time when motoring was quickly becoming a national pastime.

In the spring of 1935, Hunt met with a Colorado artist to talk about possibilities. Hunt called on Allen True, an artist who had already been commissioned to paint murals in the chambers of the state house.[20] He

18 Article titled "Meet the Senator" page 5, File: "Hunt-Personal 1950-1953" Box 19, LCH Papers

19 William T. Andrews, *A Brief History of Wyoming License Plates*, File: "License Plates" Wyoming State Archives, Cheyenne, Wyoming

20 Allen True's family has been very influential in Wyoming over decades, engaged in oil and gas development and ranching as well as politics. Allen's nephew, Diemer True, was

told True he was looking for more than a license plate. Hunt wanted a symbol, one that would represent Wyoming while advertising its attractions at the same time. True proposed alternative logos, each depicting the silhouette of a cowboy atop a bucking bronco. Hunt made the final choice and the Wyoming symbol was born.

In July of 1935, Hunt approved the new design. "A boldly embossed picture of a cowboy doing a good job of riding a wildly-bucking bronco will," said the *Wyoming State Tribune,* "adorn Wyoming's automobile license plates of next year."[21] The new license plate design was a huge success. "Secretary of State Hunt is of the opinion that the new plate not only is symbolic of our state," crowed Hunt's hometown newspaper, "but also carries with it a definite advertising value for Wyoming."[22] Artist True was paid $75 for his work.[23] The state of Wyoming cashiered a far greater profit. By December, the *Wyoming State Journal* recorded sales of the bucking horse license plate had doubled over the prior year.[24]

Hunt sent a license plate with an invoice for the fee to a Montana driver who asked, "Is it possible for one living in Montana to have a set of Wyoming automobile license plates on his car? I kind of got stuck on your 1936 plate."[25] A New Yorker who had not lived in Wyoming since "before the Spanish-American War and the Philippine Insurrection" wrote, seeking to buy a plate for his car.[26]

The plates became a popular target for thieves all over the country. The *Wyoming State Journal* warned drivers they'd "better padlock

a member of the state legislature for twenty years (1973-1993), serving as President of the Wyoming State Senate in 1991-1992.

21 "Bucking Bronc on Car Plates" *Wyoming State Tribune,* July 15, 1935

22 "Wyoming's 1936 License Plate Unique" *Wyoming State Journal,* August 22, 1935

23 *Wyoming State Tribune,* May 27, 1990

24 *Wyoming State Journal,* December 2, 1935

25 "Broncho (sic) Car Plates May Be Used in North" *Wyoming State Tribune,* November 14, 1935

26 Letter dated February 25, 1936, File: "License Plates-General-Bucking Horse Drawing-General" Box 2, LCH Papers

your buckin' bronk (sic) auto plates if you go to California."[27] A Los Angeles police officer stopped a car driven by Cheyenne doctor C.H. Welsh because it had no license plate. The officer let him go without a ticket when he learned the car was from Wyoming. "It's becoming a hard problem to protect those darn Wyoming bronc plates," he said. "Nearly every day we pick up a car without plates and find he is from Wyoming."[28]

In 1941, the Purdue Motor Club named Wyoming's license plate the "Most Distinctive" in the nation and awarded it a prize for its value in advertising the state.[29] By 1942 more than a million of the metal plates had been sold around the country.[30] Hunt's colleagues solicited his ideas for their own license plates. The Wyoming secretary of state suggested his counterpart in Colorado "place on your plate a miner's burro with its pack or a mountain design."[31] Later Colorado did, in fact, adopt the mountain design as a part of its license plate logo.

Dozens of corporations and non-profit groups asked and were freely permitted to make use of the bucking horse symbol. Lt. Edward Spevak wrote Hunt as his World War II unit prepared to head to Europe, thanking him for sending a picture of the bucking horse emblem to place on their bomber. "The 'bucking horse' is just what we needed. In a few days I will be getting a new Fortress, which is the one we will take across. As you know," the lieutenant wrote, "my whole crew wears cowboy boots, making the picture perfect."[32]

Hunt's friend Wyoming district court judge Percy Metz urged him to copyright the design before "some other state" could steal the im-

27 *Wyoming State Journal*, May 14, 1936

28 File "License Plates" Wyoming State Archives

29 File "License Plates" Wyoming State Archives

30 *Wyoming Stockman-Farmer*, April 1942

31 Letter from Hunt to C.H. Gunn, dated July 19, 1937, File: "License Plates-General-Bucking Horse Drawing-General" Box 2, LCH Papers

32 Letter to Hunt from Lt. Edward Spevak, dated February 16, 1943, LCH Papers, Id.

age. Judge Metz had returned from a road trip through the southwestern states. "No matter where I stopped, at a garage, filling station, café or parked in the street, there was a crowd around my car continuously. It (the plate) created more comment and favorable reaction than anything that the state, I think, has ever done in the way of advertising."[33] Hunt took the judge's advice and submitted an application for a copyright the following month. The original copyright was awarded to Hunt. [34] He transferred it to the State of Wyoming before leaving the secretary of state's office to become governor. [35]

The Great Controversy

Over the years, perhaps no greater controversy has occurred in Wyoming than the matter of who should get credit for designing the bucking horse symbol. On the surface, it seems to be a controversy easily settled by distinguishing between (1) those who claim to have designed the symbol from (2) those who think they can identify who the horse and the rider were from (3) and those who made the call to place the symbol on the license plate. But controversies over Wyoming myths are never that simple.[36]

There is no doubt Secretary of State Lester Hunt made the decision to place the symbol on the state's license plates. However the debate erupted when someone complained Hunt had taken credit for something done by 1st Sergeant George Ostrom of Sheridan. Ostrom claimed he designed the bucking horse symbol for a military insignia worn by Wyoming National Guardsmen during World War I. It all

33 Letter to Hunt from Judge Metz, dated January 21, 1936, LCH Papers, Id.

34 Certificate of Copyright Registration No. 22056 "Bucking Horse and Rider, by Lester C. Hunt of the United States" File "License Plates-General-Bucking Horse Drawing-General" Box 2, LCH Papers

35 *Green River Star*, March 27, 1942

36 Various claims and arguments for credit documented in File: "License Plates" Wyoming State Archives

started with a newspaper article in the *Kemmerer Gazette* on April 14, 1936, and has yet to end. "The announcement came," said the *Gazette*, " as a bombshell in the midst of the controversy raging over the state for some time as to whom (sic) originated the 'bucking bronc' now being used on Wyoming license plates as symbolic of this true western state."

A 1919 National Guard history documenting the service of the 148th Field Artillery unit of the Wyoming National Guard includes drawings of a horse named Red Wing. Sgt. Ostrom claims this animal was the model for his design.[37] Ostrom was so incensed he purchased a full-page ad in the Sheridan newspaper during Hunt's 1940 re-election campaign to criticize the secretary of state for failing to acknowledge Ostrom's role in the design. Finally, the Wyoming Militia Historical Society arrived at a Solomonic compromise during the 1990 Wyoming State Centennial. "Even if Ostrom drew the first bucking bronc in 1918 and Hunt paid True to put a bucking horse on the Wyoming license plates in 1935," the author said, "the symbolic emblem that one or both of them created is now a famous and sought after souvenir."[38]

The argument shifted to the identity of the cowboy. A Laramie businessman, Emery Miller said he had, as early as 1932, suggested Hunt use a cowboy named Marring and a horse named "Steamboat." But Hunt didn't become secretary of state until three years later. Whether the horse was "Steamboat" or not, there was also an argument over who was the rider. Calling him "the most typical cowboy I know" Hunt told Jules Farlow he had Farlow's son "Stubbs" in mind when he agreed to True's design.[39] Stubbs Farlow was a Lander cowboy who had achieved a great reputation as a rodeo performer. Later Hunt said Farlow was not necessarily the model, but that the silhouette was

37 Paul M. Davis, *History of Battery C 148th Field Artillery*, File: "License Plates" Wyoming State Archives

38 Brochure produced by the Wyoming Militia Historical Society for the Wyoming centennial (1990) File: "License Plates" Wyoming State Archives

39 File: "License Plates" Letter dated March 15, 1954, Wyoming State Archives

simply representative of all cowboys.

Forty years later, a tavern owner in Dubois said he originated the whole idea with the design of a sign over his bar. He commissioned a welder to "devise an eye-catching sign." The result was a cowboy aboard a bucking horse.

A latecomer to the design sweepstakes was Roland "Bammie" Dale of Rawlins. In 2005 Bammie (nicknamed because he was from Alabama) told the *Rawlins Daily Times* he deserved the credit. He was a 10-year-old newspaper boy when a California woman passing through town gave him a gift of a small "tarnished silver pin" in the shape of a horse and rider silhouette. As a part of a class project young Bammie "took this pin and traced around it" on a Wyoming cardboard license plate. "Guess what," he told the newspaper, "in 1936 the outline of 'Midnight' and his rider appeared on the Wyoming state license plate. Never giving credit to the original creator, a 10 year-old boy named Roland Gilder Dale."[40]

In the early 1950s "some writer from Houston, Texas, took credit themselves (sic) for putting the bucking horse on our license plate."[41] Regardless, Lester Hunt always took great pride in his role. "The idea of the Wyoming license plate was entirely original with me to the best of my knowledge," Hunt wrote to Lola M. Homsher, the Wyoming State Archivist, in August of 1953. "No other person had mentioned such a plate in my presence."[42]

Most of the people of Wyoming associated the bucking horse on their license plate with Lester Hunt. One wintry day as Senator Hunt drove along an icy road to Wheatland, he saw a car in the ditch and stopped to help. When the stranded motorist realized who this "good Samaritan" was, he said, "Well, Senator, you know...I have over my

40 "Bammie's Story of State's Bucking Bronc" *Rawlins Daily Times*, November 17, 2005
41 Letter from Hunt to Dr. Robert H. Burns, University of Wyoming College of Agriculture, File: "Hunt-Personal 1951" Box 19, LCH Papers
42 Letter dated August 24, 1953, File: "License Plates" Wyoming State Archives

door a replica of the Wyoming bucking horse which you sent me when you were governor. I want you to know I appreciated it." [43]

Senator Hunt's administrative assistant Mike Manatos was charged with the grim duty of cleaning up Hunt's affairs following the Senator's death in 1954. He sent a letter to the Wyoming State Archives in June. "One of the last things Senator Hunt did was to instruct us fully with respect to the Wyoming Suffrage Act and the original drawing of the "bucking bronco" which has so wonderfully identified Wyoming's license plates." [44] A few days later Mrs. Hunt sent the original drawing to the State Museum. "Since this license plate has become identified with Wyoming since the senator designed it, when he was Secretary of State, I thought it appropriate that the original sketch be placed in the State Museum." [45]

Lester Hunt was identified with this important state symbol thoroughly enough that a large icon of the bucking horse license plate, beautifully crafted of hundreds of flowers, graced the entrance of St. Mark's Episcopal Church in Cheyenne as mourners gathered for Lester Hunt's funeral nearly two decades after he commissioned the design.

Protecting Citizens

Hunt was adamant about making his office relevant to the people of Wyoming. He cast himself as the guardian of small investors, protecting them against corrupt corporate practices. Less than a week after being sworn into the office of secretary of state, Hunt took aggressive action against a large out-of-state mining company. He refused to approve the application of United Gas and Mining Company of Salt Lake to do business in Wyoming because of his objections to the method

43 "Driver Gets Help From Senator Hunt" *Wyoming Eagle*, October 15, 1950
44 Letter from Mike Manatos to Wyoming State Archives, File: "Bucking Horse", July 7, 1954, Wyoming State Archives
45 Letter from Mrs. Hunt to Wyoming State Archives, July 20, 1954, Id.

used to value the company stock.[46]

In his first term, he returned $26,000, the equivalent of roughly $400,000 in today's dollars, to people who had purchased fraudulent stock. Hunt involved himself in issues ranging from legislative reform to highway safety and drunk driving. He told his former legislative colleagues at the opening session of the 25th legislature in 1940, "Practically everybody admits the failure of our present legislative procedure."[47] He proposed creating a "legislative research bureau," a proposal finally accomplished in 1972. He asked that the number of legislative committees be reduced from 29 to 15 and that the time limit for introducing bills be shortened.

Hunt found real passion in addressing problems created by the abuse of alcohol. Speaking to a Cheyenne meeting of the Women's Christian Temperance Union in September 1940, he said, "My remarks this evening should be captioned "Meet a Prohibitionist."[48] Before her death, Hunt's mother, a Women's Christian Temperance Union firebrand, exacted a promise to never touch alcohol from her 10-year-old son. He kept the promise and he never "in any size, shape or form tasted liquor."[49]

As an elected official, he also took up her cause. "You and I should do all we can in every way we can to see that the whole degrading mess of alcoholic beverages are thrown overboard and step out like Knights in shining armor to battle for that dream of the eternal, sober man guiding a sober nation into the higher reaches of the Kingdom of God."[50]

46 "Hunt Refuses O.K. of State" *Wyoming State Tribune*, January 11, 1935, 1
47 Speech to Joint Session of the Legislature, File: "Government-State and National (Speeches)" Box 1, LCH Papers
48 Id.
49 Letter, File "Mimeograph" Box 23, LCH Papers
50 Speech to Women's Christian Temperance Union, September 1940, File "Miscellaneous Speeches" Box 3 LCH Papers

Hunt urged lawmakers to enact measures addressing "drunken driving" including the first proposal for what came to be known as an "open container" law. "It has been suggested that possibly passing of a law prohibiting the transportation of a bottle of liquor with the seal broken in a passenger car might help the situation."[51] Wyoming did not yet have a driver's license law but Hunt asked that if the legislature passed one it should include provisions allowing for the suspension of the driver's license of anyone convicted of driving drunk. No fines could be imposed, he demanded. "Jail time only! After all, a drunken driver is a potential murderer in every sense of the word and should be so treated."[52]

The use of public highways was expanding greatly and there were safety concerns. Hunt was the first Wyoming politician to recognize the import of the matter. In 1935 he proposed requiring those convicted of careless driving to place license plates three times the normal size on their vehicles, "thus identifying, placarding, and humiliating the public menaces by making them conspicuous."[53]

In March of 1949, President Truman appointed Senator Hunt to chair the Committee on Motor Vehicle Administration for the President's Highway Safety Conference "because of your remarkably able leadership in the highway safety movement."[54] Two years later, the Rock Springs newspaper ran an editorial entitled "Come on back, Les. We need you!" Citing heightened concerns about the growing number of highway fatalities, the editor said, "There was a time when far fewer deaths on Wyoming highways roused the state to action. One Secretary of State Lester C. Hunt carved a brilliant political career

51 Hunt's Message to open the 24th Session of the legislature, File: "Government-State and National Speeches" Box 3, LCH Papers
52 Id.
53 "Secretary Hunt Studies Reckless Driving" *Wyoming State Journal*, November 28, 1935, 4
54 Letter from President Harry Truman to Hunt, March 11, 1949, File: "Truman, Harry S." Box 37, LCH Papers

on the cornerstone of a successful campaign to reduce deaths on the state's highways."[55]

Reelection

When Hunt sought reelection in 1938, the voters responded favorably. Four years earlier the Democrats had won all statewide contests. In 1938, they lost nearly all of them. Democrats entered the campaign divided. Governor Leslie A. Miller and State Auditor "Scotty" Jack, both of whom were Democrats, engaged in open warfare. The governor accused the auditor of leaking copies of questionable travel vouchers to the Republican press. In the end, Jack refused to endorse Miller.[56] While the voters showed the Democratic governor the door in 1938, they gave Hunt a second term by a sound majority. Even so, he called the 1938 election "disastrous."[57] Having lost his friend Leslie Miller from the governorship, Hunt lamented, "The ensuing years, from some angles, may be interesting ones, but I feel that in this office, my activities will be so curtailed that I will not have the opportunity I have had in the past four years."[58]

It was not long before Hunt began sounding more like a candidate for higher office than someone content with being secretary of state. In a 1940 speech at the annual Jefferson Day dinner in Douglas, he attacked the failure of GOP Governor Nels Smith to keep a promise to repeal the sales tax on food, a bill, he said was defeated "on a straight party vote." He then blasted the legislature for its failure to "control the price of gas."[59]

55 *Rock Springs Rocket Miner*, August 7, 1951
56 Kathleen M. Karpan, *A Political History of Jack R. Gage*, Annals of Wyoming, Fall 1976, 181-182
57 "Lester C. Hunt Papers December 13, 1938 to January 30, 1939" Account Book, 1, Box 43, LCH Papers
58 Id.
59 Speech, File: "Speeches" Box 1, LCH Papers

Hunt's 1940 election eve radio broadcast included an eloquent defense of the New Deal and a third term for FDR. "To you whom (sic) in less than twenty-four hours will go the responsibility of acting as judge and jury, may I urge that you think of America first, that you think of the difficult hours ahead, and give first consideration to America, and second to party affiliation."[60] Following Roosevelt's 1940 victory, Hunt took a more aggressive posture as the leading spokesman for the Democratic Party. During a speech in Lander following the November elections, he explained to his constituents, most of whom were Republicans, the Democratic Party victory this way: "Because from Thomas Jefferson to Franklin Roosevelt our party has been the party which always is doing and we hope will always do the greatest amount of good for the greatest number of our people. Our party believes that the hungry must be fed, the jobless must be employed, and those oppressed have an opportunity to recover their economic stability. Ours is the liberal party, ours is the humanitarian party."[61]

With each speech, his intent became clearer. Hunt was itching for a fight with the Republican incumbent governor. Governor Nels Smith was a tall, handsome rancher from the northwest corner of the state. A newcomer to politics in 1938, he carried no political baggage. Dr. T.A. Larson, the state's preeminent historian, called Smith "a simple, unsophisticated, uncomplicated man who desired, as he said, to run the state as he ran his ranch."[62] Smith was remembered more for his commencement address at the University of Wyoming than for anything else. "You done good," Governor Smith told the graduates.[63]

In the four short years of his only term in office, Smith created a lot of unhappiness even within his own party. The editor of the Cheyenne

60 Id.
61 Id.
62 T.A. Larson, *History of Wyoming*, University of Nebraska Press (1965), 470
63 Id. 468

newspaper, a staunch Smith backer, acknowledged Smith had "incurred the ill will of a very considerable number of Republicans.[64] His greatest sin was the rather ham-handed way he handled the firing of a popular University of Wyoming president. Arthur G. Crane's termination followed a yearlong soap opera that included Smith's appointment of Peter Sill, a relatively unknown Laramie banker, to the university board of trustees. Legislators were puzzled by the appointment but it soon became obvious Sill's appointment had a purpose. He was there to help the governor drive out the president.[65] Crane may have been fired but he, and not Smith, retained the support of many Wyoming people.

Crane ran for the Republican nomination for the U.S. Senate the year after he was fired, coming within 500 votes of winning.[66] Smith won the gubernatorial nomination against three other GOP candidates and faced a tough general election campaign against the Democratic nominee, Lester Hunt.

Lester Hunt For Governor

Hunt had been banging away at Smith long before the 1942 campaign started. Beginning two years ahead, Hunt zeroed in on what he believed to be the failures of the incumbent. The former baseball player summed up the record of the Republican governor with these words, "The final score reads, 'No hits, no runs, many errors, a lot of foul balls, and the state left holding the saxs (sic)'."[67]

Governor Smith was out of the state when the Japanese attacked Pearl Harbor on December 7, 1941. He was onboard a train heading for Fort Lewis to visit Wyoming National Guardsmen. He got off the

64 Editorial *Wyoming State Tribune* November 6, 1942
65 T.A. Larson, *History of Wyoming*, supra. 469
66 Crane was later elected Secretary of State and became governor upon Lester Hunt's election to the U.S. Senate.
67 Jefferson Day Speech in File "Campaign 1944-1948" Box 1, LCH Papers

westbound train at Weiser, Idaho, boarding the next eastbound train for the quick return to Wyoming.[68] It fell to Acting-Governor Lester Hunt to urge Wyoming citizens to remain calm and to support the President.[69]

Pearl Harbor and America's entry into World War II may have been the catalyst for Hunt to challenge Smith in the 1942 election. Hunt wrote to E.O. Huntington of Lovell ten days after the Japanese attack, expressing concern that the Smith administration was paying only "lip service to national defense needs, Governor Smith having vetoed appropriations recommended by the feds (sic) for home defense purposes. Since a week ago Sunday the present state administration sees great possibilities in waving the flag politically ... I say very frankly that Wyoming State Government has its Wheelers and Lindberghs[70] and gave before December 7 only what cooperation and lip service that the people demanded."[71] Hunt wondered aloud how the Democrats might raise issues with the GOP administration when "politics are out" during wartime. He summoned close supporters to a "little Dutch treat dinner here (in Cheyenne) Monday night to discuss strategy for the coming campaign."

As a World War I veteran, Hunt was offended that Smith was not, in his view, fully supportive of the war effort. A year earlier, Hunt had become miffed when Smith reduced a $200,000 legislative appropriation for civil defense to $75,000.[72] Among Hunt's personal papers is this handwritten note. "Meeting of State Board in Gov. office July 20th

68 T.A. Larson, *Wyoming's War Years 1941-1945*, Stanford University Press (1954), 7

69 "Wyoming Prepares to Go on Full War Basis; Smith Interrupts Trip" *Casper Tribune-Herald*,

70 According to the Spartacus Educational website "In September 1940, Charles Lindbergh helped Burton K. Wheeler and Norman Thomas to form the America First Committee (AFC). It soon became the most powerful isolationist group in the United States. The organization was dissolved four days after the Japanese Air Force attacked Pearl Harbor." www.spartacus.schoolnet.co.uk/USAlindbergh.htm

71 Letter, File "Politics-State-1942" Box 2, LCH Papers

72 T.A. Larson, *Wyoming's War Years*, Supra. 61

moved to give only two weeks pay to men called into service. Not co-operating with Fed. Gov. in helping to build up army. Interfering with preparedness program."[73] Hunt believed he should run for governor not simply to win an election and the title but because he believed the war put the future of the nation at risk and even the governor of a small state needed to do his part.

After December 7, 1941, newspapers were filled with little other than war news. Neither the public nor the press seemed to have much appetite for the coming political campaign. Although the decision had been made, Hunt delayed his announcement until the last possible moment. He assured a constituent in March, "I do intend to be a candidate for governor."[74] In April he told a gathering of Democrats, "The people of Wyoming are interested only in the war and in ways to improve their efforts in the war. When the people are a little more interested in the coming elections, I shall have an announcement to make."[75]

Governor Smith announced his candidacy first on May 4. Hunt followed 10 days later saying, "Wyoming owes to the nation at war the most effective leadership available."[76] Hunt felt Smith had failed to exercise leadership on the war effort and his announcement emphasized his administration would cooperate fully with Roosevelt.[77] He pledged a "drastic reduction in state expenditures and personnel and the promotion of the state's resources." Hunt said, "Wyoming should capitalize in labor and health and happiness on its natural resources and discontinue sending of its potential prosperity into other states."

Other candidates joined the race. Two other Republicans and a

73 Letter, File "Politics-State-1942" Box 2, LCH Papers
74 Letter to Dr. Henry J. Peterson, UW Political Science Department dated March 16, 1942, File "Odds and Ends", Box 2, LCH Papers
75 "Hunt Delays Announcement; Says He Will Reveal Plans When Public is Interested" Wyoming State Tribune April 14, 1942, 1
76 Letter, File "Politics-State-1942" Box 2 LCH Papers
77 Dr. Hunt to be Candidate for Governor" Wyoming State Tribune May 14, 1942

Democratic challenger assured both Hunt and Smith would be contested in the August primary. There were also contests for the U.S. Senate and House and the other four state offices. In spite of all of that activity, the public was mesmerized by the war news and state politics was less than a distraction, more of an annoyance. The public didn't seem to notice even when each party chose its nominees in a primary where fewer voters participated than expected, and the expectations had been low. It was not until the month before the general election that the contest for governor piqued the curiosity of the voters. Finally, on October 19th, with only a couple of weeks until the general election, the *Wyoming State Tribune* exclaimed, "Wyoming's Political Campaign Gaining Momentum."[78]

When he announced, Hunt promised he would not "delegate important functions of state government to subordinates" emphasizing, "I will be the Governor."[79] One of the major issues in the governor's contest was the role of GOP State Chair James Griffith, a powerful player in the party. Griffith was the publisher of the *Lusk Herald*. He was not bashful about using his newspaper to promote Republicans and to bash Democrats. During the Smith administration, Griffith enjoyed his own office in the governor's suite and, according to Democrats, used it to influence public policy decisions.

Lester Hunt sized up Mr. Griffith early in Governor Smith's term. Writing in his private diary on January 3, 1939, the day after Smith's inauguration, Hunt said, "It is interesting to note how the Republican state chairman, Jim Griffith, and the new Attorney General, Ewing Kerr, seem to be taking complete charge of things, fronting for the Governor and relieving him of any of the decisions - apparently they feel he will speak out of turn, or take some action that would react to

78 Headline, page 3 of the *Wyoming State Tribune*, October 19, 1942
79 Letter, File "Politics-State-1942" Box 2 LCH Papers

the detriment of the Republican Party."[80] On January 6 he recorded it was a beautiful winter day, "but the building badly polluted with Republicans in to speed up their appointments."[81]

In stump speeches, Hunt labeled Griffith "a governor by proxy" and urged voters to go to the polls on November 3 and "rid Wyoming forever of Jim Griffith and his political racketeers."[82] Citing the Smith administration's funding of a fish hatchery in Idaho, Hunt said, "We think this is an intolerable situation and urge every citizen in the State of Wyoming to go to the polls on November 3 and oust Nels Smith and Jim Griffith for boner number 739, namely moving one of Wyoming's fish hatcheries into Idaho."[83]

The 1942 Democratic candidate for Hunt's old job as secretary of state was a popular politician named William "Scotty" Jack. He took the lead in denouncing Governor Smith. In a quarter page ad placed shortly before the election, Jack issued a "Dear Jim" letter, addressed to Griffith. The letter cited "questionable" expenditures Jack had been called on to approve while he was state auditor and Smith was governor. "Why Did I Pay the Following Claims Against the State?" the ad inquired. It listed everything from bars of soap and clothesline rope to starch and floor wax purchased for the governor's home.[84]

The intent was to make Griffith, not Smith, appear to be the real power in the administration. The ad read, "Remember Jim, how you and the money-jugglers thought you could hijack me into playing your game?" A follow-up "Dear Jim" ad referred to the "Griffith-Smith Regime" and blamed them for increased state budgets.[85]

80 "Lester C. Hunt Papers From December 13, 1938 to January 30, 1939" Account Book page 34, Box 43, LCH Papers
81 Id.
82 Speech, File "Politics-1942" Box 2 LCH Papers
83 Id.
84 "Scotty Jack says Dear Jim" *Wyoming State Tribune*, October 22, 1942, 3
85 "Scotty Jack says Dear Jim" *Wyoming State Tribune*, October 26, 1942, 3

Griffith, on the other hand, used the front page of his own newspaper, the *Lusk Herald*, to promote Smith and the editorial page to pound on Hunt. An example was the October 8 editorial entitled "Just Another Brain Storm of the Doctor's." Fellow publisher Tracy McCracken was a Democratic insider. He published the two Cheyenne newspapers, one of which had a Republican editor and the other a Democratic editor. Griffith referred to Hunt and Scotty Jack as "the McCracken ring" or "McCracken's henchmen."[86]

Griffith ran a story the week prior to the election calling the 1942 governor's race, "the shortest and most intense in Wyoming."[87] The same day he published a letter from Mr. C.M. Houser of Casper who claimed to have been told by Hunt that Hunt was running for governor only so that he could afford to send his two children to college and that after one term, he planned "to go back to Lander, and live in his house and work a couple of hours a day at his drug store and spend the rest of the time with his flowers."[88]

Because the campaign took place while the war raged, both sides questioned the patriotism of the other. Hunt had earlier asked the Department of the Army to give him a waiver from military age restrictions in order to allow him to serve during World War II. Army regulations would not allow it since he had changed his vocation and was not practicing dentistry, as when he was first commissioned.[89] Republicans claimed Hunt had "resigned his commission" in order to avoid military service. Democrats fired back. They ran ads asking, "Who's a Slacker?" raising the issue of Governor Smith's son Christy. "Why," they asked, "isn't Christy Smith, 6-foot, husky, steer wrestler, expert rifle shot, son of the governor, in the service?"[90] The Republican editor of Cheyenne's

86 "Just Another Brain Storm of the Doctor's" *Lusk Herald*, October 8, 1942
87 "Heated Campaign Finale This Week" *Lusk Herald*, October 29, 1942, 1
88 "An Open Letter from C.M. Houser" *Lusk Herald*, October 29, 1942, 9
89 "Who's a Slacker?" *Wyoming State Tribune*, October 29, 1942
90 Id.

evening newspaper, the *Wyoming State Tribune,* responded with a front-page editorial on November 1. He explained the governor's son had a medical problem that had been detected during his induction physical. Even so, the editorial said, young Smith had "sought to volunteer for the Army, that he requested immediate induction under the Selective Service Act, and that he now eagerly is awaiting induction."[91]

In the meantime, Hunt issued an "open letter" to the voters. "There is nothing surprising in these underhanded, last minute, stab-in-the-back tactics of those who are today in charge of Republican affairs. They have done the same in every election against the most honorable of our citizens, including Senator Kendrick and Senator O'Mahoney."[92]

On November 3 it all came to an end. Voters elected Lester Hunt governor. The following day Griffith's *Lusk* Herald printed only a brief front-page story acknowledging Lester Hunt had defeated Nels Smith. It was the newspaper's final mention of Hunt through and including the new governor's inaugural in January.

The decision was close. Hunt won by only 2031 votes out of more than 77, 000 votes cast. It was close enough that it was two days later before Jim Griffith, not Nels Smith, conceded. "On the face of the unofficial returns, it appears that Hunt has been elected," he told the press.[93]

The "Pitcher from Peoria" had become the Governor of Wyoming.

---

91 "Rebuke or Reward?" *Wyoming State Tribune,* November 1, 1942, 1
92 "An Open Letter To You" *Wyoming State Tribune,* October 30, 1942
93 "Griffith Concedes L.C. Hunt's Election in Race for Governor" *Wyoming State Tribune,* November 5, 1942, 1

CHAPTER FIVE

Being Governor

Dead pigeons began falling from the high ledges of the Capitol Building. State employees who had been complaining about the infestation of the birds were puzzled. They had taken their complaints to the new governor. They couldn't eat their lunch on nearby park benches without being mobbed by begging, insistent pigeons. The bird droppings left on windowsills made it impossible, or at least ill advised, to open a window for air. They asked Governor Hunt, as they had asked his predecessor, to do something to resolve this problem.

Hunt had been in office but a few days when he asked his colleagues on the Capitol Building Commission to address the pigeon problem. The commission was made up of the five top state elected officials, including the governor. The other four commission members responded with "a horse laugh."[1] The governor was outraged. If they wouldn't take care of the problem he would take matters into his own hands.

In the early hours of a cold January morning in 1943, Wyoming's new governor slowly climbed along the narrow ledges of the State Capitol Building. Inch by inch, careful to avoid falling, he walked along the icy granite. The pigeons were still asleep with wings folded across their faces. They didn't stir. In the days that followed, dead pigeons plummeted onto the lawn below.[2] When anyone asked what had

---

1 Id. 2

2 Lewis Nordyke, "*Pitcher from Peoria*", Rocky Mountain Empire Magazine, September 19, 1948, 2

happened, he just smiled knowingly and walked on without admitting or taking credit for his role.

That was Lester Hunt's style of leadership. If a job needed to get done, no matter how dirty or unpleasant, he did it. Using his own money, he bought poisoned grain and solved this problem before the sun came up. That's how he did things. That is how he saw his responsibility. It was about public service and doing what the taxpayers paid you to do. Hunt made it clear from the start he would be anything but a conventional governor.

Because of the war, he whittled down the cost and pomposity of his inaugural. There would be no inaugural ball and the ceremony was to be brief.[3] Hunt's inaugural address was only 13 minutes long. He reminded listeners of the state's responsibility to those fighting the war. More than 18,000 Wyoming men and women were then serving in the armed forces. Soon another six to seven thousand would be called. "Therefore," he implored, "it is our duty to be prepared to receive them and to assist them in returning to their usual vocations and normal peacetime activities."[4]

The governor warned "increasing federal authority over state's rights in Wyoming is progressing rapidly."[5] Although he defended New Deal policies, it would not be long before he was forced into a state's rights confrontation with the Roosevelt administration. Hunt made a good impression in his early days as chief executive. His door was open, visitors welcomed and the office filled with artifacts and symbols of Wyoming history.[6] He had a "good smile and a sort of pleasant face. Women thought he was very charming,"[7] After his first speech to the

---

3 "Simplicity Will Mark Inaugural Rites at Noon Jan. 4" *Wyoming Eagle,* January 2, 1942, 1

4 "Hunt Warns Against Loss of State's Rights As He Takes Over as Governor" *Wyoming Eagle,* January 5, 1942, 1, 20

5 Id.

6 "The Kid Pitcher from Atlanta" (Part Two) *Wyoming Eagle,* October 22, 1946, 4

7 Transcript of interview with Lester Hunt, Jr. conducted by Rick Ewig, December 29, 1979, in Chicago, 3

legislature, a Republican newsletter admitted that Hunt was "easily the best dressed Governor, and many a woman in the Chamber took a second admiring look at the new chief executive."[8]

Legislators congratulated him for his bipartisan approach to political issues. People liked his gentle, self-effacing manner. The governor loved to tell the gag-story of the day he first toured the Wyoming State Hospital, a facility for mentally ill persons. "We like you better than we did that other governor," Hunt jokingly claimed one of the inmates whispered to him. "Why?" quizzed Hunt. "Because you are much more like us than he was."[9]

He was the first to arrive at the Capitol building each morning. The *Wyoming Eagle* listed a number of other "firsts" achieved by Hunt. He was the first citizen of Fremont County to be elected to a state office. He was the first person to be elected governor after having been elected secretary of state, the usual path coming by ascension to the governorship following the death of the incumbent. Finally, Lester Hunt was the only Democrat to unseat a Republican incumbent during the 1942 elections that had been won nationwide in large part by the GOP.[10]

Hunt's First Legislative Session

The first time Lester Hunt entered the chambers of the House of Representatives was in January of 1933. Then he was one of 54 Democrats in the state legislature. They joined 35 Republican colleagues. Things had changed considerably in the 10 years since. When Governor Hunt entered the house chambers to give the Governor's Message to the 27th State Legislature on January 13, 1943, he was looking at only 27 Democrats sitting among their 56 Republican colleagues.

8 "Easily Wyoming's Best Dressed Governor" *Wyoming Eagle*, January 5, 1942, 7
9 "Lester C. Hunt-The Freshman Senator From Wyoming" written by Robert McCracken, *Rock Springs Rocket*, April 16, 1952
10 *Wyoming Eagle*, January 5, 1942, 20

Hunt's view of this grand room had changed. The view legislators had of their former colleague also changed. On this January morning Lester Hunt was there to speak. They were there to listen. The chamber filled with members of both the Senate and the House of Representatives. People of both parties gathered to listen to his ideas. "It is," he said, "our patriotic duty to leave no act undone that will assist our Commander-in-Chief, our army and our navy, in every possible way to bring about a rapid and successful conclusion of this war."[11] The governor said it was not "as partisans" that they met "but as the delegated spokesmen of all the people."[12]

Hunt disclosed revenue and expenditure data making a point that the budget could not be balanced unless the legislature was willing to find additional revenue, possibly by restoring the mill levy on property that had been removed by his predecessor. Hunt offered budget cuts of his own, offered to limit state employee travel, added an hour a day to their work schedule, and said he was open to reducing the number of state jobs. He spent a large part of his first speech to the legislature talking about post-war planning. "When our Wyoming boys return after the victory, they will return to the hills, plains, fields and mines of Wyoming." He asked, "Are we to be ready or are we to be unready, awaiting the action of the federal government or the action of great business organizations that even now are thinking of the sort of world we are to have when peace is restored?[13]

Except for a brief skirmish over his appointments, in which Hunt eventually prevailed, his first session working with the legislature was relatively unscarred by partisan politics. He had much to be happy about. His appointments had all been confirmed, a committee had been created to study his proposals for state fiscal practices reform, a

11 House Journal of the Twenty-Seventh State Legislature 1943, *Governor's Message*, 26
12 Id. 26
13 Id. 37

balanced budget was passed, and election laws were reformed. Owing only to the fact that more than a third of the Senate were Democrats-most often denying Republicans the two-thirds vote needed to override a veto-all but one of his vetoes were sustained.[14] The governor expressed satisfaction that no other governor had found it "necessary to veto as few measures that reached his desk as have I."[15]

Settling Into A New Home

There had been little time between the election and his inauguration. Hunt was busy preparing a new state budget and legislative agenda. He had little time to settle into his new home, the Governor's Mansion, a few blocks from the Capitol building. The responsibility fell largely to Nathelle. She assembled a staff, keeping Governor Smith's "excellent housekeeper-cook" and hired several wives of "men at Ft. Warren" who were living in Cheyenne while their husbands were fighting the war. "They ranged all the way from a former dancer and one who drove up with her luggage in a Cadillac to an Indian girl and one who said she was surely glad I was like anybody else. A compliment, no doubt," she wrote."[16]

Over the years, Mrs. Hunt proved to be the most inviting of hostesses. She organized small and large events, hosting everyone from Girl Scout troops to state legislators and justices of the Supreme Court. When the Western Governor's Conference was held in Cheyenne, governors including Earl Warren of California, and their wives were feted at the mansion. In 1948, President Harry Truman, the First Lady and their daughter Margaret were her guests. Weeks of planning and working with the Secret Service left Nathelle nervous but the event came off perfectly. Mrs. Hunt noted, "The President made everybody feel at ease

14 House Journal, supra. 485-488; Senate Journal, supra. 455-459
15 Senate Journal of the Twenty-Seventh Legislature of Wyoming 1943, 486
16 Autobiographical Essay of Emily Nathelle Higby Hunt, 22

and Mrs. Truman and Margaret couldn't have been more charming."

The Wyoming Cowboy basketball team took center stage in those first few months of Hunt's term. Lester Hunt was one of the biggest University of Wyoming athletics fans in the state. The governor made it a priority to attend the Cowboy's games in Laramie. According to newspaper publisher Tracy McCracken, "He was a rabid Wyoming fan, joyous in the school's victories, distressed in its defeats." McCracken called the governor, "one of the big reasons Wyoming athletics are now on such a high standard."[17] In March of 1943, in the midst of an otherwise enormous workload, Hunt joined the rest of Wyoming in watching the University of Wyoming basketball team win its only NCAA National Championship.[18]

The brief respite was followed by two of the governor's biggest controversies. The first reared its head during the session when one of Wyoming's Senators charged the state was "pampering" Japanese internees at the Heart Mountain Japanese Relocation Center in Park County. The second, one of those encroachments into state's rights of which Hunt had already warned, came when the Roosevelt administration issued an Executive Order setting aside more than 220,000 acres of Teton County as a national monument.

Heart Mountain

"What are we, you and I?" Young Paul Mayekawa asked the question rhetorically as he began the valedictory address to fellow graduates of Heart Mountain High School in May of 1944. "Are we Japs, simply in a sense as General De Witt declared, 'A Jap is a Jap'?"[19] He knew

---

17 *Memorial Addresses Delivered in Congress for Lester C. Hunt-June 30, 1954*, U.S. Government Printing Office (1955), 12, 13

18 1943 NCAA Championship, www.wyomingathletics.com/trads/hof-1993.html. Two days after winning the NCAA Championship Wyoming played the winner of the National Invitational Tournament, St. John's University. Wyoming won that game as well.

19 General John DeWitt was placed in charge of the operation to evacuate 110,000

many Americans judged the Japanese-Americans by their appearance and ancestry. "Evacuation," he said, "has proved that we cannot take citizenship for granted."[20]

The aged, yellowed copies of the *Heart Mountain Sentinel*,[21] make apparent the resiliency of those thousands of American citizens who were forced from their homes, jobs and lives on the West Coast into a camp in a desolate part of Wyoming. Page after page discloses the difficult adjustment of the internees to their new reality. Two stories demonstrate the dark irony of all that Heart Mountain represented.

One reported on "the biggest mass trial ever held in Wyoming." On June 16, 1944, sixty three Japanese-Americans were put on trial in the federal court at Cheyenne. The U.S. government accused them of not showing for their induction into the Army. The same government that had imprisoned them for being of Japanese ancestry wanted to draft them to fight that nation's war. When they refused, they were put on trial in a courtroom designed to protect the rights of American citizens.[22] Judge T. Blake Kennedy sentenced all of them to three-year prison terms. "If they are truly loyal American citizens," Judge Kennedy said, "they should ...embrace the opportunity to discharge the duties of citizens by offering themselves in the cause of our nation's defense."[23] The judge said nothing of the fact that if their country had considered the young men to be "loyal American citizens" they would not have been at Heart Mountain.

A second story tells of Purple Hearts awarded to "58 soldiers

Japanese-Americans from the wets cost to interment camps. Seventy-five percent of the evacuees were born in the United States. DeWitt said it didn't matter they were American citizens. "A Jap is a Jap," he said. David Stafford, *Roosevelt and Churchill: Men of Secrets*, The Overlook Press, Peter Mayer Publishers, Inc. (1999), 151

20 "Valedictory Address of Paul Mayekawa" entitled "Citizenship Carries Responsibility" *Heart Mountain Sentinel*, May 13, 1944

21 *The Heart Mountain Sentinel* was a newspaper published by and about the internees at Heart Mountain during the duration of their stay.

22 "Biggest Mass Trial in Wyoming's History" *Heart Mountain Sentinel*, June 17, 1944

23 "63 Evaders Get Three-year Prison Sentence" Id. July 1, 1944

who died in action in Italy." The Chief of Staff of the Pacific Army Command, Colonel Kendall J. Fielder, told their imprisoned parents, "Your boy was an American."[24] The truth is a lot of Americans didn't believe that and Governor Lester Hunt had to deal with their prejudice. The decision to imprison citizens of Japanese ancestry was made by the President of the United States, as was the decision to place thousands of the internees in Wyoming. The War Department and its War Relocation Agency had primary responsibility for the administration of the ten camps created for the relocation of Japanese-Americans. But the governors of Wyoming and the other states where camps were located were actually the officials occupying the frontlines. They, and not the President, had to deal most directly with the inevitable controversies created by these decisions.

Among the hundreds of letters Governor Hunt received from Wyoming folks are the following, representing the broad range of opinions with which the governor had to deal in the first year of his term.

Riverton Wyoming, March 5, 1943

Dear Governor

There is a bunch of us ranchers in need of farm laber, for beets, beans and peas. They have asked me to go up to the Japanese relocation at Heart Mountain, and see what can be den in regards to laber to produce these crops, on a scale for wages or share crop.

No Lester I have bin informed it takes quit some time to get things raveled out before you can do or get in touch with the superviser. Governor if you don›t mind, would you give me a letter showing Im not there for kidnapen or for sight seein but for laber to help produce for the boys in the servise.

/s/ Bert Braskit[25]

---

24 "They Proved They Were Fine, Loyal and Brave" *Heart Mountain Sentinel*, April 8, 1944

25 Letter from Bert Braskit to Hunt, March 5, 1943, (quoted as written) File: "Heart Mountain" Box 1, LCH Papers

Another constituent asked the governor for help "to get a Japanese girl to work for me." A cattle rancher "with more work to do than I can do alone," he was specific. "I would like a girl around twenty years old."[26]

Earl Kerr, president of American War Dads, was opposed to housing the Japanese internees in Wyoming. He demanded "that all Japs that were brought here be removed and that until they are they be confined to within the boundaries of the Center."[27] The Veterans of Foreign Wars of Ogden, Utah, got into the fray, sending Hunt a resolution asking, "all Japanese be placed in concentration camps and treated as prisoners of war."[28] The VFW in Rock Springs assured the governor that Wyoming veterans endorsed the Utah resolution.[29]

Governor Nels Smith teed up this political football before leaving office with his extreme rhetoric about the "Japs" and how unwelcome they would be in Wyoming. On the day after the attack on Pearl Harbor, Governor Smith wired every sheriff in Wyoming demanding that they "contact all alien Japanese and require their registration."[30] Sheriff Frank Narramore of Uinta County informed the governor "we have only one in the county." George Yamada was, wrote the sheriff, "employed as section foreman for Union Pacific Railroad at Antelope, Wyoming. Age 45 years, born in Japan, in United States since 1914, has made two trips to Japan, one in 1922, and again in 1936. Has five children all born in this country, now living in Japan. Taken there after

---

26 Letter from Mr. Phil Lechenby of Split Rock, Wyoming, to Hunt, March 26, 1943, File: "Heart Mountain" Box 1, LCH Papers

27 Letter from Earl Kerr to Hunt, July 20, 1945, File: "Heart Mountain" Box 1, LCH Papers

28 "Resolution" dated September 1, 1943 Sent to Hunt by Corporal Fred J. Grant Post 1481, Veterans of Foreign Wars, Ogden, Utah, File: "Heart Mountain" Box 1, LCH Papers

29 Letter to Hunt from F.H. Dennison, Adjutant, VFW Post 2316, Rock Springs, Wyoming, dated November 30, 1943, Id.

30 Copy of telegrams (dated December 7, 1941) and letters in response, File: "Correspondence re: Japanese Internment" Box 3, Papers of Nels H. Smith, Collection No. 09880, American Heritage Center, University of Wyoming

the death of their mother."[31] Many of the reports identified Japanese-American families that had been in Wyoming for as long as 5-60 years. Others had adult children who had been raised in the state and were currently serving in the U. S. Army. Sheriff Frank Blackburn of Park County was baffled that the governor had not asked for "a check on Alien Germans and I am wondering if anything is being done in this respect."[32]

Smith was adamantly opposed to what he called, "the location and colonization of west coast Japanese in our state unless they are interned under federal control, supervision and maintenance."[33] He reflected the opinions of many of his constituents. Most agreed with President Roosevelt's decision to imprison Japanese-Americans, but they didn't want them in Wyoming. If they had to be in Wyoming, many felt they should be strictly confined. Others thought the "importation of native-born Japanese" was an opportunity to use them for farm labor since the agricultural workforce had been depleted by "the draft and high wages in war industries."[34]

One Wyoming rancher made a darker suggestion. "If any Japs have to come here we will run them through the dipping vat. We use an arsenic dip and for Japs we will step it up to a straight arsenic."[35] Governor Smith replied. "It is most heartening to have the support of reasonable people on decisions of this character."[36]

Under FDR's order, more than 110,000 people were to be evacuated from the west coast. They had to go somewhere. Upon first hearing of the plans to relocate them to Wyoming, Smith telegrammed

31 Id.

32 Id.

33 Western Union Telegram, March 23, 1942, Box 3, Papers of Nels Smith, American Heritage Center, University of Wyoming

34 Letter from Midvale Irrigation District to Governor Smith dated March 18, 1942, Id.

35 Letter from William D. Sidley of the Silver Spur Ranch, Encampment, Wyoming, dated March 14, 1942, Id.

36 Letter from Governor Smith to William D. Sidley, dated March 30, 1942, Id.

Attorney General Francis Biddle, informing him in no uncertain terms that the state of Wyoming "cannot acquiesce to the importation of these Japanese into our state."[37] The following month, Milton S. Eisenhower, brother of Dwight Eisenhower, invited Smith and other governors to a meeting in Salt Lake City to discuss the federal government's plans to relocate the internees.[38] The states selected were announced. Notwithstanding Governor Smith's objections, the evacuees were headed to California, Arizona, Utah, Arkansas, Colorado and Wyoming.[39] The War Department[40] acquired land situated between Cody and Powell in the far northwest corner of the state. It was called Heart Mountain. The reaction varied. Some wanted the Japanese-Americans to be treated as prisoners of war, placed under armed guard. Others wanted them for farm labor and to build highways. Some merchants wanted them to spend money in their stores. Others wanted them banned from entering the nearby towns.

In his farewell speech on the day Hunt was inaugurated, Governor Smith took a parting shot, warning there would be "a serious social problem" if the Japanese-Americans were permitted to remain in Wyoming following the war.[41] As Lester Hunt became governor, the pot had been stirred, people were angry and positions were etched in stone. Wyoming's new U.S. Senator E.V. Robertson then took up the cudgel.

Robertson had an unusual resume for a Wyoming politician.

37 Telegram from Smith to Francis Biddle, Attorney General of the United States, February 21, 1942, Id.

38 Letter from M. S. Eisenhower to Governor Smith, dated March 30, 1942, Id.

39 *"Final Report Japanese Evacuation from the West Coast 1942"* US War Department, US Government Printing Office, 1943

40 The United States Department of War, often referred to as the War Department, had responsibility for the United States Army and for land-based air forces until the creation of the Department of the Air Force in 1947. The War Department existed until renamed the United States Department of Defense in 1949.

41 "Hunt Takes Oath As Governor" *Wyoming State Tribune* January 4, 1943, 7

Born in Wales, he had served in the Second Boer War from 1899 to 1902. Robertson immigrated to the United States in 1912, settling in Park County where he raised livestock on a ranch only 14 miles from Heart Mountain. He was elected to the Senate in 1942, when Hunt was elected governor. This Welsh-American had little compassion for the Japanese-Americans.

In one of his first acts as a senator, Robertson urged the *Denver Post* to "investigate the conditions" at the relocation center.[42] "Here, at Heart Mountain Relocation Center, where the War Relocation Authority is host to (thousands of) men and women of Japanese blood," The *Post* reported, "the pampered and petted charges of the government are not only being politely asked to work but are being flooded with offers of gainful employment far better than most of them, before coming to the center, ever knew."[43]

The story came on the heels of reports of the summary execution of some of the American airmen whose planes had crashed during the first American air raid on the Japanese mainland. Lieutenant Colonel Jimmy Doolittle led the April 18, 1942 raid. The news reports stirred anti-Japanese passions.

Hunt nonetheless decried the *Denver Post* story as "political" and said the reporter relied on a "disgruntled employee who was discharged about two weeks ago and went direct to the *Denver Post*."[44] The governor defended the camp. "If you can picture a town of 13,500 people and only one actual arrest in such a community over a period of several months' duration, you can realize how orderly and well managed the camp is."[45]

Senator Robertson had a much different view of Heart Mountain

42 *Congressional Record*, Vol. 89, Part 3, p. 4040, May 6, 1943
43 *Denver Post*, April 24, 1943
44 Letter from Governor Hunt to William J. Stone, dated April 26, 1943, File: "Wyoming-World War II-Gov. Hunt Correspondence" Box 36, Papers of T.A. Larson
45 Letter from Governor Hunt to Ella W. Hise, dated July 3, 1943, Id.

and its involuntary residents. Having instigated the *Denver Post's* inter-est in the story, he bootstrapped the *Post's* article into a set of facts he used to support his claim that "disloyal Japanese are being pam-pered" at Heart Mountain while Americans are being "murdered or mistreated" by Japanese soldiers. Robertson reflected the views of his constituents and many of his Park County neighbors.

Internees were harshly critical of Robertson's role in the *Denver Post* article telling the *Laramie Daily Bulletin,* "Despite repeated invitations both before and after his election, Senator Robertson has not seen fit to visit the Center. Now in the nation's capital, Senator Robertson sets himself up as a fountain of information about this Center."[46] The Japanese-Americans at Heart Mountain were not Robertson's only critics. In nearby Lovell, the editor of the *Lovell Chronicle* called the Senator's speech "tommyrot."[47]

Robertson, who openly advocated that all Americans of Japanese descent should be sent "back to Japan,"[48] continued to stir up people while Governor Hunt had to deal with the problems created by the rhetoric. For his part, the governor found the internees caused "no trouble and very little concern" to civilian authorities.[49] Nonetheless, he found himself in the middle of quarrels about the camp and its residents. In May of 1943, the town councils of nearby Powell and Cody petitioned the Hunt to halt the issuance of passes allowing internees to visit their communities.[50] Initially, Hunt asked camp director Guy Robertson (no relation to Senator Robertson) to restrict "permission

46 "Heart Editor Says Robertson Has Not Visited Jap Camp" *Laramie Daily Bulletin,* May 12, 1943

47 "Which War is Most Important" *Lovell Chronicle,* May 27, 1943

48 "Wyoming Senator Would Deport All Japs From US" *Rock Spring Rocket-Miner,* February 23, 1944

49 Letter from Governor Hunt to US Senator A.B. Chandler, dated March 31, 1943, File: "Wyoming-World War II-Gov. Hunt Correspondence" Box 36, Papers of T.A. Larson

50 "Resolution of Policy Toward Japanese at Heart Mountain Relocation Center" File: "Heart Mountain" Box 1, LCH Papers

allowing evacuees to visit Powell and Cody."[51] Robertson politely explained, "There are two sides to the question and I am sure that you will soon find a lot of the farmers and businessmen insisting that we allow the evacuees to go to work."[52]

The governor began to hear from those who disagreed with their town councils. "As you no doubt are aware of the Anti-Heart Mountain War Relocation Camp Mayor we have," wrote A.R Fryer of Fryer's Pharmacy in Powell, "there happen to be a few other details which I think should be brought to your attention at this time since our Honorable Mayor and City Council are again trying to kick up more trouble concerning said Camp and its citizens."[53] Fryer informed the governor the camp had provided an economic boom to the businesses of Park County, explaining "90% of the merchants here in Powell have been able to pay off their old debts and now buy War Bonds since this Relocation camp was built two years ago." To make himself clear this was an economic and not a social justice issue, Fryer assured Hunt the business community favored the evacuees over "these Mexican Nationals brought up from Mexico that can't even talk United States (sic), then steal you blind the minute they come into your store."

Other merchants agreed. They appreciated the extra income received from the internees and hastened to assure the governor their town council did not speak for the majority. Nevertheless, the mayor continued to insist the evacuees not be permitted to visit Powell. In August 1944, Hunt decided to commission a private investigator to determine which side was right. Hunt made this promise to the mayor. "If his report substantiates your position, I will immediately follow your suggestions with reference to asking the Heart Mountain authorities

51 Letter from Hunt to Guy Robertson, May10, 1943, File: "Heart Mountain" Box 1, LCH Papers
52 Letter from Guy Robertson to Hunt, dated May 13, 1943, Id.
53 Letter from A.R. Fryer to Governor Hunt, June 21, 1944, Id.

to discontinue allowing the Japanese to visit Powell."[54] The mayor felt certain that if the inquiries were "thorough and unbiased" his position would prevail. He agreed with Hunt's strategy.[55]

Captain William Bradley of the Wyoming Highway Patrol was dispatched to Powell. He interviewed "perhaps twenty people" chosen at random and allowed to remain anonymous. Many didn't care one way or anther, Bradley reported to the governor. Others told him, "Every Jap should be taken out and shot." Many others had no objection. Bradley reported, "I was given the impression that the larger majority of the townspeople were in favor of having the Japs come to Powell to trade." He estimated the split to be about 65% to 35% opposed to the Mayor's position.[56]

Hunt told the mayor he was now "more stymied than ever on what I should do." He promised to take "drastic action to see that the Japs leave the relocation Center and Wyoming immediately after the termination of the war." In the meantime the governor bowed out of the community controversy.[57] Regardless, the presence of so many Japanese-Americans in Park County continued to stir controversy. The governor received countless petitions and letters demanding he assure them all the evacuees would be required to leave Wyoming at war's end.

Of course, the governor had no such authority. The question of whether any of the evacuees would be allowed to remain in Wyoming had long been an issue. During the gubernatorial campaign of 1942, Governor Smith told a Cody audience he had received written assurance from the U.S. government that all internees would be required

54 Letter from Hunt to mayor O.E. Bever, dated August 8, 1944, File: "Heart Mountain Relocation Project" Box 1, LCH Papers
55 Letter from O.E. Bever to Hunt, August 12, 1944, Id.
56 Letter from Captain William R. Bradley to Hunt, dated August 22, 1944, Id.
57 Letter from Governor Hunt to Mayor Bever, dated August 31, 1944, Id

to leave Wyoming at the end of the war.[58] No such document was ever located.[59] Governors Smith and Hunt each refused to acknowledge that after the war, as American citizens, the evacuees were free to live anywhere in the country they might choose. Some, not many, chose Wyoming.

In July 1945, with the war nearly over, the Powell chapter of American War Dads petitioned the governor to "not impose these people on the Fathers and Mothers of this community now at a time when many of them are being advised of the death of their sons and daughters in our war against Japan." Governor Hunt forwarded the petition to Guy Robertson asking what "the process or method is in returning the Japs."[60]

Robertson assured the governor the camp would be closed on or before November 15. But he had run out of patience with the Park County complainers. Robertson reminded the governor the men and women at issue were U.S. citizens who had been forced from their homes. He recounted how many of their sons were still fighting and dying in the South Pacific. "758 boys from families in Heart Mountain are now fighting in our armed forces all over the world, and I venture to suggest that these boys are just as dear to their War dads and mothers as are the boys from Powell or any other community to theirs."

Robertson asked, "if some fanatical, race baiting, unthinking and unprincipled individual did not instigate the petition and by canvassing the highways and byways of Powell and by cajolery and false information prevail upon these people to sign something that sober reflection and study might cause them to hang their heads in embarrassment and shame."

The last train, filled with more than 400 Japanese-Americans, left

58 Letter from Milward Simpson to Governor Hunt, dated April 13, 1944, Id.

59 Letter from described above returned to Simpson with handwritten note from Hunt, "Dear Milward, We can find no record of any kind in this office." Id.

60 Letter from Hunt to Guy Robertson, dated July 29, 1945, Id.

Heart Mountain for the west coast on November 9, 1945. All the former residents had been relocated. The water was turned off, the boilers drained, the windows of the barracks boarded up and the mess hall closed. One of the sorriest chapters in Wyoming and U.S. history came to an end.[61]

The Jackson Hole National Monument

In 2002, Wyoming writer and poet Sam Western wrote a controversial book entitled *Pushed Off the Mountain, Sold Down the River.*[62] Western was a correspondent for the *Economist* of London and lived in Sheridan. His book suggested the state was crippled by what he called "a way-of-life mythology," in which the state sees itself as the last refuge of the cowboy, riding the range, free of concern or control. This mythology has often produced unrealistic and unhelpful confrontations with the state's largest landowner, the government of the United States. One of the dynamics of that "way-of-life" mythology is its impact on Wyoming politicians. None ever lost a vote defending states' rights while beating federal bureaucrats and agencies over the head.

In unacknowledged ways, the roots of this controversy extend beyond the state's rights debate long a part of the American political stage. Indeed, the roots are much longer and older and can be found in Europe's monarchies. According to Wyoming historian Robert W. Righter, it was there the "governing class assumed that the proletariat class had neither the aesthetic sensitivity nor the cultural sophistication to benefit from the beauty of nature."[63] Nineteenth century naturalists like George Catlin, the American painter who, in 1830, accompanied

---

61 "Special Instructions for Next Week" *Heart Mountain Sentinel Supplement*, November 2, 1945, the final bulletin issued.

62 Sam Western, *Pushed Off the Mountain, Sold Down the River*, Homestead Publishing (2002), 18

63 Robert W. Righter, *Crucible for Conservation: The Struggle for Grand Teton National Park*, Grand Teton Natural History Association (1982), 13

William Clark on a trek into the frontier, and philosopher Henry David Thoreau, raised the democratic conscience of the nation, opening the door to a dialogue about how certain lands, especially in the spacious West could be enjoyed by all.

By 1872, the notion took hold that extraordinarily beautiful lands should be set aside for the perpetual enjoyment of all. President Ulysses S. Grant signed a bill establishing the first national park, Yellowstone National Park. While the creation of the Park was popular, later proposals to expand it created the beginnings of an uproar leading to what Hunt called "a mess of a hell," the battle over Roosevelt's Executive Order establishing the Jackson Hole National Monument.[64]

In 1929, Congress had agreed to set aside the Teton Mountain Range and eight lakes at the base of the mountains as Grand Teton National Park.[65] Soon some began clamoring for an expansion of the park boundaries, seeking to protect even more land from development. When the "veil of secrecy" was lifted, the involvement of oil mogul John D. Rockefeller, Jr. was disclosed.[66] At some point in the debate over FDR's executive order, someone slipped Governor Hunt a copy of a 1923 letter exchanged between Yellowstone National Park Superintendent Horace Albright and *Saturday Evening Post* writer Hal Evarts. Albright favored expansion of the Grand Teton National Park. Evarts was one of a handful of nationally known writers whom Albright enlisted to write favorably about the idea.

The letter from Albright to Evarts explained, "We have a proposition on (sic) that is positively the most important game conservation project in America today. It is still in a very confidential status but I am

64 Letter from Hunt to Dr. John Repogle, October 14, 1944 telling him, "Things here in the Capitol are in a 'mess of a hell', but I feel I have sufficient competent legal authority to be playing my cards in such a way that I will be upheld by the courts." File: "Jackson Hole National Monument" Box 3, LCH Papers

65 "Grand Teton National Park Information Page, http://www.grand.teton.national-park.com/info.htm

66 Righter, Supra. 64-65

going to give you a hint of what it is."[67] Albright didn't identify the "we" but detailed the economic straits in which most Jackson Hole ranchers found themselves. "There is no hope of these poor people getting out of debt," Albright explained. "They have simply got to sell out or go broke."

The letter set forth the plans of the undisclosed "they," saying, "They have therefore proposed that the entire Jackson Hole be purchased, and they, being better informed than anyone else, estimate that a fund of three million dollars would buy every ranch in Jackson Hole, and with this amount of money the country could be turned back to nature and nature's children, the elk, antelope and deer."

Actually, this line of reasoning was much the same as that of former Governor Leslie A. Miller (1933-1939). Miller shared the belief that the highest and best economic use of Jackson Hole was tourism, recreation and game hunting, not ranching.[68] But to those who read the letter in the context of the dispute, it all seemed part of the plot between the federal government and wealthy easterners to destroy the ranching economy of Jackson Hole. Albright never thought his letter would be read by anyone else. He didn't help his cause by attempting to keep it secret nor by including words that sounded like the conspiracy the ranchers feared. The letter proposed acquiring "control of the *Jackson Hole Courier* (the local newspaper) which is for sale." He said a former owner who supported the "project" was interested in buying the paper again. "Of course, with the *Courier* in favorable hands the Forest Service can be taken care of," Albright wrote.

Hunt provided Wyoming Senator Joe O'Mahoney a copy of the Albright-Evarts correspondence. O'Mahoney, in turn, sent it on to Harold Ickes, the Secretary of the Interior. Ickes was forced to acknowl-

67 Letter from Horace M. Albright to Hal G. Evarts, File: "Jackson Hole Monument" Box 2, LCH Papers
68 Righter, supra. 77 citing *An Interview With Leslie Miller* by Ed Edwin, April 13, 1966, p. 8, Oral History Collection of Columbia University

edge, "There can be hardly any doubt that the cards were not being played face up on the table."[69]

Equally damaging to the supporters of the National Monument was the release of yet another letter. On February 16, 1927, Superintendent Albright wrote to John D. Rockefeller providing evidence of the financier's clandestine involvement in the secret effort to buy out Jackson Hole ranchers. As an official of the federal government, Albright advised Rockefeller, "Say nothing at the present time about the larger or ultimate plan of acquiring all of the private land holdings in the Jackson Hole."[70] The letter suggested buying land through agents, disguising their real intent and leaving no doubt that regardless of the government's intent to protect the land, their means were surreptitious at best.

Characteristic of much of Wyoming's history, the same folks who had welcomed the involvement of the federal government when it arrived in the form of "subsidies of stage routes and railroads, government explorations from Lewis and Clark and Ferdinand Hayden, military protection, and land grant colleges" saw something sinister in what they perceived as collusion between a New York millionaire and the National Park Service.[71] But, Rockefeller's involvement was more than a little problematic, bolstering conspiracy theories about the intent of the government and this wealthy easterner. Wyoming politicians, increasingly wary of Roosevelt's New Deal programs and the perceived intrusion on state matters, began to voice their suspicions.

It no longer mattered that the President and Wyoming's governor shared a party affiliation. The new Democratic governor was about to "earn his spurs" on the states' rights issue. From the beginning

69 Letter from Harold L. Ickes to Joseph C. O'Mahoney, April 19, 1943, File: "Jackson Hole Monument" Box 2, LCH Papers
70 Letter from Horace M. Albright to John D. Rockefeller, February 16, 1927, File: "Jackson Hole Monument" Box 2, LCH Papers
71 Righter, *supra.* 66

Republicans doubted he could defend the states' rights because of his staunch support for Roosevelt and the New Deal."[72] Even though Hunt had campaigned on the issue of states' rights and had spoken of it in his inaugural address, there were those who thought his relationship with FDR would hobble him when the first fight arose.

The opportunity to prove the doubters wrong came early. On March 15, 1943, a little more than two months after Hunt had been sworn into office, President Roosevelt signed an Executive Order establishing the Jackson Hole National Monument. With the authority given Presidents under the Antiquities Act of 1906 (signed into law by the other Roosevelt, President Theodore "Teddy" Roosevelt) this Roosevelt set aside 221,610 acres of Teton County as a national monument.[73] [74] The fight was on.

Governor Hunt issued a press release the following day questioning the propriety of creating the monument by executive order. On March 20 he called the Executive Order "arbitrary and a direct invasion of state's rights."[75] Hunt received countless letters from individuals and organizations across Wyoming and throughout the United States. Nearly every one of them angrily opposed creation of the monument. Resolutions objecting to the monument came from every agricultural organization in the state. The Lions Club and the Past Matrons

72 Editorial *Wyoming State Eagle,* January 5, 1942, 7

73 "Proclamation 2578 Establishing the "Jackson Hole National Monument" in Wyoming appeared in the Federal Register on March 18, 1943 (Vol. 8, Number 43)

74 "The Antiquities Act (16 U.S.C. 431-433) was the first United States law to provide general protection for any general kind of cultural or natural resource. It established the first national historic preservation policy for the United States (Lee 1970:1 ff.) Section 2 of the statute gives the President the authority to set aside for protection "...historic landmarks, historic and prehistoric structures, and other objects of historic or scientific interest that are situated upon the lands owned or controlled by the Government of the United States..." These protected areas were then designated as "national monuments" and the federal agencies assigned to oversee them were required to afford proper care and management of the resources." Accessed at www.cr.nps.gov/archeology/tools/laws/AntAct.htm

75 *Wyoming Eagle* March 20, 1943

Club of the Eastern Star of Sheridan protested the monument, as did "Chapter D of P.E.O. Sisterhood" of Cody, the Los Angeles Chamber of Commerce, and many others. Stacks of letters landed daily on Hunt's desk. From all over the country they came, from Maine to Nebraska and Florida to California, many with highly inflammatory anti-FDR language.[76]

A Wheatland man wrote on March 27, "Go to it. Let's see whether we live in a democracy or under a dictator."[77] A Teton County rancher wrote that while Roosevelt "publicly charged Mussolini with stabbing France in the back" FDR had done the same to the people of this country.[78]

Hunt made a personal, political appeal to his friends in the White House. "We lost the election of 1942," the Governor wrote, "because to a very great extent the bureaus and not the Congress or the President were running this country." He reminded Roosevelt only one Democratic candidate had won a governorship that year. That one was Hunt, who continued, "It simply is not possible to build up any interest for our cause and our Party in this state under such circumstances and I can say to you without any question of a doubt that Wyoming will be found in the Republican column by a tremendous majority, regardless of any other contributing factors unless this proclamation is rescinded if possible or the area involved reduced in line with the map enclosed."[79]

By the time Roosevelt replied, the state's anger had been ever further kindled. The controversy provided Hunt the opportunity to forge alliances with key Wyoming Republicans. Not only did he work closer

76 Numerous letters to Governor Hunt, File: "Jackson Hole Monument" Box 2, LCH Papers
77 Id.
78 Id.
79 Letter from Governor Hunt to Marvin McIntyre "Secretary to the President" March 31, 1943, Id.

than ever with the Republicans in Wyoming's congressional delegation, he found himself receiving the praise of other GOP leaders. One was Milward Simpson, a former state legislator, future governor and U.S. Senator. Simpson praised the Democrat for his efforts to protect state's rights.[80] Another GOP stalwart was Mrs. John C. Turner of the Triangle X Ranch in Teton County. "You certainly have proved worthy of the trust that we of Wyoming had in you when we voted you our Governor – you have acted like a true Westerner and Wyomingite."[81] She added, "We certainly are proud of you." Influential Republican banker Felix Buchenroth of Jackson telegrammed, "You are not only Governor in name but in fact."[82]

On April 29 Governor Hunt upped the ante, threatening to use the state's "police powers to remove any federal official from the area who enters (the National Monument) to assume authority."[83] On the same day FDR wrote Hunt addressing one of the governor's chief concerns. The President assured him there would be no interference with grazing rights and "no adverse effect upon the production of livestock, now so vital to the war program."[84] By then the rhetoric had become too extreme, the controversy so heated that even the President's assurance was insufficient. On May 4 the *Salt Lake Tribune* ran a front-page story on the debate complete with a photograph of armed cowboys riding the range as though they were hunting officials of the federal government. "Armed Jackson Ranchers Move Cattle to Monument Ranges," bellowed the headline. The cowboys were joined by actor Wallace Berry "astride a borrowed white horse and with a .30-.30 rifle in hand."[85]

Hunt's attorney general filed a lawsuit in Federal District Court.

80 Id.
81 Letter dated May 5, 1943, Id.
82 Telegram dated April 9, 1943, Id.
83 United Press International Wire Story dated April 29, 1943, Id.
84 Letter to Hunt from Roosevelt, April 29, 1943, Id.
85 *Salt Lake City Tribune*, May 4, 1943

The Wyoming congressional delegation introduced bills and amendments to the Department of Interior's appropriations aimed at blocking enforcement of Roosevelt's Executive Order. Just when it seemed no one in Wyoming supported the efforts of the federal government to protect this land, a surprising and influential voice entered the fray.

Leslie Miller had become governor in 1934 when he and Lester Hunt were among the Democratic candidates sweeping the Wyoming elections. Unlike Hunt and most Wyoming politicians, Governor Miller had long been supportive of the idea of expanding the Park boundaries. An agent for John D. Rockefeller, Jr. met with Miller early in his term and found an unexpected supporter. Harold Fabian, vice-president of the Snake River Land Company, Rockefeller's clandestine Jackson Hole realty company, reported, "I was with Governor Miller until 10:30 P.M. and the three hours were the most pleasant I have spent in Wyoming with officials in the past six years."[86]

By 1943 Miller was no longer governor, having been defeated in 1938 by Nels Smith, the man Hunt defeated in 1942. Governor Hunt was blindsided by testimony his old friend gave to the House Committee on Public Lands as it was considering legislation to block Roosevelt's order. "Seldom, if ever, in the history of Wyoming," said Miller, "has a project which should be entitled to sympathetic consideration been so grossly misrepresented."[87] The former governor defended Rockefeller's motives and assured the committee the views of many Wyoming people had been misrepresented by special interests opposing the monument. Opponents, Miller claimed, were simply shedding "rhetorical tears." Miller concluded, "The writer hereof loves Wyoming – the state has been most kind to him. He has sung the praises of its people all over

86 Righter, *supra*, 77-78

87 "Statement of Leslie A. Miler, Governor of Wyoming 1933-1939 to the Public Lands Committee of the House of Representatives on Bill H.R. 2241 Proposing to Set Aside the Presidential Order Creating Jackson Hole Monument." File: "Jackson Hole National Monument, Box 2, LCH Papers

the land. He wants, oh so much, to have them live up to the reputation he has claimed for them for fair-mindedness, generosity, for appreciation of the better things in life."

Miller promptly followed with a private letter to Hunt asking that the "fact that I may seem to disagree with you and Joe (Senator O'Mahoney) on a proposition of this kind will not have any weight in our ordinary relationships."[88] Governor Hunt assured Miller it would not but he worried the GOP would use his statement to drive a wedge between the two of them, which of course the Party attempted.[89]

Eventually the legislation sponsored by members of the Wyoming congressional delegation was either defeated or vetoed and the lawsuit Hunt pursued was dismissed. Judge Kennedy didn't want to get his federal court between either the executive and legislative branches of the federal government, nor between the federal government and his friends in Wyoming state government. It was, the judge said, "a controversy between the legislative and executive branches of the Government in which the Court cannot interfere."[90] He dismissed the state's lawsuit.

The matter continued to be a sore spot between Hunt and his friends in the White House until he became a U. S. Senator. In 1950 a compromise was reached and President Harry Truman signed a bill sponsored by Senators Hunt and O'Mahoney abolishing the national monument but including most of the land in an expansion of the boundaries of the Grand Teton National Park.[91]

88 Letter from Miller to Hunt, July 2, 1943, File: "Jackson Hole National Monument" Box 2, LCH Papers

89 Letter from Hunt to Miller, July 3, 1943, Id.

90 Robert W. Righter, supra, citing T. Blake Kennedy, *Memoirs*, 736-739, American Heritage Center, University of Wyoming. According to Righter, "Later, in his memoirs, Judge Kennedy commented that the government had given effective evidence of scientific and historic interest, indicating that he would have ruled for the National Park Service." Page 169, footnote 73

91 Larson, *History of Wyoming*, Supra. 501

Wartime Governor

Surprisingly, the lives of even small-state governors revolved around the war. Hunt's days were filled with issues ranging from a fear of Japanese attacks and the Selective Service to rationing, war bond drives and planting victory gardens. The official files from his years as governor are replete with letters, speeches and other documents reflecting how much of his time Hunt spent as a "war-governor." On May 14, 1945, the governor received a confidential communication from Major General C.H. Danielson, U. S. Army Commanding General warning the governor of "the danger of Japanese bombs brought to this country by Japanese balloons."[92] General Danielson asked that the state inform him immediately of any such incidents but asked that they not be publicized because publicity could provide the Japanese with important strategic information.

The Selective Service Act imposed a number of duties on governors to assure the conscription process provided the personnel necessary to fight the war.[93] Governors were charged with administering the act in their states. The governor offered a recommendation for the position of "State Director of Selective Service." Once appointed, the state director was expected to manage the local selective service boards, which in turn, reviewed draft classifications, ordering men into service. The governor's time was spent filling vacancies on boards, referring cases to the boards and refereeing conflicts among board members. Complicating the life of the governor, state director and local board members was a complex scheme of physical and mental standards, deferments and exceptions. This made life so difficult for local board members serving in a small rural community where everybody knew everybody that Hunt's time was consumed looking for replacements.

92 Letter to Governor from Major General C.H. Danielson, dated May 14, 1945, File: "Seventh Command" Box 3, LCH Papers
93 Section 120, Volume One of the Selective Service Act Regulations, September 23, 1940

These were thankless jobs requiring board members to determine whether friends and neighbors would stay home or go to war. When Hunt asked an old friend, Joe Spangler of Greybull, to accept appointment to the State Appeal Board, Spangler's telegrammed reply was terse. "Respectfully decline-STOP-Suggest L. McClean-STOP-Letter follows." No letter followed. Another potential recruit said simply, "I do not feel that I have the right disposition to serve on the local board."[94]

On one occasion the governor, besieged with complaints he was not appointing enough Democrats, made an attempt to do so but got the wrong person. He intended to persuade Mark Hanna, a Democrat, to serve on the Goshen County board. Hunt placed a personal phone call that was nearly concluded when he realized he was talking to Mark's Republican brother who readily accepted the appointment. The embarrassed governor decided he could not rescind the invitation."[95]

Then there were the complaints about board decisions. "Complaints come to me daily with reference to every draft board in the state," Hunt wrote.[96] There were complaints about personalities, partisan make-up of the boards, size of the boards and whether organizations like the American Legion were adequately represented. Some felt the boards gave too many deferments. Others complained there were too few.[97]

Local quarrels started easily and often and were time consuming for the governor to mediate. When, for example, one member of the Hot Springs County board died, another said he was no longer willing to work with the third who then wrote to Hunt. "He said I had objected to drafting certain farmers and that I was more interested in keeping

94 Letter to Hunt from Dr. J.A Farlienn, December 17, 1944, File: "Selective Service-Miscellaneous" Box 3, LCH Papers

95 Letter to Mark N. Hanna, dated January 4, 1944, File: "Selective Service-Organization and Administration" Box 2, LCH Papers

96 Letter from Hunt to Tony Littleton of Gillette, Wyoming, dated April 3, 1943, File: Selective Service Administration" Box 2, LCH Papers

97 Letters to Hunt, File: "Selective Service-Organization and Administration" Box 2, LCH Papers

men out of the army than in putting them in."[98]

National interest groups also sought the help of the governor to aid in their agendas. When a member of the Daughters of the American Revolution asked Hunt to join the governor of Colorado and "refuse to allow the drafting of farmers," he declined, explaining, "I intend to let the Army run the war and I will attend to the affairs of the State of Wyoming."[99]

Numerous constituents appealed to the governor for deferments from the draft for children or other family members. William Petersen, a friend from Fremont County wrote seeking help in obtaining an agricultural deferment. "I want to know if a man owning 129 acre farm, 85 acres which are under irrigating and farming the rest is pasture, and having 6 cows milking, 1 brood sow, and 20 laying hens, also 2 working horses, is deferrable?"

Corporal Waldo Hurley asked for help getting a discharge so he could return to Casper to operate the Coca-Cola Bottling Company franchise he owned. A Cokeville constituent sought a deferment for his sons so they could help on the farm. The governor commiserated with both writing, "In many ways I am in exactly the same situation as you are, only possibly in a little tougher spot." Two-thirds of the officers of the highway patrol had been drafted or had enlisted. Hunt told them that, like the farmer's sons, they were "key men, trained with long experience, taken from every department of state government." The governor added that the state institutions "are suffering terribly from a lack of manpower." As an example he said, "The tuberculosis sanatorium at Basin has thirty-one patients and only two nurses, one for day duty and one for night duty, and we are finding it necessary to not take any additional patients, for we just can't take care of them."

98 Letter to Hunt from George C. McCormick, dated February 4, 1944, File: "Selective Service Administration" Box 2, LCH Papers
99 Letter from Hunt to Evangeline Ording, dated April 3, 1943, File: " Selective Service-Organization and Administration" Box 2, LCH Papers

To the countless letters Hunt received seeking help in obtaining deferrals and discharges, the governor nearly always responded by informing the writer, "This is a matter which is entirely under the jurisdiction of the federal government and I have no authority to intercede." Occasionally, however, he felt he had no alternative.

When the Platte County selective service board sent a draft notice to Milton R. Foe, the governor was concerned. Foe was one of only two remaining lawyers in the attorney general's office. "This request is made," he wrote the board, " without Mr. Foe's knowledge or consent, and he might not accept the deferment if it were granted." Mr. Foe did not. The chair of the board answered the governor, "The contents of your letter and your request for deferment of the registrant put the board 'on the spot' as Mr. Foe in a call to this office and in a conversation with Mr. Cossman, member of this local board, had expressed himself as feeling that it was his patriotic duty to accept service when he should be called and the board felt that the registrant's expression should be given due consideration, feeling that Mr. Foe realized the future sentiment of the public in regard to those of military age who had not seen service in this war."

Hunt was also unsuccessful in going to bat for a Casper law officer. The governor wrote to Wyoming's selective service head, Colonel R.L. Esmay. "Patrolman Collier has been doing very splendid work in cleaning up Casper, and personally I fear that if he is removed the gambling, violation of liquor laws, and other vices which have been eradicated in Casper will immediately return."[100]

The demand for men to fight the war created serious hardships for Wyoming farmers and ranchers who were asked to produce more food for the war effort though hobbled by the lack of workers. A Riverton farmer pleaded with Hunt for help in obtaining a discharge for his brother so that he could help farm. "He has been in (the Army) for

100 Each letter described in this section may be found in the Hunt Papers, Supra, Box 3

almost 5 years and has been overseas for 16 months...I understand the Army needs men but we need it (sic) here on the home front too." Ralph Plant of Encampment asked the governor to use his "influence in regard to the drafting of our ranch boys into the armed forces. Of course I do not want you to misunderstand me, we all want to do all we can to bring this to a speedy close, but in these ranch boys there is absolutely no replacement for many of them."

Governor Hunt was occasionally asked to help returning veterans. A veteran from Powell sought his assistance, "While on overseas duty I met a very lovely girl in Australia and we want to be married. I want to have her come over as soon as possible. What should I do?"[101]

While some requests may seem too trivial to trouble a wartime governor, Wyoming was, and remains a small, close-knit state that most people know their governor personally. They have likely shared a meal or a drink, pictures of grandchildren and have common friends and relatives. Writing such a letter to the governor of Wyoming is not a great deal different from asking help from a neighbor. Among Hunt's papers there is no evidence he ever felt put upon with these sorts of requests.

Postwar Planning

As the news from Europe and the South Pacific improved, the governor turned his attention to postwar planning. Earlier he had made a commitment to veterans that they would not be treated like those returning from World War I, "when the ex-serviceman, after his sixty-four dollar bonus was spent, walked the streets in his shabby uniform, many of them hungry, selling apples or peddling shoestrings, wondering if it had all been worthwhile." In early 1944, Hunt engaged his administration in sufficient postwar planning to accurately estimate

101 Letter to Hunt dated July 13, 1946, FILE: "War Manpower Commission" Box 4, LCH Papers

the state would need 40 million dollars for highway construction and another 115 million dollars for reclamation and water projects.[102]

"The United States has always efficiently and effectively mobilized for war, Hunt said. "Now it is important to just as effectively and efficiently organize for peace."[103] He advocated an ambitious postwar agenda including increased production particularly in agriculture, more efficiencies in state government "in order to maintain taxes at a low level following the war and to assist where possible in rehabilitating the returned soldier, massive highway construction to encourage economic development and tourism, and water reclamation projects." Hunt proposed a large building program especially at the University of Wyoming and state institutions caring for disabled persons. [104]

The governor promised voters in the 1942 campaign that, if elected, he would devote full time to the war effort. On election night as the vote count was completed, Hunt told the press, "Nothing will be left undone and no request will be refused in making Wyoming's war effort outstanding among the states—absolutely everything is secondary until America is victorious." [105] Shortly after his election, Hunt had predicted, "we are in for a long war."[106] He knew the war effort would take constant attention from his office. He kept his campaign promise to give it that level of his personal involvement. Hunt's days were spent promoting the purchase of war bonds, advocating for enlistments, supporting salvage collection efforts, and tending his own victory garden while asking others to plant one. The governor told a Farm Bureau audience at Hillsdale, "I know very little about farming though I do

102 Telegram from Governor Hunt to the New York Journal of Commerce, February 26, 1944, File: "Post War Planning-Miscellaneous" Box 4, LCH Papers
103 Undated Speech, Id.
104 Id.
105 LCH Papers, supra. Box 2
106 T.A. Larson, *Wyoming's War Years 1941-1945*, Wyoming Historical Foundation (1993), 74

have a victory garden of some thirty to forty square feet."[107]

He apologized to the Wyoming Grange for not spending more time in their communities saying, "The war has caused in the governor's office a tremendous increase in the volume of work. All of our various drives, Red Cross, National War Fund, War Bonds, Salvage, as well as Selective Service and the appointing of committees and organizing these campaigns requires a tremendous amount of time."[108] In Newcastle, he cited the rationing of gasoline and tires as the cause for a severe reduction in his travel. In his first year as governor, Hunt had logged only 1800 miles, his predecessor more than 6000.[109]

In 1943, the governor was proud that Wyoming ranked fifth in the nation in War Bond sales, was among the largest contributors of salvaged metals, rubber, silk and nylon hosiery and kitchen fats, and that a majority of Wyoming servicemen volunteered rather than waiting to be drafted. Fewer than 3000 of 56,000 Wyoming registrants had been deemed unfit to serve, a figure below the national average. A volunteer Selective Service Board and a state defense council were mobilized in every county, along with rationing boards, nutrition and health programs, and victory garden committees.[110]

After the war, Governor Hunt, an outdoor enthusiast, admitted that "for the 12 years that I have been working for you people as a state official I have not had the pleasure of casting a single fly and have taken only one short hunting trip."[111] He didn't tell the story of that "one short hunting trip" which proved memorable. But a Fremont County writer, Blanche Schroer, did.

Schroer told the story this way, "While riding through timbered

---

107 Speech, File: "Government-State and National (Speeches)" Box 3, LCH Papers

108 Speech, October 24, 1944, File: "Government-State and National (Speeches)" Box 3, LCH Papers

109 Id.

110 Report, File: "Miscellaneous", Box 4, LCH Papers

111 Speech, March 13, 1946, to Natrona County Game and Fish Association, File: "Miscellaneous Speeches" Box 3, LCH Papers

area, Hunt came directly upon a large, antlered moose. As the horse turned sharply aside, the moose charged. Hunt, with lightning speed, jerked his foot from the stirrup on the danger side and balanced himself on the opposite side just as the moose gored the horse. The horse reared, then ran, while the moose thrashed about before plunging into the woods. Hunt was thrown backwards, one foot still in the stirrup. Horrified at finding himself being dragged over sharp terrain, he managed to grab a shrub and jerk his foot free of the stirrup.

"At the time of the danger the guide was some distance away. Before he could get into a position to act, the episode was over. But back in camp Matt (Matt McGuire, a friend of the governor) hearing of the narrow escape of his bruised friend, yelled at the guide, 'Why didn't you help?'

"Doggone it," the crusty old guide said, "if you saw a riled moose, a gored runaway horse, and a Democrat who's drilled your teeth bouncing along the ground...would you know right off which one to shoot?"[112]

On Being Governor

Hunt earned a reputation of being more than accommodating, a reputation assured by his willingness to do whatever it was he was asked to do. In 1946, a newly elected state legislator wrote to the governor asking him to call the Plains Hotel in Cheyenne to find out if "they have a room for me and drop me a line and let me know the price of it for the time I will be there." The governor stopped whatever he was doing long enough to pick up the phone, call the Plains Hotel and send the legislator an assurance he had a reservation.[113]

Hunt was adamant about hiring members of his party. As early as 1940, he complained about the failure of the federal merit hiring

112 Story, File: "Hunt, Lester C." Box 3 papers of Blanche Schroer, Collection No. 10575, American Heritage Center, University of Wyoming
113 Letter from Chas B. Chittim of Sundance, Wyoming, November 22, 1946, File "Legislature- Miscellaneous" Box 2, LCH Papers

system to employ Democrats. After eight years of a Roosevelt administration there were still "more Republicans holding appointive office than Democrats."[114] Hunt said, "The one outstanding feature I noticed during the operation of the board (Merit System Board) is that only Republicans have merit." He harkened back to Andrew Jackson who famously said, "To the victor go the spoils." Hunt felt it should go both ways. "A Democratic administration," he said, "should be 100% Democratic and a Republican administration should be 100% Republican and the continued and ultimate success of the two-party system depends on this theory."[115]

His administration worked hard to accomplish that goal, using a form titled "Application for Political Appointment." Applicants were asked very specific questions about party affiliation. "How long," it inquired, "have you been a registered Democrat?" Applicants were expected to spell out, "What service have you given the Democratic Party?" Applicants were also asked, "Did you contribute to the Democratic Campaign Fund?" It was not until the final blank on the application that an applicant was asked what "experience and qualifications have you for the position desired?"[116]

In January 1945, Hunt faced his second legislative session. The first had been made difficult by the fact that he had just defeated the Republican incumbent and was facing a heavy GOP legislative majority. This session was somewhat better for the Democratic governor. While the Republicans continued to hold solid majorities, the House was veto-proof so long as the Democrats held together.[117]

The session opened on an ominous note. The Chaplain, Rev. H.E. Sheppard, whose duty it was to swear in legislative employees,

114 Speech, File: "Campaign 1944-1948" Box 1, LCH Papers
115 Id.
116 "Application for Political Appointment" Id.
117 *Wyoming Blue Book*, Edited by Virginia Cole Trenholm, Vol. II, 374-378 and Vol. III, 52-54

fell asleep in his chair and nearly missed the entire ceremony.[118] The following day Governor Hunt gave his State of the State address.[119] He recognized the 27,000 Wyoming soldiers yet on the battlefield and commended the people of the state for their support of the war effort. Hunt told lawmakers the state's finances were good, the general fund having increased substantially while expenditures declined over the previous two years.

Hunt asked the legislature to create a juvenile court arguing, "Many of our citizens have become alarmed by the increase in juvenile delinquency throughout the State." He cited the growing need for institutional care for the elderly and requested funding for water reclamation projects, highways and airports. His speech ended with a description of his plans for postwar projects to include employing and educating the returning veterans.

The war continued to dominate the news but the legislature was back in session and kept the local reporters busy. The first bill introduced in the Senate aimed to legalize gambling. In the House a bill to create a new college in Casper made the news. The state had only one post-secondary school. The University of Wyoming was determined to keep it that way. Each house quickly took up bills recommended by the governor to reward veterans with a preference for hiring to state jobs.

Everything then stopped for a wedding. On January 19, 1946, the center of the front page of the *Wyoming Eagle* was adorned with a wedding photo. Elise Hunt and Army Lieutenant Russell Chadwick were married. Mrs. Hunt wanted the wedding to be the first ever held in the Governor's Mansion. Elise preferred a church wedding. Mother and daughter compromised. With the proud mother of the bride watching and Buddy waiting at the altar as the best man, the governor walked his daughter down the aisle of St. Mark's Episcopal Church. Afterward,

118 "Something to Swear About" *Wyoming Eagle,* January 10, 1945, 1
119 House Journal of the Twenty-Eighth State legislature of Wyoming 1945, 33-45

the reception was held at the Governor's Mansion.[120]

On the war front, the news reported major battles brewing that were hoped to bring the much-prayed-for end to the war. In Cheyenne, the political skirmishes of January 1945 received far less attention. The House initially defeated the effort to create a community college at Casper on the heavy opposition of the University of Wyoming. The proposal was resurrected several days later and passed by both houses shortly before the session ended.

The governor and the Republican majority battled over the budget. Oddly, the legislature was voting for appropriations above what Hunt had requested and outpacing revenue expectations. Hunt tried to hold the line but was eventually forced to use a line item veto to reduce the legislature's 6.2 million dollar appropriation bill by 109,000 dollars. The gambling bill was predictably defeated on what the newspaper reported to be a "thunderous 'no' vote."[121]

Back then the state Constitution imposed a 40-day limit on a legislative session. But, in those days, the 40 days did not expire until the clock above the Speaker's chair struck midnight. If there was more work to be done, the leaders simply pulled the plug, stopping the ornate clock five minutes short of midnight. The following day the clock was plugged in, struck midnight and the session actually concluded. It ended "in the early morning hours" and on a "sour note."[122] The governor was photographed sifting through ""several hundred" telegrams asking that one or another bill be vetoed.

Senate Republicans caucused for two hours the last night of the session. When they returned to the floor, most of the governor's appointments were rejected on a party-line vote.[123] As the legislature readied

120 *Wyoming Eagle,* January 19, 1945, 1
121 "State Senate Says No on Bill to Legalize Gambling" Wyoming Eagle, February 14, 1946, 1
122 "Legislature Ends Sourly as 10 Appointees Are Rejected" *Wyoming Eagle,* February 20, 1945, 1
123 "Wyoming's Dishonor" *Wyoming Eagle,* February 23, 1945

for adjournment, Governor Hunt arrived to speak. He spoke first to the Senate and then walked across to the other side of the Capitol to talk to the House. By the time he arrived at the House chamber, he regretted the words he'd used in the Senate. The governor apologized for the harsh words used to describe the Senate's treatment of his appointees. The formal record said simply, "His excellency, Governor Hunt, appeared in the Hall of the House and briefly addressed the members."[124]

Moments earlier, Hunt called the senate vote "the most contemptible action in the annals of Wyoming."[125] Standing briefly before the Senate, Hunt said, "For the first time in the 55 years of Statehood of this State, I have received treatment at the hands of this body such as no governor has ever received. That is your privilege and your prerogative, that is what makes a democracy, and I feel no resentment at the treatment given me."[126] Hunt walked from the Senate chamber after concluding, "I know you realize that I am laboring under some difficulties, but it is still a pleasure, gentlemen, to be Governor of the greatest State of all the 48 in the union."

It was nothing compared to the fist-fight between two members of Congress reported to have taken place in Washington on the floor of the U.S. House of Representatives a couple of days later. [127] Still, for Wyoming and most especially for the mild mannered, courteous Hunt, the words were harsh. Some began to question whether he was having second thoughts about seeking a second term.

A Second Term?

Second term governors, taken for granted today, were not common in Wyoming history before 1946. The first person elected to a second term

---

124 House Journal of the Twenty-Eighth State legislature of Wyoming 1945, 628

125 "Legislature Closes on Note of Sourness" *Wyoming Eagle*, February 20, 1945, 13

126 Senate Journal of the Twenty-Eighth State legislature of Wyoming 1945, 558

127 "Congressmen in Fist Fight, But Nobody is Hurt" *Wyoming Eagle*, February 23, 1945, 1

was DeForest Richards, a Republican who died in April of 1903, just a few weeks into his second term. Frank Emerson, also a Republican, was next. He first won the office defeating Democrat Nellie Tayloe Ross, the nation's first woman governor, in 1926. He was reelected in 1930. But only six weeks after his second inauguration, Emerson died of influenza.

Secretary of State Alonzo Clark ascended to the governorship but was not nominated by his party when the special election came about to fill the last two years of Emerson's term. Democrat Leslie A. Miller won that special election in 1933. Miller then became the third governor to be re-elected the following year. If Lester Hunt decided to seek a second term, he would be only the fourth person in the state's history to do so.

As late as January 30, 1946 Hunt was undecided about seeking re-election.[128] His most recent session of the legislature had been disheartening. He had accomplished a great deal over the last 14 years of public service but was uncertain he could win another term. Hunt had lived by FDR landslides but the magic of those days seemed to be over. The reality appeared this would be a good time to end what had already been an accomplished career of public service.

Early in his first term, Hunt predicted that if the New Deal continued to lose support in Wyoming and if the war ended, "the usual preference of Wyoming voters for Republican policies will probably continue."[129] By 1946, the war was over. Support among Wyoming voters for Franklin Roosevelt had eroded. The 1944 election was the first of FDR's four campaigns that he lost in Wyoming. His electoral edge steadily declined from a high of 60.6% in 1936 to 48.8% in 1944. Just as the Roosevelt landslide had taken Hunt into public office in 1932,

128 Letter from Hunt to Mr. E.L. Bennett, January 30, 1946, File: "Labor" Box 1, LCH Papers
129 Speech to the Young Men's Literary Club of Cheyenne, May 19, 1943, 5, File: "Government-State and National-Speeches" Box 3, LCH Papers

he worried that the FDR backslide might take him out if he sought a second term as governor in 1946.

By June Hunt had not yet filed for reelection. Democrats were nervous. The Republicans already had two candidates. Former Governor Nels Smith wanted his job back and State Treasurer Earl Wright was challenging him in the GOP primary. On June 3, Charles Gentry, chair of the Democratic Party in Washakie County wired Hunt urging him to run again.[130] Letters and telegrams from around the state followed. A public meeting was held in Wheatland to encourage Hunt to run.[131]

Finally, as the filing deadline dawned, Lester Hunt announced he would be a candidate for reelection. In a letter to Pat Flannery, the state Democratic Party chairman, he expressed pride in Wyoming's support of the war effort, adding "Wyoming state government is in the best financial condition of any period in the state's history."[132]

Hunt for Governor Club

By July the "Hunt for Governor Club" was organized and raising money for the fall campaign.[133] Club president Zan Lewis said the campaign needed to raise money so that Hunt would not have to use as much of his own money as had been required in 1942. "Personally, I would like to do a little better for the Governor this year than four years ago because I know his own costs ran about $6,000.00 for that campaign, and further his income during the last several years has been considerably reduced," Lewis wrote.[134]

Contributions began to flow. People sent checks and cash in

130 "Governor Hunt Urged to Head State Ticket" *Wyoming Eagle*, June 4, 1946, 2

131 "Governor gets Strong Support as Candidate" *Wyoming Eagle*, June 5, 1946, 1, 17

132 Letter to L.G. Flannery, June 12, 1946, File: "Senate Campaign and Other Campaigns 1943-1948" Box 33, LCH Papers

133 Letter to Mrs. Nelle Armitage, July 18, 1946, from Zan Lewis, President, Hunt for Governor Club" File: Campaign 1946" Box 1, LCH Papers

134 Letter from Zan Lewis to Mr. Don Beaton, August 7, 1946. File: "Campaign 1946" Box 1, LCH Papers

amounts ranging from a dollar to $500. Dr. J.M. Havely of Torrington joined the Hunt for Governor Club. "So far as I know," he typed across the top of Zan Lewis' solicitation in red letters, "Governor Hunt has gave (sic) as near universal satisfaction as could be given. Haven't heard one complaint; even from the Politicle enemys (sic)."[135]

Though he initially wavered on a decision to run, Hunt assured supporters he was ready to campaign hard. He studied the campaigns of successful gubernatorial candidates around the country. Using some of their ideas, he adopted a strategy of identifying certain voter groups, targeting them with specific leaflets discussing their interests, whether they be veterans benefits, health care, welfare and labor, education, business, or agriculture and including reprints of favorable comments from newspapers around the state.[136]

Mr. V.P. Noonan of the Pabst Sales Company of Chicago joined the club, sending a check for $5.00 and some helpful information. "I just came back from Rock Springs, Kemmerer and Rawlins," Noonan reported. "Things around Kemmerer looks (sic) pretty good but in Rock Springs it's any body's (sic) guess, it really looks like the Governor will have to go over there and shake hands with every coal miner. Rawlins looks bad especially around the bars; they blame the Governor because gambling is closed. They are also saying he is a dry. I have been unable to find out who is putting this information out."[137]

Hunt's reelection campaign emphasized his work in support of the war effort, improved funding for education and people with disabilities as well as his efforts to diversify the state's economy,[138] noting, "Under my administration far greater appropriations have been made for education than ever before." Funding for the University of Wyoming increased by nearly 50% under Hunt and Casper College,

135 Letter from Dr. J.M. Havely, July 22, 1946, File: "Campaign 1946" Box 1, LCH Papers
136 Letter from Hunt to Mrs. Susan J and Patrick J. Quealy, August 24, 1946, Id.
137 Letter from V.P. Noonan to Zan Lewis, August 3, 1946, Id.
138 "Speech to Democratic Meeting-Casper-August 5, 1946" Id.

Wyoming's first community college, was established under his watch. "May I be so presumptuous as to suggest," Hunt wrote, "that education never had a better friend in the Governor's office."[139]

Hunt took special pride in helping to fund programs to assist the elderly and the disabled. He said, "Always a believer in taking care of those of our unfortunate people who, through no fault of their own, are in dire distress and need assistance, I submit that no other administration has ever remotely approached the benefits this administration has made available to dependent people." He cited increases in old age assistance payments from $26.72 to $43.31 per month, aid to dependent children from $34.67 to $71.50 and aid to the blind from $33 to $43.57. Hunt promised, "I will continue my interest in these unfortunate people who must have society's help to prevent suffering."

While "addressing a large, enthusiastic gathering of Carbon County citizens" Hunt emphasized the importance of water development and creating new industries in Wyoming. He proposed that the state process rather than export its natural and agricultural resources.[140] Previously Hunt had sarcastically tagged Wyoming the "Santa Claus State." He took up the theme in this campaign, complaining Wyoming was guilty of giving away its natural resources. "We have been unmercifully exploited by eastern interests," Hunt claimed, "There are more millionaires in Colorado made by Wyoming oil than there are millionaires in Colorado rich from Colorado minerals."[141] In 1944, he told the Denver Rotary Club he was discouraged "that we have no manufacturing in our state. In our homes, in our offices, and on our farms, you can search in vain and find nothing manufactured in Wyoming."[142]

139 File: "Campaign 1944-1948" Id.
140 Undated news release headed "Campaign 1946" File: Campaign 1944-1948" Id.
141 Speech, File: "Government-State and National-Speeches" Speech "Omaha, Nebraska" dated January 29, 1944. Box 3, LCH Papers
142 Speech Denver Rotary Club, March 9, 1944, 4, File: "Government-State and National-Speeches" Box 3, LCH Papers

Yet, the governor was an optimist. He believed strongly the post-war years would bring great prosperity. Bank deposits had increased by 250% since the war began. Hunt predicted the end of the war would bring thousands of tourists. The state, he predicted, "will enjoy the greatest volume of business ...Wyoming has ever enjoyed."[143] Hunt sought reelection with that same sense of optimism, but his optimism was not merely a strategy for an election campaign. He was optimistic by nature and had espoused an optimistic view of the state's future through much of his first term. In his second year as the state's chief executive, Hunt said the state's farmers, ranchers, mineral developers and others should expect continued prosperity. "Your state is a young state with a great future," He declared.[144]

A year and a half later, in 1945, the governor proclaimed, "It is a great pleasure to report to you as the war ends, we find the people of the state in perhaps the very best financial condition that has ever prevailed in Wyoming." Hunt believed that on the near horizon were years in which "thousands of new homes would be built in Wyoming, both on the farms and in the cities, new farm machinery will be purchased, the businessmen will expand and increase their stocks, new cars will literally sell like hotcakes and there will be, no kidding this time, two cars in every garage and two chickens in every pot."[145]

In mid-September, a Republican Party poll claimed Hunt would lose in November. The poll predicted the Republican nominee, Earl Wright, would beat Hunt by more than 10,000 votes.[146] Hunt ramped up his campaign, traveling even to an event in Lusk, Jim Griffith's hometown.

On the evening before the 1946 election, Governor Hunt asked

143 Speech to the Valley Chamber of Commerce, Torrington, Wyoming dated February 25, 1946, Id

144 Speech to the Wyoming Grange, Buffalo, Wyoming dated October 24, 1944, Id.

145 Speech to the Farm Bureau Convention, Evanston, Wyoming, Nov. 3, 1945, Id.

146 "GOP Victory Seen in Poll Taken in Wyoming" *Lusk Herald*, September 19, 1946, 4

voters for one more term. He reminded them of his accomplishments during eight years as secretary of state and the four he had served as governor. He was especially proud of the way in which Wyoming had supported the war effort. "In some activities, such as the purchase of war bonds, we often led the nation," he said. "And may I extend to you my fellow citizens, my deep appreciation for your splendid cooperation with my office during my trying years as your war governor."[147]

In a lengthy radio address, Hunt covered issues ranging from post-war planning to improved economic conditions for agriculture and resource development, highway, airport and hospital construction and improved educational and health care standards. Hunt said his first term had seen the state achieve "its soundest financial condition in history." The governor added, "We find ourselves in this postwar era in the happy situation of having sufficient funds to carry out all the plans and programs I have mentioned on a strictly cash, pay-as-you-go basis, quite different from the situation a few years ago when the main issue in the campaign was the overdraft."

Hunt concluded the 1946 campaign radio address with an appeal to voters in both parties, "The Wyoming voter is an intelligent elector, and the fact that in Wyoming we have elected seven Democratic and seven Republican governors that the Wyoming voter does his own individual thinking when he is in the voting booth. And if you feel that my administration has measured up to your expectations, then tomorrow I shall be deeply grateful for an expression of your confidence."[148]

The voters did just that. Lester Hunt was reelected by a wide margin despite the fact that Republican candidates won all four of the other state offices that year. [149] Hunt doubled the margin of his 1942 victory and became the first Democrat ever reelected to a second full

147 "Radio Address-Monday Evening November 4, 1946" File: "Campaign 1944-1948" Box 1, LCH Papers
148 Id.
149 "1947 Wyoming Official Directory and 1946 Election Returns" 76-79

term as governor.[150]

Although the Republican Party dominated Wyoming politics, Lester Hunt had become one of the most popular public servants in Wyoming.

150 "Hunt's Vote Strength Tops 1942 Margin" *Wyoming Eagle*, November 7, 1946, 1

CHAPTER SIX

Good Governors Make Great Senators

Lester and Nathelle Hunt joined friends celebrating while the votes were counted on that November night in 1946. It soon became clear he had won a second term as Wyoming's governor. At the same hour, Joe McCarthy was likewise celebrating his election to the United States Senate. The elections of 1946 in Wyoming and in Wisconsin made certain the paths of Lester Hunt and Joe McCarthy would cross.

McCarthy was assured a seat in the Senate when he won the Republican Party nomination. The establishment had encouraged its favorite, Walter G. Kohler, to seek the nomination. Kohler, a popular businessman who later became governor of Wisconsin, was recently divorced. McCarthy learned early that a tragedy in the family life of an opponent provided opportunity and threatened to make Koehler's divorce a campaign issue. Koehler stayed out of the race to avoid the pain that would cause his family.[1]

Robert La Follette, Jr. was McCarthy's primary opponent. He had served in the Senate since elected upon the death of his iconic father in 1925. Although his father's heir to the leadership of the Progressive Party, he disbanded the party and rejoined the Republican Party in 1946, setting up a contest with McCarthy. It's one of those ironies of history that McCarthy, who talked little about the threat of Communism

1 Robert Griffith, *The Politics of Fear,* University of Massachusetts Press (1970), 8

in that campaign, defeated a fellow Republican who made it an issue.

Earlier, "Young Bob" as he was called, advised his father to repudiate the Communists who were about to endorse his father's Progressive Party. He was decades ahead of McCarthy on the issue and a far more articulate anti-Communist spokesperson. Nonetheless, the vehemence with which Young Bob defended labor and civil rights brought contrived claims he had Communist leanings. Senator La Follette formed a Committee on Civil Rights to investigate the abuse of workers' rights by business leaders. Some said that proved he supported the Communists workers' agenda. The "Red-baiting" of Young Bob started long before McCarthy.[2]

The tragic irony is that Robert La Follette, Jr. was added to the roll of those who chose to voluntarily end their own lives rather than be victims of McCarthy's witch-hunts. By 1952 the junior senator from Wisconsin had become the Joe McCarthy that history knows best. La Follette, whom progressives hoped would make another run at McCarthy, had reason to fear he would be investigated for having unknowingly employed Communists on the staff of the Civil Rights Committee two decades earlier.

Historian Patrick Maney described Young Bob's torment. "Who were the Communists on your Civil Liberties Committee?' La Follette imagined McCarthy asking him. 'And what did you do about them?' La Follette worried about how he would answer such questions. Perhaps, he confided to friends, he would have to admit that he hadn't done enough. Maybe, he said, he should have called in the FBI."[3]

On February 24, 1953, Robert La Follette committed suicide. Maney erroneously, though understandably, surmised it was La Follette on whom Allen Drury modeled the suicide of his fictional senator, Brigham Anderson, in his Pulitzer Prize winning novel, *Advise and*

2 Patrick Maney, *Joe McCarthy's First Victim*, The Virginia Quarterly Review, Summer 2001, p. 529-536
3 Id.

Consent.[4]

But in November 1946 there were still more than two years before Hunt became a senate colleague of Joe McCarthy's and four years before McCarthy discovered the power of the Communist issue. On election night in 1946, both Hunt and McCarthy celebrated their victories, each pleasantly unaware of what the gods had in mind for them.

Governor Hunt Begins a Second Term

Inauguration Day was January 6, 1947. Mrs. Hunt was there along with Elise Hunt-Chadwick and Lester C. Hunt, Jr. American flags hung in the rotunda of the Wyoming Capitol building. A massive state flag was unfurled behind the podium at which Lester C. Hunt would take the oath of office for the fifth time. In 1933, he had been sworn in as a member of the legislature. Twice he had taken the oath as secretary of state. Today Hunt would be sworn in as governor for a second time. This was only the fourth time in the state's history that had happened. Two of the other three, Frank Emerson and DeForrest Richards had died in office before completing their second terms.[5] Hunt would not complete his second term either but for a different reason.

Hunt began his second inaugural address by acknowledging the election had left him surrounded by Republicans. The other four state elected officials were, for the first time in his public service, all members of the other party. He pledged to work with them, asking that they do the same.[6] The governor raised concerns about health care, juvenile delinquency, services for the elderly, and added, "our schools are experiencing one of their most trying periods." Hunt concluded

4 Id. Drury himself described Senator Hunt's ordeal as "the suggestor from whom Brig, in the workings of the novelistic mind, in part emerged." See *Capitol Style* Magazine, May 1998, page 9

5 "Hunt Becomes Third Man to be Governor Second Time" *Casper Tribune-Herald*, January 6, 1947, 2

6 "Hunt Voices State Aims at Inaugural" *Wyoming Eagle*, January 7, 1947, 1, 8

eloquently, "To look toward horizons and reason and plan for the future is not only the privilege of every state-elected official, it is the duty of every citizen."[7]

It's not clear when Hunt began thinking about running for the U. S. Senate. In January of 1947, that campaign was more a year and a half away. The editor of the *Wyoming Eagle,* a strong Hunt backer, was still looking forward to the "rapid strides" he anticipated the state would make under Hunt in the coming four years.[8] He thought Hunt should remain governor. Following the Jackson Hole monument fight, the governor was increasingly annoyed with Washington's attack on states' rights. In the fall of 1946, Governor Hunt received instructions from a Washington bureaucrat whose job it was to enforce the Hatch Act, a new federal law forbidding public employees from participating in certain kinds of political activity. Harry Mitchell, the president of the U. S. Civil Service Commission, sent Hunt a poster demanding it be posted in all state offices.

The poster displayed the word "WARNING" in large, dark letters across its top. It informed public employees of what they could not do and of the harsh penalties for failing to follow the law.[9] Hunt was incensed. "My dear Mr. Mitchell," he fired back a letter. "The posters you sent would be quite appropriate to post in Russia where people don't expect to exercise their rights of citizenship as they do in a democracy like the United States." Hunt suggested the poster be revised "emphasizing what an American citizen can do with reference to political activity under the Hatch law instead of attempting to impress him with the fact that he can do nothing and is a non-entity as far as citizenship is concerned." The governor offered to post it only if Mitchell would "prepare the poster as it should be."[10]

7 Id., 8
8 Editorial "Good Citizenship" Wyoming Eagle, January 10, 1947, 7
9 Poster, File: "War Manpower Commission" Box 4, LCH Papers
10 Letter from Hunt to Harry B. Mitchell, dated September 16, 1946, Id.

Confrontations like these germinated the thought in Lester Hunt's mind that he should consider running for the Senate. For now he focused on his responsibilities as governor. The legislature was returning to the Capitol for another session.

As the governor opened the Twenty-ninth Session of the Legislature with his State of the State address, the harshness of the words he had spoken when last they met were forgotten. He thanked the legislators for "the many assurances of cooperation I have received from the members of this distinguished body."[11] The governor then laid out his plans for an aggressive agenda.

Hunt wanted a state-federal partnership for the construction of new hospitals, increased funding for highways and airports, a reorganization of the National Guard and reformed election laws. He told legislators that over the years, their amendments to the election code had made it "more and more difficult to exercise (the) right of franchise, until voting today is so complicated and even mystifying to some people that many of our citizens refuse even to attempt to vote."[12] He bemoaned the fact that many of the members of the legislature ran unopposed. Hunt suggested increasing house terms to four years "to make membership in the House more attractive."

The governor renewed his recommendation that the legislature create a retirement program for state employees. Hunt wanted the state to study the feasibility of processing agricultural products, particularly wool, in the state rather than shipping the raw resources to other states, "which is," he told the Joint Session, "definitely to the disadvantage of the economy of Wyoming and the prosperity of the individual wool producer."[13]

The state was blessed with a 6.2 million dollar surplus. Hunt asked

11 "Governor's Message" *Journal of the Twenty-Ninth State Legislature of Wyoming* 1947, 29
12 Id., 36
13 Id., 39

that the bulk of it be used for necessary construction at the University of Wyoming and the state institutions. As he prepared to depart the chamber, the governor said, "Ours is a great and God-blessed state with many opportunities yet undeveloped and untouched. It is for you and me, as best we can, to light the torch of inspiration and to lead our people to higher planes of social, political, and economic life." He and the GOP majority then set off...in different directions. The headline in the Casper newspaper said it all. "G.O.P. Assails Hunt Speech."[14] The Republican leaders issued a statement calling into doubt their willingness to give the governor the money he wanted to build public projects.[15] As telegraphed, the majority defeated most of the Hunt building proposal.[16]

Near the end of the session, the governor and the legislature battled over the budget. The legislature approved more spending than the governor thought available revenue would support. Hunt sent a "strongly worded" letter to legislative leaders warning their action would result in a tax increase for the citizens.[17] The Speaker of the House responded for the Republicans, calling the expenditures "necessary" and arguing, "the state's income has always exceeded the estimates of state officials."[18]

Unlike two years earlier, when all of Hunt's appointments had been rejected, the Senate confirmed all of them.[19] In the end, they also came to an agreement on the budget. The six million dollar surplus at the beginning of the session was spent down to $259,790.06 by the time

14 *Casper Tribune-Herald*, January 20, 1947, 1

15 "GOP Leaders Outline Legislative Program" *Wyoming Eagle*, January 15, 1947, 1, 8

16 "Senate Blocks Building Fund" *Casper Tribune-Herald*, February 11, 1947, 1

17 "Gov. Hunt Burns Legislators" *Casper Tribune-Herald*, February 20, 1947, 1

18 Id., 2

19 "Senate Okays Appointments of 60 Men to State Posts" *Casper Tribune-Herald*, February 245, 1947, 5

the session adjourned.[20] They also rejected the first attempt to pass a so-called "right-to-work" law that was intended to weaken organized labor in the state. The governor was forced to veto seven bills. The legislature overrode him on only one. The lawmakers, who had voted down an increase in the beer tax, passed a bill increasing the gasoline tax. After they left town, he vetoed it.[21]

Thinking About 1948

In the summer and fall of 1947, Hunt relaxed. He and Nathelle took a cruise to Hawaii. They spent the New Year holiday in California, attending the 1948 Rose Bowl. Hunt made the national news when he and California Governor Earl Warren, soon-to-be the GOP candidate for vice-president, slipped away from security officers to sit on a curbside to watch the parade. They were the source of some anxiety until officers "hauled the two back to the reviewing stand."[22] It was his time of calm before the storm.

Lester Hunt liked being governor and was comfortable in the role of chief executive. He told the Wyoming Stockgrowers Association the people of Wyoming had been "exceedingly generous" in electing him to a second term. Hunt said it seemed there were never enough hours in the day but that he always listened to callers as they told their stories. "A governor must be patient, he should be and must be tolerant," he said. However, the governor acknowledged an important lesson he'd learned while in office. "I do find in my work," he said, "that more mistakes are made by saying yes than by saying no."[23]

In those days, the legislature was in session for only 40 days every

20 "State Financial Commitments Leave Fund Balance of $259,700" *Wyoming Eagle*, February 25, 1947, 1

21 "Hunt Vetoes Bill to Hike Gas Tax" *Casper Tribune-Herald*, March 2, 1947, 1

22 "Under the Dome" *Wyoming State Journal,* January 15, 1948, 8

23 "Speech to Wyoming Stockgrowers Association" Lander, Wyoming, June 4, 1947, File: "Government-State and National-Speeches" Box 3, LCH Papers

other year. The other twenty-two and a half months belonged entirely to him. Even though the other four of his elected colleagues were of the other party, they got along well and worked as a team. Observers said, "Harmony at the Capitol is at an all-time high."[24]

Except for two years in the legislature, Hunt had been in the executive branch his entire career. He was comfortable with the job and the people around him were comfortable with him. Hunt was relaxed enough to admit to a May, 1947 bankers' convention, "I find generally speaking, many people don't agree with what I have to say - perhaps that will be the case this morning - if so, speak right up. I like an argument."[25] He was well liked and could say something like that and still receive applause.

Leaving the comfort of a small state where he was at the top of the political ladder to go to Washington where he'd become one of 526 members of the legislative branch, and a freshman at that, gave him pause. Governors decide while legislators debate. Governors act quickly and decisively. Legislators stall, obfuscate and quibble, hobbled by parliamentary rules and by committees. It's impossible to overstate the differences between the two jobs.

And then there were Washington politics. He experienced a limited amount of partisanship as governor but in Wyoming, everyone knows everyone else. There may be six degrees of separation among the people of the world but far fewer degrees separate Wyoming people from one another. Your son might marry your adversary's daughter. Your uncle may be a business partner of your opponent. Partisanship in Wyoming was different in kind and degree from what Hunt knew of the nation's capitol.

Before he had time to make his own decision, a movement to draft

24 "Under the Dome" *Wyoming State Journal,* April 15, 1948, 1
25 Speech to Wyoming Bankers Association, May 12, 1947, File: "Government-State and National-Speeches" Box 3, LCH Papers

Governor Hunt to run for the Senate became public at the end of 1947.[26] No sooner had that kind of talk begun when Hunt realized for the first time in his political life the wind was not at his back. If he decided to run, he'd have to buck a strong head wind. The governor was only a year into his second four-year term. Running for the Senate meant choosing to resign the governorship either before the election or waiting to see whether he won and then, if victorious, submitting his resignation. That question caused Hunt's decision to become a source of serious discord within his own party. Whether Hunt resigned to run or waited until after getting elected to the Senate, his successor would be a Republican. Secretary of State Arthur G. Crane was next in line.

If Hunt resigned before the election, Crane would serve as governor only until a special election in November. If Hunt awaited the outcome of the election and then resigned, Crane could serve as governor for the final two years of Hunt's term. Party leaders believed they had a better chance to elect a Democrat if Crane served only a few months than they would if he was given two years of incumbency before a contest.

The unhappiness of Democratic Party leaders could be summed up in a single word: patronage. It's the governorship, not a senate seat that provides a party with the opportunity to put its partisans into important jobs. As governor, Hunt made it a priority to hire and appoint Democrats to key positions. A Governor Crane would reciprocate, appointing members of his party to replace many of them. While the matter was the subject of closed-door political meetings, the "private" discussions frequently found themselves written about in newspapers across Wyoming. As 1947 came to an end and 1948 dawned, the issue was the main topic of conversation.

The talk "centered around the possibility of a primary between Thurman Arnold and Governor Lester Hunt next year."[27] Arnold was a

26 "Labor Launches Draft Hunt Move" *Wyoming State Journal*" December 23, 1947, 2
27 "Under the Dome" *Wyoming State Journal*, December 30, 1947, 7

national figure. Assistant U.S. Attorney General Thurman Arnold was one of the best known "trust-busters" of the post World War II era.[28] Born in Laramie, he had served as the town's mayor and in 1921, was the only Democrat in the Wyoming state House of Representatives. On the opening day of the session, as the Republicans returned from their caucus, Arnold announced the Democrat had caucused the night before "in a phone booth." He announced the results of his deliberation. "I have known Thurman Arnold all my life. I would trust him as far as I trust myself." He then put his own name in consideration for speaker of the house.[29] He received only one vote. Arnold was well liked in Wyoming long before becoming a well-known nationally.

However, what the speculators didn't know is that two weeks before the newspapers named him as a potential candidate, Arnold had mailed a letter to Democratic Party powerhouse Tracy McCracken acknowledging rumors that he might run, telling McCracken he had nothing to do with the rumors but would be interested in running only if Hunt didn't run. "If he does decide to run I would forget about it completely, Arnold wrote."[30] There would be no Hunt-Arnold primary contest. Yet, some unhappy Democrats were still stirring those waters.

Early in 1948, as Hunt began thinking seriously about a senate campaign, he took a January trip to Washington. The trip raised more discussion about his plans. Upon his return, a reporter inquired whether he had "picked out his seat in the Senate while he was there." The governor laughed, leaned back in his high-backed chair, and did not answer the question.[31] The talk got the attention of Senator E.V. Robertson, the incumbent against whom Hunt would be running. In

28 Larson, *History of Wyoming*, Supra. 450

29 "Thurman W. Arnold: America's Amazing Mr. Trustbuster" Rawlins daily News, June 11, 1952

30 *Voltaire and the Cowboy: The Letters of Thurman Arnold*, Edited by Gene Gressley, Colorado Associated University Press (1977) Letter from Arnold to McCracken, dated December 12, 1947, page 377

31 "Under the Dome" *Wyoming State Journal*, January 29, 1948, 2

January, Robertson said, "The toughest opponent a senator can have in a campaign is the governor of the state." Nonetheless, he predicted he would be reelected.[32]

In February Hunt finally admitted publicly he was considering running against Robertson.[33] "Wyoming," the governor said, "may emerge as the key state in determining the political make-up in the 82nd Congress."[34]

Robertson "did not hesitate to identify himself as a right-wing Republican."[35] Not yet a candidate, Hunt, nonetheless, began pounding away on what he viewed as Robertson's "radical" record. After acknowledging an interest in the senate race, Hunt spoke in Casper. He recounted the history of the Great Depression and reminded listeners of the successes of the New Deal telling the audience, "It is difficult to visualize again the almost unbelievable misery and despondency of that time, the cold smokestacks of closed factories, the bread lines and the bank lines, the farm strikes and the sheriff's' foreclosure sales, yes, and the suicides and the suffering." The governor recalled trains filled with hobos, highways lined with hitchhikers, "people destitute and homeless."[36]

He claimed Republicans "made the United States Senate ridiculous in the eyes of the people" as they attempted to undo the New Deal. Hunt trained his sights on Senator Robertson. In a speech he said, "Most unfortunately in the Senate of the United States for the last six years, as far as voting is concerned, Wyoming has had no voice. With one brilliant, outstanding senator from Wyoming voting one way and the junior senator voting the other, Wyoming's votes had just as well

32 Id.

33 "Hunt Considers Senate Candidacy" *Wyoming State Journal*, February 5, 1948, 8

34 "Hunt May Decide to be Candidate for U.S. Senate" *Wyoming Eagle*, January 31, 1948, 12.

35 Larson, Supra. 510

36 Speech "Jefferson-Jackson Day Dinner-Casper, Wyoming, February 10, 1948, File: "Government-State and National (speeches)" Box 3, LCH Papers

never been cast. On practically every issue, the progressive, forward-looking positive vote of Senator O'Mahoney has been nullified by the reactionary special interest, isolationist vote of the junior United States Senator."[37] He closed by telling his cheering audience, "As Wyoming goes, so goes the Senate. Senator Joe needs a friend."

Two days later Robertson spoke to a GOP Lincoln Day Dinner in Cheyenne. He saw it differently. Robertson predicted he'd win reelection, calling the Democratic Party "splintered."[38] Robertson was correct. The national party was badly divided. The truth was that the Democratic Party had been trending in the wrong direction even before Harry Truman became President. Between the 1932 Roosevelt landslide and the 1944 election, Democrats lost a total of 90 seats in the House and 18 in the Senate.[39] FDR's untimely death exposed fissures that had long existed. The potent New Deal coalition was destined to dissolve in the postwar world. Henry Wallace, who served as Roosevelt's vice-president from 1941-1954, challenged Truman on the left. A group of southerners, displeased with Truman's civil rights ideas, divided the party from the right. Wallace ran for President as the Progressive Party candidate. The Dixiecrats nominated Strom Thurmond. It was difficult to imagine how Harry Truman could survive.

Wyoming Democrats were just as splintered. As Hunt pondered his decision, some Democrats began conspiring either to keep him out of the senate race or push him into resigning early. The editor of *The Wyoming Eagle*, a normally reliable Hunt supporter, fanned the flames writing that a "vote for Hunt for senator is also a vote for a Republican governor (Crane)." The editor gave a highly complimentary profile of Thurman Arnold, calling him "one of the most potent figures in public life." He also named Scotty Jack as another potential candidate.[40]

37 Jefferson-Jackson Day Dinner Speech, Id.
38 "Senator Robertson Sees 1948 Victory" *Casper Tribune-Herald*, February 12, 1947 page 1
39 *History of U.S. Political Parties*, Edited by Arthur M. Schlesinger, Jr. Chelsea House Publishers in association with R.R. Bowker Company (1973), 2676
40 Editorial "Wyoming Will Elect A Senator" *Wyoming Eagle*, February 6, 1948, 16

William "Scotty" Jack was a well-liked politician and businessperson. He was elected state auditor in 1934 when Hunt was first elected secretary of state. Before losing a race for governor in 1954, Jack won seven straight campaigns,[41] serving three terms in the legislature, one as Speaker of the House, and two terms as state auditor.[42] Tossing Jack's name out as a potential primary opponent was no idle threat.

To be certain, not all Democrats were unhappy with the governor. Fremont County Democrats endorsed him in February.[43] Hunt's hometown newspaper interviewed friends of the governor who were angry about the speculation that Hunt would have a primary contest. They were particularly displeased with the *Wyoming Eagle* editorial and its promotion of Arnold and Jack adding, "The Jack-Hunt race would be a torrid affair with no holds barred."[44]

In March, rumors of the discord among Wyoming Democrats were confirmed. Citing unnamed but "authoritative sources" a reporter disclosed Hunt will "probably announce himself as a Democratic candidate for the U.S. Senate around mid-April." The story predicted the announcement would not be well received by some Democrats. "Earlier reports indicated disharmony was creeping into Democratic ranks over Hunt's plans to run for the Senate without first resigning his job as governor and permitting s gubernatorial election next fall," the article continued.[45] The angst brewing among the party faithful exploded during a heated meeting at the governor's office in March. Party leaders stormed the governor's office, threatening that if he refused to resign early, affording them an opportunity to run another Democrat in November, they would support Scotty Jack in the primary.

41 Larson, Supra. 519

42 Obituary of William "Scotty" Jack, *Lusk Herald*, April 16, 1970

43 "Endorse Governor Hunt" *Wyoming State Journal*, February 26, 1948, 7

44 "Under the Dome" *Wyoming State Journal*, February 12, 1948, 2

45 "Hunt to Announce Candidacy for Senate in April" Wyoming Eagle, March 20, 1948, 1, 10

They intended to work to defeat Hunt.

The "top secret" meeting was quickly leaked to the press.[46] Such threats, especially when made public, are seldom successful with men like Lester Hunt and so it was with this one. It didn't take long after that meeting for Democratic Party stalwarts to get in line.

The Decision

Labor had already lined up. In January, the Wyoming Brotherhood of Railroad Trainmen joined other unions and announced it wanted the governor to become a senator.[47] In May, the Laramie County Democratic Central Committee went public, backing the governor for the Senate.[48] The public airing of the intra-party fight caused all the players to sit up and think about what was at stake.

There was a great deal at stake. The 1946 elections resulted in Republican majorities in both houses of Congress. It was the first time since before the Great Depression that Republicans had controlled the House.[49] The Democratic Party's defeat was attributed to the disdain for President Truman. "Not in eighty years, not since Andrew Johnson, had a President been the target of such abuse," wrote David McCullough in his Pulitzer Prize winning Truman biography. [50] McCullough recounts numerous anti-Truman jokes making the rounds in 1946. "A joke from Texas began with reflection on how Roosevelt might have handled the country's problems, then ended with the line, "I wonder what Truman would do if he were alive?"

Within a few weeks of the midterm election, the President's approval

46 "Under the Dome" *Wyoming State Journal*, March 4, 1948, 7
47 "Railroad Union to Support Hunt as Senate Candidate" *Wyoming Eagle*, January 30, 1948, 1
48 "County Demos Select Delegates to State Parley, Endorse Hunt" *Wyoming Eagle*, May 4, 1948, 1
49 David McCullough, *Truman*, Simon and Schuster (1992), 523.
50 Id. 520

rating fell to just 32%.[51] As the Republicans took over the Congress and history moved along through 1947 and into 1948, Truman's fortunes began to change and with them, so did the outlook for Democrats in the coming election of 1948. The very issues that caused people to take another look at Truman caused Lester Hunt to begin eyeing the Senate seat.

Hunt grew up in a poor home headed by a strong union supporter. Throughout his governorship, Hunt made the needs of working people, the elderly, disabled and impoverished a priority. The new Congress "was not equally solicitous of wage earners. As a matter of fact, it could work up no interest on their behalf."[52] A series of lengthy strikes dimmed public support for labor unions. In June of 1947, Congress passed the controversial Taft-Hartley Act, placing severe limitations on union activity. Truman vetoed the bill but was overridden. It became law, a rallying cry in the 1948 election and one more reason for Hunt to run for the Senate.

Taft-Hartley was only the beginning of congressional attacks on matters of significance to Lester Hunt. "The Eightieth Congress cut appropriations for welfare agencies, buried fair employment and anti-lynching legislation, refused funds for public housing and aid to education, refused to act on national health, on raising minimum wages, on higher unemployment benefits," wrote historian Bert Cochran.[53] As Hunt watched Senator Robertson vote in favor of all of these measures, his decision to run crystallized. His platform for 1948 came into focus. According to a story in the New York Times, Hunt "campaigned for the Senate on a New Deal-Fair Deal platform, pledging himself to the repeal of the Taft-Hartley Act, a minimum wage for labor, farm supports and housing for veterans."[54]

51 Id. 520
52 Bert Cochran, *Harry Truman and the Crisis Presidency*, Funk & Wagnalls (1973), 199
53 Id. 216
54 "Hunt Saw Himself As A Progressive" *New York Times*, June 20, 1954, 72

While Tom Dewey was so confident about November he planned to make only ten speeches the entire campaign,[55] Truman hopped aboard the *Ferdinand Magellan* for a whistle-stop tour that took him to hundreds of small and large communities across the country. Uncertain how much help the embattled Truman would be if he were to endorse the governor for the Senate, Hunt delayed a formal announcement until after Truman's June visit to Wyoming. Truman's entourage arrived in Cheyenne late the afternoon of June 6. The President, Mrs. Truman and daughter Margaret joined the Hunts at the Governor's Mansion a few blocks from the train station. A large crowd estimated to be more than 6000 persons greeted the President, a sign that Truman had more support in Wyoming than many believed.

"Governor Hunt and citizens of Wyoming," Truman began his remarks, "it certainly is a very great privilege and a pleasure for me to be here today. I received an invitation from Governor Hunt to call on him this afternoon, and I was most happy to accept it. I have known him a long time, and I like him, and I think he is a good Governor." Hunt presented the President a 10-gallon cowboy hat and a formal invitation to return the following month for Cheyenne Frontier Days.

"Thank you very much," Truman said opening the envelope, "The invitation says 'Mr. President, your many friends in Cheyenne, Wyoming, will be greatly honored if you can attend the Cheyenne Frontier Days, July 27-31st, 1948." Truman told the crowd of cheering Cheyenne folks he wanted to attend and hoped to be back for the rodeo. "Now," Truman said with his big Missouri smile, "I am going to see just how this hat works. [Putting it on.] That's all right!"[56] The crowd loved it. Truman returned to the train depot, boarded the *Ferdinand Magellan* and headed down the track. He had two more Wyoming stops

55 "Confident Dewey May Deliver Fewer Than 10 Speeches" *The Laramie Republican Boomerang*, August 10, 1948, 1

56 http://www.trumanlibrary.org/publicpapers/index.php?pid=1651, accessed February 11, 2012

before moving on into Utah.

The Campaign Begins

After the *Magellan* left, Hunt took a quick trip to New York. Daughter Elise and her husband had just given birth to the Hunts' first grandchild. The governor was determined to see the baby boy before the campaign started.[57]

On June 10 Hunt made it official. He was a candidate for the United States Senate. As was the custom of the day, Hunt's announcement was made in a letter to the chairman of the state Democratic Party, John B. Clark of Sheridan.[58] Hunt reaffirmed his support for states' rights and opposition to centralized government. He promised to work for veterans' housing programs and to reduce the "dangerously high national debt."

He also made it clear he was not going to give in to the threats of some of his own party. "The question has been asked-would I resign the governorship to become a candidate for the Senate? The answer is certainly not," Hunt said.[59] He would not resign the governorship unless he was elected Senator.[60] Disgruntled Democrats were free to recruit a primary opponent but, "The people elected me Governor, and the people have the right to say whether I shall remain as Governor or represent them in the United States Senate."

Hunt committed to work for new Wyoming water projects, "a very liberal and extensive veterans' housing program," and a strong national defense. "The United States has never been prepared," Hunt said, "and for such weakness we have paid dearly in the last two world

---

57 "Under the Dome" *Wyoming State Journal*" May 6, 1948, 3

58 Letter from Hunt to John B. Clark June 10, 1948, File: "Senate Campaign and Other Campaigns 1943-1948" Box 33, LCH Papers

59 Id. 2

60 "Governor Hunt Announces He's Candidate for U.S. Senator" *Wyoming State Journal*, June 10, 1948, 1

wars." He promised to work for education funding and to reduce the nation's debt. Hunt summed himself up, saying, "In all my public life, I have been constructive, liberal and progressive, but nobody has ever accused me of radicalism."

Soon Senator Robertson confirmed his intentions. He was running for a second term. But first Lester Hunt had to get by a primary opponent. In the end, neither Scotty Jack nor Thurman Arnold ran, but a little known, eccentric Cheyenne accountant by the name of Carl A. Johnson did.

The Wyoming Supreme Court Gets Involved

Mr. Johnson posed no electoral threat to the popular governor. He was not going to beat Hunt at the polls. However, Johnson had a different strategy in mind. He planned to win the nomination in the courts.

Carl Johnson was one of those characters every community has if fortunate enough. Carl was not an attorney, but for years he played one, filing numerous lawsuits against various public officials. His intent was to simply make some obscure point. He didn't seem to have a particularly active accountancy practice, lived in a small house on the south side of Cheyenne and spent his days wandering through the courthouse and the Capitol building. Carl Johnson was a fixture in Cheyenne. Often he could be seen, dressed in the same long gray woolen coat and sweater, with his gray stubble face, sitting in the law library with a tall stack of books in front of him.[61]

Once Johnson took a case all the way to the U.S. Supreme Court. The justices declined to hear his appeal. In the course of the proceedings, he asked to be excused from making copies of his brief for all the justices because, as he petitioned, he had "$400 in assets and $500 in liabilities." Johnson explained that when his father died in 1923,

---

61 From personal knowledge and experiences of the author.

he received only one dollar from his estate. He didn't do much better when his mother died in 1967, leaving him $16. He couldn't afford to make copies for each of the nine justices. Copying would have been burdensome. As with most non-lawyers who represent themselves, Johnson overwhelmed the court with paper. In the end, his case was dismissed by the state district court, the Wyoming Supreme Court and the Supreme Court of the United States. [62]

He didn't win many cases, if any. But Johnson knew the Constitution as well as most lawyers. He was aware Wyoming's had a unique provision that could be read to keep Lester Hunt off the November ballot. Article 4, Section 2 provides, "No person shall be eligible to the office of governor unless he be a citizen of the United States and a qualified elector of the state, who has attained the age of thirty years, and who has resided 5 years next preceding the election within the state or territory, *nor shall he be eligible to any other office during the term for which he was elected.*" It was that last clause that caught Johnson's attention.

He didn't campaign much. Johnson lost to Hunt by a 90-10% margin. Soon after losing the primary Johnson filed his lawsuit. When Hunt won the Democratic Party nomination, he was serving as governor. Johnson argued the governor was prohibited by Article IV, Section 2 of the Wyoming Constitution from holding any other office during his term as governor. Carl Jonson made the mistake many lay-people make. He thought those words meant what they said, that they could be taken at face value. "There is no ambiguity in the oath of office in the constitution of the state of Wyoming relative to the eligibility of the governor to seek other office during the term for which he was elected," Johnson argued.[63] The law is seldom that simple.

---

62 "Carl A. Johnson v. Laramie County School District No. 1" District Court 1st Judicial District, State of Wyoming Doc. 70 No. 300, 1972, Supreme Court of the State of Wyoming No. 4187, 1973, United States Supreme Court No. 73-10, October Term 1973

63 "Hunt's Right to Run Challenged" *The Laramie Republican Boomerang*, September 14, 1948, 1

Unlike his other lawsuits, this time Johnson had legal counsel. Two Cheyenne attorneys, Clyde M. Watts and Charles E. Lane, represented him. Watts was a prominent member of the Wyoming State Bar Association, one of its first officers when the Bar was organized in 1915.[64] Both Lane and Watts were, according to Democratic National Committeeman and publisher Tracy McCracken "staunch Republicans." It was unlikely, Hunt and his supporters thought, that a man who had inherited a single dollar bill from his father's estate and had little visible means of support could afford lawyers of the stature of Watts and Lane. The Republican Party, they said, spearheaded this lawsuit.

State GOP chairman Ewing Kerr denied the connection, calling McCracken "uninformed" and saying he was trying to divert attention from the real issues.[65] The editor of the *Rock Springs Rocket* "smelled a rat," claiming it didn't matter what "the Republican Party spokesmen may say, the court challenge of Governor Hunt's eligibility to be a candidate for senator had all the earmarks of a cheap political gesture, an attempt to remove a strong candidate from the ballot or, failing that to embarrass his candidacy."[66] In any event, neither Johnson nor his lawyers asked to be excused this time from paying to provide the court copies of his briefs. Regardless, the lawsuit was filed and posed a real threat to Hunt's candidacy.

Johnson went directly to the Wyoming Supreme Court on September 16, 1948, without first seeking the opinion of a lower court. The Court expedited the case because the general election was so near. Johnson's attorneys argued the provisions of the state constitu-

---

64 "Bench and Bar of Wyoming Chapter XXIX accessed on February 9, 2012 at http://www.rootsweb.ancestry.com/~wytttp/history/bartlett/chapter29.htm

65 "Court Gets Hunt Case Tomorrow" *The Laramie Republican Boomerang*, September 15, 1948, 1

66 "Wyoming's Supreme Court Upholds the Voters" *Rock Springs Rocket*, September 29, 1948

tion superseded those provisions of the U.S. Constitution allowing the Congress to determine the qualifications of it own members.[67] They claimed the intent of the drafters of the state constitution was that the provision applied to all public offices. "They (the drafters) also felt they wanted the Governor, who had been duly elected, to fill out his term, so that the extra duties of filling the office of Governor would not devolve upon the Secretary of State, except in the case of the death of the Governor."[68]

The Supreme Court disagreed. On September 28, the justices issued a 20-page opinion in Hunt's favor. Written by Chief Justice William Riner, the decision was based in part on "views expressed by some of the leaders in the Constitutional Convention held in 1787 in the city of Philadelphia."[69] The Chief Justice cited dozens of prior U.S. Supreme Court cases supporting the decision. "Under the decisions above reviewed, the holdings of both Houses of Congress, the persuasive utterances of lawyers, statesmen, judges, and legal authors of the most eminent authority, we conclude that the result reached in this case can not be at all in doubt," the Court wrote.

It's a historic curiosity that Joe McCarthy faced the identical challenge when he was initially elected to the Senate in 1946. McCarthy was a circuit court judge when he won the GOP nomination. Following the primary, a lawsuit was filed seeking to invalidate his victory on the grounds that a sitting judge couldn't be nominated for another office. On largely the same reasoning employed by the Wyoming Supreme Court in Hunt's case, the Wisconsin Supreme Court ruled in McCarthy's favor.[70]

As Johnson's lawsuit was dismissed, the final barrier to Lester

67 Article I, Section 5, Clause 1 of the U.S. Constitution
68 "Brief on Behalf of Relator Carl A. Johnson" filed in "Original Proceeding in Mandamus" in the Supreme Court of the State of Wyoming, No. 2432, Page 3
69 "Original Proceeding in Mandamus" In the Supreme Court of the State of Wyoming No. 2432, September 28, 1948, 6
70 "Supreme Court refuses to Bar McCarthy From Ballot: Hold Federal Rules Govern Election" *Madison Capitol Times*, September 28, 1946, 1

Hunt's name being on the November ballot was removed. The only remaining barrier for the popular Democrat was his own party's nominee for President.

The Truman Problem

No one thought Truman could win Wyoming or any other state in the west except perhaps Arizona.[71] In the end, Truman won every western state except Oregon but you'd have never predicted that by either the polls or the pols. The fear among Wyoming Democrats in the early days of the 1948 campaign was that a large margin for Dewey would drag Hunt down with Truman.

The week before the Court issued its opinion and much earlier than is customary, the *Casper Tribune-Herald* endorsed a candidate for the Senate. Their choice was E.V. Robertson. The editor concluded it would be a mistake to give both Wyoming Senate seats to Democrats when the next administration would undoubtedly be Republican. Their August 22 editorial, which Robertson then paid to print in newspapers all over the state, tied the paper's blessing to the conviction that Tom Dewey was going to win the presidential election. "Unless expert opinion is sadly in error," the *Tribune-Herald* predicted, "Gov. Thomas E. Dewey will be the next President of the United States."

The newspaper could be excused for being so certain Dewey would win. It was certainly not alone. As late as the middle of October, a *Newsweek* poll of 50 of the most widely read political writers in the country found them unanimous. They believed Truman would be defeated. "50 for Dewey, 0 for Truman."[72] But Harry Truman was, if anything, a fighter and in 1948, as boxers say, he fought way above his weight class.

Not everyone was convinced the President would lose. There was one expert who thought the *Casper Tribune-Herald* and those 50 pundits

71 McCullough, *Truman,* Supra. 657
72 Id., 694

were indeed "sadly in error." The Secretary of the U.S. Senate, Lester Biffle, told Truman, "Now listen Harry, you don't have to worry." How'd he know when the pollsters were saying the opposite? According to Truman biographer McCullough, Biffle "went around during the campaign disguised as a chicken peddler" taking his own poll. Based on his decidedly unscientific poll, Biffle knew Harry would win because, as he said, "The common people are for ya." It was the only poll showing Truman would win.[73]

If E.V. Robertson had listened to Lester Biffle, he might have avoided the mistake of hitching his wagon so tightly to Tom Dewey's. Dewey and his running mate, Governor Earl Warren, campaigned for Robertson. Each came twice to the state. Nebraska Senator Kenneth Wherry also came to campaign for his Republican colleague.[74] Wherry continued the Robertson campaign theme. "There is no question," he told a large crowd in Fremont County, Hunt's home, "but that Governor Dewey will be elected and Wyoming would receive a severe setback if it were to send another Democrat to the Senate."[75]

The front page of the same newspaper reporting on Wherry's visit described the Senate contest as "red hot." In mid-September the American Federation of Labor announced the Wyoming race was one of five Senate seats it thought the Democrats would win. The GOP promptly dispatched Tom Dewey to campaign for Robertson.[76] Hunt complained "an army of carpetbaggers" was invading the state.

Though Robertson hitched his wagon to Dewey's, the presiden-

---

73 Merle Miller, *Plain Speaking: An Oral Biography of Harry S. Truman*, Berkley Publishing Corporation (1973), 262

74 Wherry's opposition to Hunt will become more relevant to readers later in this book. Senator Wherry joined Joe McCarthy "to place the twin evils of Communism and homosexuality in the national spotlight." Randolph W. Baxter, *Senator Kenneth Wherry and the Homophobic Side of McCarthyism*, Nebraska History (2003), 119-132

75 "Eyes of Nation Are On Wyoming Sen. Wherry Tells Fremont Voters" *Wyoming State Journal*, October 26, 1948, 1

76 "Dewey Slated to Visit to Help Robertson Campaign" *The Laramie Republican Boomerang*, September 15, 1948, 1

tial candidate caused the senator some embarrassment during the Wyoming trip. Dewey was overheard "brushing the senator aside" at a campaign appearance in Rock Springs. Robertson joined Dewey on the platform at the rear of the train. They waved to a cheering crowd as they held their clasped hands high above their heads. When it came time for Dewey to address the crowd, he no longer wanted to share the platform with the Wyoming senator. Dewey spoke "in a low voice aside from the microphone as he motioned him away" audibly telling the Wyoming senator, "Go on back inside."[77]

In addition to Dewey and Warren, Senator John Bricker of Ohio, Joe McCarthy, former Minnesota Governor and perennial presidential candidate Harold Stassen and Admiral Richard Byrd all came to Wyoming to support Robertson's reelection. Hunt told an audience down the street from the Wherry-Robertson rally, "Wyoming with the highest literacy rate in the nation, doesn't need to be told by outsiders how to vote."[78]

As the campaign entered the October stretch, the candidates defined themselves. Hunt thought Senator O'Mahoney and Wyoming needed a second Democrat in the delegation. Hunt also argued, "Good governors make great senators." Robertson countered that it would be a problem for the state to elect Hunt since there would be a Republican in the White House. "Vote for the man," a Robertson ad implored, "who will be able to do the most for Wyoming under a Dewey-Warren administration."[79] The press took up those themes, repeating them throughout the fall. "There is little doubt Governor Dewey will be elected President," wrote the editor of the Laramie newspaper. "It would be indeed unfortunate for Wyoming, therefore, to send a Democrat to the Senate, both from the standpoint of the state and the nation."[80]

77 "GOP Candidate Closes Wyoming Tour With Major Talk in Cheyenne" *The Rock Springs Daily Rocket*, October 2, 1948, 1
78 Id.
79 Political ad for Robertson, *The Riverton Review-Chronicle*, October 28, 1948, 3
80 Editorial "Wyoming-Crucial Political Battlefield" *The Laramie Republican Boomerang*,

Only one Democratic Party "carpetbagger" showed up for Hunt. Shortly after the primary election, the Democratic National Committee offered to arrange for outside speakers to support Hunt. He declined the offer with one exception. Still uncertain that Truman could be helpful, Hunt used Truman's June visit as a pretext for not inviting him back. "I think it would be better for Senator Barkley to come in than for the President to come a second time.[81] "A week later Senator and vice-presidential candidate Alben Barkley came to Casper to endorse Hunt, calling him "one of the ablest statesmen."[82]

When the campaign started earlier that spring, each candidate promised they would wage a campaign on the issues and not on personalities. They did so. Except for a brief brush-up on the question of who had hired Carl Johnson's attorneys, there is no evidence the candidates did anything but talk about the issues. A nationally known columnist covering Truman's campaign took note of Wyoming's senate contest. Doris Fleeson, writing in the *Washington Star*, noted that the people of Wyoming were not displeased with Senator Robertson's "extremely conservative record" as an isolationist and one of only six senators voting against the Marshall Plan. But she said, "Democratic hopes are frankly built on the fact, as they put it, Governor Hunt is such a fine fellow."[83] It was said, Lester Hunt knew "more Wyoming residents than any other man alive."[84] The voters were left to choose between one candidate whose politics they liked, and another whom they simply liked.

September 16, 1948, 4

81 Letter from Hunt to Senator Carl A. Hatch, August 21, 1948, File "Senate Campaign and Other Campaigns 1943-1948" LCH Papers

82 "Barkley Supports Hunt," Id. page 3

83 "Tussle in Wyoming: Dewey Popular in State, Helps Robertson in Senatorial Battle, *Washington Star*, October 1, 1948

84 "Wyoming Thinks Hunt In, Barring Landslide" *Rocky Mountain News*, September 22, 1948

To the very end, Republicans, as they felt a weakening Robertson campaign, worked even harder to tie the GOP nominee to what they continued to see as a certain Dewey victory. "Friends of Governor Hunt insist that he is a fine citizen, a good governor and would be a great senator," said the editor of the *Riverton Reporter*. "But conditions will not be right for Hunt because there will be a Republican President and all he could do is function as another vote against the administration."[85]

Wyoming voters agreed they should not elect a senator from the party opposite the President. They voted for Harry S. Truman and Lester C. Hunt. On November 2, Henry Wallace finished fourth, Strom Thurmond third. Truman survived it all, upsetting Dewey. He took Wyoming's three electoral votes by a 51.6%-45.1 margin with Henry Wallace receiving less than 1% of the vote. "And that's the beautiful thing about it," said Truman about the outcome of the four-way race, "Thirty-five (electoral) votes walked out of that convention and split up the Solid South, and because of Wallace, Dewey was able to carry New York by sixty thousand votes. So I always take a great deal of pleasure in saying I won without the Solid South and without New York which wasn't supposed to be able to be done."[86]

Along with a second term for Truman came a new Democratic majority in the United States Senate. Lester Hunt was one of them. He defeated Robertson by a wider margin than Truman achieved, scoring a 57-43% victory. The irony was five years in the making but the first letter of congratulations received by Senator-elect Lester Hunt came from New Hampshire Senator Styles Bridges.[87]

Governor Hunt now endured another debate about when he should resign. The *Laramie Republican Boomerang* called on Hunt to stay home

85 "What Chance Does Hunt Have to be a Great Senator?" *Riverton Reporter*, October 28, 1948
86 Merle Miller, *Plain Speaking*, Supra. 252
87 Letter of congratulations to Hunt from Styles Bridges November 5, 1948, File "Congratulatory letters-1948" Box 11, LCH Papers

until after the coming legislative session. The editor argued Hunt's services "aren't urgently needed in Washington" but that it was critical to the state that the governor steer the state through the coming legislature.[88] For his part, Hunt said nothing and started working on the state budget that had to be ready by January. By the end of November, the governor spoke "I've never made it a practice to be late for school."[89] He resigned at the end of the year and headed for Washington.

Nathelle and the governor spent the next weeks wrapping up business, packing their belongings, and celebrating with friends, who "literally killed us with kindness," Mrs. Hunt said.[90] Nathelle learned from earlier experiences. "It was my custom," she wrote, "each time my husband was a candidate, to save newspapers for packing our belongings in case the election was lost, but in 1948, we really needed them for the move to Washington as my husband had been elected to the United States Senate."[91]

They took seriously a weather forecast predicting a severe snowstorm would hit southeast Wyoming on December 26. The storm arriving that day was the opening salvo of the famous Blizzard of '49.[92] One more day and they'd have joined thousands of people across Wyoming and the Great Plains who were trapped for days by the heavy snow and strong winds, a storm of legend in the state.

Wisely they left early on Christmas morning. Buddy, home for the holidays from his studies at Swarthmore College, joined them as they loaded the car for a road trip to Washington.

88 "Hunt is Urged to Remain on Job for Time" *Sheridan Press*, November 9, 1948

89 "Hunt Indicates He Will Resign" *Sheridan Press*, November 30, 1948

90 Autobiographical Essay by Nathelle Higby Hunt, 25

91 Id. at 25

92 Amy Lawrence, James L. Ehernberger, and Lucille Dumbrill, *Wyoming Memories: Blizzard of 1949* Annals of Wyoming, Winter 2004, Volume 76, Number 1

CHAPTER SEVEN

The Age of Suspicion

Younger drivers must find it odd to encounter the huge bust of Abraham Lincoln perched high above Interstate 80 near Laramie, Wyoming. The thirteen-and-a-half-foot bronze bust of a rather brooding Lincoln sits atop a massive, 35-foot granite base. Robert Russin, a University of Wyoming art professor, created the monument in 1959, to commemorate the highest point on the Lincoln Highway, later replaced for most travelers with Interstate 80. The sculpture has less to do with Abe Lincoln than with the old highway named for him that stretched across the United States when Lester, Nathelle and Buddy drove to their new home in Washington, D.C.

The Hunts left the Governor's Mansion early on Christmas morning. They drove the few blocks to Lincolnway Avenue, the main east-west street taking Lincoln Highway travelers through Cheyenne. There they took a left hand turn and settled in for the very long trip. The two-lane road left Cheyenne and passed through all of Nebraska, Iowa, and Illinois, Indiana, Ohio and into Pennsylvania.[1]

A 1948 road trip from Cheyenne to Washington was a far different undertaking from what it is today. There were none of the four-lane interstate highways that allow today's hurried motorists to bypass small

---

1 The Lincoln Highway Association website http://www.lincolnhighwayassoc.org/info accessed on February 25, 2012

communities. While people complain today about the crumbling part of the nation's infrastructure that is found along the Interstate highway system, the road traveled by the Hunts en route to Washington in 1948 was little more than "a well marked strip of rubble."[2]

Lester Hunt didn't record any memories of that trip but another one he took along the same rough route proved eventful. Shortly after the 1952 election, he left Cheyenne on a Saturday morning, planning a leisurely drive back to the nation's capital. A tire blew out somewhere near Atwood, Kansas. Hunt and his car careened off the highway landing some 350 yards away in a farm field. He was unhurt. The car was not so fortunate. It turned out the tow truck driver who came to his rescue was a classmate of a mutual friend, "so they treated me in fine shape. Two of the mechanics came down Sunday morning, working until two o'clock to get my car in shape so I could move along," recalled Hunt. Two more days on the road and he was back in Washington. [3]

Blown tires were simply a part of the experience on the old highway. One dramatic driver traversing the Lincoln Highway in those days figured "not a lick of work had been done on it since Lincoln finished it." Calling the trip a "terrible nightmare," he said he feared a "permanent spinal injury" if he didn't stop regularly to rest.[4]

Thankfully, there were more than a few opportunities to stop along the way even if your car was running well. From the west coast to the east, this road took travelers into, not around, more than 700 communities. It's fair to guess that the Hunts saw more than half of them on the lengthy section of the old Lincoln Highway they traveled in late December of 1948.

---

2 Linton Twiss, *The Long Long Trailer,* Vail-Ballou Press (1951), 216
3 Letter from Hunt to Edward Breece, Editor *Wyoming State Journal,* December 10, 1952, File: "News Releases" Box 26, LCH Papers
4 Id.

America In The Late '40S & Early '50S

The view Americans get driving through communities is qualitatively different from the one most of us get today driving around or flying over them. Perhaps in the days when members of Congress were required to travel across the country and see people and lives other than only those of their own states, they could view America less narrowly. Perhaps a cross-country road trip that took days and passed through small and large towns and cities, across rivers, through farm lands and within site of factories, getting a view of the lives of Americans in many states broadened their views and expanded a sense of national responsibility. Today they fly over those other states headed to Washington to speak for interests narrowly defined by their limited constituency. It's an altogether different perspective from the one opened to Lester Hunt as he and Nathelle drove across two-thirds of the United States that last week of 1948.

As the new United States senator made his way to Washington, he saw Americans on their streets, going to markets, schools, and churches. He saw then walking through parks with children in tow, holding hands with sweethearts, and talking with neighbors. He saw the smoke billowing from new factories, homes under construction, and all the other signs of a booming postwar economy. What he could not see was the fear in their hearts. He'd have read it though in newspapers all across the country as he traveled to his new job. Local newspapers expose the thoughts of the community in a way a passerby might not otherwise discern. A chain of continuous news stories from Cheyenne to Washington made apparent a palpable level of fear.

As Lester Hunt passed through Chicago, he read the most recent charges asserting there were Communists in the U.S. government and the President was attempting to cover it up. [5] Hunt took note of the re-

5 "Charges King Bared Spy Plot in Truman Talk" *Chicago Sunday Tribune,* December 26, 1948, Part 1, Page 13

fusal of John Foster Dulles to explain his relationship with Alger Hiss, whom he employed as an adviser. Hiss had recently been indicted for spying.[6] On page six of the *Chicago Sunday Tribune,* he glanced at a photograph of the native peoples of Bikini Island in the South Pacific. They were being herded from their homeland in advance of continuing tests of America's atomic bomb.

The following day the Hunts reached Canton, Ohio. Stopping for gasoline and a break, Hunt learned that one of his new colleagues, Senator Karl Mundt of South Dakota had launched a renewed spy hunt. "There are still Communists in government," Joe McCarthy's ally claimed.[7] The Canton paper also disclosed that his Wyoming colleague, Senator Joseph O'Mahoney, was being mentioned as a possibility for Senate President *pro tempore.*[8] An Ohio congressmen who had been defeated the previous month, warned his remaining Republican colleagues of Hunt's party. Saying the Democratic Party had led the United States into a "precarious pit" and that it had no confidence in "the capitalistic system," he predicted an economic collapse under their leadership.[9]

Traveling across the nation, one could take the pulse of Americans. The nation's blood pressure was high, people were afraid. Most everyone was afraid of something. Whites were afraid of blacks. People were being taught to fear homosexuals and homosexuals were being given reasons to fear law enforcement and other government officials. A growing number of Americans were anxious about organized crime. But at the center, the fear of Communism occupied the heart of American apprehension. Like a roundabout used to route traffic in all directions at a heavily used intersection, the fear of Communists was the core of

6 "Dulles Ignores Pleas To Clear Link With Hiss" Id.
7 "House To Seek Two Additional Spy Couriers" *The Canton Repository,* December 27, 1948, 2
8 "80th Congress To Hold Final Session Friday" Id. 5
9 "Bender Gives G.O.P. Advice" Id. 5

any number of other avenues of anxiety.

William Manchester called it "the Age of Suspicion."[10]

McCarthy becomes McCarthyism

Joe McCarthy and McCarthyism did not, as some claim, define the late 1940s and early '50s. Those years were defined by the resiliency of American democracy. McCarthy made many of the headlines but the ability of our system to survive him and his followers characterizes a closer examination of the times.

Demagogues don't define their times. Important and impactful ideas define the times. Demagogues have only a remote, parasitical interest in ideas. Ideas like the Marshall Plan and civil rights ultimately defined those days. Demagoguery is different. It's not the ideas that inspire people that open the door for demagoguery, but rather unanticipated events that frighten them. In recent history, the September 11 terrorist attacks are a recognizable example. Similarly the international events of the early 1950s gave rise to some of the most notorious demagoguery in the history of the United States.

Characterized by an appeal to prejudice and ignorance rather than logic and reason, demagoguery flourishes during times when people have rational cause to be concerned about events beyond their control. By manipulating their fears, demagogues give frightened people an invitation to think irrationally about difficult issues. The times in which Joe McCarthy rose to prominence were frightening for many Americans. Once-warm feelings about Russia had changed since 1943 when actor Edward G. Robinson told a Lux Radio Theater audience he was learning the Russian language. He had just returned from visiting the troops in Europe when he had this exchange with fellow actors at the conclusion of a production of "The Maltese Falcon." Robinson

10 William Manchester, *The Glory and the Dream: A Narrative History of America 1932-1972*, Little Brown (1973), 579

said, "Well, one afternoon, I broadcast six messages to the continent in French, Spanish, Rumanian, German, Danish and Italian." Actress Gail Patrick asked, "What, no Greek?" Robinson answered, "Well, I'm working on Russian at the moment, Gail. I want to be able to say 'thank you' to all the Russians I meet from now on."[11]

After the war, the admiration Americans once had for the Russians was transposed by fear. Our World War II ally had become a Cold War enemy. Americans believed Communism was a monolithic force and the Soviet Union exercised hegemonic control. Accordingly they saw a worldwide threat and conspiracy behind events that, on their own, were troubling enough. In the fall of 1949, Americans learned the Russians had built and successfully detonated an atomic bomb.[12] That news worsened in February with the arrest of a British scientist who had passed the secrets to the Russians.[13] In October 1949, an intimidating figure by the name of Mao proclaimed China to be The People's Republic of China. The media dubbed it "Red China." Within a few days, the Soviet Union formally recognized Mao's new government. Chaing Kai Chek, America's Chinese ally, had been forced from the China mainland to an island named Formosa. The North Korean invasion of the South was months away but Americans were on edge. As McCarthy began to assert his claims about Communists in the U.S. government, the international news gave people a reason to listen to the junior Senator from Wisconsin.

By the end of 1953, a Gallup poll showed the thought of Communists in the federal government raised more fear among Americans than

---

11 *The Maltese Falcon,* Generic Radio Workshop Script Library, genericradio.com. Lux Radio Theater was a popular dramatic radio broadcast of classic films in the 1930s and '40s. The hour-long radio shows were performed live before a studio audience on NBC and CBS radio.

12 McCullough, *Truman,* Supra. 747

13 David M. Oshinsky, *A Conspiracy So Immense: The World of Joe McCarthy,* Oxford Press, (2005), 103

the possibility of a Third World War.[14] Many people were willing to tolerate the questionable tactics of Joe McCarthy to ease those fears. In truth, the hunt for Communists in the U.S. government produced little but noise. Robert F. Kennedy was one of the staff members serving McCarthy. Years later he admitted the committee did "no real research." Kennedy, who along with Roy Cohn worked for McCarthy, said, "Most of the investigations were instituted on the basis of some preconceived notion of the chief counsel or his staff members not on the basis of any information that had been developed."[15] Kennedy blamed Cohn but it was McCarthy who benefited from the tactics.

Kennedy was not the only one who knew the truth. Those who knew the truth but were afraid of the confrontation wilted when it might have mattered. Neither President Eisenhower at the height of his own popularity nor Lyndon Johnson as his congressional power was ascending was willing to stake any of their chips on a fight with Joe McCarthy. When Milton Eisenhower wrote his brother in the fall of 1953, asking why the White House was unwilling to challenge McCarthy, Ike responded with a letter headed "PERSONAL AND CONFIDENTIAL." He thought the responsibility to confront McCarthy fell on those who opposed his ideas. Those who thought McCarthy wrong should, he said, "take it upon themselves to help sustain and promote their own ideas, rather than to wait and wail for a blasting of their pet enemies by someone else."[16] The President of the United States was unwilling to get in Joe McCarthy's way.

Neither was the Democratic Party leader of the United States Senate. When William White asked LBJ why he didn't do something

14 "Ridding Government of Reds Rated No. 1 Problem of U.S." *Washington Post,* December 12, 1953, 11

15 Robert F. Kennedy, *The Enemy Within,* Popular Library-New York (1960), 291

16 Letter from President Eisenhower to Milton Eisenhower, October 9, 1953, Ann Whitman Files, Box 3, Dwight D. Eisenhower Diary, Dwight D. Eisenhower Presidential Library (hereafter "DDE Library")

about "this damned fellow" McCarthy, Johnson admitted he was unwilling to commit the Democrats to a debate that would end up being what he called "a high school debate on the subject 'Resolved that Communism is good for the United States.'"[17]

The freshman senator from Wyoming concluded the Republicans were happy to reap the harvest of votes McCarthy was able to produce. He was painfully aware of what it meant to his own 1954 reelection as McCarthy helped Frank Barrett defeat Joe O'Mahoney in the 1952 Wyoming senate campaign. The Wisconsin demagogue drew what was then the largest crowd to ever attend a Wyoming political event when he came to Fremont County in October of 1952. He was there to campaign not so much for Barrett as against O'Mahoney. Hunt knew McCarthy posed the same threat to his own reelection in 1954. The responsibility for controlling McCarthy was made more difficult because Republicans "were of the opinion that the Senator would be more helpful in the campaign this fall and they do not wish to cross him."[18] In the final analysis, Lester Hunt's personal sense of integrity prevented him from, as he once wrote to a constituent, "getting down in the gutter" to fight with McCarthy.[19]

While some dodged the confrontation, there were those like Senators Styles Bridges of New Hampshire and Herman Welker of Idaho who joined McCarthy in that gutter. Senator Bridges was the first member of the Senate to welcome Lester Hunt to the "club." But it was not long before the two had a serious confrontation. Bridges openly criticized Hunt for taking a position he felt too lenient on the employment of homosexuals and others who Bridges thought were security risks in the federal government. During a hearing before the Armed Forces Committee, on which both served, Bridges accused Hunt of be-

17 Merle Miller, supra, 163
18 Letter from Hunt to Wandell Elliott, March 12, 1954, File: "Hunt-Personal-1954" Box 19, LCH Papers
19 Id.

ing willing to allow a disloyal employee to "wiggle his way into some other department if he can possibly do it."[20]

Opportunistic politicians who were willing to say anything, accuse anyone, and ruin any number of lives to achieve little but the propagation of fear characterized the Age of Suspicion. McCarthy's demagoguery held sway over the nation during all the years Lester Hunt served in the Senate. His reckless claims became the currency of fear espoused from political stages, church pulpits, the front pages and editorial pages of newspapers, academia, and popular culture. The politics of fear allowed those who could have spoken to remain quiet even as careers were destroyed and through countless suicides among those wrongfully accused of being Communists. Ironically, in some great measure, it would take the suicide of one of their own to at long last cause McCarthy's colleagues to put an end to the tragic charade.

The Red Scare

Lester Hunt was no less concerned about Communists and Communism than most any other person of his times. When he and his daughter Elise visited the campus of the University of Chicago, they entered the student lounge where Hunt saw a poster. "Free Earl Browder." Browder was an avowed Communist. He had been the Communist Party candidate for President who received 91 Wyoming votes in the 1948 election.[21] At the time Lester and Elise were visiting the University of Chicago, he was in prison for a passport violation.[22] Hunt told his daughter, "You can't go to college here. You might become a Communist!" They left for the University of Wisconsin. When they walked through that door, the same pro-Browder poster starred at them. This time Dad

20 Randolph Baxter, *"Homo-Hunting" in the Early Cold War,* Supra. 128

21 "Library of Congress memo to 'Miss Phelan" of Hunt's senate staff, September 11, 1951, File: "Immunity" Box 20, LCH Papers

22 As a special assistant to the U.S. Attorney General, Roy Cohn was the lawyer who led the grand jury investigation ending with the indictment of Browder. File 72, Box 084141, Folder No. 135, Papers of Styles Bridges

relented. Elise later graduated from Wisconsin without becoming a Communist.[23]

As Lester Hunt's senate career unfolded, the fear was genuine. The genie America had let out of the bottle at Nagasaki and Hiroshima was both consciously and subconsciously the driving force. As the Soviets acquired the technology through espionage and built their own atomic bomb, the stakes were raised. Americans envisioned scenarios involving Russian agents smuggling atom bombs into the United States in brief cases. It was honestly thought such a contraption existed and that it could destroy half to three quarters of the population of the U.S. in an instant.[24]

Political careers were made and broken on those fears. Those willing to take advantage of the fears thrived. A United States senator who was unable to earn respect enough from his colleagues to gain a significant committee assignment found fame claiming to have identified Communists throughout the government. Suddenly, it seemed the opportunists controlled the United States Senate, perhaps even the United States government.

The Lavender Scare

Francis Flanagan had reached a conclusion. Now all he had to do was find some evidence to support it. As the chief counsel for a senate committee appointed to investigate homosexuals in government, Flanagan knew what he wanted to say in the final report. Now he just needed some facts to back up his argument.

Flanagan had feet in all camps as he arrived in Washington in 1950 to serve as an investigator for the Committee on Expenditures in Executive Departments. A senator from Missouri named Harry Truman was chairman of the committee when Flanagan joined its

23 Author's interview with Mrs. Elise Chadwick, daughter of Lester Hunt, December 20, 2011
24 Merle Miller, *Lyndon*, G.P. Putnam's Sons (1980), 164

staff. They became friends. He was also a close friend, even a hunting buddy, of Joe McCarthy. But for the complaints of right-wingers about his relationship with Truman, McCarthy would have chosen Flanagan instead of Roy Cohn as chief counsel for his investigations.[25] Flanagan became the chief counsel for a new subcommittee. When the Senate adopted a resolution calling on its Committee on Expenditures to investigate government employments of "homosexuals and other sex perverts"[26] Flanagan was hired.

Shortly after reporting, Flanagan drove to the White House to confer with the President's staff. He left no doubt in their minds that his was closed. Flanagan had already reached the conclusion "that homosexuals should not be employed in government under any circumstances."[27] Though the subcommittee had been charged with determining whether homosexuals posed a security risk, its chief counsel believed they did before gathering a stick of evidence. He saw his duty as simply ferreting out the evidence to back up that preconceived notion. Flanagan firmly believed the proof was there. He was confident that if he looked into files of every federal agency, he'd find what he was looking for. While the White House believed him to be sincere, intelligent and non-political, those whose lives would be shattered by the public stigma which befell homosexuals and their families would come to view Flanagan's work far differently.

Most Americans are familiar with the Red Scare. Not near so many are aware of the "Lavender Scare" though its witch-hunts more severely impacted a far greater number of Americans. Heterosexual Americans were "learning" they should fear the "perverts" who filled federal offices. They were the homosexuals Stalin, it was said, planned to use in

25 *Lavender Scare*, Supra. 103

26 *Interim Report Submitted to the Committee on Expenditures of Executive Departments by the Subcommittee on Investigations*, U.S. Government Printing Office, November 27, 1950, 1

27 "Report of Meeting With Mr. Flanagan, Senate Investigations Staff" from Arch E. Jean June 20, 1950, File: "Sex Perversion" Box 32, White House Confidential Files, Harry S. Truman Library (hereafter "WHCF, HST)

his plot to overthrow the government of the United States.

In 1948, Alfred C. Kinsey released his extraordinary 804-page study, *Sexual Behavior in the Human Male.* Americans learned they knew little about "the birds and the bees" and what the Kinsey report taught them scared them. Kinsey's survey revealed more than many wished to know about the sex lives of husbands and wives, teens and farm boys. It revealed that 37 percent of all American males had engaged in homosexual relationships and four percent were exclusively homosexual.[28]

Now Americans added them to their growing fear list. A leading psychiatrist, Edmund Bergler, expressed the alarm felt by many. "If these figures are only approximately correct, then the 'homosexual outlet' is," he said, "the predominant national disease, overshadowing cancer, tuberculosis, heart failure, and infantile paralysis."[29]

The fear that caused the removal of thousands of men and women who were or were rumored to be homosexuals started with a 1947 demand issued to the State Department by the Senate Appropriations Committee. The letter to Secretary of State George Marshall warned of an internal conspiracy to protect Communists working for his agency. The senate committee also cautioned Marshall of the "extensive employment in highly classified positions of admitted homosexuals, who are historically known to be security risks."[30]

It cannot go unnoticed that from the beginning, names of those who would become central figures in the tawdry blackmail schemes against Lester Hunt seized on this issue. When he realized McCarthy may have bitten off more than he could chew, Senator Styles Bridges decided to use the more easily substantiated cause of removing homosexuals from government as a means of distracting the public from the

28 *Lavender Scare,* Supra. 53-54
29 Edmund Bergler, *The Myth of a New National Disease,* Psychiatric Quarterly 22 (1948), 86
30 *Congressional Record,* July 24, 1950, reprint of the June 1947 letter to Marshall on page 10806

fact that McCarthy really could not find many Communists.[31]

Bridges assembled a team to talk over strategy. Sitting around that table were Joe McCarthy and Bridges, R. W. Scott McLeod, then Bridges' administrative assistant and Nebraska Senator Kenneth Wherry.[32] Poignantly, it was during this meeting that McCarthy was found to have never even heard of Earl Browder, then the head of the U.S. Communist Party.[33] "Little Joe from Idaho," as Herman Welker became know for his close association with McCarthy, joined the group after his election to the Senate in 1950, a victory largely attributed to McCarthy's help.[34]

Their argument began with a bizarre rumor that Adolph Hitler had assembled a lengthy list of American homosexuals. Congressman Arthur L. Miller, a member of the House of Representatives from Nebraska held himself out as the expert on homosexuals in government. Miller claimed to have been informed by the C.I.A. that Herman Goering had a "complete list of homosexuals in the State Department, the Department of Commerce, and the Department of Defense and they knew whom to contact when they came over here on espionage missions."[35] By then neither Hitler nor Goering were alive. The ominous list, it was said, had fallen into the hands of Stalin who was now busily recruiting Soviet agents from among the names.[36]

Those with same-sex attraction had always faced discrimination but in earlier years they were permitted, in many communities, to have a life. One of the gay community's historians, Len Evans, has traced the history of cultural attitudes toward gays, lesbians, bisexual and

31 *Lavender Scare*, supra. 22
32 *The Life and Times of Joe McCarthy*, supra. 248
33 Id. 249
34 Id. 345, 395
35 *Congressional Record*, 81st Congress, 2nd Session, April 19, 1950, 96:5403
36 Neil Miller, *Out of the Past: Gay and Lesbian History from 1869 to the Present*, Vintage Books (1995), 259

transgendered persons. He began in the centuries before Jesus. Four hundred years before the birth of Jesus, Aristotle pronounced, "The homosexual disposition occurs in some people naturally and whether the individual so disposed conquers or yields to it is not properly a moral issue."[37] That began to change in the centuries after Jesus when theologians began to interpret the Christian and Hebrew scriptures. Even so, a 1921 incident demonstrates a high level of community tolerance.

When a group of Episcopal clergymen was accused of soliciting homosexual sex from sailors at Newport Beach, the U.S. Senate Committee on Naval Affairs investigated. Their report condemned not the homosexuals but rather the Navy and its Secretary, Franklin Roosevelt, for using "methods of entrapment."[38] Although the armed forces instituted rules to deny homosexuals admission during World War II, it also adopted regulations designed to deter gays from claiming their sexuality to avoid service. The draft rules required that anyone admitting to homosexuality be reported, i.e. "outed," to their local community draft board.[39]

The tolerance changed with McCarthy era politics. The previous "urban culture of queer conviviality" ended abruptly.[40] When Joe McCarthy, Styles Bridges, Herman Welker, Kenneth Wherry and other members of Congress launched their witch-hunts in the late 1940s, community attitudes regarding homosexuals became poisonous. The "Lavender Scare" was on. The chief of police in Miami began raiding gay bars that had been open for years. He called their patrons "maniacs and child molesters."[41] Vigilante groups formed in California

37 Len Evans, *From the Beginning of Time to the End of World War II"* File: "Gay Chronicles," 5, Box 2, Papers of Len Evans, GLBT Historical Society, San Francisco
38 Id. 50
39 Id. 56
40 Nan Alamilla Boyd, *Wide Open Town: A History of Queer San Francisco to 1965*, University of California Press (2003), 91 and 123
41 Len Evans Papers, supra. 50

to "prowl pervert hangouts." Around the country, liquor licenses were taken from proprietors who allowed gay patrons to be served. In those days, virtually all secretaries serving members of Congress were men. However, when "this great big thing, McCarthyism, came down" many of them were fired and replaced by women.[42]

As Washington began to focus on homosexuals, the greatest fear in Wyoming, judging from Senator Hunt's constituent correspondence, was Truman's proposal to send an ambassador to the Vatican. People from every part of the state, representing virtually every non-Catholic Christian denomination wrote to express their unhappiness with the idea. One said it was the most shocking thing to happen since the Reformation. Another claimed Catholic nations had proved to be the most open of all to Communism. Letters from Wyoming portrayed the papacy as a "totalitarian power." Mrs. Jack Keimy of Casper wrote, "A country where there is a Catholic majority and Catholicism rules has lost any hope for freedom."[43] It seems from Hunt's letters that virtually every Protestant in Wyoming, Methodists, Presbyterians, Baptists, Seventh Day Adventists, and Episcopalians feared Truman's appointment. If any were in favor, they didn't write a letter.

Others expressed genuine fear about what they were hearing from McCarthy about Communists in the federal government. The leader of an "anticommunist" rally in Casper told Hunt that Communists in Wyoming had threatened him. "The point is," he said, "that there are Communists everywhere...even in the state department under Dean Acheson."[44] People complained to their senator that "fair haired boys" who never worked for a living rather than "genuine Americans" ran the State Department.

42 Ted Rolfs, "Description: 1930's, 1940's, politics, McCarthy Era," 13, Oral Histories at GLBT Historical Society
43 Letter to Hunt, December 18, 1951, File: "State Department-1951" Box 35, LCH Papers
44 Letter to Hunt from Warren B. Look, December 6, 1950, File: "State Department" Box 35, LCH Papers

And yet, a careful search of the correspondence received by Senator Hunt during these years failed to turn up even a single letter expressing concern about the allegations that homosexuals were employed in the State Department. Though it might not have been an issue yet back home, it was becoming the focus of McCarthyism in Washington, D.C.

The Truman administration faced charges the Department of State had knowingly employed 91 Communists. Undersecretary John Purifoy wanted the committee to be assured they were not Communists, but rather, homosexuals. Most of the 91 had been dismissed for reasons of "moral turpitude." The dogs were unleashed. Purifoy's testimony came on the heels of statements provided the committee by Detective Roy Blick of the Metropolitan Washington Police Department vice squad. Blick was asked "how many perverts he would estimate were employed in the Department of State."[45] Blick estimated there were three to four hundred. Blick later acknowledged to State Department officials that his method of estimating the number of homosexuals was, at best, a guess. He said that what the government really needed was "a central bureau for record of homosexuals and perverts of all types."[46]

McCarthy had been unable to identify those he claimed to have on the list of Communists he held high in the air that February 1950 night in Wheeling, West Virginia. Now he and his supporters had an admission. The federal government employed homosexuals and McCarthy and others focused on them. According to one McCarthy biographer, the Wisconsin senator denounced those whom he called, "egg sucking phony liberals whose pitiful squealing would hold sacrosanct those Communists and queers." McCarthy promised to use his influence to drive them out of government.[47]

Senator Styles Bridges made some of the most irresponsible claims.

45 "Memorandum of Conversation" March 29, 1950, File: "Sex Perversion" Box 32, WHCF, HST
46 File memo by D.L. Nicholson, May 3, 1950, Id.
47 Griffith, *Politics of Fear*, supra. 89

He cried that the State Department purposely recruited "homosexuals and subversive agents" because, he alleged, "Russia wanted them there.[48] Bridges demanded an answer. "Who put the homosexuals in the State Department?" The strident New Hampshire Republican was a useful dupe for those such as FBI Director J. Edgar Hoover and others who began making frequent anonymous claims about the sexuality of others. Bridges could be counted on to pursue the allegations aggressively.[49]

Senator Wherry joined the chorus, demanding to know whether any of the 91 had been re-employed in other federal agencies.[50] At the same time, Senator Homer Ferguson of Michigan wanted names. He was angered when Harry B. Mitchell, the chairman of the U.S. Civil Service Commission, declined to provide them. "Despite the mental peculiarities with which these people are afflicted and the disgusting results of these peculiarities," wrote Mitchell in response to Senator Ferguson, "they are still human and I can see no reason why they should be hounded by the government when they are no longer employed by, or asking employment from the government."[51]

McCarthy screamed that the State Department and other federal agencies were "infested with Communists, homosexuals, and pro-Reds."[52] His complaints reached a crescendo when Wherry and Ferguson demanded a full investigation of the hiring of homosexuals among the federal agencies. Without any opposition, the Senate voted

48 Robert D. Dean, *Imperial Brotherhood: Gender and the Making of Cold War Foreign Policy,* University of Massachusetts Press (2001), 76, citing ""Bridges Wants Manhunt for 'Master Spy" *Washington Post,* March 28, 1950
49 Id. 97
50 Letter to Senator Wherry from Harry B. Mitchell, Chairman U.S. Civil Service Commission responding to Wherry's request, May 16, 1950, File: "Sex Perversion" Box 32, WHCF, HST
51 Letter from Mitchell to Ferguson, May 16, 1950, File: "Sex Perversion" Box 32, WHCF, HST
52 "3750 Perverts Working For U.S., Wherry Says" *World Telegram,* May 20, 1950

to give them what they wanted. Vice President Alben Barkley assigned the task to the Committee on Expenditures in Executive departments, a committee on which Joe McCarthy served.[53]

Gays and lesbians likely had no idea what was about to hit them. During the war, many had enlisted or were drafted, serving their country in combat. Yet, the armed forces were first federal agency to raise the concern that homosexuals were security risks. Rules were adopted banning homosexuals from service. Those rules to the contrary, the need for personnel was simply too great. Recruiters often chose not to notice signs of same-sex attraction. One obviously gay man was allowed to enter the service after being asked simply "Do you like girls?" He said yes and was given the oath and a uniform.[54] Another, so the joke goes, was asked if he "went out with girls. "No," he said, "I do not." The examiner summoned a psychiatrist to evaluate the man. "Why do you not go out with girls?" he inquired. "Because," the draftee said, "my wife won't let me."[55]

Once in, not all remained. Some 50,000 men and women received what were termed "Section 8" discharges. Thousands of others served honorably.[56] At the end of the war, many decided to relocate to larger American cities rather than return to the small communities from which they came. Larger cities afforded more anonymity and greater opportunity. Many used the G.I. Bill to go to college. Others used the opportunity of veterans' loans to buy homes and start businesses. Homosexuals became a part of the communities in which they lived. There was always a stigma but nothing like they were about to experience as Joe McCarthy and others, including the newly formed "Subcommittee to Investigate the Employment of Homosexuals and

53 *Lavender Scare*, supra. 98-99

54 Allan Berube, *Coming Out Under Fire: The History of Gay Men and Women in World War Two*, Free Press (1990), 8

55 Id. 22

56 Michael, Bronski, *A Queer History of the United States*, Beacon Press (2011), 152-175

Other Sex Perverts in Government" learned the political benefit of targeting them.[57] The Communist hunters became homosexual hunters.

The Communist issue was conflated with the homosexual issue under a common heading of "security risks." It was assumed, without any
proof, the loyalty of homosexuals could be easily compromised. The
committee's widely publicized hearings on the subject raised the fear
level and created a stigma that ruined the lives of thousands of citizens
before the fears subsided.[58] "Not surprisingly, 'Pinko fag' became the
worst insult of the era."[59]

North Carolina Senator Clyde Hoey, a Democrat, chaired the
subcommittee. He found the whole matter distasteful, telling White
House staff "it was a dirty job which he had not wanted but that he was
going to do his best to do it right, in a quiet and unspectacular way."[60]
That, of course, was not possible in the early 1950s.

Before the committee was formed and staff appointed, the
federal agencies began to panic. In the atmosphere McCarthy had
created, all began to envision themselves sitting in front of a senate
committee explaining why they had hired homosexuals. The purge
began immediately. The Central Intelligence Agency used polygraph
tests to "ferret out homosexuals on their pay rolls."[61] Bureau heads
were summoned to a seminar called "Perversion Among Government
Workers."[62] A participant reported that before taking the course,
he would "kick perverts out wherever I found them." Now, he said

57 Ironically, Senator Hunt was one of the co-sponsors of the senate resolution calling for
the creation of this subcommittee.

58 *Employment of Homosexuals and Other Sex Perverts in Government,* 81st Congress, 2nd
Session (1950)

59 www.glbtq.com/social-sciences/McCarthyism.html

60 "Memorandum For the Hoey Subcommittee Sex Pervert File" June 29, 1950, File: "Sex
Perversion" Box 32, WHCF, HST

61 "Federal Agency Spots Perverts By Lie-Detector" *The Washington Times-Herald,* May 21,
1950

62 "School Dealing With Perversion Opened by U.S." *Washington Times-Herald,* June 24,
1950

he didn't know what to do because the instructors seemed to advise retaining homosexuals in "non-sensitive" positions. The head of the National Institute of Mental Health advised agencies not to discharge employees simply because they are homosexuals, but "because they have discredited their government."[63]

State Department staff produced a hastily researched study of the "Problem of Homosexuals and Sex Perverts in the Department of State."[64] It explained the initial hiring of the 91 former employees had been the result of a policy that, until recently, "tolerated homosexuals in its employment solely because not much was known about them or who they were." Now, the memo explained, we know they are "neurotic, characterized by emotional instability, that they represent a type of regression to man's primitive instincts and that they live a life of flight from their inversion and of fear of detection." Significantly, the memo admitted the Department had no evidence that homosexual employees "have caused a breach of the security of the Department."

The Hoey committee's work got off to a rough start when chief counsel Flanagan sent written demands to all federal agencies asking that they turn over their files "concerning known or suspected homosexuals."[65] The White House ordered the agencies to refuse the request.[66] Flanagan already had the files of the Metropolitan Police Department. Detective Blick was more than willing to share names and vice squad files. The President's staff was uncertain about Hoey's views. "We don't know what Hoey's attitude is, whether he is being just a dupe of the Republicans or whether the Republican group is working up a very sordid smear campaign to the effect that the President is protect-

---

63 "U.S. Officials Asked to Take Care in Firings" *Washington Post,* June 25, 1950

64 Memorandum, June 23, 1950, File: "Sex Perversion" Box 32, WHCF, HST

65 Letter from Flanagan to Department Secretaries, June 15, 1950, File: "Sex Perversion" Box 32, WHCF, HST

66 "Files on Aberrants (sic) Closed to Hill" *Washington Daily News,* June 20, 1950

ing homos," a White House memo noted.[67] However the President's staff and Hoey came to an understanding. The agencies could disregard the request for files until and unless the committee reached a different conclusion.[68]

The next controversy was the question of whether all or a part of the hearings would be held in public or executive sessions. Senator Hoey sought the advice of the White House expressing some concern that the more conservative committee members would want a public hearing in order to score political points. The White House staff was unanimous in its feeling the hearings should be held in private. One staff member wrote, "The charges about homosexuality have struck home with far greater effect, in certain quarters, than the Communist allegations. This investigation, therefore, represents a political problem of considerable magnitude. The pressure to make political hay out of the investigation while it is going on will be very great."[69] He felt that holding any part of the hearings in public would "defeat the professed intention of Senator Hoey to conduct the entire investigation as quietly as possible."

As the committee prepared to open hearings, this issue remained unresolved. But, in the mind of the chief counsel the question of whether homosexuals posed a security risk was, without any evidence, fully resolved. When he met with White House staffers on July 8, Flanagan admitted his discussions with security officials had not produced any documentation. The CIA reported on a single World War I incident involving countries other than the United States. "Despite the lack of documentation he (Flanagan) seemed convinced that homo-

---

67 Memorandum to "Mr. Murphy" June 30, 1950, File: "Sex Perversion" Box 32, WHCF, HST
68 "Memorandum for Mr. Dawson" June 29, 1950, File: "Sex Perversion" Box 32, WHCF, HST
69 "Memorandum to Mr. Spingarn" July 3, 1950, File: "Sex Perversion" Box 32, WHCF, HST

sexualism (sic) represents a serious security threat and my suggestion that it should be squared up against other types of security threats by individuals resulting from normal sexual or non-sexual activity did not seem to impress him much."[70] The White House knew two things at that time. The State Department had no evidence of any security breach by a homosexual and the committee's chief counsel was "committed to the position that the homosexual is the most serious security threat of all." They never confronted Flanagan with the results of the State Department inquiry.

During this summer of investigation, a *New York Post* columnist did his own. He also found no actual evidence, only notions. "One was offered to me by a Harvard professor with considerable government experience. It is a theory of the relation between virility and the needs of diplomacy in the age of the atom bomb. It takes a virile man, he said, to be able to meet Russian diplomacy today. It requires the kind of toughness that an effeminate man would not have," the *Post* story read.[71] In the meantime the White House discovered Mr. Purifoy was wrong when he told the Senate committee that 91 employees had been discharged because they were homosexuals. The actual number was 115.[72] More were voluntarily leaving as the investigation gathered momentum. Department officials told the committee, "Moral degenerates are fleeing the State Department at the rate of one or two each week."[73]

In late July, the subcommittee agreed to hold its hearings behind closed doors.[74] The director of the CIA, Rear Admiral Roscoe H. Hillenkoetter, testified that homosexuals were genuine security risks.

70 "Memorandum for the Hoey Committee Sex Pervert Investigation File" July 1, 1950, File: "Sex Perversion" Box 32, WHCF, HST

71 "Scandal in the State Department: Are Homosexuals Security Risks" by Max Lerner, *New York Post,* July 16, 1950

72 Memorandum to file, July 20, 1950, File: "Sex Perversion" Box 32, WHCF, HST

73 "Perverts Fleeing State dept. Under Pressure" *Washington Times-Herald,* July 27, 1950

74 "Memorandum for the Files" July 24, 1950, File: "Sex Perversion" Box 32, WHCF, HST

War preparations, he said, intensified that risk.[75] Once again, neither he nor any other witness provided a shred of evidence.

By November the committee concluded its hearings and issued a report. The members had three objectives. They were to "determine the extent of employment of homosexuals and other sex perverts in Government; to consider reasons why (not whether, but why) their employment by the Government is undesirable; and to examine the efficacy of the methods used in dealing with the problem."[76] The subcommittee fulfilled each. Its final report left no doubt. The security of the United States, in the committee's opinion, was at stake. The final report announced, "In the opinion of this subcommittee homosexuals and other sex perverts are not proper persons to be employed in Government for two reasons; first, they are generally unsuitable, and second, they constitute security risks."[77] Flanagan had believed that from the beginning and the absence of proof didn't get in the way of a final conclusion.

While the subcommittee report assured readers its conclusion that homosexuals posed a security risk "is not based on mere conjecture,"[78] the senators cited only a single case involving a World War I Austrian soldier who, because of his sexuality, was compromised by Russian agents. Based on the questionable relevance of that one case and a great deal of "mere conjecture," the subcommittee reached a conclusion that would set into motion a nationwide fear of the potential of homosexuals to sell out their own country.[79] "Most perverts," the Hoey

75 Id.
76 *Employment of Homosexuals and Other Sex Perverts in Government* Supra. 1
77 Id. 3
78 Id. 4
79 In 1957 the United States Navy Board of Inquiry, quietly conducted its own investigation. The final report was called the "Crittenden Report after the committee chair, Navy Captain S.H. Crittenden, Jr. The Board evaluated policies dealing with homosexuals based in part on the assertions made in the final report of the Hoey Committee. The Crittenden Report concluded that there was "no sound basis for the belief that homosexuals posed a security risk" responding to the Hoey Report, "No intelligence agency, as far as can be

committee report announced, "tend to congregate at the same restaurants, night clubs, and bars, which places can be identified with comparative ease, making it possible for a recruiting agent to develop clandestine relationships which can be used for espionage purposes."[80] Having concluded homosexuals were security risks, the subcommittee then reviewed civilian and military personnel records and police records from the District of Columbia. They concluded the military exhibited a "uniform and constant pattern in ferreting out and removing these persons." Not so with civilian agencies who were criticized for being more lax.

Finally, the subcommittee targeted the District of Columbia. Its report found police, prosecution and court practices in cases of alleged homosexuality to be substandard. The committee was especially concerned that sexual acts performed by consenting adults within the confines of their own homes were not prosecutable offenses.[81] The committee recommended broader laws, harsher penalties and tougher prosecution. The final report made a recommendation that would four years later facilitate the blackmail of Lester Hunt. The senators suggested the prosecution of these particular cases no longer be the domain of the District of Columbia. They wanted a prosecutor beholden to the Senate. They wanted these cases to be handled instead by an official who got his or her job because of a senate confirmation. The United States Attorney for the District of Columbia would now prosecute cases against suspected homosexuals.[82]

The Hoey committee hearings had a dramatic impact on Americans and their attitudes toward people with same-sex attractions, expos-

---

learned, adduced any factual data before that committee with which to support these opinions" and said that "the concept that homosexuals necessarily pose a security risk is unsupported by adequate factual data. The Crittenden Report remained secret until 1976.
80 *Employment of Homosexuals and Other Sex Perverts in Government*, 81st Congress, supra. 3-5
81 Id. 16
82 Id. 16

ing them to sensational testimony from influential voices including the armed services, the CIA, and the FBI, among others. Because the committee had preconceived notions about the results, the witnesses were limited to people who supported those conclusions. The results were inevitable. This committee, as much or more than any other development of the times, created an atmosphere of distrust and disdain toward those who were or were rumored to be homosexuals. It also motivated the District of Columbia to create its special investigation unit that would soon play a role in the life of Lester Hunt.

On April 27, 1953, President Dwight D. Eisenhower signed Executive Order 10450: Security Requirements for Government Employment. The order listed "sexual perversion" as a condition for firing a federal employee and for denying employment to applicants for any government job. Homosexuality was added to moral perversion and Communism, each categorized as national security threats. Although President Truman had established broad standards for dismissal from federal employment during his administration, his policy toward dismissing homosexuals was deemed too weak. Eisenhower ordered the government to hire and retain employees only when "clearly consistent with the interests of national security." Homosexuals were outside those boundaries.

Soon FBI agents began regularly questioning civil servants and applicants for government jobs about their opinions of marriage as a means of weeding out homosexuals.[83] Political rhetoric was pitched. Americans were now attuned to the argument. Senator Wherry spoke for many. "You can't hardly separate homosexuals from subversives," he claimed. "Mind you, I don't say every homosexual is a subversive, and I don't say every subversive is a homosexual. But a man of low morality is a menace in the government, whatever he is, and they are

83 *Lavender Scare,* Supra. 36

all tied up together.[84] A separate subcommittee headed by Wherry concluded homosexuals were a "corrosive influence" on government. Wherry, a close confidant of McCarthy, was considered the head of what he called "the pervert purge."[85]

As many as ten thousand men and women lost their livelihoods as federal employees because they were or were rumored to be homosexuals.[86] But that was not enough for Bridges and Wherry, powerful members of the District of Columbia Committee who used their influence to demand stricter enforcement of laws criminalizing the behaviors of gays in the District. One result was the formation of what was crudely known as "The Pervert Elimination Campaign." The National Park Service used hundreds of undercover agents to harass and arrest gays and lesbians using the vast network of Parkland in the Washington area.[87]

The Metropolitan Police Department followed suit naming Roy Blick to head a special vice squad to target suspected homosexuals in the bars, restaurants, and the parks of the District of Columbia. Wherry considered Blick to be a "one man watch-dog" in the effort to catch "perverts" in the nation's capitol.[88] Some of Roy Blick's undercover agents were on duty the night of June 9, 1953, when Lester Hunt, Jr. walked through Lafayette Park. By then, the Joe McCarthy Lester Hunt had first met during the Malmedy hearings in 1949 had become McCarthyism.

84 Jonathan Ned Katz, *Gay American History: Lesbians and Gay Men in the U.S.A.*, Thomas Y. Crowell Press (1976), 95

85 Baxter, *"Homo-Hunting" in the Early Cold War*, Supra. 119

86 Eleanor Bontecou, *The Federal Loyalty-Security Program*, Cornell University Press (1953), 272-299

87 Lavender *Scare*, Supra. *59*

88 Baxter, *"Homo-Hunting" in the Early Cold War*, Supra. 124

CHAPTER EIGHT

Meeting Joe McCarthy

Pierre L'Enfant designed Washington to intimidate. Washington was also designed to overwhelm. From its garden-lined mall to the broad boulevards radiating out from the center of the city to its imposing monuments perfectly situated along the Potomac River, Washington, D.C. intends to intimidate and to overwhelm. It succeeds.

On a January morning in 1949, Mrs. Hunt watched, prideful, as her husband walked onto the Inaugural stand with other members of the United States Senate. She thought him to be the handsomest, best dressed of them all just as he had been back at the state house in Cheyenne. But she was no more impressed with him that day than when she first saw him take the field in his baseball uniform back in Lander in 1911.

If she were a bit intimidated and overwhelmed it was to be expected. She wondered whether he was as well. Nathelle had never known Lester to be intimidated or overwhelmed, but this was somehow different. This day demonstrated just how much their lives had changed in a matter of a few short days.

Lester Hunt had come a long way from Atlanta, Illinois and Lander, Wyoming. He was certainly prepared for his new job. After all, he had served in the state legislature, as secretary of state and governor of Wyoming. He'd been a political leader in his state during the Great Depression and World War II. Yet, as she looked out across the

National Mall to the outline of the magnificent Capitol Building and the expressive Washington Monument in the distance, and then to the faces and profiles of the men and women who joined her husband on that stand, it would have been surprising had Senator Hunt's wife not thought ominously of the distance they had traveled. It wasn't the number of miles between Wyoming and Washington. It was rather a sense of "time travel." Neither Lester nor Nathelle had experienced such a cultural change since those long ago days when each of them left behind anything familiar in their lives for an uncertain life in the Lander Valley.

The Inauguration of Harry S. Truman

The inauguration of a President is the most sacred of democratic rituals. Yet, 160 years passed from the time George Washington became the first to take the oath until most Americans could witness the event. For much of our history, only those who lived in the nation's capital or who could afford to make the trip could see an inauguration. Until 1925, most of the nation could only read about it, usually days later, in their local newspaper. Beginning when Calvin Coolidge was sworn in, they could hear the words on their radios.

January 20, 1949, was the first time they actually saw a Chief Justice of the United States Supreme Court administer the oath and a President of the United States repeat it. The Inauguration of Harry S. Truman was televised to 10 million Americans, considerably more than the total of all persons who personally witnessed the oath taking of all previous American presidents combined.[1] Americans tuned in to see grainy, black and white images on tiny television screens. Cameras panned the great national monuments and the huge crowd on the Washington Mall. They saw a blimp hovering over the U.S. Capitol.

---

1 Harry S. Truman Library and Museum, www.trumanlibrary.org, accessed on November 10, 2011.

Hundreds of American flags moved in the slight breeze.

This was the day of the improbable inauguration of an accidental President. No one ever thought Harry Truman would be President. He never asked for the job. When Franklin Roosevelt died during his fourth term, the job simply fell, not in Truman's lap, but on his shoulders. Few even in his own party had wanted him to run for the job in 1948. They wanted to draft Dwight Eisenhower. Once Truman decided to run, the party split wildly, nominating not just one candidate, but three. The Republicans nominated only one. They figured Thomas Dewey to be a sure winner.

Congressional Republicans were so certain it would be Dewey raising his right hand on inauguration morning, they agreed to a record appropriation of $80,000 for the event.[2] In 1949 that sum bought a grand celebration. And indeed it was, albeit for Harry Truman and not Dewey. Six hundred thousand visitors packed the city. A train filled with revelers arrived at Union Station every two minutes. The inaugural parade that afternoon stretched more than seven miles. A calliope played "I'm Just Wild About Harry." Truman himself led the parade. The Inaugural Ball danced well into the early morning hours of the following day.

But, the morning was set aside for swearing in the man Americans had chosen for their President. The sky above the U.S. Capitol Building was mostly clear. The sun was shining but the 38-degree temperature seemed much colder on that humid and breezy Washington day. Emily Nathelle Hunt and her guests arrived early hoping to be ahead of the large crowds everyone expected.[3]

They shivered in the cold awaiting the President who was twenty minutes late for his own inauguration.[4] Finally, he arrived and the cer-

2 Id.
3 Nathelle Hunt, Autobiographical *Essay*, 25
4 Tyler Abell, editor, *Drew Pearson Diaries 1949-1959*, Rinehart and Winston (1979), 13

emony began. Truman used two Bibles. One was a Guttenberg Bible given him by the people of Independence, Missouri. It was opened to Exodus 20:3-17, the Ten Commandments. The other, used by Franklin D. Roosevelt in his 1945 Inaugural, was opened to the Sermon on the Mount. [5]

The new senator from Wyoming watched along with fellow freshmen Lyndon Johnson, Hubert Humphrey and Estes Kefauver. "*I, Harry S. Truman, do solemnly swear...*" The senators, who had taken their own oaths earlier,[6] listened along with other members of Congress, including Wisconsin's junior senator Joseph McCarthy, as the Thirty-third President of the United States completed his oath of office and began his Inaugural Address.

> *I accept with humility the honor, which the American people have conferred upon me. I accept it with a resolve to do all that I can for the welfare of this Nation and for the peace of the world. In performing the duties of my office, I need the help and the prayers of every one of you.*

The President emphasized the challenges the nation's leaders would confront in the coming years. "The peoples of the earth," said the President, "face the future with grave uncertainty, composed almost equally of great hopes and great fears."

> *Each period of our national history has had its special challenges. Those that confront us now are as momentous as any in the past. Today marks the beginning not only of a new administration, but of a period that will be eventful, perhaps decisive, for us and for the world. It may be our lot to experience, and in a large measure bring about, a major turning point in the long history of the human race.*

5 Legislative Reference Service, Library of Congress, Facts on File, January 16-22, 1949, 21
6 United States Senate History, "Senators, 1789 to Present" www.senate.gov

Truman dutifully warned Americans of the threat posed by Communism. He asked the nation to continue supporting the recovery of postwar Europe and the work of the United Nations. "Events have brought our American democracy to new influence and new responsibilities. They will test our courage, our devotion to duty, and our concept of liberty, Truman said."

Hunt nodded in agreement as the President spoke. They each understood the threat. Hunt was there on a promise to make certain America was prepared if another war should come its way. In a speech a few days earlier to the Cheyenne Lion's Club, his first as Senator-elect, he had expressed a belief that neither World War I nor World War II would have occurred "had we been prepared."[7] He felt the United States was decidedly unprepared again. More than five years ahead of the estimates of U.S. intelligence experts, Russia had tested its first atom bomb in August. The American monopoly in nuclear weapons had ended abruptly. Earlier that summer a civil war in China had ended with Mao Zedong's proclamation of the People's Republic of China and the exile of Chiang Kai- shek along with two million other Chinese nationalists from Mainland China.

Less noticed among the events of the year, but equally ominous, was the 1949 publication of George Orwell's prophecy, *1984*. In the tradition of Isaiah, Jeremiah and Micah, Orwell warned against militarization. However, unlike the prophets of Hebrew scripture, Orwell had witnessed the penultimate accomplishment of militarism, the use of a nuclear bomb to kill hundreds of thousands and threaten an entire planet.

As with the warnings of Biblical prophets, Orwell's admonition against "chauvinism and regimentation and hysteria"[8] failed to change

7 Speech, undated, File: "National Defense Speeches" Box 3, LCH Papers

8 Christopher Hitchens, Introduction to *Animal Farm and 1984*, George Orwell, Harcourt, Inc. (2003), xiii.

a course ordained by the gods of fear. The course was set and the challenges of which Truman spoke arrived quickly. As they did, so did that which was predicted by Orwell.

Investigating Nazi War Crimes

The opening salvos in what would become known as "the Cold War" were being fired. Cleaning up the mess created by the war in Europe, Americans were holding Nazi soldiers accountable for war crimes. Well-publicized trials included gruesome evidence of German atrocities. Looking for strategic advantage in the Cold War, the Soviets charged the Americans used torture and trickery to obtain confessions from Germans who were accused of massacring American soldiers near the end of the war. The Malmedy investigation was Lester Hunt's introduction to the Senate and to Washington politics.

More than an ocean away in a beautiful valley, not at all unlike the Lander Valley of Wyoming, is the little town of Malmedy, Belgium. It sits at the confluence of the Warche and Warchenne Rivers on the southern slope of the thickly wooded and scenically charming Hohe Venn Forest. The town's odd name has a Latin origin, deriving itself from the word "malmundarium." Ironically the name means "cleansed from the evil ones." Historically, Malmedy suffered the great bad fortune of having been settled too near the Belgian-German border, making it one of the first targets of armies either invading Belgium or on their way to invade others. In earlier times, the Normans and the Romans had come. Napoleon's armies invaded in 1815. Hitler's Wehrmacht came their way darkly in 1940. Near the end of World War II, the small Belgian community unwillingly became the center of hostilities during the Battle of the Bulge, the bloodiest battle fought by American forces in that war.[9]

What occurred at Malmedy on December 17, 1944, was the subject

9 Stephen E. Ambrose, *Americans At War.* University Press of Mississippi (1997), 52.

of heated debate in Germany and the United States for many years. One account written almost half a century later described the massacre of American soldiers.

> *Twenty-one American survivors made statements to U.S. authorities in Malmédy on December 17, the same day as the massacre, and on the following day—long before there was any possibility of collusion or anybody putting ideas into their heads. They all told essentially the same story: After surrendering to a German armored column and being disarmed, they were assembled in a field just south of the crossroads. The Germans then opened fire on them with machine guns and rifles. In most cases, the survivors mentioned two pistol shots before the main shooting started. They said that soldiers then entered the field and shot anyone who showed any signs of life and that many of the bodies were kicked or prodded in order to get a response. Following this, the German column continued to drive past, with some of the vehicle crews taking potshots at the bodies lying in the field. All but one of the survivors insisted that no attempt to escape had been made before the Germans opened fire, and that the escape attempt came at a much later stage when they thought the Germans had left the area.[10]*

Senator Hunt explained the massacre to his constituents more succinctly. "The Malmedy Massacre occurred in December 1944 in the vicinity of Malmedy, Belgium, where some five hundred surrendered and unarmed American soldiers and Belgium citizens were shot down without reason."[11] Within a year after V-E (Victory in Europe) Day, a two- month-long military trial began in May of 1946 in the Dachau

10 Michael Reynolds, "*Massacre At Malmédy During the Battle of the Bulge*" Published online June 12, 2006, accessed February 26, 2012, http://www.historynet.com/massacre-at-malmedy-during-the-battle-of-the-bulge.htm
11 News Release, August 24, 1949, File: "Mimeograph" Box 23, LCH Papers

concentration camp. Verdicts included 43 death-by-hanging sentences and life imprisonment for 22 former SS soldiers who had been found to have had roles in the war crime.[12] A few others were given sentences ranging from 10 to 20 years. Despite the postwar frenzy for revenge, these verdicts were controversial. The Russians alleged confessions from some of the German defendants had been coerced, obtained through torture and illegal trickery. Stalin compared the Nazi trials to the vicious tactics of the Nazi army.

The U.S. Senate passed a resolution asking the Armed Forces Committee to investigate "reports that confessions by the German troopers were obtained under duress."[13] Committee Chairman, Senator Millard Tydings of Maryland appointed the freshman Senator from Wyoming as one of four members of a subcommittee to conduct the investigation.[14] It was a coup for Lester Hunt. It was also his rude introduction to Wisconsin's junior Senator Joe McCarthy.

Likely these two antagonists never knew how much they had in common. At the time they met, the common experiences of their youth were not apparent. Like Hunt, Joseph Raymond McCarthy had his roots in rural America. Like Hunt, McCarthy was raised in a "close, happy family – hard working, very religious, proud of their ancestry."[15] While there was a perceptible path from Lester Hunt's childhood to the values he exhibited as a man, it was not so with McCarthy. One biographer wrote, "What we know about Joe McCarthy's childhood and youth does not really explain his subsequent conduct."[16]

McCarthy had a combative personality. His father taught him to

12 The abbreviation "SS" stands for Schutzstaffel, meaning "protective squad," literally Hitler's personal bodyguard. The SS earned a reputation for brutality.

13 News Release, August 24, 1949, File: "Mimeograph" Box 23, LCH Papers

14 The original subcommittee included Senators Ray Baldwin (R-Connecticut), Estes Kefauver (D-Tennessee), Richard Russell (D-Georgia) and Hunt. Senator Russell resigned before hearings began.

15 Thomas C. Reeves, *The Life and Times of Joe McCarthy*, Stein and Day (1982), 3

16 Id. 4

box before Joe became a teenager. McCarthy disciple Roy Cohn observed that as a boxer, Joe was "Impatient of technique, his style was to come charging out at the bell and stay on the offensive, no matter how powerful his opponent, until he won or dropped."[17] He was an aggressive young man whom others avoided because of his strength and propensity to "scrap."[18] He became an aggressive senator whom others avoided for much the same reasons.

Joe was briefly tempted by the thought of becoming a professional fighter. He opted not to follow that career path, a decision much regretted by both boxing fans and his senate colleagues. Instead he took the advice of his boxing coach and stayed in college, graduating from law school and later opening a law office. In 1936, Joe McCarthy was an FDR Democrat and made no bones about it even though his boss was "a staunch Republican." McCarthy ran an unsuccessful campaign for district attorney. It was the first time Joe McCarthy would be accused of being an "unscrupulous politician who had grossly misstated the facts."[19] It wouldn't be the last.

Two years later he became the youngest circuit court judge in Wisconsin history, defeating an incumbent who had been on that bench for 24 years. He won using a strategy that even his friends called "tricky." They said McCarthy was "ruthless if you were in his path."[20] Judge McCarthy defied conventional rules then as Senator McCarthy did later. As a result, he suffered a rebuke by the state supreme court for destroying evidence. They said his conduct amounted to an abuse of judicial authority. The abuse of authority, judicial and legislative, would be McCarthy's calling card thereafter.

In 1942, McCarthy took a leave of absence from his judicial du-

17 Roy Cohn, *McCarthy*, The New American Library (1968), 13
18 Id. 4
19 Id. 23
20 Id. 28

ties to enlist in the Army Air Corps. He flew bombing missions in the South Pacific and later used the experience to bolster his political aspirations, nick-naming himself "Tail-gunner Joe."[21]

In 1946, he entered the Republican primary for the U.S. Senate against the iconic Progressive Party Senator Robert M. Lafollette, Jr. who was heavily criticized for having recently changed to the GOP. McCarthy gained ground charging that his opponent was a war profiteer who had failed to serve during the war. The charge scored though Lafollette was 46 years old and ineligible to serve when the U.S. entered the war.[22] On August 13, 1945, McCarthy won the Republican nomination. Joe's first campaigns were each cliffhangers. He was elected to the circuit court judgeship by 3986 votes in 1939.[23] He won the nomination for the U.S. Senate by only 5300 votes out of more than 400,000 votes cast. He went on to easily win the general election against token opposition and arrived in Washington in 1947 as the youngest member of the Senate. Lester Hunt arrived two years later.

McCarthy was neither a member of the subcommittee named to investigate Malmedy nor was he a member of the Armed Forces Committee. Nonetheless, he was permitted to attend subcommittee hearings and to participate. He told the subcommittee he was there "informally" as a member of the Senate Committee on Expenditures of Executive Departments.[24]

In his biography of McCarthy, David Oshinsky concluded, "Throughout the Malmedy hearings, McCarthy bullied witnesses, made scores of erroneous statements, exaggerated his evidence, and turned

21 Appleton Public Library, a biographical essay prepared by the Reference staff, based primarily on information from *The Life and Times of Joe McCarthy,* Reeves, supra accessed at www.apl.org/history/McCarthy, on November 27, 2011

22 Richard H. Rovere, *Senator Joe McCarthy.* University of California Press (1959), 97,102.

23 "McCarthy Winner By 3,986" *Shawano Evening leader,* April 3, 1939, 1

24 Transcript, *Hearings Before a Subcommittee of the Armed Forces Committee of the United States Senate-Investigation of Action of Army With Respect to Trial of Persons Responsible for the Massacre of American Soldiers, Battle of the Bulge Near Malmedy Belgium, December 1944"* Vol. I page 6.

almost every session into a barroom brawl. At the same time, however, he demonstrated that Baldwin (Senator Ray Baldwin R-Connecticut) and Hunt were no more interested in an impartial investigation than he was. Their manners were better, their tone more subdued, but they were determined to exonerate the Army at all costs, just as Joe was determined to prove its culpability." [25]

The hearing transcripts provide ample evidence to support Oshinsky's opinion of McCarthy's role as a bully but precious little to support his view of Senator Hunt. Robert Griffith wrote what the American Historical Association called "a definitive account of McCarthy's political career."[26] Professor Griffith thought Hunt's performance "inoffensive" but concluded McCarthy's to have been both ironic and prophetic.[27]

Irony was found in the fact that McCarthy was the primary advocate for the Russian argument that the U.S. Army officers in charge of the investigation had treated the Nazi defendants unfairly. "Most prophetic, however," Griffith wrote, "was the manner in which McCarthy bullied and intimidated the entire investigative committee, its staff and the witnesses who appeared before it."[28] McCarthy resorted to his old boxing strategies, blindly throwing wild punches in the hope that one or two might land.

Over the course of the spring, the subcommittee held 23 days of hearings in Washington. Senator McCarthy abused his "guest" status, dominating the proceedings. He interrupted and badgered witnesses

25 David M. Oshinsky, "A Conspiracy So Immense: The World of Joe McCarthy" Oxford University Press (2005), 76-77

26 Richard Breitman and Allan J. Lichtman, of American University, Essay entitled *"Robert Griffith: Historian of McCarthy Era United States, Perspectives on History,* April 2011 accessed on www.historians.org/Perspectives November 27, 2011.

27 Robert Griffith, *The Politics of Fear: Joseph R. McCarthy and the Senate* (1970; 2nd edition, 1987), 23-24. (Note: The book won the Frederick Jackson Turner Prize of the Organization of American Historians)

28 Id. 23

as well as his senate colleagues, targeting most particularly Senator Baldwin, the chair of the subcommittee.

Only two of the four members of the subcommittee were present as the hearings began. Chairman Ray Baldwin, a senator from Connecticut, took his seat next to Lester C. Hunt of Wyoming. Senator McCarthy was also in attendance. Chairman Baldwin gaveled the hearing to order and Kenneth C. Royall, the Secretary the Army, marched to the witnesses' table. He was placed under oath and began to testify. Only a few minutes passed before McCarthy began arguing with the witness, asking Secretary Royall to assume that American officers used physical violence and mock trials to obtain confessions from the German soldiers.[29] The freshman Senator from Wyoming looked on as the chairman repeatedly admonished McCarthy. Senator Baldwin struggled to maintain the role of chairman in the wake of McCarthy's aggressive tactics.

The Wisconsin Senator interrupted the testimony of Secretary Royall. "I don't like to get into an argument," McCarthy shouted, "but..." and then began arguing. Chairman Baldwin asked, "May I interrupt?" McCarthy ignored the request and continued his harangue.[30] Chairman Baldwin was unable to attend the second day of the hearing. Hunt assumed the chair. McCarthy took control of the proceedings, vigorously cross-examining the witness as though he were a prosecutor in a courtroom. When Hunt advised McCarthy "this hearing is not a prosecution of the witnesses before us" McCarthy threatened to leave and return to the Expenditures Committee on which he served and ask them to conduct the investigation.[31]

McCarthy screamed at one witness, telling him that if he had appeared in his old courtroom with similar testimony, "I would do one of

29 Transcript of Malmedy Hearings, supra. Vol. I, 6.
30 Id. 11
31 Id. 48

two things. I would ask that he be immediately disbarred, or perhaps, first commit him to an institution for observation."[32]

Baldwin had not been in the Senate long. He came, as did Joe McCarthy, in 1946. This was likely his, as it was Hunt's, first experience of the McCarthy the country would soon come to know. There is no transcript of private conversations between senators. Still, if you've been around politicians long you might guess accurately at those between Hunt and Baldwin during breaks in testimony. What they were experiencing was not at all the decorum senators expected from one another. Undoubtedly, while they shook their heads, they talked about strategies for controlling the junior senator from Wisconsin. If so, they were unable to develop one.

McCarthy was single-minded in his purpose. He had made up his mind before the hearings ever opened. Based on little objectivity, he decided the Army was the villain. He invited himself to participate in order to make that case. McCarthy prepared himself by reading only one-sided reports that confirmed his preconceived notion that the U.S. military officials were in the wrong.[33] "One thing the Army has proved so far," McCarthy asserted, "is that they acted with the utmost malice."[34] Defending the SS troops McCarthy claimed, "It would be hard to convince them (the Nazi defendants) that they (U.S. Army officers) were operating with malice toward none and charity toward all."[35]

McCarthy used an old trial lawyer's tactic of hoping to intimidate a witness by reminding him he was "under oath." Baldwin came to the defense of the witness. "I want to say for the benefit of the record since you (McCarthy) have impressed on the record the thought that possibly the witness is attempting to change his testimony, that this young

32 Id. 756-757
33 Reeves, *The Life and Times of Joe McCarthy*, supra, 169
34 Transcript of the Malmedy Hearings, supra. Vol. 1, 248
35 Id. 247

lieutenant gives to the Chairman of this committee the appearance of trying to tell the truth to the best of his knowledge, information and belief of a fact that occurred a long time ago and an awful lot has happened since then. Now here is a young American officer and I think something ought to be said a little bit in his behalf, said Senator Baldwin."[36] Later Baldwin demanded McCarthy cut off his examination of one witness who had appeared voluntarily but was kept for five days under McCarthy's questioning.[37]

Only two years into his first term, McCarthy was already learning to enjoy the media spotlight. Three months into his first term, Lester Hunt was already seeing the darker side of Washington politics. Hunt knew how to work with those who saw things differently in the Wyoming Capitol building. There was little grandstanding back home because there was no stage like the one on which United States senators performed. In Wyoming politics you didn't accomplish anything by putting on a show for the press. The small press corps back home knew you too well for that. A successful Wyoming politician had to learn how to persuade another by the force and clarity of an argument. Raised voices were seldom heard. Intimidation was almost never successful. Washington was different. In Washington, adversaries took a different approach to one another, particularly in the times of Joe McCarthy.

From the opening bell, McCarthy's strategy was not only to condemn U.S. Army officers but also to make headlines in the process. He learned early the tactics that would at first make him first famous and later infamous. It was sensational rather than measured statements that made the front-page. As a former trial judge, McCarthy was well aware of the suspicion with which the law views polygraph examinations. He was also aware of how much more credence the media and the public afford this questionable means of extracting information.

36 Id. 358
37 Id. 774

Thus, he vehemently pursued his proposal to require key witnesses in the hearings to undergo lie detector tests.

> *Senator McCarthy: He says he will submit to a lie detector test. The chair seems to be afraid of the results of that test.*
>
> *Senator Baldwin: That is totally-*
>
> *Senator McCarthy: I am going to finish.*
>
> *Senator Baldwin: Go ahead.*
>
> *Senator McCarthy: It is fair to say this committee is afraid of the facts…and is sitting here solely for the purpose of a whitewash of the Army....*[38]

And so it went. Day after day McCarthy dominated the proceedings. When the Washington phase of the hearings was completed, the subcommittee scheduled a trip to Germany. "We have exhausted all witnesses available in this country," Senator Hunt said, "and the chairman of the subcommittee has taken the position that a full, complete and authentic report cannot be written until the German prisoners are examined."[39] Hunt felt the number of conflicting statements offered by witnesses in Washington compelled the subcommittee to "make direct interrogation of witnesses in Germany" and physically examine the prisoners "to determine the facts."[40]

Hunt and the other subcommittee members, who now included Tennessee Senator Estes Kefauver, boarded a ship, the USS General Roe, and sailed for Germany on August 26. The hearings continued in Munich without Senator McCarthy. He was no longer participating. By the time Hunt, Kefauver, and Baldwin toured the massacre site and heard some of the most important testimony over a six-day period,

38 Id. 634
39 News release, May 31, 1949, File: "Armed Forces-Malmedy" Box 8, LCH Papers
40 News Release, August 24, 1949, File: "Mimeograph" Box 23, LCH Papers

McCarthy had withdrawn.[41]

His exit from the proceedings was as dramatic as it was premature. On May 20, the final day of the Washington hearings McCarthy issued a press release. Months before the conclusion of the investigation the Wisconsin Senator denounced the hearings as "a shameful farce."[42] McCarthy told the press the evidence would show American Army officers had torn "a page from the books of Hitler and Stalin in order to get confessions ...regardless of guilt or innocence."[43] McCarthy renewed his charge that the refusal of the subcommittee to require lie detector tests was proof his fellow senators were engaged in a "deliberate attempt to avoid the facts and affect (sic) a whitewash of the Army officers involved."[44] McCarthy accomplished his goal of making headlines with outrageous and unsubstantiated charges. The Senator then left the room and the hearings.

On July 1 he released a 28-page document entitled "Report on the Conduct of the War Crimes Trials in the American Occupied Europe." It was his personal report on the investigation. Resorting to extreme hyperbole and outrageous distortions of recent history, the Senator said he was concerned that "our government had been placed in the position of condoning a brand of brutalitarianism (sic) worse than that practiced by the most morally degenerate in either Hitler's or Stalin's camp."[45]

Unlike Baldwin, McCarthy's fellow Republican, Senator Hunt did not openly challenge McCarthy during the proceedings. Even so, McCarthy was greatly annoyed by the freshman Wyoming senator's statement published in a Wisconsin newspaper. Hunt called McCarthy's

---

41 News Release, August 24, 1949, File: "Mimeograph" Box 19, LCH Papers

42 Transcript of the Malmedy Hearings, supra, 844

43 Id. 837

44 Id. 838

45 Copy of *"Report on the Conduct of the War Crimes Trials in the American Occupied Europe"*, July 1, 1949", 10, File: "Armed Forces-Malmedy 2" Box 8, LCH Papers

attacks on the committee unfair, adding that he thought the Wisconsin senator was "hitting below the belt."[46] McCarthy's real target was Baldwin. The Wisconsin Senator was angered by Baldwin's appointment to chair the subcommittee. McCarthy was correct in pointing out it was "extremely unusual that a Republican Senator should have been appointed chairman of a committee which was controlled by the Democrats."

McCarthy also charged that prior to the "extremely unusual" appointment, Baldwin had already declared the misconduct charges "groundless." In addition, McCarthy claimed one of Baldwin's law partners was the Army major who commanded the unit "that got the confessions and statements from the accused."[47]

The transcripts of the Malmedy hearings portray Hunt as a typically reserved freshman. He had been a member of the Senate for only three months when he was given this difficult assignment. Hunt was the only member of the panel who was not an attorney. He was learning the Senate rules and procedures on the run. He asked few questions and did not offer a direct challenge to the far more aggressive McCarthy. Nonetheless, the questions posed by the freshman senator from Wyoming were objective and not designed to pursue a preconceived agenda. Hunt paid close attention to the lengthy, complicated testimony, once correcting a witness who thought it was "eight" of the defendants who had taken the stand to testify in their own defense during their trial. "I believe it was eight," said the witness. "Nine, exactly," interrupted Hunt.[48]

Neither was he reluctant to question the competency of the American attorneys appointed to represent the Germans. He asked why the defense lawyers had not offered proof to support their theories

46 "McCarthy Charges Baldwin Should Not Have Headed Malmedy Probe" *LaCrosse Tribune and Leader-Press,* July 28, 1949
47 Id. 11-13
48 Id. 1279

of abuse during the trial. "Would not the attorneys have been very negligent in their duties as defense attorneys," Hunt inquired, " if they had not developed this mistreatment at great length during the trial?"[49]

Both Senators Baldwin and Kefauver were accomplished lawyers whose expertise and experience helped ferret out the legal issues. They turned to Dr. Hunt on the critically relevant medical issues. Hunt employed his medical expertise to question whether injuries existed, if doctors, dentists or others witnessed them, and whether any injuries were reported. On the second day of the hearings in Germany, Dr. Hunt was dispatched to the Landsberg prison, forty miles west of Munich, to conduct the inquiry of the medical personnel who were examining the prisoners.[50]

As McCarthy predicted, the subcommittee exonerated the Army and the officers who took part in the trials. Hunt and Kefauver then returned to their work in the Senate. Baldwin resigned to accept an appointment as a Justice on the Connecticut Supreme Court. McCarthy began to set the stage for his witch-hunt and within a few months all but two of the Malmedy defendants sentenced to death were granted clemency.

Senator Hunt was proud of the subcommittee's work, writing to a constituent two years later, "In 1949 I was assigned to the subcommittee to investigate the Malmedy Massacre in Belgium, when charges were made that the German prisoners had been mistreated and that their confessions of guilt had been obtained under duress. The subcommittee visited the battlefield and interviewed the prisoners, studied the record of court testimony and found that the allegations of mistreatment were without foundation."[51] He was outraged when the Commanding General of the European Command exercised his discretion and com-

49 Id. 1284
50 Id. 1337
51 Letter from Hunt to Bob McCracken, July 12, 1951, File: "Hunt Personal 1951" Box 19, LCH Papers

muted most of the sentences.

On January 31, 1951, General Thomas Handy issued his decision. Of the thirteen Germans who had been given death sentences, eleven were commuted.[52] Those who would be put to death were "two prisoners to whom I cannot rightfully grant clemency. These prisoners are Schallermair and Schmidt."[53] The role they played in the deaths of thousands in German concentration camps, including Buchenwald and Dachau, sealed their fate. "Large numbers of inmates died as a result of beatings which (Schallermair) personally administered. He visited the morgue daily with an inmate dentist to extract gold teeth from the dead bodies from the camp."[54] Schmidt had been Adjutant of the Buchenwald Concentration camp at a time when an estimated 5,000 prisoners were killed each month.[55]

However, Joachim Peiper, the commander of the SS troops who massacred American soldiers at Malmedy, was granted clemency. General Handy found Peiper and ten others had acted during "a confused, fluid and desperate combat action," thus distinguishing their crimes from "the more deliberate killings in concentration camps. On that basis Handy commuted their sentences to life in prison."[56]

Senator Hunt disagreed "thoroughly and completely" with General Handy and took to the floor of the Senate to denounce Handy's decision. "In essence," Hunt exclaimed, "we have laid the ground work for the repudiation of the theory of punishment for war crimes."[57]

52 Originally 43 defendants had received death sentences but most had been commuted at earlier stages of the review process.

53 Statement "Released in Heidelberg-Today-Wednesday-5:00 a.m.-31Jan51" announcing the "Final action in the cases of 13 war criminals under his jurisdiction who are now held in Landsberg Prison under death sentence." Thomas Handy, US Army General, Commander-in-Chief, European Command, Decision, 3, File: "Malmedy" Box 8, LCH Papers

54 Id. 3

55 Id. 4

56 Id. 6

57 Congressional Record, February 26, 1951, 1580

The Malmedy investigation occupied the new Wyoming Senator during much of the initial year of his term. It provided a crash course on senate rules and procedures, introducing him to the process by which that body exercises oversight. More significantly, Malmedy was also Lester Hunt's introduction to Joe McCarthy. There is little doubt this was the genesis of Lester Hunt's disdain for McCarthy and his tactics. There are people like Lester C. Hunt for whom people like Joe McCarthy are unfathomable. In Wyoming, Hunt had not encountered people like McCarthy, people willing to say anything to get attention even as they denigrated the very democratic institution that gave them a platform. McCarthy exhibited a lack of personal integrity that was foreign to the way in which Lester Hunt lived his life and viewed his responsibility as a United States Senator.

Photo-Lander ca. 1910. Lander in 1910 shorty before Lester Hunt arrived to pitch for the town's professional baseball team. Photo Courtesy of Fremont County Pioneer Museum

Photos Courtesy of Fremont County Pioneer Museum

Hunt Family (L to R: Father William Hunt, Lester, Nila, Clyde, Mother Viola) Courtesy Lester C. Hunt, Jr.

Thanksgiving Day dinner at Governor's Mansion (date unknown) L to R: Elise Hunt, Senator Joseph C. O'Mahoney, Nathelle Hunt, Johanna Scribner (Mansion cook), Lester Hunt, Jr., Maude Higby (Nathelle's mother), and Governor Hunt. Courtesy Lester C. Hunt, Jr.

(above left) Nathelle and Senator-elect Hunt responding to letters of congratulation on Hunt's senate election-1948. Courtesy Charlotte Dehnert. (above right) Photo of Hunt courtesy of the Freemont County Pioneer Museum.

Secretary of State Lester Hunt joins **FDR** and Colorado Governor "Big Ed" Johnson on whistle stop campaign tour. Courtesy Lester C. Hunt, Jr.

(above)The members of the Special Committee of the US Senate to Investigate Crime in Interstate Commerce (L to R) Senators Charles W. Tobey (R-NewHampshire), Lester C. Hunt, Chairman Estes Kefauver (D-Tennessee), Alexander Wiley (R-Wisconsin), and Herbert O'Connor (D-Maryland).

(left) The members of the special committee of the US Senate investigating war crimes at Malmedy, Belgium meet in Berlin.

L to R: Senators Lester Hunt, Estes Kefauver (D-Tennessee) and Chairman Ray Baldwin (R-Connecticut)

Both photos courtesy of the American Heritage Center, University of Wyoming

Joe McCarthy and wife Jean (Left) with Styles Bridges and wife Doloris (Right). Photo Courtesy of the Division of Archives and Records Management. Concord, New Hampshire.

United States Senator Herman Welker (R-Idaho) Official Senate Photograph Courtesy of US Senate Historical Office, Washington, DC.

Nathelle Hunt.
Photo Courtesy of Fremont
County Pioneer Museum

Senator Hunt.
Photo courtesy of the U.S.
Senate Historical Office

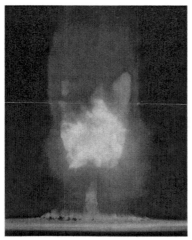

Senator Hunt, a member of the
Senate Armed Services Committee,
witnessed this explosion of an atomic
bomb at Eniwetok in May of 1951.
Later he described the experience.
"It gave me the peculiar feeling that I
was standing at the gates of Hell."

Photo courtesy of the American
Heritage Center, University of
Wyoming (Papers of Lester C. Hunt,
Box 26, Folder 819)

CHAPTER NINE

Senator Lester C. Hunt

The United States Senate has always been a rather odd democratic institution. Never intended to be representative of the people, it lends itself more readily to representing regional and special interests. The allocation of power between the two houses of Congress was a contentious matter at the Constitutional convention in Philadelphia. A compromise resulted in the purposeful distinctions between the House of Representatives and the Senate. Alexander Hamilton found significant advantage in designating "dissimilar modes of constituting the several component parts of the government." The U.S. Constitution, therefore, provided that members of the House would be selected by the voters of a given state, senators by the legislature of the state and the President by members of the Electoral College.[1]

The qualifications were made different by design. Senators are required to be older and to be citizens for a longer period of time. Representatives can serve if but twenty five years old with no less than seven years of citizenship while Senators must be at least 30 years of age and citizens for nine or more years. "The propriety of these distinctions is explained," wrote James Madison, "by the nature of the senatorial trust, which, requiring greater extent of information and reliability of character, requires at the same time that the senator should

---

1 *The Federalist Papers* No. 60

have reached a period of life most likely to supply these advantages.[2]

Of the requirements initially imposed, it was the selection of senators by state legislatures that was found objectionable most quickly. By the early nineteenth century, populists were clamoring for the popular election of members of the Senate. Nearly a century later in 1913, the Seventeenth Amendment to the Constitution was ratified. Since then senators have, like Representatives, been elected by a direct vote of the people.

The citizenship requirements never attracted much concern especially as the nation grew older. Another distinction that has remained since 1789 is that while the members of the House of Representatives are there to represent people, senators represent sovereign states. House membership is apportioned by population, on the basis of "one person, one vote." Wyoming never had a great enough population to justify even one member of the House, though all states are assured of that minimum representation. However, each state is entitled to two senators regardless of population. Thus, Wyoming has always been significantly over-represented in the United States Senate. When Lester Hunt became a senator, New York had nearly ten percent of the U.S. population. Wyoming had less than two-tenths of one percent, but enjoyed the same number of senators as New York.

The disproportionate power afforded Wyoming was further enhanced by the presence of a senior senator who had served since 1934. During a time when seniority was a chief determinant of Senate power, Joseph C. O'Mahoney ranked 14 among the 96 members. O'Mahoney served until 1953 and again from 1955-1961 when a stroke made it impossible for him to seek yet another term.

"Here It Takes Forever And A Day To Accomplish Anything"
Lester Hunt entered the Senate 91st on the seniority list, ahead of other

2 *The Federalist Papers* No. 62

freshmen as a result of having been a governor. The newcomer devoted himself to his new job every bit as much as he had to all the others he worked since his days on the Pennsylvania Railroad in East St. Louis. His office commonly answered nearly 15,000 letters and more than 25,000 phone calls a year from constituents.[3] While the most intense work in the Senate is done in committees, no senator served on more of them than Senator Hunt. Though a freshman, he was appointed to five major committees: Armed Services, District of Columbia, Interstate and Foreign Commerce, Crime Investigation, and Small Business. He chaired three of the nine subcommittees on which he served.

It wasn't only the quantity of Hunt's work that impressed colleagues. He had only been among them for a month when Senator John Stennis told him, "I am mightily well pleased with your attitude toward your responsibilities here and believe you will make rapid strides as a member of the Senate."[4] Hunt was given key committee assignments and asked to shoulder additional responsibilities as his abilities became known. He was appointed to the committee to investigate the trial of German soldiers sentenced to death for the massacre of American troops during the Battle of the Bulge. Later he was chosen by the vice-president to serve on the senate committee investigating organized crime in the United States.

But he was quickly frustrated by the difference in how long it took a senator to get anything done as opposed to a governor. "The work is so different from my work in Cheyenne, where occasionally I could really get things done, in that here it takes forever and a day to accomplish anything," he confided in friend Monte Robertson less than three weeks after being sworn into the Senate. He regretted his decision to move from the governor's office to the Senate. "Leaving the Capitol

3 "Hunt's Office Receives 14,678 Letters in year" *Wyoming Eagle*, February 20, 1952
4 Letter to Hunt from Senator John Stennis, February 20, 1949, File: "Rules and Administration Committee" Box 31, LCH Papers

Building was not a pleasant move in any sense of the word, but I am hoping after I get more into the swing of things here in Washington that I will like it better, he wrote."[5]

The senator quickly developed a routine, arriving at his office each day "between 8:30 and 9:00." In a letter to a friend, he disclosed his daily routine. "There is always considerable mail to be read and answered, and, as a rule, one or two appointments with members of the various departments regarding matters in my state or of the nation. As I am a member of several different committees, I always have a committee meeting scheduled at 10:00 until noon. Then the Senate convenes at 12:00 and its sessions last from four to twelve hours. If there is any free time left in the afternoon, it is spent in answering correspondence, research on bills pending before congress, and gathering materials for speaking engagements."[6]

Supporters and detractors alike had reason to believe Hunt would be there as long as O'Mahoney, perhaps longer. The public service ethic he learned as a secretary of state and governor carried over easily into his work in Washington. While giving tireless attention to the needs of constituents, he also worked overtime on larger matters of national significance.

Lester Hunt carried with him to Washington his long-held concerns for children. In April of 1952, he made an unannounced visit to a District of Columbia facility caring for children. "This is terrible, he muttered, 'horrible."[7] The facility had bare walls with plaster falling, and shabby furniture including discarded school desks and limited fire escape avenues. One facility for "colored girls" had no running water.

5 Letter from Hunt to Monte Robertson, January 27, 1949, File: "Miscellaneous REF-RY" Box 31, LCH Papers
6 Letter from Hunt to Miss Gail Galanis, December 19, 1951, File: "Hunt Personal 1951" Box 19, LCH Papers
7 "Hunt Wants Members of Congress to See for Themselves How DC Cares for Children" *Washington Post,* April 6, 1952, A-3

"I never heard of such a thing," Hunt challenged the D.C. Welfare director Gerald Shea. The former Wyoming governor proudly provided the *Washington Post* with a recent photograph of the similar facility in Wyoming, the Wyoming Girl's School at Sheridan. The comparison was stark. The photo of the Wyoming facility showed new furniture, carpeted recreation rooms, nicely furnished bedrooms and smiling young women.[8] Hunt was proud of the Girls School back home but outraged at the conditions he witnessed in Washington.

Senator Hunt pointed the finger at Congress, charging, "The men who pass on these institutions have never taken enough interest to take a look them over. Maybe that's why they are so neglected." He received a letter from a Washington children's advocate, Mrs. Leila M. Asinof. "God, and God alone must have guided your footsteps in paying a visit to the Loughboro Home, or Industrial Home School Annex, so-called government owned building, and you will most probably agree with the writer that in this day and age, human beings, mostly helpless waifs, who through no fault of their own in this Capitol City of our great government, have been herded together in filth, disease infested, ill-kept and ill-smelling quarters and subjected to memories of life that will remain with them forever," she wrote.

Hunt championed the cause before the Senate Appropriations Committee and after hearing from him, a powerful senator was persuaded. Lister Hill of Alabama, chair of the Committee on Labor and Public Welfare who was also the ranking Democrat on the Appropriations Committee made sure Hunt got what he wanted for the children. After listening to the first witness describe the substandard condition about which he had already heard from his Wyoming colleague, Hill told the second witness, "I don't think anyone need worry about that $86,000. Just say you're for it."[9]

8 Id.
9 Undated clipping, *Washington Star*, FILE: "District of Columbia-Reports and hearings"

Occasionally Hunt was sidetracked by the moral ethic instilled by his parents in the early days back in Atlanta, Illinois. Senator Hunt was incensed when a new fad dubbed "panty raids" sprang up on college campuses across the country.[10] He denounced the young men who participated, suggesting they should be drafted and given jobs defending America. Hunt's "panty-raid" statement brought dozens of favorable letters from soldiers in Korea. "If these collegians want to fight so much, let them come over here to Korea and fight for something worth fighting for. Signed-"The Boys on the USS Haven" May 30, 1952." Another soldier asked, "Why in hell are not these hoodlums and possibly marijuana addicts not drafted and sent to Korea. They can fight Stalin's criminal stooges there and leave American girls alone."[11]

He never relinquished claim to being a prohibitionist. A member of the Senate committee overseeing the government of the District of Columbia, Hunt was indignant when the city council allowed metropolitan Washington bars to remain open an additional two hours on New Year's Eve 1951. Hunt took a nominee for D.C. commissioner to task for his role during a confirmation hearing.

Senator Hunt: "Mr. Donohue (Nominee for Commissioner of the D of C), I believe it was the Commissioners (who) granted the plea of the liquor dealers to allow them to stay open two hours – I don't know whether it was to allow them to start drinking two hours earlier –

Mr. Donohue: After twelve o'clock.

Senator Hunt: — or to stay drunk two hours longer. But I think it

Box 14, LCH Papers

10 "The panty raids of the 1950s were one of the first major crazes to surface after the end of World War II. Functioning as humorous activities, groups of males raided all-female college residences (dormitories) to secure panties or other intimate apparel as "trophies", proof that the guys had momentarily crossed a societal barrier and occupied the forbidden territory of a co-ed's dorm room. The panty-raid craze ran from the 1950s through the 1960s." for history of "panty raids, see www.mortaljourney.com/2011/01/1950-trends/panty-raids

11 Letter to Hunt from V.V. Solte of Long Beach, CA, June 2, 1952, File: "S. J. Res 256-Code of Fair Committee Procedure" Box 11, LCH Papers

was a terrible thing to do."[12]

It didn't happen again while Lester Hunt was in the Senate.

An Eisenhower Democrat

Hunt described himself as "a political middle-of-the roader with liberal leanings." An avid New Dealer, he didn't object to being called an "Eisenhower Democrat." A month after Ike's 1952 victory, Hunt was interviewed on a nationally broadcast news program, CBS Radio's "Capitol Classroom." The Senator said, "My people in Wyoming gave General Eisenhower a thirty-three thousand (vote) majority, unheard of in my state. I feel I have an obligation to support whatever he himself suggests."[13] He gave the same advice to the Democrats who had elected him back in Wyoming. "Our party," he told a Jefferson-Jackson Day crowd in Cheyenne "should keep on working positively and constructively for the good of the country. What is best for our country should ebb our guide and our ambition. It is not WHO is right but WHAT is right."[14]

Hunt pointedly refused to accept a coveted appointment to the Democratic Steering Committee.[15] Serving on this committee would have required him to take decidedly partisan positions. He declined the prestigious position saying he "wished to remain free from any partisan obligations so that he might act independently with reference to

12 Transcript of Hearing of the Senate Committee on the District of Columbia, March 2, 1951, Volume 3, Page 213 (Request for NY Eve 1951), File: "District of Columbia 1952-1953-1954" Box 13, LCH Papers

13 Transcript of radio program, File: "Capitol Classroom-CBS Radio-12/5/52" Box 10, LCH Papers

14 Speech, File: "Jefferson-Jackson Day Speech-Wyoming-March 1953" Box 35, LCH Papers

15 "In the sixty five years since the Democratic Policy and Communications Committee (DPCC) (formerly known as the Democratic Policy Committee (DPC)) was established in January 1947, it has served as an advisory board to the Democratic Leadership and as a research, policy-formulating, and communications arm of Senate Democrats. While the DPCC's role has evolved through the years, the thread that unifies its long history is the key role it has played in facilitating communication among Senate Democrats and enhancing their ability to formulate and advance their agenda." (www.dpcc.senate.gov)

all matters coming before the Senate" and support Eisenhower as often as his "conscience" would allow.[16]

Even as a freshman from a small, rural state, Hunt was more fully involved in issues of national interest than one might expect. In the few years he served in the Senate, Lester Hunt was in the eye of several of the most difficult storms of the day. He was a major contributor to the early 50s debates over civil rights, health care reform, organized crime, foreign policy, Communism and what to do about Joe McCarthy.

Civil Rights

The "state's rights" battle cry became little more than code for the defense of segregation in the 1950s and '60s, particularly valued by southern governors and senators. Lester Hunt arrived in Washington at a time when powerful southern politicians dominated the United States Senate. The 22 senators who formed the "Southern Caucus" wielded influence far beyond their numbers. A combination of their abilities, seniority and unity created a virtually impregnable front.[17] Fresh from their walkout at the 1948 Democratic National Convention and the poor showing of Strom Thurmond, the Dixiecrat candidate for President, these Southerners were aching for the fight Truman started.

They were, from the days of the Civil War, state's rights protectors. The "state's rights" they were there to defend, however, differed in kind from those Hunt was there to protect. Yet they found common ground on one of the most significant issues of the time, the extension of civil rights to black Americans.

Judging politicians on social issues and the positions they either took or failed to take in an era far different from the one in which we

16 News Release from Hunt's office, January 6, 1953, File "News Releases" File Folder #802, Box 26, LCH Papers

17 For a compelling history of the Southern dominance of the U.S. Senate, see Robert A. Caro, *The Years of Lyndon Johnson-Master of the Senate*, Vintage Books (2003), 89-97

live and at a time when we have experienced the longer experience of history to which they were not afforded, can be tricky. An analysis seemingly fair on its face becomes problematic in the shadows cast by decades of reform.

In large measure, the differences between Truman and Hunt on civil rights may be attributed to the jobs they came to hold and the responsibilities accompanying them. The view of America is so different from the Oval Office of the White House than one gets from a seat on the floor of the United States Senate. Truman's civil rights proposals seem to reflect views sandwiched between the time he spent as a Missouri politician and his days as a former President. As a Missourian, Harry Truman had struggled with the question in his early political career. His family tree was filled with "slaveholders and supporters of the Confederacy, and his mother denounced Abraham Lincoln throughout her long life."[18] When Truman biographer Merle Miller asked him about the "extreme Southern sympathies of most of the members of your family and most of the people you grew up with," the former President sidestepped the question. Instead he went directly to the position he took in his 1948 campaign, a position that nearly cost him the election because of the way in which it split the Democratic Party.[19] As President, Truman integrated the armed services and proposed the most sweeping civil rights legislation of his era. Yet his sister Mary Jane was quick to let history know that her brother's personal views may not have been so consistent with his public policies. She told another Truman biographer, Jonathan Daniels, "Harry is no more for nigger equality than any of us."[20]

18 *To Secure These Rights*: Report of Harry S. Truman's Committee on Civil Rights" Edited by Steven F. Lawson, Bedford/St. Martins Press (2004), 10

19 Merle Miller, *Plain Speaking: An Oral Biography of Harry S. Truman,* Berkley Publishing Company (1973), 79-80

20 McCullough, *Truman,* 588, citing a Jonathan Daniels interview with Mary Jane Truman, October 2, 1949

After leaving the White House, the former President was so disdainful of the civil rights movement and its leaders that he agreed with J. Edgar Hoover that many were Communists.[21] In 1960, John Kennedy feared a late attack by the former President because of JFK's support for civil rights. He asked Truman's friend Dean Acheson to use his influence to quiet his former boss. Acheson reminded Truman that, "Your views as reported, are wholly out of keeping with your public record."[22]

There is little question of the courageous work Harry Truman did as President of the United States to advance the cause of equal rights. When the war ended, millions of veterans returned. They were celebrated for winning the war for freedom. Among them were thousands of black men and women whose hopes for their own freedom had been raised by the outcome of the war. They had helped change the world but their world had not changed. They returned to the same old segregationist attitudes they had left when they marched off to war. When veteran Isaac Woodard took a Greyhound Bus from his Army base in Georgia to his home in New York, he was wearing his uniform when the bus driver complained about his entering a washroom to clean himself up before arriving home. The police were summoned. They beat him severely, leaving him blinded from blows to his face with their nightsticks.[23]

Other similar incidents outraged President Truman. The President sought to champion the cause of civil rights but he understood the odds of getting legislation through the Southern-dominated Congress. Instead, on December 5, 1946, he issued an Executive Order creating the President's Committee on Civil Rights. Reminding Americans of FDR's famous words, Truman said, "Today, freedom from fear, and the democratic institutions which sustain it, is again under attack."

21 McCullough, *Truman*, supra, *971*
22 Id. at page 971-973, citing an Acheson letter to Harry S. Truman, June 27, 1960
23 *To Secure These Rights*, Supra. 8

Showing a stroke of political brilliance, Truman tied civil rights to the struggle against Fascism and resurrected the spirit of the late President in support of the endeavor.

After numerous hearings around the country, the Committee issued its report on October 29, 1947, a year before Lester Hunt was elected to the U.S. Senate. Opening with a restatement of the rights guaranteed all Americans in the Declaration of Independence and the Bill of Rights, the report set forth those "rights essential to the well being of the individual and to the progress of society." They are: one, "the rights to the safety and security of the person;" two, "the right to citizenship and its privileges;" three, "the right to freedom of conscience and expression;" and, four, "the right to equality of opportunity."[24] The drafters acknowledged there had been progress but then cited police brutality, lynchings, discrimination in housing, education and employment, unequal administration of justice and citizenship and the internment of Japanese-Americans as road posts showing how far the nation had to go.

The Committee anticipated the "states' rights" argument, rejecting the notion that state and local governments could solve the problem. The evidence proved, they said, that local officials perpetrated the most egregious wrongs.[25] The Committee argued this problem was urgent and the nation "cannot afford to delay action until the most backward community has learned to prize civil liberty."[26] They believed basic civil rights arose largely from federal law. The federal government should, therefore, take the lead.

The report contained 34 specific recommendations. One historian described the response, writing, "the report pushed moderates to the sidelines and propelled reactionaries to the forefront."[27] Lester Hunt

24 Id. 52-53
25 Id. 126-127
26 Id. 29
27 Id. 33, Steven F. Lawson

had one foot in each camp. He was one of the moderates on civil rights but one of the reactionaries on protecting states' rights. As Southern senators arrived in Washington in January of 1949 intent on protecting the rights of their states, so it was for Lester Hunt. The Southerners were in the midst of the civil rights battle. Hunt, as a governor, had just come off of his own fight with the federal government over the Grand Teton National Monument. Each was convinced the national government had become far too involved in state matters. Governor Hunt used harsh words about FDR's attempt to create the monument. He testified to a congressional committee. "I should like the committee to know that as chief-executive of the state of Wyoming, duly elected by the vote of a majority of the people of this state, and speaking for them as well as myself, I resent the secret, un-American, dictatorial methods used and the contempt for the duly elected state officials of Wyoming manifest in this action." Of FDR.'s Executive Order, Hunt said, "this action on the part of the federal government is a bold, un-American, and undemocratic invasion of state's rights."[28] The Southern senators believed the same about Truman's strategy. After all, Truman had created the Civil Rights Commission by an Executive order, just as Franklin Roosevelt had created the Jackson Hole National Monument.

In his first few months in the Senate, the former Wyoming governor was faced with a dilemma. He had campaigned convincingly telling Wyoming audiences that the state would benefit if it had two senators who voted alike. Now a key vote would require him to choose between going along with Joseph O'Mahoney in supporting a President of his own party or joining others who claimed the mantle of states' rights protectors.

One of the rails of power to which the Senate has clung is the rule allowing few restrictions on the length of a debate. In the beginning of the Republic, unlimited debate was not permitted in the Senate.

28 *Wyoming Eagle,* March 20, 1943, File "Jackson Hole Monument, Box 2, LCH Papers

All matters could be brought to a vote on a motion for "the previous question." A simple majority could demand the debate end and a final vote. That changed when the Senate rules were modified in 1806, and the "previous question" rule was omitted. From then until 1917, there were no rules to cut off an endless debate.[29] Together with unequal representation, unlimited debate was another way in which the Senate held itself up as the last refuge against hasty legislative decisions.

Eventually restrictions were placed on the filibuster. Senate Rule 22 was adopted in 1917. It provided for "cloture." Cloture became the process for bringing a debate to an end so that a vote could be held. Cloture was allowed if two-thirds of the Senate agreed, a high hurdle in a legislative body where each state had the same number of lawmakers. In 1949, it remained the parliamentary weapon of choice among Southern senators intent on blocking any civil rights legislation.

Unlimited debate posed threats beyond the pending civil rights matter. The leader of the Southern caucus, Richard Russell of Georgia, developed a long list of important laws due to expire in 1949, including the rent control statute Truman had struggled so hard to attain earlier. Without a vote, rents would skyrocket on March 31. Russell made clear that if the President wanted to debate cloture reform, the remainder of his legislative program would be delayed until after an extended debate on that one issue.[30]

Richard Russell had been in the United States Senate since the day Lester Hunt was sworn into the Wyoming Legislature in 1933. He knew the rules and their nuances. Russell knew how to use the rules to get things done or to stop things from getting done. Lester Hunt had been a senator for less than three months when this monumental fight

29 "Statement of Senator Claude Pepper Before the Senate Committee on Rules and Administration on Amending the Senate Rules on Cloture" January 24, 1949, File: Rules and Administration Committee, Box 31, LCH Papers
30 Robert A. Caro, *Lyndon Johnson-Master of the Senate,* Vintage Books (2002), 215-218

reached its dramatic climax. His votes on the Truman civil rights proposal and the vitally relevant cloture issues reflect the unsteadiness of
a newcomer. The freshman senator voted with the administration and
his liberal friends on the Rule 22 cloture matter but with the Dixiecrats
and southern Republicans on the question of allowing the civil rights
bill out of committee. The whirlwind created by manipulating complex
Senate rules in the face of a storm over the most significant, controversial, and complex policy proposals presented difficulties for veterans much less a freshman still learning the ropes. The entire affair
exposed both Russell's astute deviousness and Hunt's learning curve.

Wyoming constituents made it no easier. Senator Hunt received a
telegram from Reverend Charles A. Nowlen of Casper's First Methodist
Church expressing unhappiness with him for joining the southern
coalition on the cloture matter. Hunt called "mistaken" the notion
he had joined the "GOP-Dixie coalition. He said he supported the
Truman administration's position writing, "This appears on the face
as though I have switched my attitude, but nothing is further from
the truth, because my stand on Civil Rights is, and has been, with the
Administration."[31]

Hunt did vote with the administration on a parliamentary ruling
made by vice president Alben Barkley. He also voted with Mississippi
Senator John Stennis and Louisiana Senator Russell Long against reporting the Truman civil right legislation out of the Committee on
Rules and Administration.[32] He firmly believed reporting the bill to
the floor for debate would only result in a promised filibuster, which he
feared would keep the Senate from other important work.[33]

Hunt also had personal and political reservations about what
Truman sought to accomplish. While he was outraged about how

31 Letter from Hunt to Reverend Charles Knowlen, March 16, 1949, File: "Civil Right" Box
11, LCH Papers
32 Letter from Hunt to George Scales of Sheridan, March 7, 1949, Id.
33 Letter from Hunt to Katherine R. Hammond, March 14, 1949, Id.

blacks were treated in the South, he was reluctant to interfere with the rights of those states to address their own problems. Hunt told Manville Kendrick, the son of former Wyoming Senator John Kendrick, "While I do not at all approve of some of the things that happen in the South, nevertheless I think that is their business and that we of the North should not attempt to tell them how to run their state governments."[34]

Kendrick expressed an opinion Hunt was hearing from many of his constituents. It was enough for him that, "the numbers of lynchings are steadily decreasing." That, he said, was a sure sign of progress. "The program of racial equality which is putting tremendous pressure on every individual in the Nation, is basically unsound and unwise. The premise that I must accept a negro (sic) as my personal friend and social companion is very dangerous. It leads straight to miscegenation," Kendrick told Hunt. Kendrick claimed civil rights were a threat to freedom being "urged upon us by every agency, (including the Communists and Federal Government)."[35]

Urged by Kendrick to "join with the Senators from the South to stop this thing as it should be stopped now," Hunt replied, "Frankly I am of the opinion that this Civil Rights business is a come-on for votes and since it is not an issue in the state of Wyoming I do, at this writing at least, expect to go along with the southern boys as I previously did on the cloture matter." Hunt went further, complaining about Truman's decision to integrate the armed forces. He was unhappy with the Army's plan "to intermingle in sleeping quarters, at the mess, in drill and every other way, white and colored men." He said the secretary had met with the Armed Services Committee and now "may not go through with any plan to end segregation in the Army."[36]

Lester Hunt received an abrupt and rude welcome to the hardball

34 Letter from Hunt to Manville Kendrick, February 17, 1949, Id.
35 Letter to Hunt from Manville Kendrick, March 5, 1949, Id.
36 Letter from George Scales July 30, 1949, and Hunt's reply, August 8, 1949, File: "Civil Rights" Box 11, LCH Papers

politics of the Senate. He hoped the controversy would go away, telling a friend he thought the civil rights problem faced by the nation would "work itself out in time."[37] But without federal legislation, the problem could not "work itself out in time." Southern filibusters denied the nation civil rights laws until 1965 when the Senate at last invoked cloture after a 57-day debate. (In 1975, the hurdle for limiting debate was reduced from two-thirds to three-fifths.)

The entire unpleasant matter left Lester Hunt uncertain he'd made the right decision to leave the governorship for the Senate. In the midst of the firestorm, he confided to Senator Kendrick's son, who would have understood, "Can't say that I am liking the work in Washington nearly so well as I did the work in the Governor's office."[38]

Healthcare Reform

Harry Truman saw health care as a national security issue. Having just witnessed the nation desperately try to raise an army to fight the Second World War, Truman believed preparedness demanded the United States do something to improve and protect the health of its citizens. The Selective Service system exposed widespread deficits in the physical and mental health of significant numbers of military age men and women.

The U.S. was one of the last remaining nations without some form of national health insurance. The history of compulsory insurance traced back to Germany who adopted it in 1883. Austria followed in1888 and Hungary in1891. By the early 1900s national health insurance had expanded to Great Britain, Russia, Switzerland and later to Japan, Portugal, France, and Italy. By the 1940, 27 nations including most of Europe, South America, Central America and the Soviet Union had adopted some form of national health insurance.[39] The United

37 Letter from Hunt to D.D. Reed, February 15, 1949, Id
38 Letter from Hunt to Manville Kendrick, February 17, 1949, Id.
39 Library of Congress "National Health Insurance and Medical Plans" William H. Gilbert, General Research Section, February 4, 1949, File: "S.5-National Health Insurance Program

States was a glaring exception.

Truman was convinced the lack of an American program was more than a simple health care financing problem. Not long after assuming the presidency in the wake of Roosevelt's death, the President highlighted the problem for Congress. More than 5,000,000 men between the ages of 18 and 37 years called to serve in World War II had been found unfit to serve. The defects were both physical and mental. The rejection rate rose as the ages of potential inductees increased. Almost half of those between 34 and 37 were declared unfit for military service.[40]

The President added, "In addition, after actual induction, about a million and a half men had to be discharged from the Army and Navy for physical or mental disability, exclusive of wounds; and an equal number had to be treated in the Armed Forces for diseases or defects which existed before induction." It wasn't just men. More than a third of women volunteering to serve were rejected for the same reasons. Worse yet, a far higher number of Americans suffered from poor health and were never examined by Selective Service doctors.

Truman was personally acquainted with this problem. He once tried to recruit a full regiment of Field Artillery personnel to fight in World War I. "I was appalled at the large number of young men who were unfit for service," Truman said. "When a man was rejected for a physical disability it was tragic for him and for those of us in the outfit. That made me pause and think."[41] Now he had his hands on the levers of power and an opportunity to convert his concerns into public policy.

Truman spelled out the problem. It started with an unequal distribution of doctors and other medical resources. The President quanti-

Material" Box 25, LCH Papers

40 "Special Message to the Congress Recommending a Comprehensive Health Program, November 19, 1945, Harry S. Truman Library and Museum, http://www.trumanlibrary. org/publicpapers

41 David Blumenthal and James A. Morone, *The Heart of Power-Health and Politics in the Oval Office,* University of California Press (2009), 65-66

fied the challenge, saying, "About 1,200 counties, 40 percent of the total in the country, with some 15,000,000 people, have either no local hospital, or none that meets even the minimum standards of national professional associations." Likewise, he said, Congress needed to address the lack of good medical services for mothers and children, the failure of local infrastructure and the imperative to provide safe water systems, sewage disposal plants and sanitary facilities. He added the urgency of funding research to address cancer as well as mental health.

The final two issues Truman raised were related to costs. One was the financial loss attributed to illness resulting in job loss. The other problem was that many Americans did not have access to health care because they simply could not afford it. "The principal reason why people do not receive the care they need is that they cannot afford to pay for it on an individual basis at the time they need it. This is true not only for needy persons. It is also true for a large proportion of normally self-supporting persons."

These thoughts had been formulated under President Roosevelt who died before they were developed into complete proposals. That left it to Harry Truman to deliver the first Presidential message devoted entirely to American health care.[42] The most controversial provision, one that might well have gone down better if proposed by the popular Roosevelt, was a taxpayer-funded assurance that all Americans would have health care irrespective of their ability to pay. Health insurance, he said, should be compulsory and funded through payroll tax deductions.

The accidental President was already overwhelmed with crises. Labor strikes, demobilization issues, resignations of key New Deal holdovers, growing problems with Russia and China and a general sense among an increasing number of the press corps that he was not up to

---

42 Monte M. Poen, *Harry S. Truman Versus the Medical Lobby*, University of Missouri Press (1979), 64

the job, left Truman with far more to worry about than health care reform. Accordingly, his proposal, although reaffirmed in his 1947 State of the Union message, languished throughout the term he completed for FDR. It began to re-gather steam as a part of Truman's attacks on a "do-nothing" Congress in his come-from-behind victory over Thomas Dewey in 1948. As he barnstormed America en route to his upset win over Dewey, Truman heard loud and clear from average Americans. They wanted something done about health care.

Truman was better prepared in 1949 for what he knew was coming. In his 1945 message to Congress, he anticipated the main attack opponents would make. He began with a rationale for his idea. "Everyone should have ready access to all necessary medical, hospital and related services. I recommend solving the basic problem by distributing the costs through expansion of our existing compulsory social insurance system," he told Congress.

The President quickly, knowingly, and defensively added, "This is not socialized medicine."[43] The American Medical Association didn't agree. Within a few days its public relations team made it clear how this battle would be fought. "Obviously this is the beginning of the final showdown on collectivism," read the AMA's initial alert to member doctors. "Not one day dare be lost. Do not underestimate the crisis. Fight for personal freedom and professional independence."[44]

Watching from the governor's office in Cheyenne was Lester Hunt, who would find himself deeply involved four years later as a United States Senator. Before he arrived in Washington, the political environment became more enflamed by the fear of Communism. The House Un-American Activities Committee was becoming the biggest story of the era as it searched for Communists in and out of government. "In

---

43 "Special Message to the Congress Recommending a Comprehensive Health Program, November 19, 1945, Supra.

44 Blumenthal, *Supra.* 72, citing George Coleman, *Emergency Bulletin, National Physicians Committee for the Extension of Medical Service*, November 23, 1945

this context, health reformers made irresistible target. Opponents had long scorned national health insurance as 'socialized medicine.' Now the familiar critique turned treacherous."[45]

Wyoming's new senator was in office for barely three months when Truman submitted his 1949 health care message to Congress. Between his election in November of 1948 and being sworn into office the following January, Hunt tied his own hands, committing himself to opposing any health care proposal "that is not approved by the state medical and state dental associations."[46] The senator-elect acknowledged too many Wyoming people were unable to afford basic medical care and believed it wasn't enough for the medical community to simply oppose reforms. "I think I can say to you that such opposition will not be successful for any great length of time in the future, and unless our professions straighten this matter out we can expect others to do it for us, Hunt said."

Many of his constituents made it clear they were opposed to Truman's legislation. Hunt's mail ran ten to one against the proposal. The Torrington Lion's Club sent a telegram. "Any program of a compulsory, not voluntary, nature violates the Constitutional rights of our citizens."[47] A Presbyterian minister from Sheridan wrote opposing Truman's plan. "When freedom is falling all over the world, why should we as a nation see how close we can walk to the abyss of totalitarianism without going over the precipice. "[48] Some called the bill "un-American." One wrote, "Looks like we Americans are getting so soft and incompetent we even need Washington to tell us when we need a bath."[49]

45 Id. 80

46 Letter from Hunt to Dr. J.E. Carr of Sheridan, December 3, 1948, File: "National Health Care Correspondence" Box 25, LCH Papers

47 Letter to Hunt from Uno J. Korhonen, Secretary-Treasurer, Torrington Lion's Club, January 26, 1949, File: "National Health care Correspondence" Box 25, LCH Papers

48 Letter to Hunt, February 2, 1949, Id.

49 Postcard to Hunt from D.P. Wilson, Casper, May 15, 1949, Id.

When Dr. C.M. Stebner of Laramie was removed from the Veteran's Administration's list of acceptable dentists, he called it an example of what happens when "petty politicians disagree with a professional man's diagnosis." Stebner said his disqualification was an example of the kind of "political medicine" Truman's bill would impose.[50]

Senator Hunt's papers include files in excess of six inches in thickness evidencing his constituents' opposition to health care reform. There are letters, telegrams, postcards, and petitions from individuals and organizations including multiple Lion's Clubs, chapters of the Daughters of the American Revolution, V.F.W. Posts, Chambers of Commerce, and several local Business and Professional Women organizations, among others.

There were, of course, some who felt differently. A disabled piano tuner from Sheridan told his new senator that even though he was blind, he could get no help paying for necessary dental work. He wrote Hunt saying, "The era of the 'country doctor' is past and the modern doctor should not be allowed to hinder the march of progress because of selfish and personal aims in his profession."[51]

Hunt quickly became weary of the way some of his colleagues blithely tossed around the term "socialism" to stir opposition to any number of ideas. When a constituent told Hunt he was growing more concerned about how the country was moving toward socialism, the Senator objected. Hunt replied to a Laramie constituent who expressed concern about "the recent trend towards socialism," listing government programs "referred to on the Senate floor by Republican Senators as socialistic, communistic or both":

Jefferson's public school system
Women's Suffrage
Income tax

50 Letter from Dr. C.M. Stebner to Hunt, April 19, 1949, Id.
51 Letter to Hunt from Jack L. Shields, December 21, 1948, Id.

Interstate Commerce Commission
Eight hour (work) day
Workman's Compensation
Pure Food and Drug Act
Federal Reserve Act
Minimum wage
Guarantee of bank deposits
Child labor law
Securities and Exchange Act
Federal Aid to highways
Rural Electrification Administration
Soil Conservation Service
Bankhead-Jones Farm Tenant Act

"In fact," wrote Hunt, "it seems to me every time the government attempts to help the great mass of our people, we hear the cry of 'socialism."[52] But Lester Hunt honestly thought Truman's proposal was "socialized medicine." An unhappy Cheyenne constituent asked him bluntly, "Have the doctors put the squeeze on you?" The Senator said he thought the Truman bill required people to give up their freedom to choose a doctor and was, therefore, socialism.[53] He told the president of the American Dental Association, "This socialized medicine has quite an appeal to Americans, for they think they will be getting something for nothing."[54]

Hunt was fully focused on what he considered the socialist design of compulsory health insurance. When Truman nominated Anna Rosenberg to be Assistant Secretary of Defense, she was confronted

52 Letter from Hunt to Ralph E. Conwell of Laramie, May 6, 1952, File: "CA-CI 1951" Box 10
53 Letter from Hunt to H.A. Waechter of Cheyenne, October 4, 1949, File "National Health-Correspondence" Box 25, LCH Papers
54 Letter from Hunt to Dr. Leo M. Shaney, March 18, 1949, File: "Socialized Medicine Broadcast" Box 34, LCH Papers

with charges she was once a member of the Communist Party. The Armed Forces Committee, of which Senator Hunt was a member, investigated. When Mrs. Rosenberg appeared for an interrogation, Senator Hunt had only one question for the embattled nominee. He wanted to make sure she would not use her position to advocate for "socialized medicine."

> *Senator Hunt:Mrs. Rosenberg, I wanted to ask you, in your present capacity you will have no contact or no authority or no reason to make suggestions with reference to socialized medicine; is that right?*
> *Mrs. Rosenberg:No, sir, I am against socialized medicine."*
> *Senator Hunt: That is the only question I have."*[55]

Although the tradition no longer exists, for decades there was a serious expectation that new members refrain from speaking on the floor for many months. Violators of the unwritten rule were shunned. In 1906, Robert La Follette was a freshman senator although he had a prior career of more than 20 years as Wisconsin's governor and as a member of the U.S. House of Representatives. After only a couple of months as a senator he rose to speak and nearly every other member got up and walked off the floor. La Follette's wife watched from the gallery. "There was no mistaking that this was a polite form of hazing."[56]

Lester Hunt was a senator for more than eight months before offering his "maiden speech." He chose the moment to address President Truman's health care proposal. Senator John McClellan of Arkansas introduced him. "Mr. President, I yield 25 minutes of my time to the distinguished Senator from Wyoming, Mr. Hunt. Let me say, I understand this is his first time to address the Senate. I know that on this very important issue, in which he is vitally interested, and in which all mem-

55 Hearings Before the Committee on Armed Services United States Senate Eighty-first Congress Second Session on the Nomination of Anna M. Rosenberg of New York, to be Assistant Secretary of Defense November 29,1950, "Testimony of Anna M. Rosenberg" 20
56 "1878-1920 Maiden Speeches" www.senate.gov

bers of his profession are interested, all of us will enjoy his remarks."[57]

Perhaps some enjoyed them more than others. He not only broke with Truman but also with his Wyoming colleague Joseph C. O'Mahoney. At issue was a plan to reorganize health and human services. Hunt and others were opposed largely because they feared the agenda of the man Truman planned to name as director of the new agency. Oscar Ewing was the controversial head of the Federal Security Administration. Hunt told his colleagues of the near-unanimous opposition of doctors, nurses, dentists, druggists and hospital administrators to Truman's proposal. He felt certain it would not improve health care and would result in greater costs. But his real concern was Ewing.

Ewing, Hunt argued, was an advocate for socialized medicine. The Wyoming lawmaker told his colleagues Ewing had refused to "relent his advocacy of a proposed compulsory health insurance program." Hunt feared that if Truman's reorganization plans were adopted, Ewing would become the secretary of the resulting agency and use it as a "source of propaganda" for socializing medicine in the United States.

Truman's plan was rejected overwhelmingly and Hunt was given credit back home for his independence. "When Senator Hunt went to Washington," editorialized the *Laramie Boomerang*, " there were some who predicted he would rubber stamp the Truman administration. Evidently he is a man with very definite ideas of his own."

In spite of the victory, Hunt remained concerned about the large numbers of Americans who could not afford medical care. Hunt was convinced that he and the other opponents could not keep a finger in the dike forever. On January 7, 1950, he wrote to Dr. Morris Botvin, chairman of the Public Relations Committee of the Rhode Island Medical Association. "Down through the years," Hunt said with characteristic humor, "we doctors have taken a position very much like the Arkansas hound dog sitting alongside the road with his snoot up in

57 Speech, *Congressional Record*, August 16, 1949, FILE: "National Health-Miscellaneous" File Folder #772, Box 25, LCH Papers

the air and howling. Two boys were coming down the road and one of them asked the other, 'What is the matter with that dog?' The second boy answered, 'He is sitting on a cocklebur and would rather howl than move.'[58]

Speaking to the 90th Session of the American Dental Association in San Francisco on October 18, 1949, Hunt urged them and the AMA to "present a forward-looking, constructive program for health services in the United States." He said they should not simply "denounce socialization."[59] The editor of the American Journal of Orthodontics, H.C. Pollock agreed with Hunt, writing of the Wyoming senator, "He has made a profound study of the subject both in Europe and America and has a constructive message for physicians, dentists, nurses, legislators, and the public. His message is packed with common sense and is markedly void of arm waving and fantastic ideas."[60]

When Dr. Matthew R. Beljan of Cleveland, a leading national opponent of the Truman bill, thanked him for his efforts, Hunt responded, arguing it was not enough to simply defeat the Truman bill. "Unless the professions begin to do something about the vast numbers of people who cannot afford or avail themselves of adequate dental or medical care," wrote Hunt, "some form of compulsory care will be forced on us to the detriment of both the professionals and the people." Dr. Bejan asked Hunt to take on the burden of drafting an acceptable bill.[61] He did so.

On January 30, 1950, Senator Hunt introduced the precursor of what came to be known as Medicaid. Hunt's proposal, the Voluntary

58 Letter from Hunt to Dr. Morris Botvin, File: "National Health-Correspondence" Folder #764, Box 25, LCH Papers
59 Speech, File: "Hunt-Personal-1950-1953" Box 19, LCH Papers
60 Editorial, *American Journal of Orthodontics*, November 30, 1949 File: "Hunt Personal 1949" Box 19, LCH Papers
61 Letter to Hunt from Dr. Matthew R. Beljan of Cleveland, May 5, 1949, File: "National Health-Correspondence" Box 28, LCH Papers

Health Insurance Act, a brief 35-page bill, provided that anyone with an income of less than $5000 per year would be eligible for national health insurance. It was estimated the plan would meet the medical needs of eight out of ten Americans.[62] The coverage included medical and dental services, home-nursing services, hospital, and auxiliary services including prescription drugs. Patients were given complete freedom to choose providers. Those covered would be required to pay a premium based on income with a $5 deductible for each service.[63]

Although the AMA supported it Dr. Joseph C. Bunten of Cheyenne, president of the Association of American Physicians and Surgeons, found Hunt's ideas no less "socialistic" than Truman's.[64] Hunt's bill did not pass. But the AMA later adopted the idea of covering health care costs for the poor as its own counterproposal to President Lyndon Johnson's health care legislation 14 years later.[65] Combining LBJ's legislative savvy and the soundness of Hunt's proposal, Medicaid emerged in 1965 as the way in which the health care needs of the poor are being met more than half a century later.

Investigating Organized Crime

Estes Kefauver and Lester Hunt must have seemed an odd couple sitting across from the likes of Lucky Luciano, Tony Gizzo, Frank Costello, the "Camel" Humphrey, and Johnson Bucklesjaw. The tall, lanky, outspoken Senator from Tennessee and his short, stocky, soft-spoken colleague from Wyoming traveled the country in 1950 and 1951. They went *mano a mano* with some of the most notorious mobsters of the time. This improbable pair brought down some of the biggest mobsters

62 "Hunt Offers Voluntary Health Plan To Cover 79% of Nation's Families" *Rocky Mountain News,* January 29, 1950, 21

63 *Congressional Record,* Speech delivered by Hunt to Senate on January 30, 1950, File: "S. 2940-Mr. Hunt intro-January 1950 to consolidate govt. health activities", Box 24, LCH Papers

64 "Denounces Sen. Hunt Bill" *Wyoming Eagle, March 9, 1950*

65 Blumenthal and Monroe, *The Heart of Power, supra.* 164

and exposed the pervasiveness of organized crime across the nation. Kefauver and Hunt became television celebrities, seen on the screen grilling dozens of mob bosses at the height of the Mafia's power. [66]

The hearings they held in Miami, Boston, New York, Biloxi, Kansas City, Chicago, Minneapolis, and elsewhere attracted crowds that waited for hours to enter hearing rooms that had to be searched beforehand and guarded by FBI agents during the proceedings. These were the first Congressional hearings to ever be televised live, earning ratings that drove soap operas off the screen when they were in town. The reactions were strong. Hunt and Kefauver received both public accolades and anonymous death threats. The relentless pursuit of the truth by these two senators resulted in arrests, imprisonment and deportation of high-ranking crime figures and the passage of new laws designed to prevent interstate crime. It wasn't only the crime bosses who were exposed. Kefauver and Hunt embarrassed mayors, commissioners, councilmen and law-enforcement authorities who had been on the take rather than minding the store.

In the process, the two became among the best known politicians in the nation. Kefauver and Hunt might well have been their party's 1952 presidential ticket but for the Democratic Party's doomed love affair with Adlai Stevenson. Organized crime was good business. Fighting it was also good politics and, as it turned out, great theater.

Perhaps it was simply an element of "The Age of Suspicion." Americans were suddenly more aware and much more concerned about crime than ever before. When Harry Truman initially responded to heightened interest in the issue, he seemed to think the newborn hysteria was little different from that raised by McCarthy's "Red Menace." He said the crime statistics causing national concern were little more

---

66 See William Howard Moore, *The Kefauver Committee and the Politics of Crime 1950-1952,* University of Missouri Press (1974) for an excellent history of the Kefauver Committee

than "the inevitable result of wartime dislocation."[67] The President believed the solution could be found in "the gentler forces" of church attendance and a focus on home life. The administration took the position that crime was a local problem. White House complacency evaporated abruptly when the body of a known gambler was found in Harry Truman's own backyard, in a Democratic Party clubhouse near Kansas City, slumped lifelessly under a photograph of Truman.[68] The crime issue suddenly had legs.

For reasons that may have had something to do with Kefauver's designs on a presidential campaign in 1952, the national interest in crime caught the attention of the Tennessee lawmaker. He introduced a resolution asking congress to investigate organized crime. The committee was launched in May of 1950. The job of appointing senators to serve on the high profile committee fell to the vice president of the United States, Alben Barkley. Senator Kefauver was naturally chosen to chair the committee his resolution had created. The easiest choice was the Republican members. Barkley named the ranking G.O.P. members of the relevant standing committees, Commerce and Judiciary. Thus, Charles W. Tobey of New Hampshire and Alexander Wiley of Wisconsin were added.

Although the list of Democrats Barkley considered included James Eastland of Mississippi and Lyndon Johnson of Texas, the vice-president settled on Herbert O'Connor of Maryland and, improbably, Lester Hunt of Wyoming. Hunt's appointment was improbable first because he was a freshman from a small, rural state with little of a crime problem. The appointment was even more improbable, maybe problematic, because he was not an attorney. Three of the five members were lawyers. Tobey had little formal education of any kind but as the ranking member of a committee, he was, nonetheless entitled.

67 William Howard Moore, *The Kefauver Committee*, supra, 43
68 "Kefauver Crime Committee Launched" www.senate.gov

Questioning crime bosses and analyzing related evidence was a skill
the dentist from Wyoming had never studied, as had his lawyer colleagues. Lester Hunt, on the other hand, earned his appointment by
developing an early reputation for diligent, hard work. Kefauver attributed Hunt's selection to his reputation for common sense and sound
decision-making.[69]

The first of 61 hearings in 14 cities opened in Miami on May 27,
1950, behind closed and heavily guarded doors. Before the gavel
dropped, FBI agents scoured the room for eavesdropping devices and
bombs. Witnesses could be seen entering and departing, arms loaded
with files and boxes of files.[70]

Kefauver and Hunt were the only two senators who made that first
foray. They spent two days listening to dramatic testimony pointing to
widespread, organized criminal activity, mostly gambling activities. It
was apparent this level of criminal activity could not exist without the
cover provided by corrupt officials. The committee uncovered and exposed illegal campaign contributions to local pols from gambling figures. When a reporter asked Hunt whether the money that exchanged
hands was simply legal campaign contributions, he replied, "What's
the difference whether you call it campaign contributions, bribes or
protection? The gamblers donated more to local campaigns than it
cost me to get elected to the United States Senate."[71]

Florida Governor Fuller Warren was angered with the negative attention focused on his state. He prepared his own report on crime.
Warren included a section on Wyoming, targeting Hunt. He leaked a
comment to the press indicating he had documentary evidence from
Cheyenne "that is so explosive it will rock the Democratic Party all the

69 Estes Kefauver, *Crime in America,* Doubleday (1951), 2
70 "Senators Open Crime Probe Here" *Miami Herald,* May 27, 1950, 1
71 "Crime Probers Report Gamblers Aided Local Candidates in Florida" *Washington Evening Star,* May 28, 1950

way back to the Senate office building."[72]

When made public, the Warren crime report offered little that Wyoming citizens didn't already know and nothing they cared deeply about. The so-called "explosive report" disclosed that gambling was "wide open" in Wyoming during the years Hunt had been governor, that slot machines were operating in Casper with craps tables, roulette wheels and blackjack at the Cowboy Bar in Jackson.[73] Wyomingites yawned and went back to watching the televised crime disclosures Hunt and Kefauver were turning up against people with colorful names operating in America's biggest cities.

In December, Kefauver dispatched Hunt to Tampa to conduct the hearing there alone. His assignment was to identify Mafia links to several unsolved murders.[74] When the Wyoming senator ended the hearings with a finding that the evidence linked Tampa to the national crime problems, the local establishment was furious.[75] The Tampa Bar Association and the Chamber of Commerce skewered Hunt as did the local sheriff and State's Attorney, neither of whom fared too well in the stories told during the proceedings. However, newspaper editors lauded the senator from Wyoming, saying he'd done "a terrific job."[76]

Hunt ended the Tampa hearing challenging the local folks to clean up the mess he had exposed. "The gray-haired senator warned the packed Federal Courtroom that whatever is done from here out will depend upon 'an angry, aroused, and determined pubic," a Tampa newspaper wrote.[77]

The show gathered momentum as it moved on to New York where

72 "Explosive Report on Wyoming" *Casper-Herald,* August 14, 1951

73 "Gov. Fuller Challenges Senator Hunt to Wordy Duel" *Kemmerer Gazette,* July 6, 1951

74 "Mafia links with Tampa's many unsolved murders." *Wyoming State Tribune,* Dec 28, 1950

75 "Tampa Aroused, Indignant At Gambling Pay-off Tales" *Jacksonville Journal,* January 1, 1951, 1

76 *The Denver Post,* January 1, 1951

77 "Kefauver Committee Tosses Tampa's 'Sordid Mess' To Officials, Suggests Cleanup" *Tampa Sunday Tribune,* December 31, 1950, 1

the media guaranteed a sensational hearing. The committee proceedings in New York made many of the most notorious underground figures household names. Americans learned Lucky Luciano, a man pardoned by Governor Tom Dewey and deported to Italy, was "the long distance czar, or intermediary" sending drugs into the United States.[78]

Crime figure Frank Costello was subpoenaed. He walked out of the hearing in dramatic fashion after quarreling with the senators and his own lawyer. After that, the hearings became even more interesting. "Bugsy" Siegel's girlfriend Virginia Hill testified next. (She and Bugsy became a part of popular Mafia lore as a result of the 1991 film, *Bugsy*, starring Warren Beatty as Bugsy. Annette Bening played Virginia Hill.)

"Wearing a silver blue mink as if it were alive," Ms. Hill talked about her quick rise from minimum wages as a waitress to mansions in Florida, California and Mexico. "The only money I ever made was what I reported on my taxes. Other money I had was given me by the men I was going with that gave me things," she testified.[79] The committee wanted to know more about those men and the sources of their money. Virginia Hill exploded. "You goddamn bastards, I hope an atom bomb falls on all of you."[80]

While an atom bomb did not fall on any of them, they each received serious death threats. One morning Senator Hunt opened an envelope with a Boston postmark. It was unsigned but the warning was clear. If he pursued the gambling investigation "he'd meet a violent end."[81] That same day, eight "big names" were indicted in Miami as a result of the committee's work. This followed an earlier indictment of 30 oth-

78 "Luciano Linked to Increase of Smuggles Dope in U.S." *Wyoming State Tribune,* March 15, 1951, 1
79 "Costello Walks Out in Senate Crime Hearing" *Rock Spring Rocket-Miner,* March 16, 1951, 1
80 "Hotties of History: Virginia Hill, http://halloftheblackdragon.com/reel/5989/hotties-of-history-virginia-hill.html, also see William Howard Moore, supra. 191-192. Following the hearings, Hill re-married. She took her own life in March of 1966.
81 "Senator Hunt's Life Threatened By Letter" *Washington Post, September 2, 1950, 12*

ers after Kefauver and Hunt left Miami.[82] Death threats continued to arrive as the circus took down its tents in one town and raised them in the next. In each, the committee caused embarrassment to powerful and sometimes dangerous people. In March 1951, Hunt received another threatening letter warning him against "sticking my nose into other people's business."[83]

Governor Dewey was no less pleased than Virginia Hill, though perhaps less eloquent, when Kefauver suggested the New York governor should answer for his pardon of Luciano.[84] Dewey telegrammed the committee saying he would talk to the senators only if they came to him "in the Executive Mansion at Albany-or not at all" promising them a bed for the night. "Somewhat surprisingly, the senator who got his dander up was Lester C. Hunt (D-Wyo.) who ordinarily is the most placid," reported the *New York Sun Times*." Hunt fired at Dewey, "There are four of us, and three of us have served as governors of our states," Hunt replied. "I for one don't get any kick out of spending a night in the Executive Mansion at Albany."[85]

After Miami, Tampa and New York, hearings followed in New Orleans, Kansas City, Cleveland, St. Louis, Detroit, Los Angeles, San Francisco, Las Vegas, Philadelphia, Washington, and Chicago. Each produced a colorful mix of brash gangsters and embarrassed local politicians and cops. In Kansas, City, Tony Gizzo, a boastful, noisy, beer barrel of a man, appeared as though from central casting. When Senator Wiley asked him about his habit of carrying large sums of money, Gizzo was almost gleeful. "Do you want to see it?" he asked, pulling a roll of hundred dollar bills from his pocket and carefully counting them aloud to $2500.

---

82 "8 Indicted in Florida" Id.

83 "Crackpots Blamed by Senators" *Denver Post*, March 27, 195

84 "Crime Probers Seek to Deport Costello" *Washington Post*, March 19, 1951

85 "Prober 'Tells Off' Dewey on Invitation to Albany" *New York Sun Times* undated clipping, Scrapbook, Box 45, LCH Papers

During the Chicago phase, a one-time bodyguard for Al Capone testified. Philip D'Andrea said he had "heard" of the Mafia but otherwise "knew nothing." Asked whether it was believable that someone born in Sicily knew nothing about the Mafia, he replied, "If he was born in Sicily I would think so." The follow-up question, "what would you say was a principle of the Mafia," produced a candid response. "It would be a good idea to keep your mouth shut."[86]

In Chicago they met Police Captain Daniel Gilbert, "the richest cop in the world" and Tony the Enforcer. Captain Gilbert, it was said, had amassed a net worth of about $360,000 from gambling, a huge amount of money in 1950. Gilbert explained, "I bet on football games and prize fights." Asked whether he bet on elections, Gilbert said yes he did, adding, "In 1936 I think I won around $10,000 or $12,000." Tony the Enforcer was "swarthy, gorilla-like." He had a flying dove tattooed in the crease between his thumb and his trigger finger. He reported that when he "squeezed off" a shot, the dove looked as if it were flying. [87]

The names, places, confessions, denials, and accusations were dramatic. None of it was staged. These were real people. These were real crimes. Television sets were becoming a part of the living room furniture in homes across America. The Crime Committee hearings proved there was an untapped American interest in live broadcasts. Mrs. Margaret Sawyer wrote from Dover, Massachusetts telling Hunt her six-year-old son asked her, "Mommy, will you be tied up all day watching (what the child knew as) the 'Key Committee?'"[88] A teacher from Schroon Lake, New York told Hunt the televised hearings had caused her students to "realize more than ever before that they, as individuals are responsible for a democracy and what goes on."[89]

86 Mike La Sorte, *The Kefauver Crime Committee, 1950-1951,* February 2010 www.american-mafia.com/Feature_Articles_452.html
87 Kefauver, *Crime in America,* supra. 74-75
88 Letter to Hunt from Margaret Sawyer, File: "Crime Committee, Box 12, LCH Papers
89 Letter to Hunt, April 9, 1951, File: "Crime Committee, Box 12, LCH Papers

Hunt told a friend back in Wyoming that the Hooper television ratings were 26% in a morning time slot that averaged 1.25%. The Hooper rating for the hearings outscored the 1950 World Series 31.5 to 23.2.[90] Americans were enthralled with the stories they heard told by live witnesses with funny names. A writer from Manchester, New Hampshire called it "the best thing I have ever seen on TV." Thirty million Americans watched on television or listened on radio.[91] The vast amount of TV coverage brought mail from all over the nation. Cards and letters of support came from nearly every state, filling file after file of Lester Hunt's official papers. They came from individual citizens, churches, Kiwanis and many other service clubs, numerous Chambers of Commerce, business, faith and political leaders. Some even sent cash and checks to help pay the costs of the proceedings.[92]

Hunt became somewhat of a celebrity as a result of the investigation. In April 1951, he appeared on a nationally broadcast ABC "Town Meeting" entitled "How Should We Deal with Organized Crime?" There were other nationally televised new shows on which he spoke and numerous magazine and newspaper interviews. The folks in Wyoming were equally enmeshed in the drama. The Lincoln Theater in Cheyenne sold tickets to a Twentieth Century Fox documentary entitled "The Kefauver Crime Investigation." Their promotional ad blared, "Now on Film, A fifty-minute feature- no punches pulled." [93]

Lester Hunt became the unwitting victim of an unnoticed open microphone in New York. He was overheard saying to Senator Kefauver, "Who's that good-looking girl who's been sitting in the front row all day, the cute one in the white hat?" Kefauver readily picked out the woman Hunt was trying to identify. There weren't many others in that

90 "Crime Probe Rated Above World Series" *Rocky Mountain News,* March 21, 1951
91 Radio broadcast by Hunt, March 1951, File: "KSPR Broadcasts", Box 35, LCH Papers
92 See multiple letters to Hunt, File: "Crime Committee" Box 12, LCH Papers
93 Ad appearing in the *Wyoming State Tribune,* April 2, 1951

room wearing "white hats."

Their work impressed the nation's number one crime fighter, J. Edgar Hoover. The Director of the Federal Bureau of Investigation told the committee, "The very fact that we have a crime problem reflects an evil of even greater import. The American home too often does not occupy the place in our national life that it did at the turn of the century. We are in a state of moral depression. The breakdown of the home is both a cause and a result. The bad state of affairs in too many of our schools is another result. In many instances any semblance of religious training is barred and the mentioning of God is frowned upon while espousers of godless Communism carry on under the guise of academic freedom," wrote Hoover.[94]

The committee issued its "Final Report of the Special Committee to Investigate Organized Crime in Interstate Commerce" on August 27, 1951, noting, "This committee has served as a powerful searchlight, exposing widespread national and local crime conditions to public gaze."[95] In the wake of its hearings, "corrupt officials have been forced to resign, grand juries and enforcement officials have doubled their vigilance, and gangsters have gone into hiding." Citing narcotics as a major growing problem, the senators identified a need for education, prevention and treatment. They also sought tougher penalties. "A judge passing on an individual case is often tempted to be lenient, but if he appreciates the true relationship between the case before him and the over-all aspects of the drug evil, he will be more likely to mete out the punishment that is deserved," the report said.[96] The senators encouraged local communities to provide treatment.

94 Statement of J. Edgar Hoover, Director, Federal Bureau of Investigation, Before the Special Committee to Investigate Organized Crime in Interstate Commerce, March 26, 1951, File: "Crime Committee" Box 12, LCH Papers
95 "Final Report of the Special Committee to Investigate Organized Crime in Interstate Commerce" on August 27, 1951, 1, File: "Crime Committee" Box 12, LCH Papers
96 Id. 35

The members of the committee expressed surprise at the level of public interest and expressed excitement about the role of television in educating the public about the crime problem. The final report took note that, "Through the medium of television the citizens of the country for the first time had it driven home to them with dramatic and startling impact that top-ranking hoodlums and underworld leaders were in their midst and were not story-book characters."[97]

A Kefauver-Hunt Ticket?

The committee's work led to numerous citations for contempt and a great number of indictments and convictions for criminal activities. Their work also led to serious speculation that Lester Hunt would join Estes Kefauver on the Democratic ticket in 1952. When Senator Kefauver entered the race for the Democratic Party nomination many thought he would choose for his running mate the man with whom he had become close friends during the crime hearings.

In April of 1951, as the committee's work was winding down, Frank Bowron, the head of Wyoming's "Kefauver for President Club" said he was working with Kefauver's staff on the idea of naming Hunt vice-president. Bowron told the press, "The situation has become rather encouraging lately."[98] A month later, Bowron said he had "an iron-clad commitment" from the Kefauver team. John T. O'Brien, Kefauver's National Chairman had made a "commitment in writing" that if Kefauver were nominated "he would give his blessing to no other vice presidential candidate."[99] On May 12, 1953, Kefauver campaigned in Casper. Aware of the speculation, he added fuel to the fire. "Senator Hunt and I have the closest relationship of any two men in the Senate,"

---

97 Id. 19

98 Wyoming Kefauver Backers Boom Senator Hunt for Veep" *Laramie Daily Boomerang*, April 3, 1952

99 "Kefauver Reported Favoring 'Only' Senator Hunt as VEEP Running Mate" *Rawlins Daily Times*, May 6, 1952, 13

said Kefauver" Lester Hunt is, he said, "worthy of any office to which he might be chosen."[100]

Alas, it was not to be. Kefauver boldly entered the race while it was yet believed Truman would seek reelection. The first primary was held in New Hampshire. Kefauver upset Truman and the incumbent soon announced he would not seek reelection. The Tennessean then won Wisconsin without opposition. In all, Kefauver ran at or near the top in all twelve primaries. In those days, primary victories didn't mean so much as they do today. The party leaders and bosses still controlled the outcome.

Kefauver became the front-runner but arrived at the national convention short of the delegate total he needed for a first ballot victory and with a lot of political baggage. Big-city party bosses were still smarting over the embarrassment they had suffered as a result of the crime committee hearings. They joined Truman in denying Kefauver the nomination.

The Chicago convention was dramatic. Delegates couldn't agree on a nominee through the first two ballots. Kefauver held a plurality in both. But the third ballot gave the nomination to Adlai Stevenson. He lost to Dwight Eisenhower the following November. Four years later, Stevenson was again nominated. This time he lost with Estes Kefauver as his running mate.

Standing at the Gates of Hell

The Air Force plane carrying Senator Hunt and other members of congress to the South Pacific passed directly over Wyoming. Looking out the window of the aircraft, Hunt recognized the landmarks. Elk Mountain shone brightly through light cloud cover. As they passed

---

100 "Kefauver Appearance Spurs Backer's Hopes at Casper" *Wyoming State Tribune,* May 12, 1952

over Rawlins, Hunt could see cars moving on the streets of the small town. He imagined friends and constituents going about a normal day in Wyoming.[101] Within another day he would be flying over an altogether different landscape where only charred tree stumps and vaporized steel buildings remained. He thought of those Wyoming folks walking around as though life everywhere was normal.

The decision to drop an atomic bomb on Hiroshima and Nagasaki had not invoked the fear of other world leaders so much as envy. In 1949, the Soviets tested the first atom bomb outside the United States. The nuclear arms race was on and no one was advocating disarmament at a time when it might have been possible. Instead the U.S. Atomic Energy Commission (A.E.C.), encouraged by the President and most members of Congress, concluded there was an urgent need to ratchet up the research and increase the tonnage of explosives that could be delivered. The larger of the two atom bombs dropped on Japan to end World War II contained the equivalent of 21 kilotons or 21,000 tons of TNT. The explosion Lester Hunt witnessed six years later delivered 225 kilotons.

Once the decision was made to continue nuclear weapon development, it was politically and strategically necessary to detonate the bombs outside the United States. The A.E.C. identified a small chain of islands in the South Pacific as a test site. Eniwetok, a small atoll in the Marshall Islands of the Pacific Ocean, is 4400 miles west of San Francisco.[102] The island was occupied. The U.S. government herded all of its native inhabitants off the island and built new military installations to replace their homes and culture. The natives were re-

---

101 Hunt's hand written journal from trip to Eniwetok, File: "Operation Greenhouse-Eniwetok (A Bomb)" Box 26, LCH Papers

102 The U.S. government initially referred to the island as "Eniwetok." The name was a misspelling. Official references were changed in 1974 to a more accurate "Enewetak." Barton C. Hacker, *Elements of Controversy: The Atomic Energy Commission and Radiation safety in Nuclear Weapons Testing, 1947–1974*, University of California Press, (1994), 14.

placed by 3000 American troops. Their village huts were soon replaced by 197 buildings using 400,000 linear feet of aluminum, with more than 200,000 feet of pipe along with 450,000 square yards of asphalt pavement.[103]

The United States had conducted fewer than a dozen nuclear tests since the first atomic bomb was detonated in the New Mexico desert. The Americans were scurrying to find bigger and more destructive bombs after learning Russia had one. "Operation Greenhouse" was the gateway to the thermonuclear hydrogen bomb.[104] "This experiment that you will observe will be history-making," Task Force Commander General E.R. Quesada told the small congressional delegation that included the junior senator from Wyoming.

As a member of the Armed Forces Committee, Hunt was invited to witness the "history-making" test in May of 1951. To clear the time on his schedule to witness this explosion, he missed another. General Douglas MacArthur, who had recently been fired by President Truman, was returning to Washington to testify before the Armed Forces Committee while Hunt was at Eniwetok. Hunt's handwritten log of the trip discloses that as he was leaving Washington, the General and his entourage were arriving.

"Since Gen. MacArthur was to testify before the Armed Forces Committee, I was reluctant to leave," Hunt scribbled, "as I am a member of the Committee. Zan (Lewis, of Hunt's staff) took me to the airport. MacArthur arrived before we left. As I saw his four motored

---

103 "Operation Greenhouse-Joint Task Force Three" Report of the Atomic Energy Commission, File: "Operation Greenhouse-Eniwetok (A Bomb)" Box 26, LCH Papers,

104 See a 1951 documentary film on Operation Greenhouse and the detonation witnessed by Senator Hunt at http://archive.org/details/OperationGreenhouse1951 "This formerly secret film was produced through the top secret Lookout Mountain Laboratory, located in the Hollywood Hills of California, under the joint command of the United States Air Force and the Armed Forces Special Weapons Project (AFSWP). The intention of this film was for viewing by top secret oversight committees of United States Congress and leading members of the United States military."

ship come in and realizing that it costs $ to build a ship and $ to operate I wondered how long the people are going to stand for this hero to fly from coast to coast campaigning for the Republican nomination for President at their expense."[105]

The flight across the width of the country was uneventful until "about an hour before reaching Travis the air got rough and I got sick. Lost my lunch." The plane continued on to Hawaii where the party spent the night. The final note in Hunt's Eniwetok journal indicates, "Left the following morning for Eniwetok...picked up a coconut as a souvenir and bought a set of pearls for Nathelle. Rained like the devil." Military officials strongly discouraged any note taking after that time.

The briefing Hunt was given beforehand was specific. Senators were told, "When an atomic bomb explosion occurs, a tremendous quantity of energy in a variety of form is released. The energy is propagated outward in all directions. When fission occurs, the immediate reaction is intense emission of ultra-violet visible and infrared (heat) radiation, gamma rays and neutrons. This is accompanied by the formation of a large ball of fire. The largest part of the energy from the explosion is emitted as a shock wave. The ball of fire produces a mushroom-shaped mass of hot gasses, the top of which rises to about 10,000 feet in the first minute and about 30,000 feet in 5 minutes."[106]

Eye protection was required to avoid temporary blindness. "Special goggles will be provided for some while others will be asked to face away from the explosion." The primary protection against the radiological effects was, according to the briefing, to be "distance" so long as one is at least 2000 yards away.

Senator Hunt and the congressional party were roused from bed before daylight and taken to an observation site. The weather was aw-

---

105 Hunt's hand written notes journal from trip to Eniwetok, File: "Operation Greenhouse-Eniwetok (A Bomb)" Box 26, LCH Papers
106 "Operation Greenhouse-Joint Task Force Three" Report of the Atomic Energy Commission, 9, Supra.

ful. Rain poured heavily most of the day. The skies cleared just long enough to allow the test to proceed. Congressman Edward Hebert of Louisiana observed, "The sky was all lighted. There was a gigantic ball of fire on the horizon. Simultaneously there was a gust of heat across my face. The fire and the heat seemed to arrive at the same time. There was no sound."[107]

On June 13, 1951 the Department of Defense issued a statement. Lieutenant General E.R. Quesada heralded the success of the detonation that, he said, included tests on pigs, mice and dogs and steel structures. "We have again operated in and around radioactivity. Our operations have indicated to us clearly that the mysterious ghost of lingering radiation should be dispelled. The immediate radiation, blast, and heat kill and destroy. Fear of lingering residual radioactivity must not confuse or delay prompt disaster operations in the event we are attacked," the General said.

After the detonation Hunt and his colleagues flew over the target island. The Senator from Wyoming was unnerved by what he witnessed. Nothing was left but charred tree stumps. A huge steel tower built to test the impact on an office building was gone. The bomb had vaporized thousands of tons of industrial steel from the face of the earth. Over time, that test and a significant number of others left the islands uninhabitable for many years and caused personal and property damage to native peoples for which the taxpayers of the United States are yet being held accountable.[108]

107 "Like Standing at the Gates of Hell: Witness at Eniwetok Reports" *Washington Evening Star,* June 14, 1951, 1 and A-6
108 "During the period from June 30, 1946, to August 18, 1958, the United States conducted 67 atmospheric nuclear tests in the Marshall Islands, 43 at Enewetak Atoll, 23 at Bikini Atoll, and one approximately 85 miles from Enewetak. The most powerful of those tests was the "Bravo" shot, a 15-megaton device detonated on March 1, 1954, at Bikini atoll. That test alone was equivalent to 1,000 Hiroshima bombs. While the Bravo test is well known, it should be acknowledged that 17 other tests in the Marshall Islands were in the megaton range and the total yield of the 67 tests was 108 megatons, the equivalent of more than 7,000 Hiroshima bombs. For the sake of comparison, it may be noted that from

Hunt confided to a close friend, "This was the most awe inspiring spectacle I have ever witnessed."[109] Once he was permitted by the A.E.C. to speak publicly about what he saw, the Senator told a Wyoming audience, "It gave me the peculiar feeling that I was standing at the gates of Hell and a strange and disconcerting feeling came over us that we were dealing with a supernatural power that might develop into a chain reaction and keep moving toward us."[110]

Lester Hunt was not unaffected by having stood "at the gates of hell." He was more troubled than ever now about MacArthur's cheerleading for an all-out war with Russia and China. A few days after his return, he faced General Omar Bradley during a top-secret briefing on U.S.-Russian nuclear capabilities. Hunt discussed the General's estimate of the results of a U.S.-launched all-out war. Hunt said, "It does occur to me that the possible effects or results on the United States of the plans for expanding our war effort outside of Korea as suggested by General MacArthur have not been thoroughly explored, explained

1945 to 1988, the U.S. conducted a total of 930 known nuclear tests with a combined yield estimated to be 174 megatons. Approximately 137 megatons of that total was detonated in the atmosphere. In other words, while the number of tests conducted in the Marshall Islands represents only about 14% of all U.S. tests, the yield of the tests in the Marshalls comprised nearly 80% of the atmospheric total detonated by the U.S. In June 1983, a formal Agreement Between the Government of the United States and the Government of the Marshall Islands was reached. In that agreement, the U.S. recognized the contributions and sacrifices made by the people of the Marshall Islands in regard to the Nuclear Testing Program and accepted the responsibility for compensation owing to citizens of the Marshall Islands for loss or damage to property and person resulting from that testing. Under the Agreement, the United States provided to the Marshall Islands the sum of $150 million as a financial settlement for the damages caused by the nuclear testing program. That money was used to create a fund intended to generate $270 million for distribution over a 15-year period with average annual proceeds of approximately $18 million per year through the year 2001. These funds were distributed among the peoples of Bikini, Enewetak, Rongelap, Utrik, for medical and radiological monitoring, and the payment of claims." http://www.nuclearclaimstribunal.com

109 Letter from Hunt to Bob McCracken discusses senate work, July 12, 1951, FILE Hunt Personal 1951

110 "Senator Hunt Tells Lions of Witnessing Atom Bomb Blast" Clipping, Newspaper unidentified, November 29, 1951, Scrapbook, Box 45, LCH Papers

or discussed. In the event we start World War III, we must expect-for we invite-an immediate offensive against this country, namely the bombing of the United States by the Russian Air Force."[111]

Over the months following his trip to Enewetak, Hunt was anxious to paint a real picture when his Wyoming constituents urged him to support an all-out war. He had seen what they had not. He now knew what they did not. He had a responsibility they did not. If the United States launched an all-out war against China or the Soviet Union, the result would be devastating to our own citizens. "Our nation," Hunt wrote to a constituent, "would learn the effects of an atomic war within itself and anyone who has seen the devastation wrought by the bombings in World War II knows the devastation in this country would be horrible if Russia sent planes over New York, Washington, Chicago and other metropolitan areas; and a good percentage of the Soviet bombers would get through."[112]

When another constituent questioned why the United States was so fearful of the Russians, Hunt, who had felt that "strange and disconcerting feeling came over us that we were dealing with a supernatural power that might develop into a chain reaction and keep moving toward us" responded, saying, "It is not the fear of Russia that dictates every precaution possible against World War III, it is just good common sense."[113]

Ironically, in the face of the dilemma, Hunt became an optimist on these matters. After the United States built and tested a hydrogen bomb in 1954, he recalled his morning in the Marshall Islands watching the detonation of that "atomic colossus." He reached the yet- to-be-demonstrated conclusion that "in the face of the tremendous increase

111 Memorandum from Committee hearing, File: File: "Operation Greenhouse-Eniwetok (A Bomb)" Box 26, LCH Papers
112 Letter from Hunt to Phil Little of Clearmont, Wyoming, February 6, 1952, File: "Foreign Policy" Box 16, LCH Papers
113 Letter from Hunt to Earl Davis of Lander, August 28, 1951, Id.

in the kill capacity of bacteriological and atomic warfare, there is definitely a trend in the world today toward the peaceful solution of the differences between the ideologies of the Communistic and the free world."[114]

Foreign Policy

Lester Hunt was gone long before the United States fully made its fateful commitment to Viet Nam. But the seeds of that commitment were being sowed while he was yet a senator and a member of the Armed Forces Committee. Less than two months before his untimely death, Hunt spoke about his own growing uneasiness of developments in what he called "Indo-China." He acknowledged that as early as 1954, under President Eisenhower, administration officials were already calling on the U.S. to send ground troops. The Armed Forces Committee received a top-secret briefing from the Chairman of the Joint Chiefs of Staff in January 1954. Hunt said he painted a "gloomy picture." Eisenhower had recently decided to send more warplanes and technical advisers to Southeast Asia. The United States was already spending more than $2 billion a year trying to stave off the inevitable.[115] Others were demanding Americans use nuclear weapons to end the conflict. Hunt opposed the use of atomic or hydrogen bombs. Having seen one detonated, he felt the United States "cannot, as a peace loving nation, take it upon ourselves to drop a bomb, wantonly killing and maiming thousands and accomplishing no military objective, only causing tremendous human suffering."[116]

The Senator believed a solution could start with the French giving independence to the Vietnamese. America's Korean experience con-

---

114 Radio broadcast, April 1, 1954, File: "KSPR Broadcasts" Box 35, LCH Papers
115 Letter from Hunt to Tracy McCracken, February 8, 1954, File: "Hunt-Personal-1954" Box 19, LCH Papers
116 Radio broadcast, April 22, 1954, File: "KSPR Broadcasts" Box 35, LCH Papers

vinced him that U.S. military intrusion would be futile. Hunt called the times "troubled" but second-guessed his earlier support for the Korean War. "As a Monday morning quarterback, I feel we made a mistake in ever going into Korea. However, at the time, like everyone else, I felt it was the thing to do and that we must stop Communism some place along the line, and I have since, in Armed Services Committee meetings, urged the immediate withdrawal of all our troops from Korea," Hunt wrote.[117]

Yet, Hunt recognized what many of his time did not. The United States was already in a no-win situation. The Senator told a radio audience candidly, "We indeed find ourselves in a dilemma. We face the loss of the entire Asiatic world if we ignore Indo-China or we face the possibility of becoming ourselves involved if we do not ignore it."[118] There can be no certainty about how he would have approached the subsequent, acrimonious debate over Viet Nam, but the second senate term he'd have undoubtedly been elected to serve, if he had lived, would have put him in the midst of the fateful decisions the United States made by the end of that decade.

McCarthy and McCarthyism

The second clause of Article One, Section 6 of the U.S. Constitution protects those who serve in Congress from those who do not. "The Senators and Representatives shall receive a Compensation for their Services, to be ascertained by Law, and paid out of the Treasury of the United States. They shall in all Cases, except Treason, Felony and Breach of the Peace, be privileged from Arrest during their Attendance at the Session of their respective Houses, and in going to and returning from the same; *and for any Speech or Debate in either House, they shall*

117 Letter from Hunt to WW Porter of Byron, Wyoming, January 19, 1951, File: "P-1951" Box 27, LCH Papers
118 Radio broadcast, April 22, 1954, supra.

not be questioned in any other Place." (Emphasis added.)

The final few words of the clause reflect the framers' desire to ensure free discussion of controversial issues in Congress. They immunized members of Congress from lawsuits and liability for statements made in House or Senate debates. The freshman Senator from Wyoming sought to change that. He proposed amending the Constitution to strike out the words of immunity, i.e. "and for any Speech or Debate in either House, they shall not be questioned in any other Place." In the alternative he proposed a statute to allow civil suits against members of Congress who defamed a citizen.

Lester Hunt learned earlier than most Americans how willing Joe McCarthy was to play fast and loose with the facts. He was introduced to McCarthy early in his own senate career. During the Malmedy hearings in the spring of 1949, Hunt watched as McCarthy made wild charges against high-ranking military officers with little or no facts to support him. That was before the 1950 Wheeling, West Virginia speech when McCarthy took the strategy to an unimaginable level. He was willing to say anything about anyone regardless of the truth and the Constitution of the United States gave him complete cover. McCarthy ruined reputations, caused people to lose their careers, drove some to suicide and left good men and women with reputations in irretrievable shreds. There was nothing the victims could do. Members of congress were immune even when they lied.

As he introduced the legislation, Hunt provided a detailed history of immunity, tracing it back to old England and the need to protect members of parliament from kings seeking revenge. He said the ancient protection had been abused. "If a member of the Senate having a deep seated and malicious hatred of any person and with full knowledge of the falseness of our word, rises in our places on the senate floor and charges that enemy with evil, vile and contemptible crimes, yes, charges him with treason to his country, or calls him a Communist, we need have no fear for we are not subject to arrest, or punishment and no civil suit can make us pay for the destruction of our enemy's character, the loss of a good reputation, ruining his business or standing in his home community or for any unfair, unjust, evil consequences which may follow from our intemperate and immoral remarks," Hunt said.[119]

Prominent journalist William S. White covered the speech for the *New York Times*. He reported Hunt's words "stirred considerable interest" among his colleagues. "The time has arrived," Hunt announced, "when the American citizen wishes no longer to tolerate such highhanded, irresponsible action. He will no longer be deprived of his reputation, his position, his home and family without the right to defend himself."[120]

There was, of course, no mistaking about whom Hunt was speaking. Hunt's immunity bill was considered an "ad hominen attack on both McCarthy and New Hampshire Senator Styles Bridges" according to a report in one Wyoming newspaper.[121] The term ad hominen, in Latin meaning literally "at the man," was accurately used. Lester Hunt was often openly critical of his Wisconsin colleague and had done battle with Bridges as well. He said McCarthy was using "the big lie technique," a not-so-subtle but stinging reference to the propaganda strategies of Adolph Hitler and Joseph Goebbels.[122] McCarthy's response was to travel to Riverton, Wyoming, Hunt's backyard, and tell a large crowd that the Democratic Party had become the "Commie-crat Party" and no longer represented "loyal Americans."[123] Hunt confided in his friend and former U.S. Senator Bill Benton that he was "saddened" by

---

119 Transcript of speech, File: "Immunity" Box 11, LCH Papers

120 "Curbing Congress on Slander Urged" *New York Times,* December 22, 1950

121 Editorial, Wyoming Eagle September, 22, 1950, Scrapbook Jan 1, '50-Jul 1, '52, Box 45, LCH Papers

122 "Hunt Censures Big Lie" *Rawlins Daily Times,* September 26, 1952, 1

123 "Senator McCarthy Attacks 'Commie-crats in Government" *The Riverton Review,* October 16, 1952, 1

the reception McCarthy received in Hunt's home county.[124]

Lester Hunt felt Americans were entitled to believe that when members of Congress spoke, their words were truthful. "A situation confronts us when we of Congress are no longer able to control our own members by the rules of justice and fair play," Hunt told a nation-wide television audience. "Then we must take drastic steps to control them." On September 24, 1951, he appeared on an ABC program, "On Trial." His proposal to eliminate blanket immunity for members of Congress was a subject of great national interest.[125]

Hunt and Senator John Stennis debated the topic on the NBC news program, "The American Forum of the Air" on September 2, 1950. During another nationally broadcast of the same radio program on Sunday, November 23, 1952, Hunt was asked by moderator Theodore Granik about efforts to remove Communists from government. Hunt discussed his proposed legislation to repeal congressional immunity. "That is the only way a man whose name is smeared can clear his name," the senator from Wyoming explained, "because otherwise he has no chance. He is deprived of job opportunities, he is put in a position in his community where he is an outcast."[126] More people each day were looking for a way to curb McCarthy's irresponsible behavior and Hunt's proposal struck a chord.

The Wisconsin press took delightful note. Reprinting an editorial from the *Davenport Daily Times*, the Madison paper reported Hunt's bill was popular among his colleagues and others. "It is receiving strong support among those that fear the foundations of a free society are being awakened by a device originally conceived to bulwark it," the newspaper said.[127] The *Des Moines Register* called Hunt's bill, "A little

124 Letter to William Benton from Hunt, March 22, 1954, File: "Hunt-Personal-1954" Box 19, LCH Papers

125 Transcript, File: "Immunity" Box 20, LCH Papers

126 Transcript, File: "Hunt-Personal-1953" Box 19, LCH Papers

127 "An Immunity Threatened by its Abuse" *Madison Capital Times,* January 19, 1951Series

soap and water to wash out the mouths of some Congressmen."[128] A *Washington Post* editorial called McCarthyism a "betrayal of freedom." The newspaper supported Hunt's proposal, saying anyone "interested in practical reforms" should consider Hunt's ideas.[129]

Not everyone agreed, though most sympathized with the need to control McCarthy. The *Los Angeles Times* thought the Communists would "heckle and harass their Congressional opponents with false arrests and phony lawsuits" if Hunt's law was enacted, though the paper did think Congress needed to police its own members.[130]

Hunt's proposal received extensive coverage in newspapers across the country. His remarks, printed in dozens of newspapers, resulted in letters of support from many places. Californian Marguerite Angelo Smelser wrote to her new senator, Richard Nixon. "I didn't vote for you, but congratulations anyhow! Senator Nixon, the swashbuckling antics of Senator McCarthy, his smear campaigns, his incredibly high handed attempts at coercion of radio advertisers and newspapers, seem to me to be a great danger to America." She asked Nixon to support the Hunt bill.[131] A young state senator from Wisconsin named Gaylord Nelson sent a proposal to Senator Hunt. Nelson was sponsoring legislation similar to Hunt's in the Wisconsin state legislature to allow defamation suits against legislators.[132]

One of McCarthy's constituents encouraged Hunt. "Thank you for doing something about the way congressional immunity is be-

12, Reel 2, Papers of Joseph R. McCarthy, Marquette University

128 "Senator Wants Legal Soap and Water to Wash Mouths of Some Congressmen" *Des Moines Register,* December 25, 1950

129 Editorial, *Washington Post,* January 6, 1952

130 Editorial, *Los Angeles Times,* July 21, 1951

131 Letter from Marguerite Angelo Smelser to Richard Nixon, copied to Hunt, January 11, 1951, File: "Immunity" Box 20, LCH Papers

132 Letter from Nelson to Hunt February 13, 1951, File: "Immunity" Box 20, LCH Papers (Gaylord Nelson served as Governor of Wisconsin and in the U.S. Senate from 1963-1981. He is credited with founding Earth Day.)

ing abused," wrote Eva Anderson of Eau Claire. "McCarthyism must be stopped."[133] For his part, McCarthy quickly defaulted to his talking points. Hunt's bill, he said, "would "make it impossible to convict Communist agents."[134]

Hunt's proposals were never enacted and members of Congress continue to be immune for anything they say on the floor of the House and Senate. But Lester Hunt was one of the few who were willing to so directly confront the blatant dishonesty of Joe McCarthy and those like Senator Styles Bridges who turned McCarthy into McCarthyism.

133 Letter from Eva Anderson to Hunt, January 7, 1951, File: "Immunity" Box 20, LCH Papers
134 "Hunt's Proposed Ban For Witnesses Hit by McCarthy" *Denver Post,* Dec 22, 1950

CHAPTER TEN

The Longest Year

The longest year of Lester Hunt's life began on a warm June evening in 1953 when his namesake walked into Lafayette Park, the
shady tree-lined plaza on the north side of 1600 Pennsylvania Avenue
in Washington D.C. Lafayette Park was first intended to be a part of the
spacious White House grounds. President Thomas Jefferson instead
had Pennsylvania Avenue laid between the park and the executive
mansion. Its strategic location, so near the view of the President, has
made it a center of all sorts of activity over the years. Those seven acres
have, from time to time, been used as "a race track, a graveyard, a zoo,
a slave market, an encampment for soldiers during the War of 1812,
and many political protests and celebrations."[1] In February of 1859, the
park was a crime scene. A congressman, Representative Daniel Sickles,
shot and killed the man with whom his wife was engaged in an affair.
The man was Philip Key, the son of Francis Scott Key, writer of the
"Star Spangled Banner." Key's lawyer was Edwin Stanton, who became
Lincoln's Secretary of War. Stanton obtained an acquittal arguing his
client was rendered temporarily insane by his wife's infidelity.[2]

1 "Lafayette Square Historic District" http://www.nps.gov/history/nr/travel/wash/dc30.
htm
2 "Crime History: Congressman shoots, kills prosecutor in Lafayette Park" *Washington
Examiner,* February 27, 2012, http://washingtonexaminer.com/local/crime/2011/02/
crime-history-congressman-shoots-kills-prosecutor-lafayette-park/11100, accessed March
15, 2012

Given its proximity to the White House, the park has been an especially important stage for political protest theater. During the Gulf War, President George H. W. Bush was annoyed with an anti-war demonstration in Lafayette Park. An "incessant" drumbeat used by protestors was so loud he ordered the drums silenced. "Those damned drums are keeping me up all night," Mr. Bush told a group of visiting congressmen.[3] Not long after, a federal court held the park was a public place. The whole point of free speech was to get the attention of the President. The beat went on.[4]

Lafayette Park has always been a delightful venue for socializing and from the early years of the Republic, Washington D.C. provided a vibrant social environment for gays and lesbians "despite periodic crackdowns by the police and government."[5] In the 1890s, Lafayette Park was the destination point of an annual "drag dance" where hundreds of gay African-American men dressed in female attire filled the park after a "dance" through the city. For many years and certainly during the first half of the twentieth century, it was a well-established gathering place for Washington's gay community.[6] The park offered a serene, comfortable place for harmless socializing among the beautiful trees and picturesque statues of President Andrew Jackson and Revolutionary War heroes.

Although police would occasionally breakup actual sexual encounters among both heterosexuals and homosexuals, they paid little heed to other social and romantic antics.[7] Nor was there any serious threat to the lifestyle of homosexuals elsewhere in the city. "Gay men and lesbians in the nation's capital in the 1930s and 1940s enjoyed a com-

3 "War in the Gulf: The Drums of Protest" *New York Times,* February 6, 1991
4 "Noise Limit Struck Down" *New York Times,* July 1, 1992
5 *glbtq: An Encyclopedia of Gay, Lesbian, Bisexual, Transgendered, and Queer Culture,* http://www.glbtq.com/social-sciences/washington_dc.html, accessed March 12, 2012
6 *Lavender Scare,* Supra. 47
7 Id. 46-49

fortable working environment in the federal government and a vibrant social life in the fast growing city."[8]

Tolerance never moved fully to acceptance. As a result, gays and lesbians were always one demagogue away from becoming targets. The change occurred over time and could, in part, be attributed to the openness increasingly experienced by gays and lesbians. The growing tolerance of homosexuality was bound to collide with religious beliefs and political opportunism.

Lester Hunt, Jr.

To distinguish Lester Hunt from his namesake, they called him "Buddy." Buddy was eight years old when the family moved to Cheyenne and a life of full-time politics. In the summer of 1945, Buddy completed his junior year in high school. He was only one credit hour short of graduation and his father, somewhat surprisingly at least to Buddy, agreed to allow him to earn that credit at a summer typing class. As his father prepared to run for the United States Senate in 1946, Buddy prepared to start his college career.

Feeling it was not appropriate for the child of a governor and Senate candidate to go to college out of state, he enrolled at the University of Wyoming. By the time he was part of the way through his sophomore year, his advisor recommended Buddy look to another college for a more rigorous academic challenge. Young Lester made a lasting impression on University of Wyoming professor Henry Peterson who recommended him for a Rhodes Scholarship. Peterson described Hunt as "one of those exceptional students whom teachers come to prize over the years because they appear only too infrequently."[9] The professor cited Buddy's academic achievement, saying he was less inter-

8 Id. 51
9 Letter from Henry J. Peterson to Dr. Ottis Rechard, Dean of the Liberal Arts College, University of Wyoming, August 8, 1949, File "Miscellaneous P" Box 29, LCH Papers

ested in grades than in learning. Calling him a "serious student (who) yet displays a normal sense of humor," Peterson said young Hunt had a personal character that "seems to be developed in a well balanced way." His letter of recommendation concluded, "In my judgment Lester shows unusual promise of outstanding achievement."

Professor Peterson also recommended Hunt attend Swarthmore College. A few miles south of Philadelphia and founded by the Quakers in 1864, its alumni include Alice Paul, a suffragist and founder of the National Women's Party; Michael Dukakis, the former governor of Massachusetts and 1988 Democratic Party nominee for President; and novelist James A. Michener among five Nobel Prize winners and eight MacArthur fellows. Lester Hunt, Jr. thrived in that environment. "Swarthmore," he recounted, "was often called the 'Little Red School House' because the school was generally very liberal. The American Friends Service Committee offered students the opportunity to get involved in local activities, especially in Philadelphia. I went quite often with them to protest restaurant segregation. We would occupy a restaurant in the morning, order some food, and then refuse to leave until they took down the sign in the window that in one way or another told blacks not to come in."[10]

Swarthmore was known not only for its commitment to social justice but also for a commitment to academic rigor. Young Lester was up to the challenge, graduating with a bachelor's degree in history in June of 1949. An adventurer at heart, he found the Office of Education in Washington had a program placing those who wanted to teach in American schools around the world. He accepted a teaching job at the Ruston Academy in Havana, Cuba in 1949, after teaching a year in Mexico City.[11] Although he briefly toyed with the idea of earning a PhD in history, he soon felt the tug to the clergy.

10 Lester Hunt, Jr. responses to questions of author, December 7, 2011
11 "Buddy Hunt Will Teach in Havana" *Wyoming Eagle*, August 27, 1949

Buddy enrolled in the Episcopal Theological School. Today known as the Episcopal Divinity School, the college is located in Cambridge, Massachusetts, and is associated with Harvard University. It was established in 1974 in the merger of Philadelphia Divinity School, which was founded in 1858, and Episcopal Theological School, established in 1867. The school is well known for progressive teaching and political activism. Faculty and students were often involved in many of the social controversies of the time. This appealed greatly to Hunt.

He had not involved himself much in politics before attending the University of Wyoming where he became a part of protests against school's board of trustees' attempt to censor books. In October of 1947, the board ordered an examination of all books used in the social science courses to determine which might contain "subversive or anti-American doctrines."[12] Criticism came from far and near. Arthur Schlesinger called it a "crude" investigation by "ill-informed trustees.[13] "The *St. Louis Post Dispatch* called the trustee's action "an insult to the good sense and patriotism of the faculty" and "an affront to the intelligence" of the students.[14] Newspapers in 20 communities followed suit, heavily criticizing the trustees.[15] The fear level of the administration was so high that students were hired by the university to monitor the lectures of a young history professor who it suspected of teaching anti-American doctrine.[16] That professor was Gale W. McGee. He was elect-

12 "Fifth Freedom-To Learn" *Laramie Republican Boomerang*, November 13, 1947, 4

13 Arthur M. Schlesinger, *The Vital Center*, Houghton Mifflin Company *(1949)*, 205

14 "SAD Story from Wyoming" Reprint of *St. Louis Post Dispatch* editorial in *Laramie Republican Boomerang*, December 30, 1947, 4

15 *Common Sense*, January 19, 1948, *Common Sense* was a short-lived publication by University of Wyoming students. Its sole purpose was opposing the book investigation. Its first edition was published on January 19, 1948. Its last was in the spring of 1948. One of the student editors/owners was W.G. Urbigkit who later became a state legislator and a member of the Wyoming Supreme Court.

16 "The Textbook Controversy at the University of Wyoming 1947-1948" Summary of Constitution Day Lecture by UW History Professor Phil Roberts, September 18, 2006, accessed on March 24, 2012 at http://uwacadweb.uwyo.edu/RobertsHistory/UW_text-

ed to the United States Senate a decade later and served for 18 years.

Young Lester Hunt was the son of the governor who appointed several of the university trustees including Tracy McCracken. It was Hunt's good friend and fellow dentist, Dr. P. M. Cunningham, who made the motion to conduct the investigation.[17] It's doubtful Lester Jr. would have refrained from getting involved. There are those who recall him writing letters to the editor of the UW student paper, *The Branding Iron,* in opposition to the book investigation. Curiously, none of the editions of the campus newspaper from the weeks of that controversy survived. "If I didn't do it," Hunt said many years later, "I wish I had. I wouldn't be surprised if I did. I hope I did."[18]

It all ended when the board, looking for a face-saving way out of the quagmire they had created, appointed a group of 15 professors to review some books and report back. Among the 15 were T.A. Larson and Gale McGee. They read 64 books and informed the board they found no anti-American or subversive information in any of them. "That's fine," said McCracken. "Now the people of Wyoming will know that even though subversive teaching may be practiced at other schools, there is none of it in Wyoming."[19]

Lester and his fellow students went back to class and the matter was put to rest. It was, however, one snapshot of the climate of fear pervasive in the country, arriving in full force in Wyoming as young Hunt made his way through the university. At Swarthmore, he was even more involved in political activity, including high profile petition drives and marches objecting to Joe McCarthy's tactics. "We saw freedom being destroyed right before our eyes so we were pretty active," the younger

book_controversy_1947.htm

17 *Common Sense,* January 19, 1948, *supra.*

18 Ewig interview of Hunt, Jr. December 29, 1989, 7

19 "UW Faculty Committee Maintains Book Probe Hearing Still Needed" *The Laramie Republican Boomerang,* January 21, 1948, 1

Hunt later said."[20]

Buddy's political activity did not escape Joe McCarthy's notice. An elevator operator in the Senate Office Building alerted young Hunt to a conversation he'd overheard. The operator told Lester, Jr., "McCarthy was on his way down and he was talking about you and this and that, and (how) he's about to take your father on because of you and your activities."[21] There is little reason to doubt the statement was made. As intriguing a person as McCarthy knew himself to be, he would not have said something so sensational in the presence of an elevator operator unless he believed and hoped it would be repeated. It was either a threat or a warning.

Lester Hunt, Jr.'s politics would not have appealed to Joe McCarthy. One might wonder whether they appealed to his father. Young Hunt was quite liberal. The first time he was old enough to vote in a Presidential election was 1948. He attended a Socialist Party rally, listening to Norman Thomas make "a rousing speech." At a rally for Henry Wallace, he heard Paul Robeson sing a worker's song in five languages. "Since I am a pragmatic voter," Hunt said during an interview, "I did vote for Truman because I was one of those who thought he needed every vote to be able to win. If I had been an ideological voter I would have voted for Wallace."[22]

In truth, Lester Hunt was not troubled by his son's political views. "He never tried to stop me and he never sort of tried to change my mind," young Hunt recalled of his father many years later. "I think he thought I was a little hotheaded and impulsive, and that I should keep my powder dry and do other things, but I don't think he disapproved in the sense that he didn't always agree, but he could leave it be."[23]

20 Ewig Interview, Supra. 7
21 Id. 8
22 E-mail from Lester Hunt, Jr. to the author, March 5, 2012
23 Ewig interview, Supra. 8

June 9, 1953

It is one of life's ironies that a year beginning with Lester Hunt, Jr.'s arrest, ended with Joe McCarthy's self-immolation. It was June 9, exactly a year to the day after Hunt's arrest that Joseph Welch asked Joe McCarthy the question the rest of the country was finally prepared to answer. "Have you no sense of decency, sir, at long last? Have you left no sense of decency?"[24]

But that was a very long year away and on June 9, 1953, American politics still marched to Joe McCarthy's drum, though some like Lester Hunt, Jr. marched to a different drummer. Hunt was 25 years old. Americans were as stirred up by what David K. Johnson labeled the "Lavender Scare" as they were by the Red Scare. Homosexuals were deemed a significant threat to national security no less than Communists. Same-sex attraction was seen as a disease, a mental illness. The American Psychiatric Association was two decades away from removing homosexuality from its long list of mental illnesses.

Over time, the medical community's views of same-sex attraction have been, may we say, schizophrenic. Dr. Sigmund Freud believed all humans were bisexual. He responded to a distraught mother who had written to him about her son's attraction to other men. "Homosexuality is assuredly no advantage, but it is nothing to be ashamed of, no vice, no degradation, it cannot be classified as an illness; we consider it to be a variation of the sexual function produced by a certain arrest of sexual development. Many highly respectable individuals of ancient and modern times have been homosexuals, several of the greatest men among them (Plato, Michelangelo, Leonardo da Vinci, etc.). It is a great injustice to persecute homosexuality as a crime, and cruelty

24 *Special Senate Investigation on Charges and Countercharges Involving: Secretary of the Army Robert T. Stevens, John G. Adams, H. Struve Hensel, and Senator Joe McCarthy, Roy M. Cohn, and Francis P. Carr, Hearing Before the Special Subcommittee on Investigations of the Committee on Government Operations, United States Senate*, 83rd Congress, June 9, 1954, U.S. Government Printing Office, 2429

too, Freud wrote."[25] Freud's successors were not so sure. Increasingly, science was used to corroborate religious and political views. After the Second World War, medicine was moving toward parity with religion and law. Author John D'Emilio who studied the sexual attitudes of the times, wrote, "In important ways they reinforced the cultural matrix that condemned and punished persons who engaged in homosexual activity."[26]

It was in the early 1950s that McCarthy gave way to McCarthyism. A major component of McCarthyism was a crackdown on homosexuals. There were too many rumors about McCarthy's own sexual attractions for him to take the lead in this battle. An Army lieutenant told Senator William Benton he had been "picked up" by McCarthy in D.C.'s Wardman Park, taken to the senator's home and sodomized while intoxicated. He claimed to know other servicemen who'd had the same experience with the Wisconsin senator.[27] The primary political responsibility for pursuing homosexuals, fell then to Senator Styles Bridges among others.[28] Journalist Westbrook Pegler, who responded to Martin Luther King's "I Have a Dream" speech by saying it is the duty of all Americans to "practice bigotry,"[29] urged Bridges on, arguing, "Homosexuality is worse than Communism.[30]

It was not only self-identified gays and lesbians who were targeted. Targets also included single people who were viewed suspiciously for either living alone or non-intimately with persons of the same sex. The

25 "Facts About Homosexuality and Mental Health" University of California-Davis website http://psychology.ucdavis.edu/rainbow/html/facts_mental_health.html, citing American Journal of Psychiatry, (1951), 107, 786

26 D'Emilio, *Sexual Politics,* 17

27 Staff Memo from Ralph Mann to Senator Benton, dated January 3, 1951, Papers of William Benton, File: "Senate Privileges and Elections" Box 4, Correspondence of Senator William Benton of Connecticut relating to his efforts to have Joseph R. McCarthy of Wisconsin expelled from the United States Senate, Wisconsin Historical Society Archives

28 *Lavender Scare,* Supra. 3

29 http://www.spartacus.schoolnet.co.uk/USApeglerW.htm, accessed March 16, 2012

30 *Lavender Scare,* Supra, 35

persecution of gays, lesbians, bisexuals and those rumored to be so, became a cultural pursuit. The lives and liberty of people with a same-sex attraction were at risk. One of the risk-takers was Lester Hunt, Jr.

Only a risk-taker would have walked through Lafayette Park in 1953, looking for a homosexual encounter. The park was filled with undercover cops as well as gang members who came for the sport of "knocking off a queer." There were others who wanted to roll someone, anyone and take all their money.[31] A widespread scam targeted straight men, luring them into compromising situations. The scam began with a victim looking to meet new acquaintances. They'd invite him to a nearby hotel where he'd be drugged and then photographed with a young boy in what would appeared to be a sexually compromising position. The photo was then used to extort great sums of money from the target. Victims were loathe to report the crime because they would be viewed as homosexuals in a time when avoiding the stigma was worth any price.[32]

By far the greatest threat was posed to gay men. Some were beaten rather than arrested by the undercover officers if not by the gangsters.[33] Simply being present in a known "gay cruising" area or making eye contact with an undercover cop could result in an arrest.[34] Perhaps because he had been away at college, Buddy had not gotten the word.

It was around 10:15 that night when he arrived at the park. Moments later he made eye contact with John Costanzo, an officer with the morals division of the Metropolitan Police Department. Hunt testified the stranger was "swaggering" as he walked and was "trying to attract my attention." Hunt thought Costanzo was "soliciting me."[35] A reasonable person reviewing the facts would be inclined to conclude

31 *Lavender Scare*, Supra.153-154

32 "The Vilest of the Rackets" Lloyd Wendt, *Esquire Magazine*, April 1950, 53

33 Id. 164

34 Id. 61

35 "Senator Hunt's Son Convicted on Morals Charge" *Washington Post*, October 7, 1953

Hunt had been entrapped. In fact, that's the argument his lawyer made, unsuccessfully.

Entrapment is a legal word of art, defined and re-defined over many decades of court decisions. In the final legal analysis, in order to avoid a conviction with an entrapment defense, the defendant must prove two elements. The first is inducement. Did a government agent "induce" or pressure him to commit an illegal act? There is little question Hunt had been induced. Costanzo's job was to induce men to engage in illegal behavior. That's what he was in the park to do. However, there is a second element. Hunt would have to persuade the judge he had no predisposition to commit the crime. He was unable to do so. More than 25 years later, he accepted responsibility for his role. "No," he said in response to being asked whether he had been framed. "I wasn't framed. I guess technically it was entrapment, but I was ready for the trap."[36]

Days later, Hunt and his father's administrative assistant Mike Manatos met with Roy Blick, the head of the D.C. vice unit. A recorded statement was taken and he and Manatos departed, believing the matter had been handled and the criminal charges would be dismissed. Hunt left for Cuba where he had enrolled in a summer practicum with the Episcopal parish in Havana. When he returned in the fall he learned the charges had been resurrected, not dismissed. His case would go to trial after all. As a result, he was not permitted to re-enroll in the fall. The seminary enforced a strict rule denying admission to anyone thought to be homosexual.

A two-day trial was held in October of 1953. Judge John Malloy heard the evidence, rejected the entrapment defense and found Hunt guilty of the charges.[37] A $100 fine was levied and paid. The ordeal of the very public trial behind him, Lester Hunt, Jr. then left Washington for

36 Ewig interview, 13
37 October 7, 1953 *Washington Post*, Supra.

Chicago unaware of the political intrigue stirring among Washington's power brokers.

A 2nd Term for Senator Hunt?

The defeat of his friend and colleague Joe O'Mahoney in 1952 weighed heavily on Lester Hunt. Joe McCarthy had played a key role in defeating O'Mahoney and the Red Scare issue as well as his personal conflict with McCarthy loomed as problems for Hunt in the coming campaign. Shortly after the '52 election, Hunt told a friend he was likely not going to seek a second term, explaining, "With the way the tide is running, and I am anticipating there will not be much change in two short years, you can realize I am giving serious consideration to bowing out of the picture two years hence."[38]

Two years ahead of the election, the GOP set its sights on defeating Hunt.[39] Wyoming was an overwhelmingly Republican state that had just gone big for Dwight Eisenhower. Even as Republicans were in the process of defeating Joe O'Mahoney in 1952, they had reason to believe that Hunt was equally vulnerable.

Hunt was not so concerned about how Buddy's arrest and conviction would impact the campaign as he was about the general political climate. He told his colleague Ernest Gruening, the governor of Alaska, that the "conditions must be favorable in 1954 or I do not think I shall be a candidate." He was also concerned about the costs of a campaign. "If I were a wealthy man, the situation would be different," Hunt wrote, "but I don't feel justified, at my age, gambling $10,000, $12,000 or maybe $15,000 on the questionable possibility of being reelected."[40]

He began exploring career options outside of the Senate.

38 Letter from Hunt to Al Harris, December 16, 1952, File: "Miscellaneous 'H' 1952" Box 19, LCH Papers

39 "Senate Republicans Eye 1954" *Christian Science Monitor,* November 10, 1952

40 Letter to Governor Ernest Gruening from Hunt, April 9, 1953, File: "Hunt-Personal-1953" Box 19, LCH Papers

Senator Hunt was awarded the highest honor of his profession when the American Dental Association gave him the Scroll of Honorary Membership at its national convention in October. He became only the eighth person to receive the award in the organization's 100-year history.[41] During the convention, he met with officials of the association. As a dentist and a popular member of the Senate, Hunt would make an effective lobbyist for the organization. No formal offer was made. All agreed it would be best for Hunt to run again. They believed his standing with his colleagues would suffer if he took this job instead of seeking reelection. "My standing with the Democratic members of the Senate," Hunt wrote, "would not be near as good as it would be if I did run and was defeated."[42] His future appeared secure whether he won in 1954 or lost. Though subtle, it was certain the association was interested in hiring Hunt if he was available after the campaign.

Six weeks earlier he asked his friend Jack Gage to speak to a supporter of William Henry Harrison. Harrison was Wyoming's lone member in the House of Representatives. When a state has only one house member he or she runs the same statewide campaign as a senator, only three times as often. House members shake the same number of hands, kiss the same number of babies and eat the same "rubber chicken" dinners every two years. The Senate candidate rides that circuit only once every six years. House members can be formidable opponents for an incumbent senator in a state with only one. Speaking of Harrison, Hunt pointed out, "He has recently completed two statewide campaigns, has gained a wide, and the newspaper man he has in his office constantly keeps the papers supplied with releases."[43]

As early as May of 1953, speculation had begun to focus on the 1954 Senate race and the possibility of a Hunt-Harrison showdown.

41 News Release, October 5, 1953, File: "Hunt-Personal-1953" Box 19, LCH Papers
42 Letter to P.M. Cunningham, D.D.S., October 29, 1953, File: "Hunt-Personal-1953" Box 19, LCH Papers
43 Letter to Jack Gage, September 16, 1953, File: "Hunt-Personal-1953" Box 19, LCH Papers

Lester Hunt, it was said, "is considered certain to run again." The editorial said, "Wyoming's senior senator is considered one of the few candidates left in the state who can command votes from both parties."[44] The editorial reported Harrison had been talking to party leaders about running for the Senate. Hunt asked Gage to speak to one of his and Harrison's mutual friends, Homer Scott. He hoped Scott could persuade Harrison to stay in the House.

The timing of Hunt's request of Gage is significant. Coming only a few months after his son's arrest and a few weeks before his trial, it is a clear indication Buddy's problems had not given him pause about his political future. Hunt was confident after a recent trip around the state, telling a friend he was "inclined to deviate some from the usual underestimation of my own possibilities and say in all candor and honesty that as of today I am of the opinion I would be returned to the Senate."[45]

Hunt's health, humor and spirits were good. "Old age," he said, "is beginning to show itself around the corner (but) we are in fairly good health." He and Nathelle had just celebrated their 36th wedding anniversary. "Nathelle got ambitious the other day and bought a piece of furniture she calls a 'love seat' and since I am only home part of the time, I hope it won't see too much use," Hunt joked.[46] On a recent evening, he and Nathelle stayed late at a White House event, dancing into the night to the Marine Corps Orchestra. He said, "I thought it would be something to talk about for the next fifty years that we had danced at the White House."[47]

44 "Speculation in State Shifts to '54 Congressional Races" *Wyoming State Tribune,* May 27, 1953
45 Letter from Hunt to E.D. Nicholson, September 24, 1953, File: "Hunt-Personal-1953" Box 19, LCH Papers
46 Letter to Mr. and Mrs. C.L. Griffin from Hunt, February 8, 1954, File: "Hunt-Personal-1954" Box 19, LCH Papers
47 Id.

Early in 1954, Richard Nixon afforded a high honor to the Wyoming senator. The vice-president had the responsibility to choose a member of Congress to read George Washington's Farewell Address on the floor of the Senate as a part of the celebration of Washington's birthday. Nixon, on the recommendation of Majority Leader Lyndon B. Johnson, selected Lester Hunt. In announcing Hunt's selection, the vice-president pointed out, "Only one other Wyoming senator has ever delivered the Farewell Address to the Senate, and that was Senator Joseph C. O'Mahoney in 1934."[48]

Hunt assured party leaders he would make a decision on whether or not to seek reelection no later than January of 1954, "so as to give the party a whole year to get another candidate lined up."[49] That deadline came and went without a decision. Near the end of January, he sounded as though he would prefer to retire. He asked advice from party activists such as Henry Watenpaugh, a former Democratic state legislator but cautioned him saying, "I am not looking for encouragement, Henry. Fact of the matter is I would appreciate some discouragement if I could get enough to justify my getting out of the game."[50]

That spring Hunt commissioned a poll, measuring his support against four possible GOP contenders. The poll told him he would likely be reelected.[51] It was another clear indication his son's troubles would not affect the campaign. A few days later he wrote his old friend Oscar Hammond in Laramie asking him to chair the "Hunt for Senate Club." On April 15 he made it official.

In a letter to state Democratic Party chairman J.J. Hickey, Hunt

48 News Release, February 10, 1954, File: "Hunt-Personal-1953" Box 19, LCH Papers

49 Letter to C.L. Griffin, January 6, 1953, File: "Hunt-Personal-1953" Box 19, LCH Papers

50 Letter from Hunt to Henry Watenpaugh, January 25, 1954, File: "Hunt-Personal-1953" Box 19, LCH Papers

51 Report on poll, April 5, 1954, File: "Hunt-Personal-1953" Box 19, LCH Papers. File: "Hunt-Personal-1953" Box 19, LCH Papers

said, "Being deeply concerned over the future of America and knowing what seniority in the United States Senate means to Wyoming, and having no desire to shirk the responsibility I feel is mine, I am today announcing my candidacy for reelection to the United States Senate."[52] Simultaneously his office issued a news release touting his years of community and public service. It discussed his senate service and work on national defense and other matters, saying, "I have always endeavored to place the national interest as a force superior to any group or regional selfish interest." Hunt concluded by stating he had "reason to believe that the people of the great State of Wyoming have approved my public service and will endorse the action I am taking today."

Hunt told Hammond that while the choice to run again "was a rather tough decision," he could not "bring myself to letting down those fine friends, like yourself, who have stood by me all through the years."[53] He said he'd be in Wyoming soon to open the "Hunt for Senate Club."

If Hunt had any doubts that he would be reelected, the letter he received from pollster Herbert O'Connor at the end of April settled those concerns. O'Connor informed Hunt that "voter response" to him was much higher than it had been for Senator O'Mahoney in 1952, when O'Mahoney lost to Frank Barrett. "Most important to me was the definite written report made on the basis of the survey that as of this time you unquestionably would be reelected if you run for another term," Hunt wrote.[54]

On June 4 Lester Hunt stunned everyone when he announced he had decided to withdraw from the Senate race. Less than two months had come and gone since he first announced, saying then, "Having no

52 Letter to J.J. Hickey, April 15, 1954, File: "Hunt-Personal-1953" Box 19, LCH Papers
53 Letter from Hunt to Oscar Hammond, April 9, 1954, File: "Hunt-Personal-1953" Box 19, LCH Papers
54 Letter to Hunt from Herbert R. O'Connor, April 30, 1954, File: "Hunt-Personal-1953" Box 19, LCH Papers

desire to shirk the responsibility I feel is mine, I am today announcing my candidacy for reelection to the United States Senate."[55] William Harrison, his strongest potential opponent, had already bowed out. Polls proved Hunt would be overwhelmingly reelected. The filing deadline for a new candidate was just days away. Hunt was backing out of a race he was sure to win. "Regret exceedingly at this date to advise you," Hunt wrote to state Democratic Party chairman J.J. Hickey, "that due to personal reasons beyond my control, namely health, I am compelled to withdraw my announcement as a candidate for reelection to the United States Senate." He called it "the decision I am forced to make."[56]

People across Wyoming and around the country were shaken by the sudden news. "My goodness," one letter exclaimed, "dear Senator Hunt, you have given us all a terrible shock."[57] While disappointed, they first expressed deep concerns about Hunt's health. "Your illness has us all greatly concerned and we are first most anxious for your health and well-being, but," wrote supporter Robert Lowe, "secondly we are also gravely concerned about your withdrawal from politics."[58] Hunt did not make public the nature of the health problems he said necessitated his exit. He told one friend he had not been feeling well "for something like a month" and that he needed time for a rest to regain his health.[59] Privately he told his old running mate Scotty Jack that he had been making daily visits for the last week to the Bethesda Naval Hospital. He said he had not received a "final verdict" but did not

55 Letter to J.J. Hickey, April 15, 1954, File: "Hunt-Personal-1953" Box 19, LCH Papers

56 Letter from Hunt to J.J. Hickey, June 4, 1954, File: "Hunt-Personal-1953" Box 19, LCH Papers

57 Letter to Hunt from Dr. May H. Barker of Greybull, June 14, 1954, File: "Hunt-Personal-1953" Box 19, LCH Papers

58 Letter from Robert Lowe to Hunt, June 10, 1954, File: "Hunt-Personal-1953" Box 19, LCH Papers

59 Letter from Hunt to Frank Gill, June 10, 1954, File: "Hunt-Personal-1953" Box 19, LCH Papers

think he would "need to undergo extensive surgery, possibly none."[60]

Others were left to believe the illness must be serious "or otherwise," a concerned constituent wrote, "I am sure it would not have required you to take the extreme step of withdrawing from the election."[61] A constituent said, "What we regret most personally is the indication that your health has been seriously impaired."[62] Expressions of concern were not confined to Wyoming. A woman from New York wrote, "You have given the best years of your life, your strength and your health for this great government of ours. Now all we could wish and hope for is that you should regain your health."[63]

Many of those who wrote still called him "Doc." One letter read, "I trust, Doc, your health will improve with some much needed rest and easing off the pressure."[64] "Dear Doc," wrote Pat Flannery, a former Democratic Party chairman, "I can only say that I hope very much the final word on your health will be much better than you apparently anticipate and allay all cause for concern."[65] Two weeks before his death, Hunt spoke optimistically. He assured one close friend that he felt he would soon "get our health back if possible and enjoy the remaining years that we may have to live."[66]

On June 10 Hunt told Fred Marble of Cheyenne he was looking for-

60 Letter from Hunt to William "Scotty" Jack, June 5, 1954, File: "Hunt-Personal-1953" Box 19, LCH Papers

61 Letter to Hunt from George Guy, June 9, 1954, File: "Hunt-Personal-1953" Box 19, LCH Papers

62 Letter to Hunt from D.P.B. Marshall, June 14, 1954, File: "Hunt-Personal-1953" Box 19, LCH Papers

63 Letter from Mrs. Joseph Ryback, June 11, 1954, File: "Hunt-Personal-1953" Box 19, LCH PAPERS

64 Letter to "Dear Doc" from George Wicke, June 8, 1954, File: "Hunt-Personal-1953" Box 19, LCH Papers

65 Letter to Hunt from L.G. Flannery, June 8, 1954, File: "Hunt-Personal-1953" Box 19, LCH Papers

66 Letter from Hunt to Mr. and Mrs. Earl Burwell, June 5, 1954, File: "Hunt-Personal-1953" Box 19, LCH Papers

ward to a few months' rest after which he would give more thought to the future.[67] Two days later, he wrote another letter to Scotty Jack. "One cannot look too far in the crystal ball these days, but it is my intention at this time to eventually return to Lander, and while I can't take up where I left off, I feel I can find something to keep me occupied."[68] A return to Lander was atop Lester Hunt's list. He began telling those who expressed concern about his health and future that he and Nathelle planned to take a month's vacation when the Senate adjourned later that year. After that, he said he would "return to my home in Lander."[69]

The man who had served in public office for 22 years wanted to make sure historians had access to his records. On June 10 he wrote to Dean Krakel, the archivist for the University of Wyoming. Lester Hunt wanted his papers placed at the university's library. He told Krakel they would be sent to him "the first of January 1955, when the Senate term expires."[70]

On June 12, Hunt wrote a personal letter to Zan Lewis, his close confidant and former aide. It was a week before he died. "Nathelle and I just decided it was best to get out and then when the Senate adjourns, take at least a month to get to feeling better," Hunt said. In mid-June Hunt wrote several letters to fellow dentists around Wyoming and elsewhere. He wanted to thank them for the support they had given him over the years. A June 18th letter from Hunt to Mary Ash of Sheridan, said, "I shall always be grateful to the fine people of Wyoming for the honors they have bestowed on me for nearly twenty-two years. Only hope that my efforts on their behalf have at least partially repaid them

67 Letter from Hunt to F.W. Marble, June 10, 1954, File: "Hunt-Personal-1953" Box 19, LCH Papers
68 Letter from Hunt to Scotty Jack, June 12, 1954, File: "Hunt-Personal-1953" Box 19, LCH Papers
69 Letter from Hunt to E.C. Rathwell, June 12, 1954, File: "Hunt-Personal-1953" Box 19, LCH Papers
70 Letter from Hunt to Dean F. Krakel, June 10, 1954, File: "Hunt-Personal-1953" Box 19, LCH Papers

for their support."

The final letter Lester Hunt wrote before his death was written also on June 18. He told a friend, "One of the pleasant aspects of this work I have been in is to have made and retained friends who are so considerate and thoughtful as to drop me a line at this time."[71]

The following morning, Lester C. Hunt took his own life.

71 Letter from Hunt to Mrs. Martin Weeg, June 18, 1954, File: "Hunt-Personal-1954" Box 19, LCH Papers

CHAPTER ELEVEN

Following the Facts

When journalist and novelist Allen Drury wrote *Advise and Consent,* his 1959 fictional account of Lester Hunt's ordeal, he opened the chapter immediately following the account of Senator Brigham Anderson's suicide with these haunting words, *"Now it is 4 A.M. and ghosts walk."* [1]

The truth took on a ghost-like quality during the few years Lester Hunt spent in Washington. Occasionally it could be seen, an apparition haunting some but not all. Among those who were haunted, some wanted to tell the truth about Lester Hunt's death, while others were not anxious to hear the truth. On the other hand, those who were not haunted had good reason to make certain the truth was not told.

A few months before his death, Senator Hunt wrote to Secretary of the Army Robert Stevens, a favorite target for Joe McCarthy's abuse. Stevens had just undergone another public ordeal of answering McCarthy's allegations when Hunt expressed his regret over the clash between the secretary and the Wisconsin senator. "You were trying valiantly to carry out the thoughts expressed by Abraham Lincoln when he said, 'I am not bound to win but I am bound to be true." Hunt comforted Stevens.[2] Truth mattered to Lester Hunt. It was what

---

1   Allen Drury, *Advise and Consent,* Opening line to chapter immediately following the fictional suicide of Senator Brigham Anderson, Doubleday (1959), 551

2   Letter from Hunt to Robert T. Stevens, February 29, 1954, File: "Hunt-Personal" Box 19, LCH Papers

he'd learned from those days in Atlanta and Lander, a value he carried with him to the state house in Cheyenne and to the U.S. Senate.
Nonetheless, for many the truth of what happened to him in the final
year of his life would not be told for decades.

Early attempts to tell the truth

Drew Pearson was the first to tell the truth, at least the parts of the truth
he knew. But there wasn't much of a market for it in the days, weeks,
and years following Hunt's death. Pearson was a nationally syndicated
journalist who wrote a muckraking column titled *Washington Merry-Go-
Round*. The column had, at best, a mixed reputation for truthfulness
though it was responsible for uncovering many a Washington secret.
Three days after Hunt died, Pearson became the first to tell the truth.

Pearson was unaware that the scandal reached the Eisenhower
White House. Those documents were still classified and not yet available to the public. But Pearson was the first to say publicly what was
well known among insiders in Washington. He blamed two powerful Republican senators in Hunt's suicide: Senators Herman Welker
(R-Idaho) and Styles Bridges (R-New Hampshire).

Senator Herman Welker, "Little Joe from Idaho"

Bridges and Welker were among the first and the last of Joe McCarthy's
supporters. In December of 1954, when two-thirds of the Senate voted
to censure McCarthy, these two joined 20 other Republicans, including
Senator Frank Barrett of Wyoming, stood by the discredited Wisconsin
lawmaker.[3] From the time Welker was elected in 1950, he had aligned
himself closely with McCarthy. The relationship earned him the deri-
sive nickname "Little Joe from Idaho."

---

3   Roll Call of Senate Vote on Senate Resolution 301, December 2, 1954, File 47, Box
077153, Folder "McCarthy Final Tally" Papers of Styles Bridges (Wyoming's other senator,
Joseph O'Mahoney, voted "aye")

Welker was a lawyer and a farmer. He moved to California but returned to Idaho following World War II. He served two short years in the state legislature before his election to the United States Senate. Welker was neither a workhorse nor a show horse. He was a relatively nondescript senator who was known for little else but his far right positions. He was also famous for his arrogance. Once a witness politely requested to "beg your indulgence" when he had a hard time hearing the senator's question. Welker replied, "You'd better beg!"[4]

In his last months in the Senate, Welker's detractors claimed a serious drinking problem interfered with his work and his judgment. One afternoon Senator Barry Goldwater felt the need to quiet Welker. The Idaho senator was humming and singing as he presided over the Senate. According to a page who witnessed the incident, Goldwater told his colleague that he was "in no condition" to "be in that seat." Welker challenged Goldwater to "come up and do something about it," Goldwater just turned and walked away.[5]

The rumor of Welker's alcohol problem was so pervasive that during his 1956 campaign for reelection, Welker was forced to offer a $1000 reward to "anyone proving Senator Welker has taken a drink of intoxicating liquor in 19 years."[6] No one claimed the reward but a 32-year-old Boise Lawyer named Frank Church claimed Welker's senate seat the following November. Herman Welker turned out to be a one-term senator. He was defeated by Church in 1956 and died the following year.[7]

---

4   Center for Labor Education & Research, University of Hawaii, http://www.hawaii.edu/uhwo/clear/HonoluluRecord/articles/v9n22/Gadabout.html

5   "Paging History" by Maureen Dowd (her brother Martin was the page involved), *New York Times*, September 6, 2011

6   "Newcomer Pressing Welker Hard At the Close of Idaho Senate Race" *New York Times*, November 2, 1956

7   *Biographical Directory of the United States Congress*, http://bioguide.congress.gov

Senator Styles Bridges

Styles Bridges was no run-of-the-mill politician. He was both a show horse and a workhorse. At the time he targeted Lester Hunt, he was the President *pro tempore* of the Senate, chairman of the powerful Appropriations Committee and a former chairman of the Republican Senate Campaign Committee.[8] He was the governor of New Hampshire when he was elected to the Senate in 1936. In 1952 he was selected by his GOP colleagues to serve as minority leader. He declined to stay in the job when Eisenhower became President and his party won a majority of the Senate seats. He then became the President *pro tempore*. Under the succession laws at the time, Styles Bridges was third in line to become President of the United States following the vice-president and speaker of the house. He was considered the "most important man in the United States Senate"[9] and "one of the five or six most powerful men in the world."[10]

Finding yourself in his sights was no small problem.

Access to power provided Bridges with access to wealth. Although fond of Bridges, Washington columnist Jack Anderson, who worked with Pearson before taking the *Washington Merry-Go-Round* by-line, called him "an incorrigible crook."[11] Said Anderson, "I don't think he considered himself corrupt but he was."[12]

James J. Kiepper, who taught at Columbia and the University of Albany while playing a major role in Republican politics, was Bridges' biographer. Kiepper's business cards identified himself as "Editor/Biographer-U.S. Senator Styles Bridges." After editing the Senator's papers, he wrote a flattering biography entitled *Styles Bridges: Yankee*

8   James J. Kiepper, *Styles Bridges-Yankee Senator,* Phoenix Publishing (2001), 146
9   "Senator Styles Bridges: New Hampshire Yankee" *American Mercury Magazine,* August 1954, reprinted in the *Congressional Record,* August 1, 1954, 13293-13296
10   Kiepper, Supra. 195
11   Kiepper, Supra. 187
12   Id.

Senator" in 2001. Kiepper glossed over Bridges' responsibility for the Hunt suicide but made room in his book to fully discuss some of the other darker angels of Bridges' character.

The New Hampshire farmer arrived in the U.S. Senate rather poor by comparison to most of his colleagues. Shortly after arriving he filed a federal income tax return reporting earnings of $12,508.51, of which $12,000 was his senate salary.[13] But he left the Senate and this life on the same day in 1961, apparently quite wealthy. The year before he died, Bridges reported income of $55,084.08. Over the intervening years, his Senate salary had increased to $22,500. His non-government income went from a few hundred dollars more than $23,000.[14] If Kiepper's information is accurate, there may have been a great deal more income which was not reported.

Most senators, including Hunt, complained their government salary was insufficient to make ends meet.[15] Bridges found a way to stretch it. He left an official estate of as much as half a million dollars when he died in 1961, the rough equivalent of nearly $4,000,000 today. The formal accounting did not include massive amounts of additional cash he left lying around at a number of locations to be retrieved by his wife following his death. Kiepper reported the senator's staff and some friends "were given valises and asked to keep them at home. In the event of the senator's death, the valises were to be turned over, unopened, to Doloris (Bridges' wife)."[16]

After his funeral, Doloris retrieved "six large manila envelopes

13   1939 Federal Income Tax Return for Styles Bridges, File 119, Box 095063, Folder "1939 Income Tax" Papers of Styles Bridges

14   1960 Federal Income Tax Return for Styles Bridges, File 120, Box 060024, Folder "1960 Income Tax Return" Papers of Styles Bridges

15   In a letter to constituent Jack Smith of Cody, February 3, 1954, Hunt wrote, 'I have found that my salary has not been sufficient since I have been in the Senate to compensate me for the necessary expenses I have incurred with my duties as a Senator." File: "Congressional Salaries" Box 11, Papers of Lester Hunt

16   Id. 189

and one small letter-sized envelope" from the New Hampshire Savings Bank in Concord.[17] Doloris later acknowledged receiving "a million dollars in cash, money that was never accounted for." Following her death, as much as another $100,000 in cash was discovered "behind a bookcase in the cellar of Bridges' home."[18] Clearly, public service had been very, very good to Styles Bridges.[19]

The so-called "Yankee Senator" became known most for how long he served. Colleagues called him "the Gray Eminence."[20] He died of a heart attack in 1961, just a few weeks before completing a quarter of a century in the Senate. Lyndon Johnson attended his memorial as he had Lester Hunt's.[21]

Pearson's column

"Hunt had been living under the fear of political blackmail in connection with his son," Pearson wrote a few days after Hunt's death."[22] Pearson had long been aware of the threats made against Hunt by some of his colleagues. He knew who they were and what they had threatened if Hunt refused to resign from the Senate. Pearson regretted having not reported the story earlier. "Perhaps if I had brought the whole thing into the healthy light of day," Pearson wrote with regret, "Senator Hunt might have adjusted himself some time ago and might be alive today." However, Hunt had made a personal appeal to Pearson, asking him not to write the story because of the emotional

---

17   Id. 199

18   Id. 189

19   In 1962, Deloris sought to replace her late husband but was defeated in the Republican primary. Democrat Thomas McIntyre won Bridges' seat in the November election. He served until 1979.

20   Kiepper, Supra. 231

21   Id. 233

22   "Walker Threatened Hunt's Son With Trial-Pearson" *The Laramie Daily Bulletin*, June 23, 1954

toll it would take on his family.[23] He was no longer restrained. Pearson had many but not all of the facts that have been corroborated over the years. He learned, for example, that following Buddy's arrest, the prosecutors made a decision not to charge him because it was a first offense. However, Senators Welker and Bridges threatened to have his son prosecuted if Hunt did not resign immediately.

Hunt's seat was critical. The 96-member Senate was effectively tied between the two parties.[24] While there were 48 Democrats and 47 Republicans, there was one independent, Wayne Morse of Oregon who usually voted with the GOP.[25] Vice-president Richard Nixon was available to cast tie-breaking votes when necessary. One seat made a difference. If Hunt resigned, his replacement would undoubtedly be a Republican given that Wyoming's Republican Governor C.J. "Doc" Rogers, would make the appointment. Hunt told Pearson the previous December of the threat. He and Nathelle "debated it for a week" before deciding he would not permit himself to be "blackmailed" out of office.

Pearson revealed that the heat was then turned higher. Senator Bridges joined Welker in pressuring the District of Columbia police and prosecutors to re-file the charges they had earlier dismissed. Pearson said the senators met with police detective Roy Blick, head of the vice squad. According to the column, they "handed him an envelope" allegedly containing his unsigned resignation. Blick, according to Pearson's sources, was given a choice of prosecuting young Hunt or facing the political realities.

As a result, Lester Hunt, Jr. was prosecuted and convicted. The fol-

23 Id.
24 Neither Alaska nor Hawaii had yet been admitted to the Union.
25 The slim Republican majority was precarious. Many expected Morse to change parties soon and he did. He had been elected and reelected as a Republican in 1944 and 1950. In 1956 he was reelected as a Democrat. (Biographical Directory of the United States Congress http://bioguide.congress.gov)

lowing spring, even in the face of continuing threats, Hunt announced he was a candidate for reelection. But he remained nervous about the threats. "Mrs. Hunt," the senator said later, "hardly survived the trial. She didn't eat for a week." Pearson reported Hunt's words, "If the opposition brings this up in the senate race,' he told this column, 'I shall withdraw."

Pearson also reported Hunt had undergone medical examinations after which he announced on June 4 he had decided to withdraw for health reasons. "But I am sure that on top of this," the column concluded, "Lester Hunt, a much more sensitive soul than his colleagues realized, just could not bear the thought of having his son's misfortunes become the subject of whispers in his reelection campaign."

Following the publication of Pearson's column, a second columnist, Marquis Childs of the *Washington Post*, confirmed key facts from the Pearson story. In a column entitled "Smears and Tears Plague the Senate," Childs blamed what he called 'the McCarthy-Welker faction of the party."[26]

Bridges and Welker each made a cynical appearance at a June 30 Senate memorial service held for Hunt. After Lyndon Johnson delivered an eloquent remembrance of the man whom he called "one of God's kindly men" Senator Bridges rose to speak. "Mr. President," he began, "I wish to pay tribute to the distinguished late Senator, Lester Hunt, of Wyoming." Bridges recounted his acquaintanceship with Hunt, how they had served together on the Armed Forces Committee, and of his "personal knowledge of the outstanding contributions which he made as a member of that committee." Bridges ended with, "Today I join my colleagues who have paid tribute to this man who had demonstrated the best qualities that should characterize an American."[27]

26   Marquis Childs, "Smears and Tears Plague the Senate" *Washington Post*, June 30, 1954
27   *Memorial Services Held in the Senate and House of Representatives of the United States, Together With Remarks Made in Eulogy of Lester C. Hunt, Late a Senator From Wyoming,* United States Government Printing Office, (1955) 15, 16

Senator Welker's eulogy followed. "Mr. President," he said, "indeed this is a dark day." The Idaho lawmaker called Hunt "truly emblematic of all that was good in America." Welker added, "that had he lived, I venture to say he could have been the senior Senator from Wyoming as long as he lived, or as long as he desired."[28]

Efforts to discredit Pearson

Having memorialized Lester Hunt, Welker and Bridges teamed with other McCarthy allies and went after Pearson. McCarthy made no bones about his disdain for the columnist. There were few knick-knacks in the senator's office but one was a framed, white sledgehammer. It was inscribed "For Drew Pearson Only."[29] The day after the Republican senators first saw Pearson's column, they went on the attack. On June 21 they telegrammed the Bell Syndicate, a New York enterprise that delivered articles and columns to newspapers around the country. Among them was the weekly Pearson column. Bridges threatened that "if your syndicate or any of your papers under contract with you carry the Drew Pearson story with respect to the undersigned and the late Lester Hunt that you and each of you will be held strictly accountable."[30]

Bridges then went after Pearson's sponsors, the Capital Transit Company. The company owned and operated all streetcars and buses in Washington and depended heavily on political connections to maintain its monopoly. The corporate president undoubtedly wanted nothing to do with a fight with a man of Bridges' power. Without taking time to adequately investigate the facts, Mr. J.A.B. Broadwater

---

28   Id. 20, 21

29   Newspaper story, "The Private Life of Joe McCarthy" *The American Weekly*, August 16, 1953, Papers of Joseph R. McCarthy Series 12, Reel 8, Marquette University.

30   Telegram from Senator Bridges to Bell Syndicate President, June 21, File: 43, Box 076123, Folder: 112 "Hunt-Senator Lester C." New Hampshire Division of Records, Management and Archives, Concord, New Hampshire (hereinafter "Papers of Styles Bridges)

promptly apologized for airing the Pearson allegations of Bridges' role in Hunt's suicide. "Being fully aware of your long and distinguished record of public service both in the United States Senate and your own state, we do not believe you would be a party to a plan to intentionally injure one of your colleagues," wrote Broadwater. He assured the unhappy Senator that if he'd reviewed Pearson's comments ahead of the telecast, he would have censored him. And then he did. He told Bridges the company would cancel its contract with Pearson.[31]

Broadwater felt he needed to do even more penitence. Capital Transit purchased a quarter-page ad in the *Laconia Evening Citizen* on July 20, 1954, reprinting the apology letter in full. It was a follow-up to that newspaper's challenge to Publisher Loeb to prove the case he claimed to have in his July 17 editorial defending Bridges and Welker.[32] The same ad was placed in newspapers throughout the nation at presumably enormous cost to Capital Transit's shareholders.[33]

Senator Barry Goldwater joined the anti-Pearson chorus. He inserted the Capital Transit apology in the Congressional Record adding, "The sponsors of the Pearson telecast, the Capital Transit Company, recognizing the gross errors in the telecast, have written to the Senator from New Hampshire (Mr. Bridges) and the Senator from Idaho (Mr. Welker) apologizing for the telecast."[34]

On August 26, under an editorial offering its readers free "Let's Get Out of the U.N." buttons, the *Colorado Springs Gazette* printed a column by syndicated columnist Holmes Alexander. A Washington writer for the McNaught Syndicate, Alexander wrote a column entitled, "Pearson

31 Letter to Bridges from J.A.B. Broadwater, July 12, 1954, File: 43, Box 076123, Folder: 112 "Hunt-Senator Lester C." Papers of Styles Bridges

32 *Laconia Evening Citizen*, July 20, 1954. File: 43, Box 076123, Folder: 112 "Hunt-Senator Lester C." Papers of Styles Bridges

33 "Pearson's Radio Sponsor To Beg Bridges Pardon" *New Hampshire Sunday News,* July 18, 1954

34 *Congressional Record,* July 20, 1954, 10562-3

Spreads a Lie." Relying on nothing but the denials of Bridges and Welker, Alexander said there was "no truth in Mr. Pearson's charges." He added the words from a letter written by an unidentified man who claimed to have walked down a Senate hallway with Hunt and Welker a few days before Hunt killed himself. The man said the "jovial conversation" among the three of them was proof that Welker was not guilty.[35]

Riding the middle rail was the editor of a California newspaper, the *Tulare Times*. After repeating Pearson's allegations, he admitted he was "inclined to believe them up to a certain point." He thought Bridges and Welker were guilty of using Buddy's problems to force Hunt to resign, but he didn't believe they had "death in mind." He proposed a novel solution, calling on Wyoming's Republican Governor C.J. "Doc" Rogers to pull the rug out from under Bridges and Welker by appointing a Democrat to replace Hunt "just to see where the loudest squeals come from."[36]

The harshest criticism of Pearson expectedly came from William Loeb. He was a McCarthy supporter, Bridges ally and the influential publisher of the *Manchester Union Leader* in Manchester, New Hampshire. Loeb personally penned an editorial entitled "Pro-Communist Attack on Bridges." Loeb predicted, "This dirty, unfounded accusation will soon be exposed for the baseless lie it is."[37] Unlike Pearson, Loeb was working without the facts, using only his political prejudices to acquit Bridges.

Bridges sought to stretch the evidence to force the columnist's bosses to kill Pearson's June 23 report.[38] Among the allegations in the column was an assertion that the two senators approached Detective Blick in Bridges' office where they demanded the detective's resigna-

35 "Pearson Spreads a Lie" *Gazette Telegraph-Colorado Springs,* August 26, 1954, File: 43, Box 076123, Folder: 112 "Hunt-Senator Lester C." Papers of Styles Bridges
36 "Fatal Politics" *Tulare Times,* June 22, 1954, 5
37 "Pro-Communist Attack on Bridges" *Manchester Union Leader,* July 15, 1954
38 *Drew Pearson Diaries 1949-1959* Edited by Tyler Abell, Holt, Rinehart and Winston (1974), 322-323

tion. On July 9 Blick signed an affidavit denying Bridges called him to his office regarding "the so-called Hunt case." The detective also denied Bridges handed him an envelope or demanded his resignation."[39] Neither fact was central to the question of whether Bridges and Welker had hounded Lester Hunt into suicide.

Yet it seemed the two senators had been successful in ending any search for the truth.

A "pall of gloom" but no investigation

"I can think of few events which cast a greater pall of gloom over the Senate," Lyndon Johnson lamented, "than the untimely and tragic death of our beloved colleague, Lester Hunt." Despite Johnson's strong words, the Senate never undertook an ethics or any other investigation to learn the truth. Hunt was buried and replaced by a Republican. The majority shifted only momentarily to the GOP. The following November, Joseph O'Mahoney won the seat back for the Democrats. Justice has seldom been so poetic as it was on a January 1955 morning. Custom required the President *pro tempore* to swear in newly elected senators. Styles Bridges administered the oath of office to Wyoming's new senator.[40] In the end, hounding Lester Hunt to his death gave Bridges and his party a majority for a brief six months.

Other attempts to tell the story

Any lost ghosts hanging around for the truth to be told had a long wait. It's not that people didn't know the truth. In 1959, Allen Drury was a reporter who covered the Senate for United Press International. As a journalist, Drury stayed away from reporting the story. Yet he knew

39   Affidavit signed by Roy Blick, Inspector, Morals Division, Metropolitan Police Department, July 9, 1954, File: 43, Box 076123, Folder: 112 "Hunt-Senator Lester C." Papers of Styles Bridges
40   Kiepper, Supra. 204

enough of the truth to write a fictional account of the incident. Drury's book, *Advise and Consent,* won a Pulitzer Prize and became a popular movie. The book tells a story of the blackmailing of a U.S. Senator in the midst of a bitter fight over the confirmation of the President's nominee for Secretary of State. His adversaries learn the Senator once engaged in a homosexual relationship. The result is the suicide of Senator Brigham Anderson, fictionally of Utah. Ironically, even cruelly, the villain is portrayed as a senator from Wyoming.

One of the people who most did not want to revisit the story was, understandably, Mrs. Hunt. It was her husband, her family, and her personal tragedy. Mrs. Hunt was adamant. She did not want the "blackmail" story to be told. Perhaps she truly believed her husband took his own life because of health problems. Perhaps she was determined that the story of Buddy's arrest not be retold time and again as it would be if the suicide were fully investigated either by law enforcement or historians. Perhaps the stigma of suicide and the overall pain of the entire ordeal was simply too burdensome and she preferred it all be forgotten. She refused to discuss it and didn't want others doing so.

In 1964, a decade after Hunt died, Wyoming historian T.A. Larson wrote what became the preeminent textbook on the state's history. Larson's book, *History of Wyoming,* has been the mainstay for high school and college history courses alike since its publication in 1965. Larson's research confirmed the story told by Drew Pearson in the immediate aftermath of Hunt's death. In 1964, he conferred with Mike Manatos, by then an administrative aide to President Lyndon Johnson. Manatos, Hunt's former administrative aide who was the first to find the Senator's body, assured Larson that the "Pearson column was quite accurate except that I know of no health problem that Senator Hunt had at the time of his suicide."Manatos and others provided Dr. Larson with additional facts corroborating Pearson.

Larson sent a draft of that section of his proposed book to Mrs.

Hunt for her review. The draft relied heavily on Pearson's account and added facts he had gathered from a few other sources. Although more than a decade had come and gone, the matter of her husband's very public death was yet too awful. Mrs. Hunt responded to Larson through her attorney. Mr. J.J. Hickey served as Wyoming Democratic Party chairman when Hunt was in the Senate. Now Hickey represented Mrs. Hunt. He informed the historian he had read "the proposed statement by you in your forthcoming book."[41] Hickey said he found "the contents of the statement are not factually accurate." Hickey threatened litigation if that version of the story found its way into a published book. "I would advise you," Hickey wrote Larson, "that the inaccuracies of the statement might subject you to some action on behalf of those who might be injured by its circulation." Hickey derided Pearson as a writer "who has, in times past, been known to have made false statements in his column and subsequently has retracted them." Larson was bluntly asked to limit his historical explanation of the suicide of Senator Hunt to "no more than his ill health."

Larson quickly acceded. Dr. Larson was not only a history professor at the University of Wyoming but was also actively involved in Democratic Party politics. He served in the Wyoming legislature from 1977-1984. His relationships with the Hunts and others in the party made it difficult for him to ignore Mrs. Hunt's entreaty. Two days after receipt of the Hickey letter, Larson assured him he would refrain from telling the story. "Since, however, Mrs. Hunt apparently thinks that she, rather than Bridges and Welker would be hurt, I am going to say as little as possible, since I have not the slightest desire to hurt her feelings," Larson assured Hickey.[42] As a result, students of Wyoming history have for decades learned little more than the simple account of

41   Id. Letter from T.A. Larson to J.J. Hickey dated February 28, 1964, File: "Lester Hunt" Box 18, Larson Papers
42   Id. Letter from T.A. Larson to J.J. Hickey dated February 28, 1964, File: "Lester Hunt" Box 18, Larson Papers

the Senator's death written by Dr. Larson in his textbook, "In June 19, 1954, Senator Lester C. Hunt, overwhelmed by political and personal problems, committed suicide."[43]

It is interesting to note that despite Hickey's direct request, Dr. Larson's history did not allude to the questionable claim that Senator Hunt suffered from health problems. Although Hunt spoke of health concerns as his reason for withdrawing from the Senate race, there is evidence that was a pretext. Larson would have certainly been aware that Drew Pearson had written an account of what had been told to him by a "Dr. Calvert" at Bethesda that there was "nothing wrong with (Hunt's) health."[44]

In 1980, Manatos told historian Rick Ewig he was not aware of anything that would substantiate stories of Hunt's health problems.[45] While Hunt told friends that he had been undergoing several days of medical tests at Bethesda Naval Hospital, Manatos said he knew only of the senator's annual visits to the hospital for a physical examination.

What Manatos remembered of this matter years later conflicts with what he told reporters on the day of Hunt's death. However, on that dark day, Bethesda officials basically confirmed Manatos' 1980 version. In the hours following the Senator's suicide, reporters sought to confirm whether Hunt had any serious health problems that may have contributed to his decision. Bethesda officials said the only record they had of treating him was "on June 3 when Senator Hunt received treatment for hemorrhoids."[46] The Senate physician told a somewhat different, though equally benign story. Rear Admiral George R.W. Carver said Hunt had been examined at Bethesda. Urologists were probing

43   T.A. Larson, *History of Wyoming,* University of Nebraska Press (1965), 520
44   Pearson Diaries, 321
45   Letter from Manatos to Rick Ewig, April 30, 1980
46   "Senator Hunt Found Shot in Office, Dies" *Washington Star,* June 19, 1954

a possible kidney infection.[47] Obviously, neither condition would have been particularly serious, much less life threatening.

For his part, Senator Hunt had earlier "toned down the wild-fire speculation on his physical condition." Following the announcement he had decided not to seek reelection because of health problems, friends and supporters assumed his health problems must have been serious if they forced him out of the campaign. "I am not quite at the threshold of death,' Hunt said laughingly, 'but I am not in as good physical condition as I'd like to be."[48]

In writing this book, every attempt was made to locate Hunt's medical records. Requests were made under the Freedom of Information Act to Bethesda and the National Archives. When they were unsuccessful, the help of the office of Wyoming Senator John Barrasso was enlisted. His staff also made repeated inquiries of several federal agencies and eventually learned the records were destroyed 30 years after Hunt's death.[49]

After Larson's book was published, the search for the truth was called off for nearly two decades. In 1983, Wyoming historian Rick Ewig wrote a brief history of Hunt's demise. *McCarthy Era Politics-The Ordeal of Senator Lester Hunt,* published in the spring of 1983, may have been the first time many of the people of Wyoming learned that one of their senators had committed suicide. After Pearson, Dr. Larson was the first to unearth many of the unseemly details, but Ewig was the first to publish them.[50] The following account benefits greatly from Ewig's

47   "Services Set Today For Senator Hunt" *Washington Times-Herald,* undated clipping, File: "Republican National Committee" Box 191, Eisenhower Library

48   Id.

49   The following is the text of an email received by the author from Daniel Gallegos, Military Liaison for Sen. Barrasso. "I contacted Bethesda and went from records to Patient Administration to Death Certificate and finally correspondence. There I learned that back in the 50's the hospital would hold the records for about 30 years than destroy them. I am sorry I could not be of more help."

50   Rick Ewig, *McCarthy Era Politics-The Ordeal of Senator Lester Hunt,* Annals of Wyoming, Vol. 55, Number 1, Spring 1983,

courageous work and adds additional facts that have, over time, come to the surface.[51]

Following the facts

Lester C. Hunt, Jr. was arrested on June 9, 1953. The young man was taken to the office of the Morals Division on the Fifth Floor of the Municipal Center in the District of Columbia. He was photographed and fingerprinted. Hunt's name was recorded in the Bond and Arrest List maintained by the department and available to the press and the public.[52] Hunt spent a night in jail, too embarrassed to call his parents.[53]

The following morning, the arresting officers, John F. Costanza and N.C. Vasile, presented the case to assistant U.S. Attorney Kitty Blair Frank. She authorized "the issuance of an Information charging Hunt with soliciting for a lewd and immoral purpose."[54]

Lester Hunt was not particularly well liked around the District of Columbia police department. A year earlier he publicly called the department "corrupt" claiming "the graft and dishonesty of the (D.C.) police are comparable to any of the situations uncovered by the Kefauver Committee."[55] But that didn't preclude a key officer from extending a kindness to the senator. Sometime after the Information was issued, Roy Blick telephoned Senator Hunt's office to let him know his son was in trouble.[56] Mike Manatos met personally with Blick. Young Hunt was

51   James J. Kiepper relied almost entirely on Ewig's account in the brief section of his biography dealing with Bridges' role in Hunt's death. *Styles Bridges: Yankee Senator,* Phoenix Publishing (2001), 145-147

52   "Memorandum: Hunt Case" From Bill Reisinger, File: Senator Lester Hunt, F155, 3 of 3, Papers of Drew Pearson, Lyndon Baines Johnson Library and Museum (hereafter "Drew Pearson Papers)

53   "Confidential Memorandum" Dated December 21, 1953, F155, 3 of 3, Drew Pearson Papers

54   Reisinger memo, Supra. 1

55   "This Week in the US Senate" *Riverton Review,* April 17, 1952 page 4

56   "Confidential memorandum" Drew Pearson Papers, Supra.

present. "I met briefly with some police official with my father's chief of staff," he recalled many years later. "There was a discussion in which a tape recording was played of the officer's report. Not much was said and the meeting ended. I was never told why we were meeting or what might or might not happen."[57]

Manatos explained to Blick that the senator's son was undergoing psychiatric treatment and informed the detective the young man was a seminary student.[58] At the time Buddy was enrolled in the Episcopal Theological School in Cambridge, Massachusetts. Blick, who achieved a reputation in the gay community for his ruthlessness, uncharacteristically promised Manatos he would "see if we could get the case thrown out."[59] Blick was not known for his generosity in these cases. Ben Bradlee, then a reporter, later the publisher of the *Washington Post*, called him "a nasty little man" who enjoyed getting press coverage. [60] He got ink by boasting of "how on one night he led a raid on Lafayette Park that resulted in the arrest of sixty-five homosexuals."[61]

For whatever reason, this time Blick was magnanimous and good to his word.[62] Soon "the Information was withdrawn at the request of Inspector Blick." Prosecutor Frank supported Blick's decision. The assistant U.S. Attorney gave the press a hand-written statement "to the effect that the defendant was a particularly disturbed individual under medical care for which reason prosecution offered little hope of cure and correction." Frank concluded the matter should be dismissed without prosecution.[63]

---

57   Transcript of responses of Lester C. Hunt, Jr. to questions posed by the author.

58   Transcript of meeting between Detective Blick and attorney Ford, File: 43, Box 076123, Folder: 112 "Hunt-Senator Lester C." Papers of Styles Bridges, 2

59   Id.

60   Charles Kaiser, *The Gay Metropolis 1940-1946*, Houghton Mifflin (1997), 71

61   *Lavender Scare*, 87

62   Prior to the mid-70s the Episcopal Theological School, where Hunt was enrolled at the time, had a strict policy of expelling gay students. Blick may have been made aware of the policy and attempted to save him from that penalty.

63   Id., 1

By now rumors were flying around Washington. When Bridges got wind, he conducted an investigation of his own. This is a man who had once carefully admonished his Senate staff, "Never put anything on paper that you don't want the whole world to read."[64] So it is more than a little significant that among his papers is an undated, hand-written note headed "Lester C. Hunt." Senator Hunt's home address is noted along with the following. "Arrested soliciting prostitution as a queer-June 9-June 10, 1953. Taken out on bond 5 A.M. in morning Police Court $500 bond (word indecipherable) by Ryan, gone to Cuba-Lafayette Park."[65]

Senator Bridges promptly arranged a meeting with Blick. A court reporter was in the room as an attorney named Charles Ford questioned the detective. Ford and another lawyer, Edward B. Williams, were hired by Bridges to represent him after the Drew Pearson column was published.[66] Both Ford and Williams were prominent and powerful lawyers with impressive credentials and connections. It was no accident Bridges chose Ford to represent him in this matter. Bridges was aware that Ford and Hunt had crossed swords before. Bridges' official papers include a file on Lester Hunt's death. Among the documents in that file is a newspaper clipping from June of 1952, two years before Hunt died. The clipping tells a story of the dramatic confrontation between Senator Hunt and attorney Ford during the Kefauver Crime Committee hearing in Washington. Ford was representing the D.C. police chief who was accused of financial irregularities. Ford was described as "his neck reddening from obvious anger, gripped the witness table where he was sitting, and rose slowly to his feet" to respond to a barrage from Hunt. The Wyoming senator had just said "there would be a lot less crime in the United States" if criminals were not protected by what he

---

64   Kiepper, Supra. 189
65   Handwritten memo, File 43, Box 076123, File No. 112 "Hunt, Senator Lester C."
Papers of Styles Bridges
66   Reisinger Memo, Drew Pearson Papers, Supra, 2

called "criminal attorneys."[67]

In addition to Bridges and Ford, Senator Welker joined the meeting. Ford asked Blick to explain why he had met earlier with Bridges and Welker. The detective told Ford, "It was 15 or 20 days after he (Lester Hunt, Jr.) was arrested. I was sent over by the Chief."[68] Blick said they met in "an ante-room in the United States Capitol" because "Senator Bridges and Senator Welker wanted to talk to me."[69]

In the days following Buddy's arrest, Senator Bridges was told that the "Lester C. Hunt" who had been charged with soliciting sex from an undercover officer was his fellow senator. Scott McCleod, a former FBI agent, was also once an administrative aide to Bridges.[70] Bridges introduced him to McCarthy who was so impressed he helped him get the job of security officer for the State Department. McLeod saw his primary duty there as identifying and removing anyone who might possibly be a homosexual, telling *Newsweek,* "I am required to show that a man looks like a duck, quacks like a duck and walks like a duck-not whether he is actually a duck."[71] McCleod earned a reputation for aggressively hunting homosexuals in government jobs. He ended hundreds of careers, justifying his harsh tactics by saying no one had a right to a government job "so if he loses his Government job, he hasn't lost any right."[72] McLeod once visited Wyoming on a speaking tour while Hunt was in the Senate. He told his audience that Americans

67   "Senator Hunt and Ford Clash Over Criminal Lawyer Tactics" Clipping from unidentified newspaper, File 43, Box 076123, Folder 112 "Hunt, Senator Lester C." Papers of Styles Bridges

68   Ford interview transcript, File 46, Box 076123, Folder 112 "Hunt, Senator Lester C." Papers of Styles Bridges

69   Id, page 1

70   For a discussion of R. W. Scott McLeod and his relationship with Bridges and Joseph McCarthy, see David K. Johnson's book, *The Lavender Scare: The Cold War Persecution of Gays and Lesbians in the Federal Government,* University of Chicago Press (2004), 124-131

71   "Interview with R.W. Scott McLeod: 'We're Cleaning Up the Mess in the State Department" *Newsweek,* February 12, 1954, 4

72   Id. 71

"aren't interested whether loyalty risks are drunks, dope fiends, sex perverts or Communists."[73]

Shortly after Hunt's arrest, McLeod ran into Bridges. Apparently believing it was Senator Hunt who had been arrested, he asked his former boss "why he didn't clean the homos out of the Senate."[74] Bridges immediately set out to learn more. Thus it was that Welker began the meeting by asking whether Senator Hunt himself had gotten into trouble. Inspector Blick cleared up the confusion.[75] He explained the confusion arose from the fact Hunt and his son had the same name. Welker asked about the status of the case. The detective couldn't recall the exact charge but said the assistant district attorney had ordered a *"nol pros."*[76] The charges had been dismissed. Young Hunt was not going to be prosecuted. Blick explained the reasoning behind that decision.[77]

Previous to those days, such charges were seldom if ever pursued. Suspected homosexuals would be brought to the station house and questioned. Cops hoped they would name others. Bond was forfeited and the suspect was never required to appear in court. Even innocent citizens followed this ritual in order to avoid the publicity that would convict them in the minds of others if they went to trial.[78] But that had changed. The attention given the issue by Congress meant the politicians were able to exercise more "prosecutorial discretion" than the prosecutors. Congress had transferred the duty to pursue these cases from the District of Columbia prosecutor to the U.S. Attorney, over

73   Id. at page 135

74   Papers of Drew Pearson, File: Lester Hunt, Folder 155, 3 of 3, LBJ Library

75   Transcript of Ford interview with Blick, Papers of Senator Styles Bridges, Supra, 1

76   Slang for a Latin term, *Nolle prosequis*, it is a legal meaning "to be unwilling to pursue" used in many common law criminal prosecution contexts to describe a prosecutor's decision to voluntarily discontinue criminal charges before trial.

77   Transcript of Ford interview with Blick, File: 43, Box 076123, Folder: 112 "Hunt-Senator Lester C." Papers of Styles Bridges, Supra, 1, 2

78   Robert D. Dean, *Imperial Brotherhood*, supra, 79

whom they had more influence and control.

Thus Blick had reason for deep foreboding as he left the meeting with a clear impression that Bridges and Welker were not pleased with either him or the decision.[79] Welker and Bridges began to use the clout they had as members of the Senate Committee on the District of Columbia. They called Robert Murray, the Chief of Police, to "demand an explanation."[80] Chief Murray said he was not aware of the facts but would "immediately contact the officer who handled such a charge."[81]

The two senators had a second meeting with Blick the following day. It was then Welker revealed he had heard rumors that Blick had taken a bribe to fix the case.[82] An acquaintance of the two senators told them the day before that "the Hunt case had been fixed by Blick and it was suggested that $2000 had changed hands in order to accomplish this."[83] He didn't say whose hands had participated in the alleged exchange. Blick denied doing anything illegal. Welker told him that "if there was anything crooked about it, God help you."

But in the face of such allegations made by two senators who had control over his department and perhaps his job, Blick angrily defended his handling of the case. "Everything I have done in this case was open and above-board. The man was charged, he was booked, and as I stated before that I have yet to take a theological student or minister, regardless of the religion or race because it would break down the religious foundations here in this country and if I was doing wrong they could get someone else for the job."[84]

Blick then left his second meeting with the senators. But Bridges and Welker were not done with Blick. After dinner, Blick was relaxing

79 Transcript of Ford interview with Blick, Papers of Styles Bridges, Supra, 2
80 Id., 2
81 Id., 1
82 Id., 2
83 Reisinger Memorandum, 1
84 Transcript of Ford interview with Blick, Papers of Styles Bridges, Supra, 2

with his family when the phone rang. Police officers dread those late evening phone calls and Blick was especially unhappy to receive this one. It was Senator Welker. He demanded Blick return to the Capitol immediately. This time they claimed to have "proof that there was $2000 passed to kill the case."[85] Welker pretended to think someone would be "so stupid as to pay $2000 for a charge that would only cost $25 or $35." Again Blick denied anything improper had influenced his decision to drop the charge.

As the third meeting ended, Welker put his arm around the detective's shoulder. There were suddenly ten or twelve other men at the door. Blick assumed they were reporters. As the reporters listened, Welker told Blick, "I am behind you if you are right, but if you are wrong you've got somebody who will fight against you."[86]

The affidavit Blick executed on July 9 said Bridges "did not call me to his office to discuss the Hunt case." It's true he did not. Welker summoned Blick. The sworn affidavit also acknowledged that at no time did they ask for his resignation as the Pearson column had claimed.[87] These were peripheral to the more serious charges. In the context of the real crime, this affidavit was akin to Willy Sutton denying he jaywalked on his way to the bank. Yet, it was important to Bridges to prove that at least some part of the Pearson story lacked foundation.

In any event, Inspector Blick was soon relieved of any responsibility for the case. The next thing he knew, someone had re-filed the Information and a warrant was issued for Lester C. Hunt, Jr.'s arrest.[88] Assistant U.S. Attorney Kitty Frank was also replaced. The case was assigned to Kenneth Wood who told the press he was "mystified" that the case had been dropped. "I have been unable to get a definite answer

85   Id., 3
86   Id. 3
87   Statement signed by Roy Blick, July 9, 1954, File: "Hunt, Senator Lester C." File 43, Box 076123, Folder 112, Papers of Styles Bridges
88   Id. 4

why those charges were dropped."[89] Although signed by Wood on June 30, 1953, it was not until October 2 that the criminal complaint was formally filed with the court.[90]

The delay might be attributed to the fact that at the time the charges were renewed, Buddy was, as indicated on Bridges' handwritten note, in Cuba for the summer. He was doing fieldwork related to his studies at the Episcopal Theological School. Buddy "was told to return to Washington and that the case would go to court."[91] However, the delay also afforded Bridges and Welker additional time to coerce Senator Hunt into resigning.

It was during this period that Welker asked an acquaintance to tell the Senator that "if Hunt would retire from the Senate at the end of this term and not run for reelection next year, the charges against his son would not be prosecuted."[92] The "acquaintance" of whom Welker made the request was Glenn "Red" Jacoby. Red Jacoby was the popular and influential Athletic Director at the University of Wyoming. He took the job while Hunt was governor, serving for 27 years, from 1946 until his death in 1973. He and Hunt had become close when they partnered to raise private funds to build UW's athletic facilities, War Memorial Stadium and the Fieldhouse. Jacoby was legendary in Wyoming for hiring successful football coaches such as Bowden Wyatt, Phil Dickens, Bob Devaney and Lloyd Eaton. Jacoby was posthumously elected to the National Association of College Athletic Directors Hall of Fame, the University of Wyoming Hall of Fame and the Idaho Sports Hall of fame.[93]

89   "Senator's Son Is Charged on Morals Count-Lester Hunt Seized Here June 9" *Washington Post,* July 4, 1953

90   Reisinger memo, 2

91   Transcript of responses of Lester C. Hunt, Jr. to questions posed by the author.

92   "Confidential Memorandum" from the LBJ Library, Papers of Drew Pearson, Supra.

93   Wyoming Athletics Hall of Fame Class of 1993, http://www.wyomingathletics.com/trads/hof-1993.html, accessed February 18, 2012

Because of their shared Idaho roots, Jacoby knew Welker.[94] The two grew up together and were close childhood friends. Jacoby also considered Lester Hunt close, telling him once, "friendships such as yours are surely honored and the source of much satisfaction to me."[95]

Welker telephoned Jacoby. He asked his friend to relay the threat to Hunt, telling Jacoby that if Hunt refused to resign, his son's name and the facts of his case would be smeared all over Wyoming.[96] Drew Pearson's staff confirmed Jacoby's involvement. Jacoby, they learned, took part in several three-way phone conferences. Styles Bridges often joined him and Welker to talk about the matter.[97] Many years later, Joseph Kimmitt, an administrative assistant to Montana's Senator Mike Mansfield who came to the Senate the year before Hunt died, also confirmed the story. "They had the coach of the University of Wyoming football team (sic), the name escapes me now, but he was a highly respected man—they gave him the mission of telling Hunt that if he ran, they were going to expose his son."[98]

Jacoby later told Manatos he refused to be the go-between. In a personal conversation with Manatos, Jacoby did acknowledge calling Tracy McCracken for the purpose of informing him of the plot. McCracken then, according to Jacoby, took the matter to Joe O'Mahoney who relayed it to Senator Hunt, "who after spending some difficult hours,

94   It follows that Welker would have been close to Jacoby. Herman Welker was a sports fanatic. According to one source "he was instrumental in bringing Hall of Fame slugger Harmon Killebrew to the Washington Senators. Killebrew was not the first major league ballplayer Sen. Welker discovered. Several years earlier, he told Griffith about a pitcher from Idaho named Vernon Law, but Law signed with the Pittsburgh Pirates after Bing Crosby, who owned stock in the Pirates, wrote to Law's mother praising her son." Al Eisele, editor, *The Hill, http://www.huffingtonpost.com/al-eisele/killebrews-death-highligh_b_865327.html,* Posted May 22, 2011, accessed March 2, 2012
95   Letter to Hunt from Jacoby, May 16, 1949, Box 22, LCH Papers
96   Letter from Mike Manatos to Rick Ewig, April 30, 1980
97   Paper of Drew Pearson, File: Lester Hunt, File 155, 3 of 3, LBJ Library
98   Joseph Stanley Kimmitt, Secretary for the Majority (1965-1976), Secretary of the Senate (10977-1981), Oral History Interviews, February 15, 2001 to October 9, 2001, Pages 35-36, Senate Historical Office, Washington, D.C.

finally declined."[99] Hunt decided that although it would be difficult to face his friends and supporters back in Wyoming, "he wasn't going to be blackmailed out of running for reelection."[100]

Lester C. Hunt, Jr. was then tried and convicted on October 6, 1953.

Senator Hunt was present throughout the trial. He listened as the undercover policeman told the story of how Buddy had "asked him to commit an immoral act after the two fell into conversation June 9 in Lafayette Park." He heard his son admit "that he and Costanzo were going to Hunt's home...for the purpose of committing an 'unnatural act' when the policeman flashed a badge and arrested him."[101]

An observer thought the defense should have prevailed, "since the police officer obviously was trying to entrap Hunt."[102] But the defense did not prevail. Senator Hunt sat in the courtroom listening as Judge John J. Malloy announced his son had been convicted. "The charge here is one of the most degrading that can be made against a man," Malloy proclaimed as he sentenced Buddy to a one hundred dollar fine or thirty days in jail.[103] Hunt paid the fine.

Friends who witnessed Hunt and his wife struggle through the legal proceedings were painfully aware of how distressed they were. The Senator and his wife faithfully sat through the entire trial. One of their friends who watched with them said it was the first time he had "seen a man die visibly."[104] Manatos said, "The trial of Buddy Hunt proved to be a heart-rendering (sic) experience for the Senator, not so much as to whether there would be a fallout politically, but because he felt so deeply that it was a reflection upon his family. He believed that had

99   "Confidential Memorandum" Papers of Drew Pearson, LBJ Library
100   Id.
101   "Senator's Son Convicted on Morals Charge" *Washington Post*, October 7, 1954
102   "Confidential Memorandum" December 21, 1953, Papers of Drew Pearson, LBJ Library
103   "Senator Hunt's Son Found Guilty of Sex Charge" *Washington Times Herald*, October 7, 1953, 5
104   Id.

he not been a senator, the ordeal could have been avoided."[105] Buddy would have never been convicted, Hunt believed, if he had given in to Bridges and Welker.

By the end of October, Hunt was thinking seriously about leaving public office. He spoke to the head of the American Dental Association about the possibility of working for them, perhaps as a lobbyist. He went so far as to discuss the matter with Senator Robert Kerr of Oklahoma, a Democrat who was elected to the Senate at the same time as Hunt. Kerr advised him his standing with colleagues would be served best by running rather than bowing out. "I think Bob is right," Hunt wrote to P.M. Cunningham, a dentist friend in Cheyenne. "My Democratic colleagues would not feel as kindly toward me if I were not a candidate as they would if I did try and then was defeated."[106]

If friends took note of Lester Hunt's ordeal, his enemies most certainly did not miss it. The story of Welker and Bridges' involvement was not the best kept secret in Washington but those who knew tried to keep it a secret. Only decades later were some willing to talk about those dark secrets. In 1990, a one-time administrative assistant to Arizona Senator Carl Hayden admitted during an oral history interview with the Senate Historical Office that the blackmail was common knowledge. Roy Elson, later a candidate for the Senate, thought Bridges "might be a little crooked." He said, "For instance, the (Lester) Hunt suicide. He and Knowland,[107] I think, they were threatening to expose Hunt's son as a homosexual, to force him out of the race. Finally he announced he wasn't going to run again, but he still blew his brains out. As I remember the time period, you sort of knew what was going on

105   Letter from Mike Manatos to Rick Ewig, April 30, 1980
106   Letter from Hunt to P.M. Cunningham, File: "Hunt-Personal-1954" Box 19October 29, 1953, LCH Papers
107   Referring to California Senator William Knowland. However, Elson was likely mistaken in his memory. The author has not found any evidence whatsoever of any involvement on the part of Knowland.

behind the scenes, and later some of it was confirmed. You could never really put your finger on it, but I think that the pressures that were put on him, particularly by those two gentlemen, caused him to break."[108]

According to Elson, a top member of the New Hampshire senator's inner circle, Chet Wiggins, confirmed rumors of Bridges' involvement. "I'm trying to think who else told me some of the background on that. Oh, Wiggins, Chet Wiggins was Bridge's administrative assistant," recalled Wiggins. "I think Chet one drunken—I mean one day when we had a few drinks—made some comments that sort of confirmed the politics that were involved at that time."[109]

While most kept quiet, there were exceptions such as Pearson and William M. Spencer, the chairman of the board of the North American Car Association and a Hunt confidant. He angrily confronted Welker and Bridges when the transcript of the June 30 Senate memorial service was made public in December. Spencer read it and was outraged that Welker and Bridges had participated in the eulogy. "I was shocked when I read this," Spencer wrote.[110] A few weeks before he died, Hunt had confided in him. Spencer knew "in detail the diabolical part you played following the unfortunate and widely publicized episode in which his son was involved."

Hunt had told Spencer all of the grisly details. "It seems apparent," Spencer said to Welker, "that you took every advantage of the misery which the poor fellow was suffering at the time in your endeavor to turn it to a political advantage." Spencer knew Bridges was equally guilty. "I understand, too, from Senator Hunt that Senator Bridges

108   Roy L. Elson, Administrative Assistant to Senator Carl Hayden and Candidate for the United States Senate, 1955-1969, Oral History Interviews, April 27 to August 21, 1990, Pages 67-68, Senate Historical Office, Washington, D.C.

109   Id. 67

110   Letter from William M. Spencer to Senator Herman Welker copied to Senator Styles Bridges, December 29, 1953, File: "Correspondence-December 1954-Personal" Box 83, Papers of Joseph C. O'Mahoney, Collection No. 275, American Heritage Center, University of Wyoming

had been consulted by you and approved of your action in the matter." Spencer copied Senator Bridges with his letter. Neither senator denied the letter's serious allegations.

In December 1953, Drew Pearson wanted to expose the two but it was Senator Hunt who dissuaded him. At Hunt's request, Pearson's friend and colleague, Tracy McCracken, pleaded with the columnist not to do it. Hunt told Pearson's partner, Jack Anderson, the trial had been an agony for his wife and that another story would only add to her misery.[111]

Though the trial and the accompanying publicity was behind them, Hunt believed the matter would be used against him in the coming campaign. He confided to Pearson that, "he could not bear to face his colleagues in the Senate." Hunt's hair turned completely white in a few short months.[112]

During December a strange and sinister event took place, leaving the Hunts fearful of what their enemies were capable. On December 11 or 12, someone broke into the Hunt's home and ransacked it.[113] The Hunts were out of town. While they were in Wyoming for the holidays and a much-needed rest, someone went looking for something in their Washington home. In the dark of a late Friday night or equally dark early Saturday morning someone never-to-be-identified, cut through a back porch screen. They broke two windows and unlocked the door. When neighbors whom the Hunts had asked to look after the house came by the next day, "They found the apartment totally ransacked, every drawer turned upside down, every cranny had been looked in."[114]

---

111   *Drew Pearson Diaries 1949-1959,* Holt, Rinehart & Winston (1974), 321
112   Id.
113   "Senator Hunt's Home Entered and Ransacked" *Washington Post,* December 13, 1953, 27
114   Interview of Lester C. Hunt, Jr. conducted by Rick Ewig, December 29, 1979, in Chicago, 17

Hunt said the apartment had been "completely torn apart."[115] Only a couple of token items were taken, a camera and a pair of binoculars.[116] Buddy believed "it was obviously some kind of a search."[117]

This incident was more than a little alarming to both Lester and Nathelle. The impact of having been the victim of a burglary is recognized by psychologists to leave behind enormous emotional baggage. Victims of burglaries often compare the experience to rape. A stranger entered their personal domain uninvited and took from them that which was most important, a sense of personal security they could not find anywhere else during those awful days.

Lester Hunt had not only been emotionally raped but he believed the "rapist" was someone who wanted his soul. This crime was neither random nor coincidental. Hunt knew what he didn't want to say to Nathelle or others. This stranger had a darker motive than simply to take a camera and a pair of binoculars or other property that did not belong to him. Hunt knew the burglars were looking for something that didn't exist. But yet he feared that those to whom the burglars were responsible could manufacture what they didn't actually find. Was the break-in simply designed to scare him and his wife? Were they searching for some kind of evidence with which to further torment him? In his heart, he knew who was responsible. Colleagues whom he had trusted were involved. Trust may be too strong a word. But Hunt never before expected his political adversaries to be capable of what they were in fact doing to his life. He and Nathelle were now left to contemplate what might come next, how far these people were willing to go.

No arrests were ever made nor any suspect identified. Nonetheless, the Hunts were unnerved by the incident. They suspected the phones

---

115   "Lowe Says Hunt Faced GOP Conspiracy" *Rawlins Daily Times,* July 1, 1954, 1

116   Letter from Hunt to Detective Frank E. Wright, Metropolitan Police Department, December 21, 1953, File: "Hunt-Personal-1953" Box 19, LCH Papers

117   Id. 17

in his office were tapped as well.[118] It was clear to Senator Hunt that although his refusal to resign had resulted in his son being convicted, that was not enough for those who were pursuing him relentlessly. His personal ordeal was far from over. By now Hunt had become so depressed he began taking lunch alone at his desk rather than joining colleagues in the Senate dining room.[119]

Early in the New Year, the chairman of the Democratic Senate Campaign Committee, aware of the Hunt's troubles, encouraged the Wyoming senator to run for another term. Earl Clements (D-Kentucky) surveyed Wyoming and thought Hunt would be easily reelected despite the publicity surrounding the trial. Clements was confident that if Hunt's opponents used the matter as a campaign issue it would backfire "to the point they will forever leave their opponent's personal misfortunes out of a political campaign."[120]

An April 5 poll proved Clements right. Hunt held a substantial lead over all potential opponents in every county of the state. He received 54.4% with the remaining 45.6% divided among all four potential GOP candidates.[121] The pollster reported, "as of this time you unquestionably would be reelected if you run for another term."[122]

Was President Eisenhower involved?

On April 15, Lester Hunt, in the face of all his personal problems, announced he would seek a second term. Welker and Bridges, who had held out hope that Hunt would bow out, renewed their plotting.[123]

118 "Lowe Says Hunt Faced GOP 'Conspiracy" *The Rawlins Daily Times,* July 1, 1954, 1

119 "Welker Threatened Hunt's Son With Trial-Pearson" *Laramie Daily Bulletin,* June 23, 1954, 1

120 Letter from Senator Earl Clements to Joseph C. O'Mahoney, File: "January 18, 1954" Papers of O'Mahoney

121 Letter from Herbert R. O'Connor, April 30, 1954, File: "Hunt-Personal-1954" Box 19, LCH Papers

122 Id.

123 "Confidential Memorandum" Papers of Drew Pearson, Supra.

The stick hadn't worked and so now they held out a carrot. With the approval of the Eisenhower White House, Hunt was offered an alternative. If he would leave the senate race, the President would appoint him to a high-paying job as Chairman of the Federal Tariff Commission. In 1954 a senator was paid $12,000 a year. The chairman of the Tariff Commission received $15,000.

A single page found among Eisenhower's official papers is headed "L.C. Hunt, Senator-Possibilities."[124] The document bears a notation verifying it was "Received May 3, 1954-Central Files." It lists eight executive branch jobs. Someone who likely had the authority to commit to a presidential appointment placed a mark near "Tariff Commission: $15,000—Six year term."

The Senator had tired of the confrontation with his powerful and incessant adversaries. This offer sounded like a way to end the ordeal and allow him, Nathelle and Buddy to move on with their lives, escaping the situation with dignity. Hunt discussed the offer with his friend, former Wyoming Governor Leslie A. Miller. He told Miller an "emissary from the Republicans" had relayed the offer to him. The *quid pro quo* was quite specific. Hunt must resign and agree not to run again for the Senate, though they didn't object if he ran for governor. The messenger believed President Eisenhower had signed off on the offer, which would have been necessary. The position required a Presidential appointment and Senate confirmation. The offer must have been preceded with the necessary political assurances. If Hunt agreed to resign and permit Republican Governor C.J. Rodgers to appoint a successor, the President would appoint him to a six-year term on the Tariff Commission.[125]

Hunt asked his staff for advice. All but one objected, as did Miller.

124   Eisenhower, Dwight D.: The Dwight D. Eisenhower Presidential Library and Museum Records as President, White House Central Files, Alphabetical File, "Hunt, Lester C."
125   T.A. Larson interview of Leslie A. Miller conducted October 9, 1966, Box 18, T.A. Larson Papers

"You can't do that, " he told his friend. "You couldn't face your friends in Wyoming." Hunt would be forced to explain how he had gotten an important job in exchange for turning control of the Senate over to the Republicans. Miller believed Hunt wanted to take the offer but asked him to sleep on it and to talk to Joe O'Mahoney. O'Mahoney gave Hunt the same recommendation he had received from Leslie Miller. The next afternoon, Hunt called the emissary and declined the offer.[126] After his death, a close political ally, State Representative Stan Lowe of Rawlins, lauded Hunt's refusal to take the job. Lowe said Hunt had been "true to his integrity, he refused to be bought off."[127]

At some point in this time period, Senator Welker let it be known that while many Wyoming newspapers had refused to run the story of Buddy's trial,[128] he would make sure the information found its way into every mailbox in the state.[129] He had printed 25,000 flyers to send to Wyoming voters.

The walls closed in around Lester Hunt. He was publicly committed to a campaign for reelection. Friends had already contributed thousands of dollars. But he knew that continuing to campaign exposed his wife and son to an ordeal he could not willingly permit them to suffer. Initially he had reluctantly decided to simply push forward with his plans to seek reelection. He flew to Cheyenne with the announced intentions of filing his formal candidacy with the secretary of state's office but returned to Washington having decided not to do so. "Something must have taken place in Cheyenne," Mike Manatos said years later. "The only explanation Hunt had was that he just wanted to

126   Id.

127   "Lowe Says Hunt Faced GOP Conspiracy" *Rawlins Daily Times*, July 1, 1954, 1

128   Rick Ewig, *McCarthy Era Politics: The Ordeal of Senator Lester Hunt*, Annals of Wyoming, Vol. 55, Number 1, Spring, 1983, see footnote 45 for a listing of those newspapers that carried the story and those that did not.

129   "Smears and Tears Plague the Senate" Column by Marquis Child, *Washington Post*, June 30, 1954

get away from it all."[130]

On June 4 Hunt sent a letter to Joe Hickey, the Wyoming Democratic Party chairman. "Regret exceedingly at this date to advise you that," he wrote, "due to personal reasons beyond my control, namely health, I am compelled to withdraw my announcement as a candidate for reelection to the United States Senate."[131]

A few days later, Hunt asked Leslie Miller to come to his office for a visit.[132] He began by sharing the April poll results, assuring Miller he could be reelected. Fear of losing was not behind his decision to withdraw. He wanted Miller to know why. Hunt explained Buddy's trial and the threats emanating from it had "almost killed" Nathelle and him. He said he had been diagnosed with in his kidney. It was operable, but one kidney would have to be removed and he knew the recuperation period would render a political campaign impossible.

On Friday evening the two old friends went to dinner. They sat in the parking lot talking for nearly an hour as Hunt told Miller the whole story of how he was being pressured by Bridges and Welker. He called it "blackmail." Hunt was aware the two senators were telling others that Inspector Blick had taken a bribe to halt Buddy's prosecution. They had also made known their plans to distribute 25,000 copies of the story of Buddy's arrest and conviction throughout Wyoming.[133]

Saturday Miller flew back to Wyoming after spending a week with Hunt. Senator and Mrs. Hunt drove him to the airport. They hugged and Miller left.

The following Thursday, Hunt's old friend Joe O'Mahoney dropped by for a visit. He found Hunt "pale and depressed." On Friday, Senator

---

130   Letter from Mike Manatos to Rick Ewig, April 30, 1980
131   Letter from Hunt to J.J. Hickey, June 4, 1954, File: "Hunt-Personal-1954" Box 19, LCH Papers
132   Notes from an interview Larson conducted with Leslie Miller on October 19, 1966, Box 18, T.A. Larson Papers
133   Id.

McCarthy told the press he intended to investigate a fellow senator "who had fixed a case."[134] Given those allegations and the relationships between McCarthy and Welker, Hunt may well have believed McCarthy had turned his sights on him. Did McCarthy think Hunt was involved in bribing Blick? After Hunt's suicide, Senator Karl Mundt of South Dakota was quick to deny McCarthy was referring to Hunt.[135] However, neither he nor McCarthy named the senator to whom the threat was aimed, nor did they ever investigate any of their other colleagues for such a charge.

"But one would have to know whether a friend of the desperate man had not that very day addressed him indifferently," Camus wrote in his discussion of suicide. While McCarthy was no friend to Hunt, Camus' words are haunting. Lester Hunt may well have wondered whether it was he to whom McCarthy was referring. McCarthy's threat fell upon the ears of a desperate man as all the walls were closing in on him. Speaking of the one who may have "that very day addressed him indifferently," Camus added poignantly, "He is the guilty one."[136]

In any event, it was early the following morning when Lester Hunt voluntarily ended his life.

Blackmail is, of course, a crime. The elements of the crime include threatening a person to reveal embarrassing, disgraceful or damaging facts (or rumors) about a person to the public, family, spouse or associates unless paid off to not carry out the threat. The evidence would likely cause a reasonable person to conclude that Bridges and Welker attempted to blackmail their colleague. The evidence is seemingly direct and unrelenting. They put unbearable pressure on Lester Hunt in order to achieve a temporary and narrow political gain. However, the foregoing leaves open one other question.

134 *Drew Pearson Diaries, supra. 321*
135 "Hunt Takes Life in Senate Office" *New York Times,* June 20, 1954, 72
136 Camus, *Myth of Sisyphus,* Supra. 5

Was Joe McCarthy complicit?

In a court of law there are two kinds of evidence on which a person may be convicted. One is direct evidence, the kind that most probably convicts Bridges and Welker. The other is circumstantial. There is a popular but erroneous belief that defendants in criminal cases cannot be convicted by circumstantial evidence. It was, by coincidence, in 1954, that the U.S. Supreme Court ruled, "circumstantial evidence is intrinsically no different from testimonial [direct] evidence."[137] There is no legally meaningful distinction between the kind of direct evidence that implicates Bridges and Welker and the circumstantial evidence pointing to the likely involvement of Senator Joseph McCarthy. Indeed, if circumstantial evidence is permitted in criminal courts, is it not even more persuasive in the historical record?

The same circle of plotters that encircled Senator Hunt in the last year of his life had, long before, allied with Joe McCarthy around the issue of homosexuals. Those men, whom history provides direct evidence of involvement in the Hunt matter, were integrally involved with McCarthy. They shared philosophies, motives and tactics. As incriminating or more so is the fact that the Hunt blackmail was not the first time McCarthy and Roy Cohn, his right-hand man, had used the same tactic.

When Cohn and his boss were accused of using their influence to obtain special treatment for Cohn's friend David Schine who had been drafted, General Max Reber was called to testify. McCarthy blindsided the General, asking about his brother. Sam Reber had once been the Acting Deputy U.S. High Commissioner in Germany. Roy Cohn's own biography of McCarthy tells part of the story. McCarthy, admits Cohn, asked whether the General was aware his brother had been forced to resign because he was found to pose a security risk, code for homosex-

---

137   *Holland v. United States*, 348 U.S. 121, 75 S. Ct. 127, 99 L. Ed. 150 (1954)

ual.[138] The part of the story Cohn failed to disclose was that McCarthy and Cohn had heard a rumor that Samuel Reber had engaged in a homosexual relationship as a college student years earlier. Because Reber had heavily criticized Cohn's work, they threatened to expose him unless Reber resigned his State Department job.[139]

As the staff director for Senator McCarthy, Cohn readily resorted to using allegations or rumors of homosexuality to destroy reputations. According to historian John D'Emilio, Cohn's way of hiding his own homosexuality was to employ cruelty to other gays.[140] In his decidedly unflattering portrayal of Roy Cohn, Nicholas Von Hoffman saw the Reber incident as presaging the Hunt episode and demonstrating the "*modus operandi*" of McCarthy, Bridges and Cohn. "Roy's role (in the Hunt matter), if any, in the crime can only be guessed at. The *modus operandi* was the same as that used against Samuel Reber," concluded Von Hoffman. "Hunt had been a quiet, persistent but rational foe of McCarthy's." Von Hoffman went on to describe the relationship between Cohn and Bridges as being close enough to have facilitated the joint involvement of the two in the Hunt blackmail. He quoted an unidentified Congressman. "There was no question at all that they were extremely tight. He could get 'im on the phone any time he wanted him; he'd brag about different things that Bridges would do. They were very, very close."[141]

In his biography of Hubert Humphrey, Columbia University Professor Carl Solberg, who carefully studied the facts surrounding Lester Hunt's death, concluded, "the suicide of Wyoming Senator Lester Hunt (occurred) under the most intimidating McCarthyite

138   Roy Cohn, *McCarthy*, The New American Library (1968), 146
139   Neil Miller, *Out of the Past*, supra. 267
140   Miller, Id. 267
141   Nicholas Von Hoffman, *Citizen Cohn: The Life and Times of Roy Cohn*, Bantam Books (1988) initially published by Doubleday (1968), 231

innuendos."[142]

To be fair, Senator Hunt's closest aide, Mike Manatos, seemed willing to exonerate McCarthy years later. More than a quarter of a century after Manatos found his boss's body, he was asked by historian Rick Ewig whether McCarthy played a role. Manatos replied, "No. As a matter of fact Joe McCarthy was asked to join in the 'get Hunt' activities and reportedly angrily defended Hunt as an honorable man. He would have had no part of the effort."[143]

That differs considerably with multiple other reports of the conflict between Hunt and McCarthy. No doubt there was a high level of acrimony between the two. The website of the United States Senate includes a history of this tragedy that implicates McCarthy. Its version of this story begins, "In the early 1950s, Senator Joseph McCarthy's politics of fear victimized many people. Chief among them was Wyoming Senator Lester Hunt." The Senate history continues, attributing motive to McCarthy. "Hunt quickly crossed swords with Wisconsin's Joe McCarthy." Later, "Disgusted with McCarthy's witch-hunting tactics, Hunt publicly branded him 'an opportunist,' 'a liar,' and a 'drunk.' McCarthy privately vowed to get even."[144] The senate historian readily acknowledges what was commonly believed in the halls of the Senate. McCarthy had a role in "one of the foulest attempts at blackmail in modern political history."

Remembering McCarthy's elevator speech promising to get even with Hunt because of his son's political activity, there is little question McCarthy would have taken special interest in the opportunities offered by young Hunt's arrest. The Wisconsin senator was likewise

142   Carl Solberg, *Hubert Humphrey-A Biography"* Norton Press (1984), 157; also see letters exchanged between University of Wyoming history professor Dr. T.A. Larson and Solberg regarding the Hunt suicide, File" "Lester Hunt" Box 18, T.A. Larson Papers

143   Letter from Mike Manatos to Rick Ewig, April 30, 1980, 5

144   http://www.senate.gov/artandhistory/history/minute/Senator_Lester_Hunts_Decision.htm

displeased with Hunt's attack on the congressional immunity that protected McCarthy from libel suits. Hunt called his colleague's tactics
"unscrupulous." Hunt openly deemed McCarthy guilty of using "the
big lie technique."[145]

Lester Hunt, Jr. was well aware of his father's disdain for McCarthy.
He said it was "the use he made of his senate position my father really
resented. The guy was an opportunist, and a liar, and a drunk." He recounted a story of a time when the two senators were forced into close
quarters. "I remember once they'd gone someplace and the plane
was forced down in Pittsburgh. They were forced to share a hotel. He
(Senator Hunt) was in the fits. You thought he had just been with a
murderer or a Nazi. He felt unclean about being associated with that
person. He really had a strong distaste for him personally."[146] Young
Hunt said his parent's home overlooked McCarthy's backyard allowing
them to witness "McCarthy guzzling away with his girlfriend in the
backyard."[147]

Hunt made no secret of how he felt about Joe McCarthy. He told
a supporter that when asked whether he might run for President,
McCarthy declined, saying he felt he could be more effective in the
Senate. "No doubt that is true," said Hunt, "for as a Senator he is
now acting Secretary of State, Acting President, and the Chief High
Executioner of department heads, while in the White House, he would
merely be a President."[148] No doubt a man like Lester Hunt could not
countenance a man like Joe McCarthy.

Readers are left to deliberate. History is left to judge. We do know
Lester Hunt was "loyal and true, and he served his state and nation well."

145   "Hunt Censures Big-Lie" *Rawlins Daily Times,* September 26, 1952
146   Transcript of an interview with Lester Hunt, Jr. conducted by Rick Ewig, December
29, 1979, in Chicago, Illinois, 3
147   Id. 4
148   Letter from Hunt to Charles E. Hanner, July 15, 1953, File: "Hunt-Personal-1953"
LCH Papers

Senator Styles Bridges said so at Hunt's Memorial Service. Likewise, we know Lester Hunt was sufficiently beloved that he "could have been the senior Senator from Wyoming as long as he lived." Senator Welker said so at the same Memorial Service. Senator Joe McCarthy, unlike Welker and Bridges, had the good grace to not attend.

It was Hunt's friend from Colorado, Senator Ed Johnson who made what might be rightfully considered a closing argument before the jury of history.

Lester Hunt was a warm-hearted friendly soul. In his beloved Wyoming he respected and loved everyone, and everyone respected and loved him. Politics to him, as was his religion, was based on warm friendship, courtesy, kindness, gentleness, and good will toward all men.

He was ill prepared for the cruel, brutal, rough aspect of national partisan politics. He thought evil of no one, and his gentle nature was shocked into panic, that persons whom he liked and respected would destroy him in the cause of national partisan politics when he was wholly without guilt.[149]

---

149   *Memorial Services for Lester C. Hunt*, supra. 16, 21, and 24

CHAPTER TWELVE

Afterword on the Nature of Suicide

Albert Camus believed, "There is only one truly serious philo-sophical problem and that is suicide," which he said was "illegitimate."[1] Even so, Camus admitted all "healthy" people have thought of taking their own lives. For him, the question was simply about the meaning of life. That which can be deemed a reason for dying is also "an excellent reason for living." Yet there is a footnote left among the pages of his erudite musings that some suicides can be "honorable." He cited "for example, the political suicides of protest, as they were called, during the Chinese revolution."

"It is a safe assumption that virtually everyone who desires death also simultaneously desires life," Thomas Joiner wrote in his book *The Myths About Suicide.* "The suicidal mind," according to Joiner, "is characterized by ambivalence, with competing forces tugging at the suicidal individual from the sides of both life and death."[2] Camus en-visioned this dilemma asserting itself when one is divested of all illu-sions. Existence itself becomes an absurdity and suicide the solution. Even then, Joiner says, there is an ongoing competition in the mind between living and dying.

One of the myths Joiner refutes helps us to understand Lester

1   Albert Camus, *The Myth of Sisyphus and Other Essays,* Originally published in France as *Le Mythe de Sisephe,* Translated by Justin O'Brien, Vintage Books (1991), 3

2   Thomas Joiner, *Myths About Suicide,* Harvard University Press (2010), 64

Hunt's life and letters in the days before his suicide. His letters displayed certain hopefulness, even optimism about the future. He told friends that when the Senate adjourned, he and Nathelle would take time to rest, they would return to their home in Lander and live out the remaining years God would give them. After reading these letters, his suicide is even more shocking. How can someone so hopeless about his life talk so hopefully about the future?

Joiner says ambivalence is characteristic of the mind of one considering voluntary death. It stands to reason, he says, that such ambivalence would be observed in those days and weeks leading up to the potentially fatal act. It is not uncommon for people to make plans for jobs, trips and relationships in the days and weeks before their deaths by suicide. "It would be surprising," argues Joiner, "if they didn't."[3]

This book is not intended to provide a clinical understanding of suicide. In fact, one of the most unfortunately impenetrable myths about suicide is that just about anyone can understand it. Special note was taken of an aside in Joiner's helpful book. Dr. Joiner is the Robert O. Lawton Distinguished Professor of Psychology at Florida State University. He is also the son of a father and maternal grandfather who voluntarily ended their lives. As a result, he is rightfully sensitive, at times angered, about the easy explanations some people give for the suicide of others.

Joiner tells of actress Halle Berry's suicide attempt. As she sat in the car awaiting death by asphyxiation, she said she began to think clearly enough to reason that taking her own life "would be an incredibly selfish thing to do." Joiner also recounts the advice offered by a Presbyterian minister who said in 1805, that suicide is generally prompted by "the most sordid and unworthy selfishness." As a Presbyterian minister myself , I have been appropriately cautioned by Joiner's warning that, "those interested in the truth about suicidal behavior not prioritize the

3   Id.

comments of Hollywood stars or even Presbyterian ministers, whatever their other merits may be."[4]

Yet, this book cannot be complete without at least a limited survey of the literature about suicide to the extent it applies to Hunt's death. This writing attempts to be respectful of both history and science, without exaggerating the limited knowledge of the author. The story of Lester Hunt's death inevitably raises questions about the nature of suicide. Why do people choose to end their own lives? Why did he? Perhaps the most interesting question to ponder is how did those who brought such despair to Hunt's life continue to live their own with the weight of such contemptible behavior around their necks?

Allen Drury's fictional telling of the Hunt story, *Advise and Consent,* answered the latter but not the former questions. "As it was," Drury narrates, "he was the ideal sacrifice. The ruthless and the righteous could rejoice equally, for the one could say, 'See? He stood in our way.' And the other could say, 'See? He broke our rules.' And they could join hands and dance around his bier. And for that, was a man to stop judging when he had been chosen to judge? How could society continue if all whose hands were soiled with human living permitted themselves to be forever after paralyzed?"[5]

The ruthless, but unfortunate consequence necessitates the question, "Why Hunt and not another? Was he the 'ideal sacrifice?" Perhaps someone had to be sacrificed for the sins of Joe McCarthy, Styles Bridges and Herman Welker among others. But, Ben Franklin believed, "Nine in ten (of us) are would-be suicides." Italian poet and novelist Cesare Pavese said, "No one ever lacks a good reason for suicide." Even Abraham Lincoln was so concerned about his own suicidal tendencies that for a time he refused to carry a knife in his pocket.

4   Id., 43
5   Drury, *Advise and Consent,* Supra. 546

His close friends believed it possible he would take his own life.[6] Yet, in relative terms, few people take their own lives. While each is an unbearable tragedy, the Centers for Disease Control and Prevention (CDC) says the number of lives ended by one's own hand are little more than one percent of all deaths in the United States.

When someone dies it seems obligatory for us to assign a reason or a cause of death. Humans have an innate revulsion to death. We need to know its cause. By knowing, we might avoid that outcome in our lives. For most deaths the cause lacks the spiritual implication it has with suicide. Death by cancer, stroke or heart attack is logical and physical. Death by suicide defies logic. Suicide is of the mind or spirit and not the body. Death by disease can be explained through medical science. Doctors can examine a corpse and see the cause. They can explain it to us and we can understand. Suicide is different. Its cause cannot be determined with an autopsy. There is no scientific explanation to satisfy our minds. As a result, suicide is most easily, though superficially, explained through conjecture or myth or fear. The events surrounding suicide often lead to a parade of speculation about the reasons. When the victim is a public person, much of the speculation comes from those who have no direct evidence, including biographers writing decades after their subject dies.

Is suicide a voluntary act?

One of the most accepted notions about those who take their own lives is that self-inflicted death is a voluntary act. Whether this is a myth or not is highly debated. Most certainly, there is a characteristic of voluntariness to the act that cannot be denied. However, it may be argued that the same is true of deaths resulting from the abuse of alcohol or drugs, the use of tobacco, and other lifestyle choices that the CDC says

---

6   Joshua Wolf Shenk, *Lincoln's Melancholy: How depression Challenged a President and Fueled His Greatness,* Houghton Mifflin (2005), 23

are 25 times more likely than suicide to lead to the end of a life.

The writings of Father Ron Rolheiser open new windows into the way we see suicide. He is a widely read Catholic theologian who has seen the pain and guilt left by the myths which inevitably wash up in the wake of a suicide largely because of cultural expectations and religious views. Rolheiser has written extensively on the spiritual dimensions of self-inflicted death. He doesn't accept the supposition that death by suicide is any more voluntary than is death resulting from cancer. Just as cancer is the result of a breakdown of the body's physical immune system, so suicide is a breakdown of the emotional immune system. Rolheiser says, "A person who falls victim to suicide dies, as does the victim of a terminal illness or fatal accident, not by his or her own choice. When people die from heart attacks, strokes, cancer, AIDS, and accidents, they die against their will."[7] The same, he argues, is true of self-inflicted death.

Reading Senator Hunt's correspondence with close friends and confidants as recent as the day before his death gives the reader a sense of what Father Rolheiser teaches. More than half a century later, all we have is the impression left by those writings and it is that Lester Hunt's death may have surprised him as much as anyone. To the end, Hunt answered letters from constituents, talked about issues being discussed in the Senate and spoke with enthusiasm about a future that seemed to anticipate years, not days or hours. At his most depressed, Lincoln could have been diagnosed as distressed and impaired. At the same time, his behaviors demonstrated exceptionally good mental health.[8] He, like Lester Hunt, was productive, engaged in fulfilling relationships and appeared to friends to be coping with adversity.

On the day before Hunt killed himself, Earl Clements, a senator

---

7   http://www.ronrolheiser.com/columnarchive dated 2011-07-24 "Struggling to Understand Suicide" accessed on October 23, 2011

8   Shenk, Supra. 25

from Kentucky, visited with him for several minutes on the floor of the Senate. Hunt exhibited "no sign of disturbance, no evidence of concern or worry of any kind on his part."[9] Clements and Hunt talked about the future. "But," said Clements, "as the fateful event of the following morning revealed, he was talking in terms of the next day and I was thinking in terms of the next year."

The events of a person's life leading to suicide are more complex than is often acknowledged. The cause is often listed as concrete and simple. Financial or legal problems or medical or other personal pain are to blame, it is said. The real cause is more complex, found farther upstream in the life of the deceased. It's not possible to understand why some people end their own lives unless you know more about their lives. In an ultimately important way, voluntary deaths are fully intertwined with their lives in a manner not manifest when a person dies in other, more conventional ways.

Lester Hunt's suicide raises a number of questions. Science provides some insight but it hardly gets us over the hurdle and above the speculation. In the end, we can measure that which researchers have concluded with the facts known to us. In the final analysis, we are still left to guess. The issues that quickly surface in the story of Lester Hunt include stigma. How has the inordinate amount of stigma over voluntary death affected the societal value claim to have for finding the truth? How is it possible that a set of events, despite their enormity, can reduce a lifetime of success to the compulsion to end one's life? What impact did the prior suicide of Hunt's brother have on his choice? Is suicide contagious or genetically determined? Finally, how is Lester Hunt to be defined? Is he to be defined by the final hour of his life or by all that he accomplished personally and politically before that June morning? This question implicates our own values as much or more than his.

9   *Memorial Service of the U.S. Senate,* June 30, 1954, Supra. 33

The history of suicide

In 1830, the man who was the duc de Bourbon and the Prince de Conde killed himself. Louis Henri Joseph was part of the House of Bourbon, French nobility as descendants of the crusader French King Louis IX. He hanged himself, but the French newspapers refrained from offering any hint of suicide, attributing his death instead to apoplexy. One newspaper said he had been assassinated. In 1844 Louis-Gabriel Michaud, a French biographer, explained, "It is impossible to announce that the duc de Bourbon committed suicide, that the last of the Condes hanged himself. In pronouncing these words we would believe we were unworthily calumniating the memory of that prince."[10]

St. Augustine wrote, "This we declare and affirm and emphatically accept as true. No man may inflict death upon himself at will merely to escape temporal difficulties."[11] From then, the Catholic church, among others, has responsibility for promulgating such stigma around voluntary death that families who experienced it were compelled to avoid the hearing or the telling of the truth. Apparently it didn't seem odd to the early church fathers that the Bible told the stories of several suicides without including a single word of condemnation. The most familiar is the suicide of Judas. The Gospel of Matthew records that after betraying Jesus, Judas repented, returned the bribe money and hanged himself."[12] The Gospel does not criticize the choice Judas made to end his own life. Neither are the suicides of Saul (1st Samuel 31:4-5), Ahitophel (2nd Samuel 17:23), or Zimri (1st Kings 16:18) condemned by Biblical writers. The story of Abimelech implies not too subtly that assisted suicide is a more honorable way to die than some alternatives. When a woman inflicted a mortal wound on Abimelech by throwing

10   Georges Minois, *The History of Suicide,* English Translation by Lydia G. Cochrane, Johns Hopkins University Press (1999), 316
11   St. Augustine *The City of God, Books I-IV,* Translated by Demetrius B. Zema and Gerald G. Walsh, New York-Fathers of the Church (1950), Book 1, chapter 26, p. 61
12   Matthew 27

a millstone from a tower onto his head, the dethroned king "called to the young man who carried his armor and said to him, 'Draw your sword and kill me, so people will not say of me, 'A woman killed him.'"[13]

The absence of scriptural support did not prevent many theologians from espousing a doctrine declaring suicide to be a sin. Perhaps this was another example of ways in which early Christians sought to differentiate themselves from the Romans. In the Roman Empire voluntary death was the fodder of heroic stories. Politicians and military leaders were glorified for having volunteered to end their own lives.[14] As the Christian Gospels were being written in the decades after the crucifixion of Jesus, an impressive number of Roman politicians committed suicide in very public ways.

During the Middle Ages, suicide was considered not only a sin, but also a criminal act of such revulsion that the dead body of a suicide victim was often brutalized. The estate of the deceased was confiscated by the state. Curiously, the epic poems of early French literature championed a different view of the suicides of aristocrats. The *chansons de geste* (songs of heroic deeds), depicted voluntary death as the way in which people kill themselves "because they have been vanquished and find it unbearable." These suicides are made to sound heroic and admirable.[15] If this sounds confusing, that's because it is. History is filled with examples of how church doctrine differs from cultural practices. Yet it is church doctrine that often finds itself written into the law.

By the fourteenth century a condemnation of suicide found its way into Dante's description of Hell which is largely responsible yet today for perceptions of the punishment awaiting sinners. Those who killed

13   Judges 9:54

14   Minois, Supra. "In certain years the number of voluntary deaths among men in active politics was impressive. There were nineteen such deaths in 43 B.C. and sixteen the following year; sixteen in A.D. 65, twelve in 66. These heroic suicides by falling on one's sword or by slitting one's veins are reported admiringly by Roman historians as illustrations of the supreme freedom of individuals who rose above their fate." Page 53

15   Minois, Supra. 13

themselves were, according to Dante, sentenced to the Seventh Circle of Hell where those who were violent are housed eternally. Suicide victims are guarded by Minotaur and left in the Middle Ring of this Circle. There they are transformed into bushes and trees, gnarled and thorny and fed upon by winged witches known as harpies.

Emile Durkheim was a Frenchman generally credited with establishing sociology as a discipline in the nineteenth century. It was not until his landmark work, *Le Suicide*,[16] that lawmakers and others began seriously questioning the premise for criminalizing suicide. Durkheim opened a door that permitted an understanding of suicide based on science and research rather than on ancient and questionable religious notions. He attempted to replace, or at least augment, the theological with the sociological. Durkheim believed a society was far more than a collection of individuals. He thought it included the influence of written law and moral precepts. Together those elements of societal relationships create a cultural force. These forces or currents have, he concluded, more influence on the decision to take one's own life than any individual's personal motivation.[17] Accordingly, suicide is not so much a crime as an inevitable societal phenomenon.

But by the 1950s most U.S. states had laws criminalizing suicide.[18] The continuing stigma was sufficient cause to preclude close friends and family from seeking the truth about the role of others in bringing about Lester Hunt's death. While the cause of death of a United States Senator could not be hidden, attributing the motive to health problems would limit the amount and nature of any inquiry that followed.

In this regard, the views of the authorities presiding over the atroc-

16   Emile Durkheim, *Le Suicide*'Published in 1897, English Translation by John A. Spaulding and George Simpson, and published under the title *Suicide: A Study in Sociology*, Free Press (1951)

17   Robert Alun Jones. *Emile Durkheim: An Introduction to Four Major Works*. Sage Publications, Inc., (1986), 82-114.

18   Suicide: Legal Aspects – Bibliography, http://law.jrank.org/pages/2180/Suicide-Legal-Aspects.html accessed February 19, 2012

ities of the French Revolution are worthy of reflection. Those the revolutionary government planned to behead were forbidden from committing suicide under penalty of the confiscation of their estate from otherwise rightful heirs. Suicide historian Georges Minois explains, "The prisoner sentenced to death who killed himself deprived them of an opportunity to display their authority."[19] Likely it never occurred to those who wished, in a manner of speaking, to "behead" Lester Hunt that he might volunteer to end his own life rather than allow them to do so.

The impact of his brother's suicide

On April 8, 1952, Clyde Hunt, Lester's brother, awoke early on that Tuesday morning, took his .22 caliber rifle and left the ranch house he shared with his wife, Lillian. She thought Clyde was going out to shoot troublesome porcupines. Instead Clyde shot himself. When Lillian found him, he had two bullet wounds in his head. One bullet grazed the top of his head while the other penetrated his right temple. Clyde was a prominent Colorado rancher. His death was ruled a suicide.[20] Sociologists, psychiatrists and others believe that to be an event to be considered as a factor contributing in some measure to Lester Hunt's decision.

Countless studies document "a greatly elevated rate of suicide among the family members of those who commit suicide."[21] Dr. Kay Redfield Jamison, an acknowledged expert on the subject, believes the evidence demonstrates that those who kill themselves by violent means, such as gunshots, most often have a family history of suicide. While suicide is partly explained by psychiatric disorders, there is a

19   Minois, Supra. 304
20   "Senator Hunt's Brother is Killed by Rifle Bullets" *Rocky Mountain News,* April 9, 1952, and Senator's Kin Dies of Gunshot" *Denver Post,* April 9, 1952
21   Kay Redfield Jamison, *Night Falls Fast: Understanding Suicide,* Alfred E. Knopf (1999), 169

400-600 percent increase in risk following the death by suicide of a close family member.[22]

However, Karl Menninger, one of the most distinguished psychiatrists of the twentieth century, found no conclusive evidence of any genetic or hereditary connection to familial suicides.[23] Menninger surmised the existence of "unconscious death wishes" among family members. If one committed suicide, the death wish was realized. The aftermath produced, according to Dr. Menninger, "a suddenly and overwhelmingly strong wave of guilt feelings which replaced the now gratified murder-wish." The "culprit," as Menninger refers to the survivor, inflicts self-punishment by taking his or her own life.[24]

Harvard researcher Thomas Joiner believes genes tell part of the story, though of lesser importance than non-genetic factors.[25] Dr. Jamison, on the other hand, reads the evidence as suggestive of a genetic predisposition, but not conclusive.[26] Perhaps more helpful is Dr. Edwin S. Shneidman's *Autopsy of a Suicidal Mind."* As he recounts the facts surrounding an actual suicide, Dr. Shneidman gives credence to both genetic factors and circumstance. "Genes and fortune bent (a former patient he calls) Arthur to this end," he writes, "chronically skating near the precipices of the deep canyons of life, and one day tripping and falling in."[27]

There is no reason to believe Lester Hunt was "chronically skating near the precipices." He didn't use, much less abuse, alcohol or drugs. He didn't engage in risky behavior and his performance in pub-

22   "Peripubertal suicide attempts in offspring of suicide attempters with siblings concordant for suicidal behavior" Brent DA, Oquendo M, Birmaher B, Greenhill L, Kolko D, Stanley B, Zelazny J, Brodsky B, Firinciogullari S, Ellis SP, Mann JJ, Am J Psychiatry. 2003 Aug; 160(8): 1486-93.

23   Karl Menninger, *Man Against Himself,* Harcourt, Brace & World (1938), 53

24   Id. 53-54

25   Thomas Joiner, *Myths About Suicide,* Harvard University Press (2010), 235

26   Jamison, Supra. 170

27   Edwin S. Shneidman, *Autopsy of a Suicidal Mind,* Oxford Press (2004), 163

lic office gave no hints of any serious mental illness. Instead, his life evidenced a high level of resiliency. Yet not only did his brother kill himself, he did it in the way Lester Hunt chose to kill himself, with a gunshot to the head from a .22 caliber rifle. Perhaps the precipice about which Shneidman warned is the one opened by Clyde's death. Logically it would seem there must be a connection. It is not as simple as believing that if a loved one commits suicide, others in the family will follow suit. However, there is something about the suicide of one family member that seems to give permission to others to voluntarily end their lives notwithstanding a weighty social stigma to the contrary. The documented high rate of suicides among family members causes most scientists to believe the tragedy does not strike at random.[28]

Evaluating the lives and deaths of more than 4200 suicide victims and comparing them to 80,000 others, researchers in Denmark concluded that factors such as mental illness and prior familial suicides operate independently of one another. "Though we cannot conclude that there is a genetic factor associated with suicide, the findings from this large population-based study do suggest that the aggregation of suicide in families is likely due to a genetic factor rather than other non-genetic factors," Dr. Ping Qin says. "And this genetic susceptibility is likely to act independently of mental illness."[29] Qin is lead author and a researcher at the National Centre for Register-based Research at Aarhus University in Denmark.

Menninger is just as certain that when dates of death correspond and methods are the same, familial suicides are not coincidental.[30] Even so, that does not necessarily mean there is a genetic cause. Jamison argues that neither genetics nor predisposition provide a complete an-

---

28   David Lester, *Making Sense of Suicide: An In-depth Look at Why People Kill Themselves*, Charles Press (1997), 29

29   "Suicide Risks Run in Families" http://www.healthyplace.com/depression/suicide/ suicide-risk-runs-in-families/menu-id-68/ accessed October 1, 2011

30   Menninger, Supra. 53

swer. However, when coupled with hurtful circumstances that another person might suffer but survive, could a person for whom the door has been cracked open by the suicide of a brother, might more readily find cause for self-inflicted death? Though he believed suicide was an "illegitimate" manner in which to deal with life, Camus recognized the situational fragility of some people. "But," he wrote, "one would have to know whether a friend of the desperate man had not that very day addressed him indifferently."[31] Is it that simple? A predisposition coupled with an unfortunate encounter at the particularly sensitive moment? Jamison refers to the research conducted by Dr. John Mann of the New York State Psychiatric Institute to explain the relationship between factors creating a predisposition to suicide and the circumstances actually triggering it. Jamison explains, "Several factors influence the predisposition to commit suicide and together they act to establish a threshold for suicidal behavior." Family history is one of the factors Jamison identifies.

She also discusses the "protective factors" that help some people withstand even catastrophic events without taking their lives, factors that include "financial security, strong social supports, or a good marriage." Lester Hunt seems to have been blessed with each. "In the presence of a strong predisposition to suicide, however, these protective factors," says Jamison, " may be of limited value."[32]

Menninger explains it differently but arrives at the same conclusion. It is for him, a question of "diminished immunity and resistance." The person's mind "strives to make the best possible bargain with conflicting sources of reality, instinct, and conscience." It falls on the "ego" to limit the destruction to the "least serious, least costly, sacrifice." But Menninger admits, "For this task, the capacity and the wisdom of the ego vary greatly in different individuals."

31   Albert Camus, *The Myth of Sisyphus*, Supra, 5
32   Jamison, Supra. 199

Dying for Joe McCarthy's sins

While few people take their own lives for a single reason, there is reason to conclude that Lester Hunt would not have done so but for the villainous behavior of Joe McCarthy, Styles Bridges and Herman Welker. The historical facts provide a clear and obvious roadmap. McCarthy's diaries, letters, journals and notes are deposited at Marquette University in Milwaukee. But by agreement with the family of the late Senator, these records, with the exception of newspaper clippings, are sealed until the death of his daughter whom Joe and Jean McCarthy adopted in 1957, when she was five weeks old. Once McCarthy's papers are opened to public scrutiny, historians may have direct evidence of his involvement. Even so, ample history is available to demonstrate the way in which he created the poisonous atmosphere in which a crime of this sort was inevitable.

In the end, they assured this gentle man had no alternative. Their plot had no other possible outcome. Those who study suicide find the most common denominator to be the victim's loss of control over his or her life. "The experience of being suicidal and making a suicide attempt could be understood in the overall theme of "being in want of control." According to experts, this theme has "a double entendre of not being in control as well as wishing to regain control."[33] Those who complete the attempt are obviously unavailable for study. However, those who have made a serious, though unsuccessful attempt, speak about how events had filled their lives with chaos and unsolvable problems. Their present is so out of their control that they cannot imagine a future any different. The primary motivation becomes seeking an end to the suffering.

By June 19, 1954, Lester Hunt's life was rendered so out of con-

33   Katarina Skogman Pavulans, PhD, Ingrid Bolmsjo, Anna-Karin Edberg and Agneta Ojehagen, *Being in Want of Control: Experiences on the Road to, and Making a Suicide Attempt,* International Journal of Qualitative Studies on Health and Well-being, 2012, 7:10.3402. ghw.v710. 16228, www.ncbi.nlm.gov/pmc/articles/PMC3345936/?tool=pubmed

trol by those who sought his political demise, volunteering to end his own life must have seemed the only way for him to regain any sense of control.

A coward's way out...or a hero's?

Often it comes as no surprise when someone takes his or her life. Just as often, it is not simply surprising but inexplicable. Meriwether Lewis, a national hero even during his own time, captured the imagination of the nation with his exploration of the frontier. Is it permissible, even possible, to attribute cowardice to his suicide when he exhibited such courage during his life? In dispelling the value-laden myth that suicide is cowardice, Thomas Joiner exhibits the Lewis suicide.

In his book *Undaunted Courage*, Stephen Ambrose tells of the night Lewis killed himself. "Lewis began pacing in his room. This went on for several hours," Ambrose writes." Lewis got out his pistols. He loaded them and at some time during the early hours of October 11 shot himself in the head." Lewis did not die quickly. He survived two gunshots, one to his head, and the other to his chest. Hours later, he was found "busily cutting himself from head to foot' with his razor." When a friend came to his aid, Lewis said, "I am no coward; but I am so strong, it is so hard to die." Curiously, Lewis said he wanted to kill himself in order to deprive his enemies of the opportunity.[34]

Joiner counts as a myth the notion that taking your own life is either easy or cowardly. Death is so counterintuitive, he argues, that ending your life is anything but an easy way out. Humans have survived all these centuries because of an inherent will to live. Remaining alive is fundamental to our evolving nature, psychologically and physiologically. Suicide is not "the stuff of ease and cowardice." Joiner says. "No, death by suicide requires staring the product of millions of years of

34 Stephen E. Ambrose, Undaunted *Courage: Meriwether Lewis, Thomas Jefferson and the Opening of the American West,* Simon & Schuster (1996), 475

evolution in the face and not blinking; it is tragic, fearsome, agonizing, and awful, but it is not easy."[35]

If not cowardice, is it then heroic? Origen of Alexandria, one of the greatest Christian theologians candidly observed, "If we are not afraid of words and pay attention to things, we might say, finding no other expression that fits the facts, that divinely (in a manner of speaking), Jesus killed himself."[36] Just as a person who drives down a highway at night with no headlights and veers into the path of a truck, Jesus was fully aware that the road he traveled would end in his death. He chose to veer into the path of the Roman authorities with full knowledge of the consequences. To those for whom the Gospels matter, his death is deemed heroic.

Dr. Jamison recounts the heroic nature of voluntary death among ancient Greeks where killing oneself was viewed as honorable under certain circumstances such as refusing to renounce ideas, to avoid being captured by an enemy or to stand against injustice. Although Aristotle denounced suicide as cowardly, Socrates drank the poison, preferring his own death to disowning his own beliefs.[37] As was written of Bruno Bettelheim[38] following his suicide, "He may have committed suicide precisely because, with the onset of old age and physical diminution, that faculty of thinking freely had declined in him. It was less and act of despair than one of courage to follow his life principles to their logical conclusion."[39]

35   Joiner, Supra. 28-29

36   *Commentary on the Gospel According to John: Books 1-10*, trans. Ronald E. Heine Catholic University of America Press (1989), cited at Minois, Supra. 24

37   Jamison, Supra. 12-13

38   Bettelheim, an Austrian-born American child psychologist and writer who was born in 1903 and died in 1990 gained an international reputation for his work on Freud, psychoanalysis, and emotionally disturbed children. Among numerous other works, Bruno Bettelheim wrote *The Uses of Enchantment*, analyzing fairy tales in terms of Freudian psychology and the emotional and symbolic importance they hold for children.

39   Minois, Supra. 324, Page 324 citing Odile Odoul, *Bruno Bettelheim est mort*, in *Angora*, special edition, *Artour du suicide*, (June 1990), 89

An act of courage? Heroic? Heroism, it seems, is integrally an element of mythology. Mythology is, at its core, an exposition of truth. Joseph Campbell is probably the most eloquent purveyor of the notion that a working knowledge of sacred stories of crucifixions and resurrections, virgin births, self-sacrifice and other manifestations of gods and God, transcend the divine and allow us to better understand the nature of heroism. "The image that comes to mind," Campbell told an interviewer, "is a boxing ring. There are times when you want that bell to ring, but you are the one who's losing. The one who's winning doesn't have that feeling. Do you have the energy and strength to face life? Life can ask more of you than you are willing to give. And then you say, 'Life is something that should not have been. I'm not going to play the game.'"[40]

More likely than not, Lester Hunt would never have considered himself a hero, most particularly on his final day on this earth. But the characteristics of his life, and not his opinion of himself at that dreadful moment, dictate the result. Campbell counted among those characteristics both reaching the mountaintop and knowing when to quit. He was asked whether the hero's journey in life equates to the mountain quest. "Yes, indeed, Campbell readily acknowledged, "and one part of the mythological motif of the hero's journey is acquiescence. And the hero is the one who knows when to surrender and what to surrender to."[41]

Emile Durkheim called suicide "the ransom-money of civilization, providing a provocative description of such a heartbreaking act."[42] Those words also lead to more questions. With the suicide of Lester Hunt, who or what was being held hostage? Who paid the ransom? What was accomplished by the payment? Durkheim's theory was set-

40   Joseph Campbell, *The Hero's Journey: Joseph Campbell on His Life and Work"* New World Library 1990), 65
41   Id., 12
42   Durkheim, English Translation, Supra. 367

tled on the foundational thought that suicide arises from the very same characteristics on which a society depends in order to progress. In any community, a certain level of homogeneity is required for the maintenance of stability. However, limited amounts of a "spirit of renunciation" and "the taste for individuation" are also necessary. They test the commonly held beliefs, challenge the status quo, and bring growth where in their absence there would be only a diminishment.

But they are also the generators of suicide in a progressive culture. When some renounce the beliefs that many around them hold, they alienate themselves. It is that alienation that opens the door to the alternative of ending one's life voluntarily. The suicide of some of its members is the price societies must necessarily pay in order to achieve progress. Freedom-of-thought was held hostage by McCarthyism. Durkheim might have seen Lester Hunt's life as the ransom that had to be paid in order to secure its release.

Gathering to Remember

They gathered in an anteroom of the old church. Entering through the front door of St. Mark's Episcopal, the senators passed by a large floral arrangement in the shape of a Wyoming license plate, displaying the bucking horse design Hunt created. It was one of those symbols that meant so much to Lester Hunt and the people of Wyoming.

The vice-president appointed a large delegation of Hunt's colleagues to attend the funeral service in Cheyenne. It was a sad and silent group. Earl Clements, the senator from Kentucky who had rushed to the hospital to be with Mrs. Hunt on that awful day, sat with his head in his hands. Senators Mike Mansfield of Montana and Mike Monroney of Oklahoma joined Lyndon Johnson of Texas and Estes Kefauver of Tennessee. Hunt's longtime allies Joe O'Mahoney and Tracy McCracken were also there.

McCracken broke the silence. He was the first to talk about the vile blackmail, speaking with disdain about Styles Bridges and Herman Welker.[1] He didn't need to speak at length. Everyone in the room was aware of the ugly details. They knew better than most that Lester Hunt was just one more victim of the McCarthy years. They knew. McCracken, the publisher of the two Cheyenne newspapers and others around the state, said he had refrained from publishing the story because he feared for Mrs. Hunt's reaction. She had been through enough and didn't need to read that on the day she buried her husband.

They talked of the job offer from the White House that Hunt had turned down. Clements said the emissary was Victor Johnston,

---

1 "Memo to DP (Drew Pearson) from JA (Jack Anderson), Papers of Drew Pearson, File 155, 3 of 3, LBJ Library

a former member of the staff at the Republican Senate Campaign Committee. The offer had apparently stirred up trouble in Colorado for Eisenhower. Key politicians in that state wanted one of their own to get the job. They spoke of the months of threats Hunt endured, the break-in at his home, the needless and vindictive trial of his son, and the pain politics exerts on their families.

As they visited among themselves, Nathelle, Elise and Buddy arrived joining hundreds of Hunt's people from all over Wyoming. The service began. It was time to lay Lester C. Hunt to rest.

McCarthy is censured

After Lester Hunt's death, the pall Lyndon Johnson said was cast over the Senate shrouded the continuing debate over what to do about Joe McCarthy. The shocking suicide of their beloved colleague from Wyoming sealed the fate of the Wisconsin demagogue. All of Washington was numbed by the horrifying reality. What some had sanctioned and others had ignored for the last five years had created this tragedy. Others had committed suicide as a direct result of McCarthy's brutal tactics. This was different. Hunt was one of their own.

The debate lasted until December but Hunt's June 19 death determined the outcome. In December, Bridges and Welker eulogized McCarthy much as they did Hunt the preceding June, standing with their comrade until the very end. But two-thirds of the senators voted overwhelmingly to censure the Wisconsin senator. Within three years, Joe McCarthy was dead.

Hunt's family

It took Nathelle a couple of years after her husband ended his life to decide what to do with hers. She spent time in Lander. At times she drove herself to Spokane where her daughter Elise lived with her husband Russell and their children. There were women who offered to join her for those long, cross-country drives but she said, "I had learned from experience that women who do not drive are poor navigators and want to talk all the time, so I sped across the country by myself."[2]

She moved to Chicago where she lived with Buddy until he married in 1959.

Then she went to Spokane to be near her daughter. In 1961, Nathelle joined thirteen other accomplished women for the first all-woman People to People trip under President Eisenhower's international initiative. She met Madame Chaing Kai Chek as her group traveled more than 50,000 miles across ten nations.

Back in Spokane, Nathelle honored an admonition passed down to her. "There's an old saying," she said, "that families should not live so near each other that they can see the smoke from their chimneys." She lived in a small apartment three miles from Elise's home, close enough to spend ample time with grandchildren and far enough away she never saw the "smoke from their chimney."

Emily Nathelle Higby Hunt died in Spokane on October 13, 1990. She was 95 years old.

Following a wedding in Cheyenne while her father was governor, Elise Nila Hunt Chadwick moved to New York. Later she and her family moved to Spokane. Her husband was a mining consultant. They have three sons and a daughter. At the time this is written, she is 90 years old.

In truth, the life of Lester C. Hunt, Jr. is worthy itself of a book. Today he and his wife live in Chicago where Buddy went following his father's death. His father's old friend and a McCarthy adversary, William Benton, helped him get a job editing radio programs at the University of Chicago. Benton had been a Senator from Connecticut and was the editor-in-chief of the Encyclopedia Britannica.

Buddy Hunt recalled, "When I came to Chicago, I got to know

2   Nathelle Hunt's autobiographical essay, Supra. 28

Nick von Hoffman's wife Ann who worked in an office at the University in the same building as I did.[3] She told me about Nick's interest in organizing in a neighborhood adjacent to the university. It had recently changed form Caucasian to Black and Puerto Rican. Since I had learned some Spanish in my teaching activities in Cuba and Mexico, I offered to volunteer."

Hunt had done more than "learn some Spanish." He was fluent, having spent "several years in the mountains of pre-Castro Cuba teaching the children of poverty-racked peons."[4] He met Saul Alinsky while volunteering in the Spanish speaking community in Chicago. Among von Hoffman's many books is a biography entitled *Radical: A Portrait of Saul Alinsky*. It describes the work of these three men in Chicago's poorest neighborhoods.[5] They were "community organizers" long before Barack Obama used that term to describe his qualifications for President.

"In 1983, I decided to become a community organizer," said Alinsky. "There wasn't much detail to the idea. When my classmates in college asked me just what it was a community organizer did, I couldn't answer them directly." Alinsky explained it was about working for change. "That's what I do," he said, "I'll organize black folks at the grass roots for change."[6] Von Hoffman admitted, "The real organizing was done by Lester Hunt who spoke fluent Spanish, and Juan Sosa, who worked at the Sherwin-Williams paint plant on the far southeast side of the city."[7] Hunt worked on community justice projects in Chicago: Butte,

3   Nicholas von Hoffman is known for his work as a commentator in a CBS "60 Minutes" segment entitled "Point-Counterpoint." In 1974 at the height of the Watergate investigation, von Hoffman colorfully referred to President Richard Nixon as "a dead muse on the floor. He was fired. Von Hoffman has written numerous books including *We Are the People Our Parents Warned Us Against* and *Citizen Cohn: The Life and Times of Roy Cohn*.
4   Nicholas von Hoffman, *Radical: A portrait of Saul Alinsky*, Nation Books (2011), 2
5   Id.
6   Id. 20
7   Id. 2

Montana; and with the Chelsea Community Council in New York. He worked, as well, for the Bishops' Committee for the Spanish Speaking, a national committee of Roman Catholic Bishops whose mission was, Hunt said, to "drum up church support for the Farm Workers - Cesar Chavez was on Saul's staff in the days when I was."[8]

During this time Lester met Rogene. Nathelle approved, commenting, "They both are highly intelligent and honestly intellectual people who are always doing worthwhile things."[9] They have been married for more than half a century. One of their two daughters lives in Chicago, the other in Tucson. Lester and Rogene spend considerable time with their two granddaughters. Both live in Chicago.

Lester retired in 1987 from the Richard J. Daley College, one of the City Colleges of Chicago, where he was associate professor of history. He was a member of the faculty for 20 years. Those who have met Lester Hunt are impressed with his intellect, his vitality, and his sense of humor. I spent delightful time with him in September of 2011. He took me on a walking tour of downtown Chicago. When we arrived at the bottom of a long set of stairs, he politely asked whether I preferred the elevator. It was his choice, I said. "I always take the stairs," Lester said, "because I know that if I can make it today, I will be able to make it tomorrow."

As of this writing, Lester C. Hunt, Jr. is 85 years old...and still taking the stairs.

8   Hunt's responses to author's questions, December 7, 2011
9   Letter from Nathelle Hunt to Charlotte Dehnert of Lander, Wyoming, August 6, 1983

Acknowledgements

Honestly, I never so much wanted to write a book, as I wanted to tell this story. It has been a long and wonderful experience made even more so by the many people who have guided me along the way. The American Heritage Center at the University of Wyoming is a special place staffed by special people. It is where the 51 boxes of Lester Hunt's papers, speeches, diaries and memos are housed. The Center's staff has been most gracious in accommodating many requests. From the September day in 2011 when I first stumbled into their research room, not knowing much about where I was headed to how to start, they have been courteous and helpful.

I am especially thankful for the support and direction I received from the beginning of this project from Lester Hunt, Jr. He has been as intellectually honest as his mother and father would have thought, encouraging me always to "follow the facts" even though the story is undoubtedly painful for him. I would not have undertaken this book without his encouragement. I am also appreciative of the help I received from his sister Elise Chadwick. The short time I spent with her on the telephone offered me a genuine sense of the loving parents who raised both her and Lester. Her memories permitted me to explain a part of what Lester Hunt meat to those closest to him.

Al Simpson graciously agreed to write the foreword. Al and I have been friends since I was first elected to the Wyoming legislature in 1970. I was 22 years old and he was one of my mentors. He provided me with an important reference letter when I applied to law school at the University of Wyoming. Now he has done the great favor of writing the introductory pages for this book. I am grateful to him for years of friendship.

University of Wyoming historian Rick Ewig provided immeasurable assistance. Rick is the president of the Wyoming State Historical

Society. In 1983, he wrote a revealing essay entitled "McCarthy Era Politics: The Ordeal of Senator Lester Hunt." Rick graciously and unselfishly gave me copies of his research files, opening avenues to my work that might not have otherwise been accessed. Without his 1983 essay, Hunt's story may never have been told.

Katie Rahman and others at the Laramie County Library have spent countless hours chasing books, microfilm and documents around the country, responding to my requests, which were at times more like a fishing expedition. I am also indebted to Carol Thiesse, director of the Pioneer Museum in Lander, Wyoming; the staff of the Wyoming State Archives; Don Ritchie, the director of the U.S. Senate Historical Office; Mary Burtzloff, the archivist at the Dwight David Eisenhower Library in Abilene, Kansas; Jim Armistead of the Harry S. Truman Library in Independence, Missouri; Claudia Anderson, the Supervisory Archivist at the Lyndon Baines Johnson Library at the University of Texas; Bill Kemp of the McClean, Illinois Museum of History; Burma Hardy of the Coe Library at the University of Wyoming; and Stephen Thomas and others at the New Hampshire Office of Archives and Records Management.

The day I spent with Dr. Marjorie Bryer of the GLBT Historical Society in San Francisco was critical to my attempt to convey a complete understanding of the hell Joe McCarthy, Styles Bridges, Herman Welker, Kenneth Wherry and others created for homosexuals in the Cold War era. I am grateful to her and the GLBT Historical Society for their work to assure this history is collected and told.

Kristi Wallin deserves my gratitude. Kristi is a member of the staff of Wyoming Senator John Barrasso. She introduced me to Don Ritchie, her friend at the Senate Historical Office and she and her colleague Daniel Gallegos put in an extraordinary amount of time searching through numerous federal archives for Senator Hunt's medical records. Kristi also volunteered for the rather painful task of reading a very early manuscript of this book.

I imposed on the time of two longtime friends to read and edit. Ken Burns and Mark Junge never complained (out loud) about correcting typos and grammar. They are each excellent writers, insatiable readers and good friends. Thanks go to Kathie Lowry who made the mistake one day of telling me how much she enjoyed proofreading. I am so grateful to her for making a final run through the transcript and locating those last (more than a) few typos, correcting my grammar and giving me confidence in the final product.

JoAnne Kennedy is a successful writer who encouraged me when I continued to become confused about this whole writing and publishing experience. Nominated for a RITA Award by the Romance Writers of America, her encouragement was special. Another writer, Charlotte Dehnert of Lander was helpful. Charlotte was one of the first Wyoming journalists to dig into this story. She wrote an eye-opening series on Lester Hunt for the *Wyoming State Journal* in 1984. Charlotte has her own manuscript of a book on Hunt's life that I hope will be published as well.

As a first-time book writer, I had no idea about either the amount of time this would take, nor what it would cost. Accordingly, I was especially grateful to the Wyoming State Historical Society when they awarded me a grant from the Lola Homsher Endowment.

I will be eternally grateful that I found my old friend K.T. Roes who owns WordsWorth Publishing Co. K.T. took on the project of editing, and publishing the book and, with her great expertise and knowledge of Wyoming politics and people, added immeasurable value to this book.

There is also, of course, my family. I imposed on son Pete, his spouse Andrea, daughter Meghan and her husband Josh to read the book as I was writing it. They assured me it was good as you might expect from family. But I love them for their support and cheers. And to my wife, Patricia. She has been encouraging me to write this story for many years. She recognized from the start that Lester Hunt's story should be told. Pat has been patient and supportive through the long days of research and writing, the trips around the country, the disappointments when rejection letters were received and when I questioned whether I could get this done. She was as she has always been from the day we married.

Finally, I want to give thanks for Lester and Nathelle Hunt. We all have failed to acknowledge the contribution of many of Wyoming's historical figures. Like comets, they shoot across the big sky, only to burn out and be forgotten. These two served the state well. They were good, decent, honest public servants. Telling their story has been my great pleasure.

Bibliography

Abel, Tyler, ed. *Drew Pearson Diaries 1949-1959.* Holt, Reinhart and Winston, 1974

Alvarez, A. *The Savage God: A Study of Suicide.* New York: Random House, 1970

Ambrose, Stephen E. *Americans At War.* University Press of Mississippi, 1997

Ambrose, Stephen E. *Undaunted Courage: Meriwether Lewis, Thomas Jefferson and the Opening of the American West.* Simon & Schuster, 1996

Appleton Public Library, Appleton, Wisconsin. A biographical essay prepared by the reference staff, based primarily on information from *The Life and Times of Joe McCarthy,* Reeves, supra. www.apl.org/history/McCarthy

Augustine, Saint. *The City of God, Books I-IV.* Translated by Demetrius B. Zema and Gerald G. Walsh, New York-Fathers of the Church

Author Anonymous. *History of Logan County: Its Past and Present,* reproduction of 1923 book. Nabu Publishing, 2010

Baseball Encyclopedia. 9th Edition. MacMillan Publishing, 1993

Baxter, Randolph W. *Senator Kenneth Wherry and the Homophobic Side of McCarthyism,* Nebraska History, 2003

Bergler, Edmund. *The Myth of a New National Disease.* Psychiatric Quarterly 22, 1948

Berube, Allan. *Coming Out Under Fire: The History of Gay Men and Women in World War Two.* New Press (1990)

Boyd, Nan Alamilla. *Wide Open Town: A History of Queer San Francisco to 1965.* University of California Press (2003)

Bronski, Michael. *A Queer History of the United States,* Beacon Press (2011)

Bruinius, Harry. *Better For All The World: The Secret History of Forced Sterilization and America's Quest for Racial Purity.* New York: Vintage Books, 2007

Camus, Albert. *The Myth of Sysiphus and Other Essays.* Originally published in France as *Le Mythe de Sysiphe.* Translated by Justin O'Brien. Vintage Books (1991)

Caro, Robert A. *The Years of Lyndon Johnson: Master of the Senate.* New York: Vintage Books, 2002

Cicero, Quintus Tullius. *How To Win An Election: An Ancient Guide for Modern Politician.* Translated by Philip Freeman. Princeton and Oxford: Princeton University Press, 2012

Cochran, Bert. *Harry Truman and the Crisis Presidency* Funk & Wagnalls, 1973

Cohn, Roy. *McCarthy.* The New American Library, 1968

Corber, Robert J. *In the name of National Security: Hitchcock, Homophobia, and the Political Structure of Gender in Postwar America.* Durham-London: Duke University Press, 1993

Cousineau, Phil, ed. *Joseph Campbell: The Hero's Journey: Joseph Campbell on His Life and Work.* Novato, California: New World Press, 1990

Dean, Robert D. *Imperial Brotherhood: Gender and the Making of Cold War Foreign Policy.* University of Massachusetts Press (2001)

D'Emilio, John. *Sexual Politics, Sexual Communities.* Chicago-London: University of Chicago Press, 1983

Drury, Allen. *Advise and Consent.* Doubleday, 1959

Durkheim, Emile. *Suicide: A Study in Sociology.* Edited by George Simpson. Translated by John A. Spaulding and George Simpson. The Free Press, 1951

Eaklor, Vicki L. *Queer America: A People's History of the United States.* The New Press, 2011

Evans, Len. *From the Beginning of Time to the End of World War II*"File: "Gay Chronicles," Papers of Len Evans, GLBT Historical Society, San Francisco

Ewig, Rick. *McCarthy Era Politics-The Ordeal of Senator Lester Hunt.* Annals of Wyoming, Vol. 55, Number 1, Spring 1983

Federal Register. "Proclamation 2578 Establishing the Jackson Hole National Monument" March 18, 1943 (Vol. 8, Number 43)

Fried, Albert. *McCarthyism: The Great American Red Scare.* New York-Oxford: Oxford University Press, 1997

Gressley, Gene M. ed. *Voltaire and the Cowboy: The Letters of Thurman Arnold.* Boulder: Colorado Associated University Press, 1977

Griffith, Robert. *The Politics of Fear: Joseph R. McCarthy and the Senate.* Amherst: University of Massachusetts Press, 1970

Griffith, Robert and Athan Theoharis, eds. *The Specter: Original Essays on the Cold War and the Origins of McCarthyism,* New York: New Viewpoints-A division of Franklin Watts, Inc. 1974

Gutierrez, Gustavo. *On Job: God-Talk and the Suffering of the Innocent,* Orbis Books, 1997

Hacker, Barton C. *Elements of Controversy : The Atomic Energy Commission and Radiation safety in Nuclear Weapons Testing, 1947–1974.* University of California Press, 1994

Harry S. Truman Library and Museum, www.trumanlibrary.org

Hart, Jack. *Story Craft: The Complete Guide to Writing Narrative Nonfiction.* Chicago-London: University of Chicago Press, 2011

Hamilton, Alexander, James Madison and John Jay. *The Federalist Papers.* The New American Library, 1961

Hochschild, Adam. *To End All Wars.* Houghton Mifflin Harcourt, 2011

Hokanson, Drake. *The Lincoln Highway: Main Street Across America.* Iowa City: University of Iowa Press, 1999

Hunt, Lester C. Collection No. 270, 50.51 cu. Ft. (51 boxes) This collection contains subject files and other materials related to his political and personal life. American Heritage Center, University of Wyoming

Hunt, Lester C. Jr., Unpublished Genealogy of Families of Lester C. Hunt and Nathelle Higby Hunt, 45 pages

Hunt, Nathelle Higby, Unpublished Biographical Essay, 29 pages

Jamison, Kay Redfield. *Night Falls Fast: Understanding Suicide.* New York: Alfred A. Knopf, 1999

Johnson, David K. *The Lavender Scare.* Chicago-London: University of Chicago Press, 2004

Joiner, Thomas. *Myths About Suicide.* . Cambridge, Massachusetts-London: Harvard University Press, 2011

Jones. Robert Alun. *Emile Durkheim: An Introduction to Four Major Works.* Sage Publications, Inc., 1986

Kaiser, Charles. *The Gay Metropolis 1940-1946.* Houghton Mifflin, 1997

Karpan, Kathleen M. "A Political History of Jack R. Gage," *Annals of Wyoming* Vol. 48 No. 2 (Fall 1976): 167-253

Kefauver, Estes. *Crime in America.* Garden City, N.Y.: Doubleday and Company, 1951

Kennedy, John F. *Profiles in Courage,* Harper and Row (1955)

Kennedy, Robert F. *The Enemy Within,* Popular Library-New York (1960)

Kiepper, James J. *Styles Bridges: Yankee Senator.* Sugar Hill, New Hampshire: Phoenix Publishing, 2001

Larson, T.A. Collection No. 400029, 19.5 cu. Ft. (41 boxes). The T. A. Larson papers consist of material he collected or generated during his time as a professor of Wyoming history at the University of Wyoming from 1936 to 1975. Other material comes from his years of service as a Wyoming State Representative from 1976 until 1984 and with his service to the Wyoming State Historical Society. Much of the collection relates to the histories of the West, Wyoming, and the University of Wyoming. American Heritage Center, University of Wyoming

Larson, T.A. *History of Wyoming.* University of Nebraska Press, 1965

Larson, T.A. *Wyoming.* W.W. Norton & Company, 1977

Larson, T.A. *Wyoming's War years 1941-1945.* Wyoming Historical Foundation, 1993

La Sorte, Mike. *The Kefauver Crime Committee, 1950-1951.* www.americanmafia.com/ Feature_Articles_452.html. February 2010

Lawrence, Amy, James L. Ehernberger, and Lucille Dumbrill. *Wyoming Memories: Blizzard of 1949.* Annals of Wyoming, Winter 2004, Volume 76, Number 1

Lester, David. *Making Sense of Suicide.* Philadelphia: The Charles Press, 1997

Lucas, Donald S. "Bibliography on Homosexuality" Papers of Donald S. Lucas, GLBT Historical Society, San Francisco

Mallon, Thomas. *Fellow Travelers.* New York: Vintage Books, 2008

Manatos, Mike. Letter to Rick Ewig, April 30, 1980. In author's files

Manchester, William. *The Glory and the Dream: A Narrative History of America 1932-1972.* Little Brown, 1973

McCullough, David. *Truman.* Touchstone Simon & Schuster, 1992

McQueen, Kevin. *Carrie Nation: Militant Prohibitionist: Offbeat Kentuckians: Legends to Lunatics.* McClanahan Publishing House, 2001

Menninger, Karl. *Man Against Himself.* New York: Harcourt, Brace & World, 1938

Miller, Merle. *Lyndon: An Oral Biography.* New York: P.G. Putnam's Sons, 1980

Miller, Merle. *Plain Speaking: An Oral Biography of Harry S. Truman.* Berkley Publishing Corporation, 1973

Miller, Neil. *Out of the Past: Gas and Lesbian History from 1869 to the Present.* New York: Vintage Books, 1995

Minois, Georges. *History of Suicide: Voluntary Death in Western Culture.* Translated by Lydia G. Cochrane. Baltimore-London: Johns Hopkins University Press, 1999

Moore, William Howard. *The Kefauver Committee and the Politics of Crime 1950-1952.* Columbia: University of Missouri Press, 1974

Nugent, Walter. *Into The West.* New York: Alfred A. Knopf, 1999

O'Mahoney, Joseph. Collection No. 275, 398.95 cu. Ft. (405 boxes) This collection contains subject files and other materials related to his political and personal life. American Heritage Center, University of Wyoming

Omega, Ryan. *The Spiritual Consequences of Suicide.* LA Occult & Paranormal Examiner, July 1, 2009

Orwell, George. *Animal Farm and 1984.* Harcourt, Inc., 2003

Oshinsky, David M. *A Conspiracy So Immense: The World of Joe McCarthy.* Oxford University Press, 2005

Poen, Monte M. *Harry S. Truman Versus the Medical Lobby: The Genesis of Medicare.* Columbia-London: University of Missouri Press, 1979

Pearce, Ralph M. *From Asahi to Zebras: Japanese American Baseball in San Jose, California.* Japanese American Museum of San Jose, 2005

Philbrick, Nathaniel. *Mayflower.* Penguin Books, 2006

President's Committee on Civil Rights. *To Secure These Rights.* Edited by Steven F. Lawson. Boston-New York: Bedford/St. Martin's, 2004

Quinnett, Paul G. *Suicide: The Forever Decision.* New York: Crossroad Publishing, 2004

Reeves, Thomas C. *The Life and Times of Joe McCarthy.* New York: Stein and Day, 1982

Reynolds, Michael. *"Massacre At Malmédy During the Battle of the Bulge"* Published on-line June 12, 2006, http://www.historynet.com/massacre-at-malmedy-during-the-battle-of-the-bulge.htm

Righter, Robert W. *Crucible for Conservation: The Struggle for Grand Teton National Park.* Grand Teton Natural History Association, 1982

Roberts, Phil. *The Great depression and the New Deal in Wyoming.* http://uwacadweb.uwyo.edu/ROBERTSHISTORY/great_depression_and_the_new_dea.htm

Ross, Davis R.B. *The Democratic Party 1945-1960,* essay in Volume IV of *History of U.S. Political Parties.* Edited by Arthur M. Schlesinger, Jr. Chelsea House Publishers in association with R.R. Bowker Company (1973)

Schlesinger, Arthur M. *The Vital Center.* Boston: Houghton Mifflin Company, 1949

Schroer, Blanche Collection No. 10575, Personal Papers, American Heritage Center, University of Wyoming

Shenk, Joshua Wolf. *Lincoln's Melancholy: How Depression Challenged a President and Fueled His Greatness.* A Mariner Book, Boston-New York: Houghton Mifflin Company, 2005

Shneidman, Edwin S. *Autopsy of a Suicidal Mind.* Oxford University Press, 2004

Smith, Nels H. Collection No. 09880, Papers, 1926-1943 (bulk 1938-1943) 13.05 cubic ft. (30 boxes). This collection contains subject files and other materials related to his political and personal life. American Heritage Center, University of Wyoming

Solberg, Carl. *Hubert Humphrey: A Biography.* New York-London: W.W. Norton & Company, 1984

Stafford, David. *Roosevelt and Churchill: Men of Secrets.* The Overlook Press, Peter Mayer Publishers, Inc., 1999

Stevens, Jason W. *God-Fearing and Free.* Cambridge, Massachusetts-London: Harvard University Press, 2010

Thiesse, Carol, Traci Foutz and Joe Spriggs. *Images of America: Lander.* Arcadia Publishing, 2010

Trenholm, Virginia. Editor, *Wyoming Blue Book.* Wyoming State Archives and Historical Department, Volumes I-III, 1974

Trenholm, Virginia and Maurine Carley. *Wyoming Pageant.* Bailey School Supply (1951)

Twiss, Clinton. *The Long Long Trailer.* Vail-Ballou Press, 1951

United States House of Representatives. *Employment of Homosexuals and Other Sex Perverts in Government,* 81st Congress, 2nd Session, 1950

United States Senate History, "Senators, 1789 to Present" www.senate.gov

United States Senate. Transcripts. *Memorial Services Held in the Senate and House of Representatives of the United States, Together With Remarks Made in Eulogy of Lester C. Hunt, Late a Senator From Wyoming,* United States Government Printing Office, 1955

United States Senate. Transcript. *Hearings Before the Committee on Armed Services United States Senate Eighty-first Congress Second Session on the Nomination of Anna M. Rosenberg of New York, to be Assistant Secretary of Defense November 29,1950* United States Senate. Transcript. *Hearings Before a Subcommittee of the Armed Forces Committee of the United States Senate-Investigation of Action of Army With Respect to Trial of Persons Responsible for the Massacre of American Soldiers, Battle of the Bulge Near Malmedy Belgium, December 1944* United States Senate. Transcripts. *Special Senate Investigation on Charges and Countercharges Involving: Secretary of the Army Robert T. Stevens, John G. Adams, H. Struve Hensel, and Senator Joe McCarthy, Roy M. Cohn, and Francis P. Carr, Hearing Before the Special Subcommittee on Investigations of the Committee on Government Operations, United States Senate,* 83rd Congress, June 9, 1954, U.S. Government Printing Office

United States War Department. *"Final Report Japanese Evacuation from the West Coast 1942"* U.S. Government Printing Office

The Virginia Quarterly Review, Summer 2001

Von Hoffman, Nicholas. *Citizen Cohn: The Life and Times of Roy Cohn.* Bantam Books, 1988

Von Hoffman, Nicholas. Radical: *A Portrait of Saul Alinsky.* Nation Books, 2010

Ward, Geoffrey and Ken Burns. *Baseball: An Illustrated History.* New York: Alfred A. Knopf, 1994

Wendt, Lloyd. *The Vilest of Rackets.* Esquire Magazine. April 1950

Western, Samuel. *Pushed Off the Mountain-Sold Down the River: Wyoming's Search for Its Soul.* Moose, Wyoming-Denver-San Francisco: Homestead Publishing, 2002

White, Thomas W. *How to Identify Suicidal people: A systematic Approach to Risk Assessment.* Philadelphia: The Charles Press, 1999

Williams, Walter L. and Yolanda Retter. *Gay and Lesbian Rights in the United States: A Documentary History.* Westport, Connecticut-London: Greenwood Press, 2003

Wilson, A.N. *Tolstoy.* New York-London: W.W. Norton & Company, 1988

Woody, Ralph Jerome. *The United States Senate Career of Lester C. Hunt,* Master of Arts Thesis, University of Wyoming (1964)

Wyoming State House of Representatives. House Journal of the Twenty-seventh State Legislature of Wyoming, 1943

Wyoming State House of Representatives. House Journal of the Twenty-eighth State Legislature of Wyoming, 1945

Wyoming State House of Representatives. House Journal of the Twenty-ninth State Legislature of Wyoming, 1947

Wyoming State Senate. Senate Journal of the Twenty-seventh State Legislature of Wyoming, 1943

Young, Katherine A. and Virgil M. Young, Producers, Designers, Writers, and Websters in cooperation with Boise State University. *On the Oregon Trail.* education.boisestate.edu/compass

Zion, Sidney. *The Autobiography of Roy Cohn.* New York: St. Martin's Press. 1988

337

Index

CPSIA information can be obtained at www.ICGtesting.com
Printed in the USA
LVOW121547230613

339845LV00017B/821/P